*Type*SENSE

MAKING SENSE OF TYPE
ON THE COMPUTER

THIRD EDITION

SUSAN G. WHEELER

GARY S. WHEELER

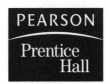

PEARSON

Prentice Hall

Upper Saddle River, New Jersey 07458

Library of Congress Cataloging-in-Publication Data

Wheeler, Susan G.
    Typesense: making sense of type on the computer/Susan G. Wheeler, Gary S. Wheeler.—3rd ed.
    p. cm.
    Includes bibliographical reference and index.
    ISBN 0-13-219010-9
        1. Computerized typesetting. 2. Computerized typesetting—United States. I. Title: Typesense. II. Wheeler, Gary S.
        III. Title

    Z253.3.W48 2007
    686.2'2544—dc22

                                                                                2005053462

Editor-in-Chief: Sarah Touborg
Acquisitions Editor: Amber Mackey
Editorial Assistant: Keri Molinari
Director of Production & Manufacturing: Barbara Kittle
Managing Editor: Lisa Iarkowski
Production Editor: Jean Lapidus
Copy Editor: Barbara DeVries

Manufacturing Manager: Nick Sklitsis
Prepress & Manufacturing Buyer: Sherry Lewis
Cover Design: Bruce Kenselaar
Cover Printer: Courier/Stoughton
Compositor: Susan G. Wheeler
Printer/Binder: Courier Companies/Stoughton

Credits and acknowledgments borrowed from other sources and reproduced, with permission, in this textbook appear on appropriate page within text.

Pearson Education LTD.
Pearson Education Singapore, Pte. Ltd
Pearson Education, Canada, Ltd
Pearson Education—Japan
Pearson Education Australia PTY, Limited
Pearson Education North Asia Ltd
Pearson Educación de Mexico, S.A. de C.V.
Pearson Education Malaysia, Pte. Ltd

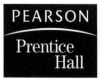

10   9   8   7   6   5   4   3   2   1
ISBN   0-13-219010-9

CONTENTS

FOREWORD

I'VE BEEN AN ENTHUSIASTIC FAN AND ADVOCATE OF *TypeSense* since its first edition. And, as I recently reviewed the many changes and greatly expanded content of this edition, I've finally figured out the reason for my continuing enthusiasm.

The author, Susan Wheeler, is an educator! This gives Susan a different perspective on communications in general, and writing a reader-friendly book in particular, than type designers, graphic designers, or full-time writers.

Every day—and, I suspect, at home, *every night*—Susan devotes herself to clarifying and organizing complex topics and—most important—*relating them* to her students' needs.

Simply put: to write—and rewrite—a book as good as *TypeSense,* knowledge and passion are not enough. You have to have an intuitive *empathy* for your readers' needs. You have to be someone in constant touch with those who don't know as much as you do, and you must know how to effectively communicate your knowledge and passion to others who may not be as involved with your subject matter as you might like.

In other words, to write a book like *TypeSense,* you have to:

+ *Understand* the baseline of the typical readers' previous involvement with type, and what they probably already know (regardless of its correctness).

- *Relativity:* you have to be able to relate typeface designs and arcane terms to your readers' goals and tasks, so they'll understand when specific designs and techniques are applicable, and how to apply them correctly.

- *Be as concise and visual as possible;* you have to recognize that—in a high-stress, attention-starved society—*reading time is limited,* and that concise writing must be matched by numerous, informative visuals that communicate more, in less time, than words alone.

The Love Connection. Most of all, *you have to really love your topic.* It takes real love and dedication to write and lay out your own book, tweaking each illustration and each page to perfection (hoping that a tiny change on page 35 doesn't throw off every page that follows!).

You have to not only create clear and meaningful illustrations, but scale them and place them adjacent to the text they support. Line endings and page breaks have to be constantly fine-tuned, not just for content, but for appearance.

A book like this represents craftsmanship in a society that puts a premium on "efficiency," "savings," and low-cost "outsourcing."

Continuing Growth. Each edition of *TypeSense* has more to teach, and—accordingly—becomes more valuable than the preceding edition. I stopped counting when I reached 100 additions and improvements, and just started reading for information and for pleasure.

As it should be. You're in good hands with Susan Wheeler, and your clients will thank you for it! ∽

Roger C. Parker
Dover, NH

Over a million and a half readers throughout the world own copies
of books written by Roger C. Parker, including the classic *Looking
Good in Print: A Guide to Basic Design for Desktop Publishing.*
His books have been translated into over 37 languages.
Visit his design blog at *www.rcpdesign.info.*

PREFACE

M Y ENDURING FASCINATION WITH TYPEFACES—the beautiful
shapes, diverse styles, and the typographic artwork created from them—
is something I enjoy sharing with others. Working with type, however,
can be daunting for beginning design and typography students or new
publication design students. All the details, rules, stylistic variations,
and interrelationships feel overwhelming at first. How can anyone remember everything? *TypeSense* makes understanding type easier by
taking readers from the broadest decisions, made first in a document or
design, to the detailed decisions, made later in the design's development.

This book divides the explanation of type into five usage areas: on a
page (chapter 3), in a paragraph (chapter 4), in a sentence (chapters 5
and 6), as a design element (chapters 7, 8, and 9), and in a publication
(chapters 10 and 11). These chapters are introduced by a brief historical
review of typesetting systems and important typographers (chapter 1)
and the requisite terminology for describing and discussing type (chapter 2). An extended discussion of evaluating typography, proofreading
procedures, and using proofreaders' marks is included with the appropriate usage chapters. A glossary, select bibliography, and two appendices (a compendium of proofreaders' marks and Adobe Systems' character access charts) conclude the book.

Unlike the typography books that focus on one aspect of type, such
as typesetting, typographic design, or publication design, *TypeSense* explores all these areas. The book has a unique, comprehensive approach

that makes it an excellent starting point for the study of type. For example, unlike type books that dazzle their readers with abundant design examples, *TypeSense* takes this one step further by explaining the design's development from thumbnails to finished art. Explaining and demonstrating the typographic design process from start to finish, discussing the choices and challenges encountered by designers, helps students work through their own designs. The historical overview enables students to understand the evolution of current terminology and the benefits of today's technology.

The third edition updates the digital type technology information to include OpenType and adds two new, example-filled, publication design chapters that explain and demonstrate the interrelationship of individual type decisions as applied to books, magazines, and newsletters. There are many new typographic designs, some improved chapter figures, and an appendix of character access charts to make typesetting easier.

There are several people to acknowledge for their contributions to this edition. My husband and coauthor's keen editorial eye and writing expertise improved the content, structure, and quality of my writing. As a graduate student in computer science, my son Kyle provided the answers to all my technical computer questions. As a law student, my son Kieran provided the legal cases and precedents to clarify the discussion on type piracy and legal protections for type designers. Thomas W. Phinney, Program Manager for Fonts and Core Technologies at Adobe Systems, helped clarify the digital typography passages with his vast knowledge in that area. Any confusion or error in this book, although unintentional, is mine alone. The reviewers, Charles D. Johnson from the University of Northern Iowa and Carol A. Straka from Moraine Valley Community College, provided a detailed student- and instructor-usage perspective beyond my own. My editor Amber Mackey helped me make this edition as beneficial to students and faculty as possible. And last, I want to acknowledge the University of Cincinnati—Raymond Walters College and its design students for providing an atmosphere that encouraged my research and creative work in typography, while providing an opportunity to pass along what I learned to others.

Susan G. Wheeler

INTRODUCTION

———❦———

THE EVOLVING
COMPUTER
TYPOGRAPHER

WORKING WITH TYPE, THE BEAUTIFULLY DESIGNED letterforms, figures, punctuation marks, and ornaments in a typeface, has never been more satisfying—more fun—than it is today. There are many avenues to explore from typesetting a complex document that communicates a thoughtful, provocative, informative message to creating a unique typographic image as personal artistic expression. Powerful, type-sensitive software and high-quality typefaces containing innumerable glyphs are seamlessly integrated in the digital environment. Type professionals create well-designed, artistically crafted type documents that captivate the mind and eye. These *type artists* benefit from ongoing developments in technology and digital typography's coming of age.

In the early 1980s, digital typography and microcomputers became available for business and private use. The type on these computers looked both to the past and the future, as they transitioned from what was, to what was to come. There were rough-edged, bitmapped letterforms comparable to shapes made by shading squares on graph paper; monospaced letterforms harkening back to manual and electric typewriters; and typefaces with a limited range of characters.

As the computer industry grew, it maneuvered itself to play a significant role in the graphic arts field. Hardware and software leapfrogged over one another in a race to attain the quality demanded by graphics professionals. Output-device manufacturers worked to provide sufficient resolution to render professional-quality typographic and graphic images reliably, quickly, and accurately. At the same time, software developers and display manufacturers worked to achieve accurate on-screen representation of images and type, so designers could see and plan what emerged from their printers or imagesetters.

As printer, display, and software technologies improved, digital typography too was evolving from infancy to adulthood. The role of bit-mapped fonts was refined, not as standalone fonts, but in conjunction with outline fonts to provide information necessary for their use and organization. Typewriter-like, monospaced type fonts were appropriate for utilitarian purposes, such as tabulated lists and forms, but not for professional-quality print documents. Type font formats, such as Post-Script Type 3, came and went as PostScript Type 1 (PST-1) fonts, and later TrueType (TT) fonts, surpassed them in quality and availability.

When the initial realignment of available type technologies stabilized, the second phase of the digital type evolution began. With high-quality output, accurate display, and well-defined software readily available, it was time to consider what came next. What more was necessary, desired, and possible? What had been overlooked?

A digital typeface is created from a single font, or image source. This infinitely scalable computer code description replaced multiple type cases filled with metal fonts necessary for each typeface size and other forms of metal and photographic typesetting. Gone were the nuanced design alterations carved into those metal fonts by the punch-cutter that improved output quality in small or large sizes. Also missing in the digital typographer's toolbox were the alternate letterforms, or glyphs, required in high-quality typesetting found in those same obsolete type cases.

To meet those needs, digital type fonts, called expert collections, and multiple master technology were developed. Expert collections included more glyphs, such as text figures, additional ligatures, swash letters, and small caps that expanded the available glyphs of a standard 256-character font file. The new digital typographer had to learn when and how to use these additional glyphs as they assumed the responsibility previously shouldered by foundry typesetters. In addition, multiple master technology enabled the digital typographer to create stylistic variations or optical weight adjustments for improved output at specific sizes, just as the punchcutters did for metal type.

The expansion into increased capabilities, however, was still rooted in some limitations. Available PST-1 and TT fonts were platform specific, purchased either for use on an Apple Macintosh or PC. Accessing letters with a keyboard varied slightly from platform to platform, so a document created on a PC would appear with some different characters when displayed on a Mac, and visa versa. Creating documents in different languages, or including multiple language references in the same document, required accessing separate type fonts. Each of these idiosyncrasies was manageable, but over time became cumbersome as application software became more sophisticated and powerful. The advances of the second phase soon evolved as well.

The computers and software of the 1980s initiated an interconnectedness of business and industry around the world. With computer networks and Internet access, the documents on a screen in Kansas, for example, were sent easily to a screen in France or Hong Kong. Boundaries of software, platforms, language, and font formats needed to be removed. In the digital type arena, this manifested itself in the removal of many limitations, such as character count, computer platform, and language, and the expansion of features, such as typefaces designed for specific sizes. Integration of software and font format features to manage and operate multilanguage, multiplatform, multiglyph typefaces has taken digital typography into its adulthood.

ℰ

TODAY, NEW OR REVISED SOFTWARE APPLICATIONS, font formats, and the professionals in front of the keyboard have an increased sensitivity to type. New type-savvy software works with new font formats, such as OpenType, to access over 64,000 glyphs with an internal "intelligence" that frees the type artist from implementing many glyph substitutions manually. This *type sense* enables type artists to typeset, manipulate, design, and create typographic documents and graphics on a professional level using tools that facilitate creativity. The result is a typographic environment within which type artists produce functional, aesthetically pleasing typographic documents and typographs that are both a joy to create and behold.

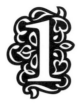

FROM THE
FOUNDRY
TO THE
COMPUTER

Typography is the art and process of working with and printing from type. Creating type, arranging type, designing type—all fall within its scope. In the discipline of typography there are two major categories of practitioners: those who produce type and those who set type. Type producers create objects, forms, or computer files from which letters are recreated. High-quality type produces distinctive and legible letters (as well as symbols, figures, and punctuation marks) each time it is used. These letters are consistent in style and structure. Typesetters work with and arrange type to create readable words and paragraphs on a page. They pursue typographic quality. Their pages of type are easy to read, uniform in color, and enhance, not confuse, the communication contained in them. To attain typographic quality, typesetters need legible, reusable letters and symbols in a variety of styles. They also need control of the horizontal space between letters in a word or a line (*letterspacing*) and control of the vertical space between lines within and between paragraphs (*leading* or *line spacing*). All three factors aid or hinder a typesetter's ability to achieve a high level of typographic quality. Most often the work and goals of both type producers and typesetters intersect.

At the time of Gutenberg's invention of the first practical reusable type in 1454, typography was perceived by its practitioners as an invisible art form. Type (and the letters it recreated) was a vehicle that delivered a message and, as with religious texts, was eloquently illuminated. Gutenberg's first type was designed to look like handwriting. Readers,

Typography … remains a difficult, subtle, and exacting art. And even though a certain degree of technical skill is relatively common, typographic mastery is the province of the perceptive and the prerogative of the few.

————————————Rand
Design, Form, and Chaos

1

Character *A basic, minimal, readable structure used to identify a letter, figure, punctuation mark, or symbol that serves as a component of written language.*

Glyph *A stylized visual representation of a character or combination of characters.*

Alphabet *A set of letters or other characters (arranged in a customary order) with which one or more languages are written.*

Typeface *The distinctive, visually unifying design of an alphabet and its accompanying punctuation marks and numbers. It includes all point sizes of that typeface, such as Minion Italic.*

Type family *All stylistic variations of a single typeface, including light, medium, bold, extra bold, and italic, such as Minion.*

Font *Originally defined in foundry type as all the sorts needed to produce the letters, numbers, and punctuation marks of one size of one specific typeface, such as 12-point Minion Semibold. Evolved to mean the entity, such as the matrices, film, or digital file, necessary to create all the glyphs of a typeface, regardless of size.*

accustomed to handwritten books, would have viewed with suspicion any new typeset books with foreign-looking letterforms. Typeset copy that recreated a handwritten appearance made readers comfortable with what they saw. For example, Cardinal Bessarion (1389–1472), a noted Greek scholar, collector, and diplomat, referred to typography as an invention "by the barbarians of a German city." Frederick, Duke of Urbino, another fifteenth-century Florentine scholar, would not include any printed works in his extensive personal library (Morison, 1926).

Today's typeset copy continues this role as message bearer. After finishing a novel, a reader is not likely to praise the type designer for a legible typeface—consistent in style and structure. Nor would the reader praise the typesetter for the page's typographic quality—uniform in color with skillfully crafted line breaks. Instead, the reader might compliment the author on the clarity of the content or the cleverness of the prose. *Type? What about it?* In this example, type achieved functional invisibility. Well-set type delivers an author's ideas and thoughts with a clarity of voice equal to that of a skilled orator. Poorly set type decreases readability, garbling the message like a speaker mumbling to the floor, and increases the chance the text will not be read at all.

For the four hundred years following Gutenberg's invention, type producers and typesetters were separate artisans. Each practiced a craft that demanded skilled knowledge of specific tools, materials, production techniques, and aesthetic principles. As Gutenberg's methods were refined and as the craft of typography evolved, the interests of these two artisans influenced one another. The materials of type limited or enhanced the typesetter's abilities. For example, the range of typefaces available in the late fifteenth century was limited in part by what shapes were possible to be cast from a metal alloy. Foundry type production techniques could not achieve the halftone or illustrated typefaces available with the phototypography production techniques of the 1960s. In addition, phototypesetting techniques freed typesetters from the limited control of line spacing and letterspacing of their linecasting typesetting machines of the early 1900s.

Today's digital type technology for type production and typesetting involves many interdependent electronic components, software, and skills. Digital type combines the design variety and typesetting capabilities of phototypography with the craftsmanship of foundry type and the speed of mechanized linecasters. Typographic quality achieved by digital typesetters is affected by hardware resolution, software interfaces, application capabilities, and functional characteristics of available digitized typefaces. Poor typographic quality can result from hardware problems, software problems, interface problems, user problems, or combinations of any and all. Today's type artist cannot achieve typographic quality without knowledge of both aspects of the discipline—type production and typesetting.

The current vocabulary of type is an amalgamation of all the type production and typesetting methods from Gutenberg's time forward. The word *leading,* which once referred to the lead material used in a typesetting procedure, now refers to the *visual* result achieved by the lead strips used in that original procedure. For today's type artist, who might be unfamiliar with type's history, using the name of an inert metal as a term to describe the horizontal white space beneath letters on a glowing cathode ray tube (CRT) or flat liquid crystal display (LCD) may be confusing or unfamiliar (and hard to remember). Although the materials and type-production techniques have changed, typesetting principles are the same. The terminology describing them is rooted in techniques and developments of the past.

———————————————
JOHANN DA SPIRA
(d. 1470)
WENDELIN DA SPIRA
German brothers, printers, and type cutters. Created the first roman typeface while working in Venice; first used in 1469. Based on the southern humanist hand used in Italy and preferred by Renaissance scholars.
∾

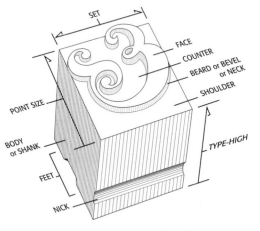

FIGURE 1-1: *Type sort with identified components*

JOHANN GUTENBERG OF MAINZ, GERMANY, is recognized as the inventor of the first practical, movable, reusable type (c. 1454). Gutenberg was an entrepreneur, an engraver, and a goldsmith. All his characteristics came to bear on his invention—the development of a metal-casting technique for reproducing pieces of hard, durable metal type, called *foundry type.* Gutenberg's foundry type was cast from a metal alloy of lead, tin, antimony, and copper. Each piece of foundry type (fig. 1-1),

METAL TYPE

called a *sort,* represented a single character in a type font. While the English-language alphabet consists of 52 letters (upper- and lowercase), a typical foundry type font with figures, punctuation marks, spaces, ligatures, and alternate characters could include 150 sorts. Gutenberg's first type font contained over 300 sorts. He believed many unique characters and ligatures duplicating the flourishes and distinctive character of handwriting were needed to assure acceptance by his readership.

Foundry Type

Nicolas Jenson
(c. 1420–80)
French type cutter and printer. Designed a roman letter style in 1470, while working in Venice, that smoothly integrated capital and miniscule letters and maintained even letter and line spacing. Served as a model for future roman type.

Foundry type was the primary means of setting type through 1890. Individual fonts were kept together in a shallow drawer, called a *type case.* Each case was divided into small compartments, one for each font character. A compartment's size and location were standard, determined by frequency of use. A skilled typesetter quickly selected letters and spaces from the case by hand and positioned them (from right to left and upside down) in a metal composing stick (fig. 1-2), set to the proper line length, held in his other hand. When a single type line was complete, a thin strip of lead was placed on top of it. The lead strip ran the length of the type line and separated one line from the next. The lead was only as high as the type body, so it was not high enough to contact the inking roller and did not print. Leading (available in different thicknesses) enhanced readability by isolating lines of type between the horizontal bands of white space it created on the page. Type set without leading was *set solid*—solid type, no leads.

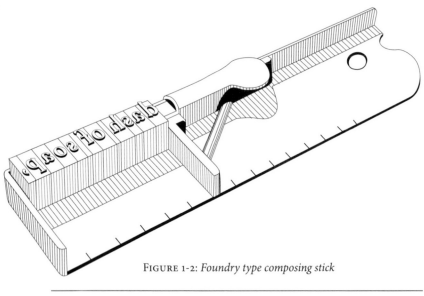

FIGURE 1-2: *Foundry type composing stick*

After filling the composing stick with several lines of type, the typesetter transferred the type to a larger type tray, called a *chase.* This procedure was repeated several times until the entire page was set and the chase contained all the required sorts. Once all the type was positioned correctly, the typesetter locked down the chase to prevent the type from moving out of position. Copies of the type, or *proofs,* were made on a proofing press by running an inked roller across the face of the type, laying paper on top of the inked type, and applying even pressure. The procedure transferred the inked letterforms to the paper. Foundry type was developed to withstand repeated impressions and to produce crisp, accurate letterforms.

Letterspacing in foundry type had limited flexibility. The amount of space on either side of a letter was determined by the width, or *set,* of the type sort's body. If adjacent letters were too close together, the typesetter would insert a thin space (or hair space) between their type sorts. If a pair of letters was too far apart, the solution was not so simple. With the type's set predetermined, moving two letters closer required carving away some of the type's metal body. Typesetters were unwilling to permanently alter sorts, unless they were for display type, where letterspacing problems would be more visible. Such alterations for text type were not usually cost-effective. For the most frequent problem letter pairs, however, type designers developed ligatures. A *ligature* was a single character (and a single sort) created from the physical union or the designed alteration of two or three separate letters. Ligatures for the letters *f-f-i, f-f-l, f-f, f-i,* and *f-l* were common, and still are. Improving text letterspacing using ligatures was faster than altering each offending sort.

Another solution for tight, adjacent letters was actually to extend the portion of the letter (the lowercase italic letter *f* was the usual recipient of this treatment) beyond the body of the type. The sort for such an overly friendly letter contained a kern. The *kern* was the portion of a letter that extended beyond the type body. When the lowercase *f* was positioned adjacent to a lowercase *o,* for example, the *o*'s body supported the *f*'s kern. The kern had to be supported or it would break under the pressure of the proofing press. Removing letterspacing from between letters in foundry type required customized sorts, but there was a limit to how many a type founder would include in a font.

GUTENBERG'S FOUNDRY TYPE TECHNIQUE survived without major revision until the end of the nineteenth century when various parts of the process were mechanized. As foundry type production became more

WILLIAM CAXTON
(1421–91)
English merchant-diplomat turned printer. In 1476 established the first printing house in England to produce English-language books. His interest in printing was an extension of his work translating French literature into English for the Duchess of Burgundy.

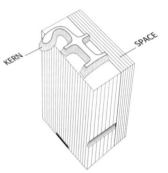

Foundry type sort with kern and word space

CAST TYPE

PHOTOTYPOGRAPHY

mechanized, foundry typesetting came under scrutiny for a mechanized alternative as well. In 1884, Ottmar Mergenthaler (1854–99) invented a typecasting system in Baltimore, Maryland, that challenged the use of hand-set foundry type for text composition. Mergenthaler's Linotype linecaster enabled operators to enter copy using a typewriter-style keyboard. The linecaster operator controlled all typesetting and typecasting operations within the typesetting machine from the keyboard.

With each keystroke, a lightweight reusable letter matrix, or *mat*, dropped from its place within the *magazine* (compartment of matrices) located above the typesetter's head. A metallic tinkling sound accompanied each matrix as it made its way from the magazine to the assembling line. Once all the matrices and spaces were in place on the line, the operator flooded the matrices with molten lead, creating a single line of type, or *slug*. After the slug cooled, the slug and matrices separated. The slug moved into position in the *galley* (similar to a foundry type chase) and the matrices returned to the magazine. When making corrections, the Linotype operator would recast an entire line and replace the original slug with the corrected one. While the linecasting procedures sound logical, it was a mechanical marvel that all steps were accomplished within a single, although ungainly looking, machine whose operator sat in front of a keyboard.

Several type manufacturers developed typecasting machines by mechanizing different stages of the typesetting procedure; these included the Monotype and the Ludlow casting machines. Typefaces designed for use in typecasters were more stylistically limited than their foundry type predecessors. Letters could not extend beyond the edge of the type body. The delicate handling required by a kern, for example, was impractical with these typecasters. The set of an italic *f*, for example, was more narrow than its foundry type counterpart. These design differences enabled foundry type to continue as an alternative form of typesetting for display (since linecasters seldom set type above 14 points) and for text typesetting. Although foundry typesetting was slower, the technique produced higher typographic quality when set by an experienced typesetter and remained in demand for some text jobs. Mechanized linecasters became the standard for jobs where speed was paramount, such as setting newspapers.

BOTH FORMS OF METAL TYPE, FOUNDRY AND CAST, coexisted for more than seventy years without a major challenge to their production techniques. During this period, typesetters worked within the limitations of both. Although handsetting made it more expensive, foundry type provided clear reproductions of a wide variety of typefaces that were suitable for display type. Cast type provided speed for setting type. Its shortcomings—standardized letterspacing and type design limitations—were offset by the increased speed for setting large quantities of text. In the 1950s, interest grew in an otherwise overlooked type production technique—phototypography. Phototypesetting exceeded the speed of the linecasters and its range of type designs and letterspacing controls went far beyond that of foundry type.

Phototype production simplified the lengthy production process required for making foundry sorts or linecaster matrices. As long as an artist could draw the typeface on paper, it could be converted to a font— as film. A phototypesetter used a single film font to reproduce a single letter thousands of times. If the film font was not scratched or otherwise damaged and if the components of the photomechanical process remained clean and regularly maintained, the type set was crisp and true.

Phototypesetting machines varied from manufacturer to manufacturer, but the principle for setting phototype was the same. Phototypesetting used a light source, a film font, a lens and/or a prism, light-sensitive photographic paper, and chemical developer. The film font was a film negative—the letterforms were clear and the remaining areas were solid black. Light passed through the clear letter shape and exposed that area on the photographic paper. Lenses and prisms inserted between the film and the light-sensitive paper changed the style, size, and weight of the projected letter image. After the typesetter exposed all the letters on the paper, the paper was placed in a chemical bath for developing. The chemical developer changed the exposed areas to solid black, and the unexposed areas (protected by the black film) remained white.

In some display phototype systems, the operator positioned and exposed each letter individually on the photographic paper after inserting the proper lens for letter style, size, or weight. Such precise operator-controlled letterspacing enabled the artist to specify, or experiment with, unique letterspacing treatments. An operator could position a letter at any distance from another letter, at varying distances from another letter within the same word, or on top of another letter. As with metal foundry type, such labor-intensive typesetting was more costly.

The faster keyboarded phototypography systems used sizes ranging from 4 to 36 points, depending on the manufacturer. Setting the type employed two different procedures—entering the copy and formatting codes, and setting the type. First the operator entered the copy on a

CLAUDE GARAMOND
(C. 1490–1567)
French type designer and punch cutter. Credited with establishing the first type foundry where type was designed, produced, and sold. Designed italic typefaces to complement roman type and established type family relationships.

≈

WILLIAM CASLON I
(1692–1766)
British patriarch of influential type-founding family. Started as a gun-barrel engraver. Caslon typeface became the British printing standard after its introduction in 1725. Used for the first printings of the Declaration of Independence and the Constitution of the United States.

≈

JOHN BASKERVILLE
(1706–75)

*English printer and typographer. A
perfectionist, he designed his own
printing press, made his own ink,
and devised a method, called hot
pressing, for making paper smooth.
All this was necessary to print his
fine-stroked types. Although
criticized by many of his
contemporaries, Baskerville's
printing improvements had
a profound effect on the
industry's future.*

∾

PIERRE SIMON FOURNIER
(1712–68)

*French punch cutter, typographer,
and printer. Developed a point
system for measuring type used for
printing music in 1735. This was the
first numerical type-sizing system.
Fournier's point measured
0.0137 inch. Designed and cut
147 original alphabets.*

∾

keyboard and proofed it on the display screen. All type formatting codes, or instructions, for the job, such as size, letterspacing, leading, and style, were typed in also. The keyboard operator saved the copy and codes to a disk, cassette, or paper tape (depending on the manufacturer). The operator then inserted the disk into a separate typesetting machine and checked that the required typefaces were installed in the machine. Some typesetting jobs were limited to a maximum number of faces due to the machine's storage capacity.

Once initiated, the type was set according to the information on the disk, using a mechanized phototypesetting procedure. Following the information on the disk, the machine located a letter on the film, set the lens for the required size or weight, set the prism to position the letter correctly on the paper, and triggered a light burst. The projected letter shape of light passes through the lens and the prism and exposes the photographic paper. Once every letter was exposed, the machine sent the paper through a chemical bath to develop the image on the paper. The set type emerged from the typesetting machine as black letters on white paper (or film, if available).

Phototypography was viewed originally as only an alternative means of setting type, but designers soon realized that phototypography offered an alternative means of *using* type. New capabilities, such as letter distortion and infinite control of letterspacing, caused designers to take another look at type and triggered a new form of graphic expression. Designers used type as an illustrative component, a graphic element, and a means of visually conveying an idea. Master type designer Herb Lubalin (1918–81) was part of a typographical movement in the 1960s that began probing the previously unexplored uses of this type.

The ease with which phototype was produced gave new life to the decorative and novelty typeface designs of the 1800s and the wooden typefaces popular from 1830 to 1870. New typefaces were made from any object (animal, vegetable, or mineral), any substance, any geometric or organic design element, and from any vantage point. This explosion of interest in type prompted the foundation of the International Typeface Corporation (ITC) in 1970. At the outset, ITC was set up to coordinate typeface development and to offer type designers financial and artistic protection for their designs. While ITC was successful with its first goal and initiated a typeface revival of sorts, the goal of type design protection was more elusive.

Piracy has plagued type designers from the beginning. Legal protections, if available, were inadequate. During the Renaissance, Aldus

Manutius received a patent from the Venetian Senate and a papal decree in an attempt to protect his typefaces from piracy. Both were ineffective. In the mid-1800s Edwin Starr, an American type founder, invented a procedure that used an electrotyping technique to produce copper matrices from existing type sorts. This facilitated the plagiarism of foundry type designs. Starting in 1911, type designers in the United States could copyright their designs, but the 1976 Copyright Revision Act removed this protection. European countries, such as England, Germany, and France, however, have copyright laws protecting these creative works. These European copyrights are recognized in the United States under the 1886 Berne Convention. A design patent is available for a typeface in the United States for a period of fourteen years. The process, however, requires the designer to meet a high burden of proof to determine if the design qualifies as sufficiently original. In 1931 Oswald Cooper lost his patent on Cooper Black by failing to satisfy the requirements of a design patent. Frederic Goudy also had a patent invalidated. Trademark protection is available in most countries, including the United States, but it only safeguards the typeface's name. This limited protection has resulted in multiple names for a single typeface. Currently, copyright protection in the United States extends to software, and digital typefaces fall under that rubric. This is the primary means of safeguarding this form of intellectual property. Type designers continue to denounce the pirating of their designs. As technology continues to improve, it is impossible to safeguard their creative property without adequate legal recourse to discourage typeface piracy.

EVERY SUCCEEDING TECHNOLOGY FOR type production and typesetting has added new possibilities for type and artistic expression. Each also has built on the foundation of goals common to all, such as legibility and readability of text and language, effective communication, and a desire to transparently provide the vehicle connecting writer to reader. The Monotype linecasting machine relied on the manual placement of matrices before casting a line of type. Early phototypesetting machines, such as the Intertype Fotosetter, looked and operated remarkably like Mergenthaler's Linotype linecasting machine. Matrices were dropped into position and were exposed line-by-line on photographic paper.

Transition from one typesetting technology to another proceeds smoothly if what is *new* operates similarly to what is *old*. This similarity minimizes the operator's decrease in productivity by forming a bridge from what was to what is. Before digital typography became available to

FRANÇOIS-AMBROISE DIDOT
(1730–1804)
Member of a famous French family of printers and type founders. Revised Fournier's point system for measuring type. Developed in 1785, the Didot point (0.01483 inch) currently is used on the European continent.

~

DIGITAL TYPOGRAPHY

a new breed of typesetter (the type artist) in the early 1980s, computerized typesetting machines used digital font descriptions from which to expose letter shapes on photographic paper.

Digital typography is the last step in a journey that brought typesetting capabilities from the foundry to the computer screens of type artists in studios and offices. Today's type artists follow a tradition of typographic principles previously passed along to succeeding generations of typesetters by skilled typographers working in type foundries. Today's type production techniques influence the typographic quality these type artists strive to attain. There are many sources of digital typefaces, from the well-established manufacturer to the newly minted enthusiast. For type artists with limited funds seeking to expand their typeface collections, the type manufacturer's name can steer the novice font buyer away from the end product of the novice type designer.

Digital typography defines individual letterforms as a mathematical description—a mathematical graphic recipe. The description directs the computer to position key points, to connect those points with lines, and to bend those lines to shape the letter's outline (see fig. 1-3). *Digital* means using numbers to describe something, such as letter shapes. People's homes and offices are connected by digital addresses called telephone numbers. The number, rather than a name, identifies the person's location and enables the connection. The digital identity that enables the computer to locate and display the correct glyph is called *character encoding.*

Digital fonts are structured in two different forms: bitmapped fonts and outline fonts. A bitmapped font, or *screen font,* defines letters as groups of dots arranged on a grid with x, y coordinates, also known as raster images. Each letter's shape is defined as preset pixel locations on a grid, or *bitmap.* Just as art students create designs on graph paper by carefully darkening each grid square, so too does the computer remember a letter's shape as selected pixels (the grid squares) on a bitmap (the computer screen or printed page). Bitmapped fonts usually have a fixed, low resolution. This resolution gives diagonal and curved edges a stair-stepped, rather than a smooth, edge when printed. Type artists do not use bitmapped fonts for print-media output, but these fonts form an essential partnership with most outline font formats.

An outline font, also called *printer font* or *scalable font,* defines letters as objects, also known as vector objects. Each letter's shape is a mathematical formula containing point locations and shaped, connecting line segments. Outline fonts are not locked in a preset resolution.

GIAMBATTISTA BODONI
(1740–1813)
Italian printer, type designer, and typographer. Court printer for the Duke of Parma. Approached typographic printing as a means to create art, rather than to communicate a written message. An admirer of Baskerville's, Fournier's, and Didot's work, Bodoni cut one of the first modern typefaces.

∿

DARIUS WELLS
(1800–75)
American printer and inventor. Credited with starting the wood type industry in 1828 after inventing the lateral router to mechanize wood type production. Used European boxwood due to its close grain, light weight, and durability.

∿

CHAPTER ONE

The resolution of the display or output hardware determines the smoothness of the letters' edges. Type artists should use outline fonts and high-resolution imagesetters for professional-quality typesetting.

Additional layers of rendering and rasterizing software stand between the digital typeface files and quality screen or printer output. This software reads the instructions contained in the typeface font files and facilitates optimal output. Different output devices require different software to interpret the descriptive information. For a CRT monitor, the optimal rendering of glyphs uses grayscale anti-aliasing or, more accurately, whole-pixel anti-aliasing. This software manipulates pixel tints or colors to optically smooth glyph edges. On an LCD screen, color anti-aliasing, or sub-pixel rendering, controls three different color bands within a single pixel to smooth glyph edges. Many, but not all, operating systems and applications support this capability. Printers and image-setters of varying resolutions require different amounts of assistance from this category of software for high-quality typographic output. Some of this software is type-format specific, able to read certain font file formats more accurately than others.

Printer fonts come in several file formats written in different computer languages. The major printer font formats are PostScript Type 1, TrueType, and OpenType. These font formats have different strengths, features, and characteristics. While most font formats can coexist on a single computer system, a type artist must be aware of potential surprises (or problems) triggered by this coexistence. A good rule of thumb is never to open the same typeface in two different formats if it is identified with the exact same name. Minion Regular as *MinioReg* (PST-1) and *MinionPro-Regular* (OT) can be opened simultaneously without adverse results due to the name difference. Type-utility software, such as Font Reserve or Suitcase, provides an easy way to organize and manage fonts and formats. They enable the type artist to open individual or sets of typefaces as needed, thereby limiting the amount of RAM allocated to typefaces, and to open the best font format for the document.

POSTSCRIPT TYPE 1 FONTS (PST-1), INTRODUCED IN 1984 by Adobe Systems, are outline fonts written in the PostScript language. Each font file contains a maximum of 256 characters. This character limit is a result of the 8-bit character encoding system used by this format. Consequently, in a single type family (Times, for example), each family member (roman, italic, bold, and bold italic) is a separate font file. Each family member displays alphabetically as a separate entry in an application's

WILLIAM MORRIS
(1834–96)
*British designer and writer.
A driving force in the Arts and
Crafts movement of the nineteenth
century. He devoted his later years
to reviving typographic quality in
printing and type design.*

∾

NELSON C. HAWKS
(1840–1929)
*American businessman,
typographer, printer, and inventor.
Responsible for developing,
promoting, and shepherding to
adoption the American point
system, despite the resistance and
competitive suspicion of the
American type foundry
community. Adopted
in 1892.*

∾

PostScript Type 1

font menu. Some software manufacturers, such as Adobe, cluster all family members in a submenu under the type family's name. For example, *Times* appears in the font menu with *Roman, Italic, Bold,* and *Bold Italic* listed in a type family hierarchy in the submenu. When working with large font families, this font-menu structuring is a must. For applications lacking this capability, software is available to enhance type menu performance.

For type artists seeking access to more typeface family members, such as semibold or black, many typeface packages come with more than the basic four. Each is a separate file. For access to additional characters within a single type font, type manufacturers, such as Agfa Monotype, offer expert collections as extensions of select typefaces. Purchasing a typeface and its expert collection offers the type artist additional glyphs that could not fit in the standard 256-character file. Expert collections include glyphs such as small caps, titling caps, text figures, fractions, swash letters, and ornaments. Using an expert collection increases the level of typographic quality a type artist can achieve with this font format.

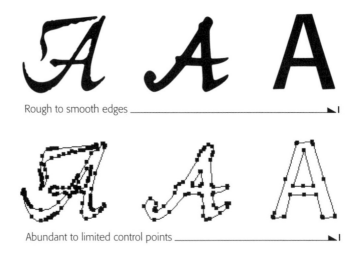

Rough to smooth edges ⟶

Abundant to limited control points ⟶

Figure 1-3: Control points determine letter-edge quality

The type artist accesses the glyphs from any of the standard or expert font files through one or multiple keystrokes. This form of keystroke glyph access is called *keyboard mapping*. A prescribed sequence of keystrokes is mapped to a single glyph and consistently produces it on screen. For example, depressing the Shift and *a* keys simultaneously produces the capital *A*. On the Macintosh, simultaneously depressing the Shift, Option, and hyphen keys activates the em dash. Character access charts listing the keystrokes required for accessing different glyphs are available for standard and expert Mac and Windows typefaces (see Appendix B). Type artists must specify either the Mac or Windows version of this file format when purchasing a typeface.

PST-1 font files range in size from approximately 35 to 50 kilobytes (KB). This keeps the amount of hard disk space and printer RAM devoted to fonts at a minimum. To display and print PST-1 fonts, the type artist needs two items: the typeface's outline font file and the font suitcase containing the typeface's bitmapped fonts. Type artists using Mac OS X will see identical icons for a typeface's font suitcase and outline font. The icon names, however, indicate their identity. Using the Times family, for example, the font suitcase name is spelled out completely—*Times.* The outline font names are abbreviated—*TimesRom, TimesIta, TimesBol,* and *TimesBolIta.*

PST-1 font files (the outline font file) contain information required to render each typeface for display or printer output according to the type designer's specifications. These specs fall into two information categories—outline and hints. The outline information uses cubic bézier mathematical formulas to describe each letter's shape. Bézier equations use control points and control point handles to delineate the outline of each letter. This technique results in fewer control points along the letter's outline path without jeopardizing the accuracy of the typographic forms and keeps printing time reasonable (see fig. 1-4). The number of control points within the same type format depends upon the intricacy of the letter's outline (fig. 1-3).

Hints are special instructions that maintain the quality of a typeface's typographic features for low-resolution output and for small type sizes. Some hints pertain to a single letter and others pertain to the entire typeface. A typeface's design nuances so easily seen at 96 points might not be worth rendering at 6 points. For example, a cupped serif on a 6-point typeface might be impossible to render on a 300-dpi printer. Instead of the gentle bowing curve typical of a cupped serif, such a printer might make the serif appear as if a rectangular bite was taken out of it. (Cupped serifs do not lay flat on the baseline. They bow slightly with the ends extending below the baseline.) The hints for that typeface could instruct the printer to render the bottom of the serif perfectly horizontal, thereby eliminating the problem.

Hints include information concerning character alignment (making sure all the letters sit on the baseline correctly), curves and strokes (creating the most visually accurate curves or strokes with different resolutions), and other visual subtleties in a typeface design. Hints in this font format describe specific glyph or typeface characteristics in a horizontal and vertical direction. Hints could aptly be called "notes on nuances." No matter what the term, hints are the next best thing to having the type designer on site adjusting the output quality for the best possible results.

Before displaying or printing a typeface within an application's file, each device must receive a displayable or printable form of the typeface. As with PostScript graphics files in general, the original font file must be translated accurately and completely. The translation of PST-1 fonts is done by a PostScript interpreter. The interpreter is a piece of software that contains the necessary description instructions to render the outline information and apply the hinting instructions included in the outline font. On the Mac platform, the bitmap fonts, located in the font suitcase, provide the *metric data* necessary for character spacing, style linking, and typeface menu names. On the Windows platform, the metric data is in the .pfm file. In the past, the interpreter was a stand-alone piece of software installed into the system by the type artist. This capability is now part of the current Mac and Windows operating systems.

The strength of PST-1 hinting is its interaction with the interpreter. PST-1 hints identify specific letter or typeface characteristics to be adjusted for optimal output. As the interpreter's ability to render a characteristic is enhanced in a subsequent system upgrade, the output of that characteristic improves. For type artists with extensive PST-1 typeface collections, the interconnection of hinting and interpreter improves the output quality of their typefaces with each interpreter upgrade.

PostScript printers contain the PostScript interpreter in their ROM chips or on a cartridge or board installed in the printer. Preparing a PostScript file for printing is called raster image processing, *rip-ing*, or rasterizing. A non-PostScript printer requires the computer and its operating system to rasterize the file for printing. Referring to this software as an interpreter, rather than a rasterizer, acknowledges its use with the display as well as the printer.

To read, understand, and render all the nuances contained in these PostScript files, a high-volume type artist with PST-1 fonts should have a high-resolution PostScript printer for professional-quality output. Surprisingly, printing PST-1 fonts from a PostScript-compatible printer can be more unpredictable than printing from a non-PostScript printer. With the latter, the interpreter in the operating system reliably rasterizes the font for the printer.

As display technology expanded to include LCD screens, enhanced interpreter capabilities were needed for displaying type due to the LCD's unique pixel structure. These new font renderers use sub-pixel anti-aliasing to enhance on-screen typographic display by as much as 300 percent. Adobe's CoolType font renderer, built into many of its applications, works with PST-1 as well as TT and OpenType fonts on most major computer platforms.

 Originally the PostScript Type 1 font format was Adobe's proprietary format. Beginning in the spring of 1989, Adobe licensed the Type 1 font-production software to other large typeface manufacturers, such as Linotype, Bitstream, and Monotype, but eventually released the software to the public. The PostScript computer language is still the pride and property of Adobe. The move away from PST-1 as Adobe's own opened up this font format to wider distribution by other manufacturers, but also opened the door to a wider range of typeface quality. Not all typefaces are created with the same eye for detail. For the type artist with limited typeface funds, staying with the larger type manufacturers is a safer path to take for ensuring the purchase of quality typefaces.

As an interesting footnote to PST-1 fonts and a harbinger of what was to come, Adobe introduced multiple master (MM) technology in 1991. While not a new type format, multiple master technology enabled a type artist to create additional Adobe PST-1 typefaces within a type family by adjusting a maximum of four design attributes, called *design axes*. The design axes were weight, width, optical size, and style. A type artist working with a MM typeface offering the weight design axis, for example, used a software interface to manipulate two master typeface outlines from each end of the axis (light and bold). The artist could create a new typeface at any point between the two stroke weight extremes. This range of options was called the *dynamic range*.

When typography entered the digital realm, type sizes were scaled from a single master. Hinting was included to compensate for the small-size and low-resolution situations that would jeopardize output of the typeface's more delicate design characteristics. The most significant MM axis, the optical size axis, addressed the weakness of this one-size-scales-all system. It enabled the type artist to create a typeface with optimal legibility for any point size within the dynamic range. It was a return to the days when each foundry type *font* (according to the true definition of the word) received the punch cutter's individual attention and expert adjustment. Adobe stopped manufacturing MM fonts in 1999 and is slowly phasing out software support for its capabilities. Fortunately for type artists, the OpenType file format incorporates some of the benefits MM fonts made available, specifically optical size. (See "OpenType" later in this chapter.)

TrueType

TRUETYPE FONTS (TT), INTRODUCED IN 1991, were developed by Apple. TrueType fonts are outline fonts that use quadratic *b*-spline mathematical formulas to delineate type outlines. This mathematical system describes shapes more simply than cubic béziers, but can result in more control points (fig. 1-4) along the letterform's outline (path) than the PST-1 fonts. TrueType fonts are larger font files than PST-1, as much as 50%, due to their storage structure for outline information and hinting techniques. When purchasing this font format, type artists must specify the computer platform on which it will be used.

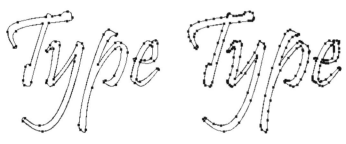

PostScript Type 1   TrueType

FIGURE 1-4: *Letraset's Pristina typeface in two different formats converted to outlines in Illustrator*

HERMANN ZAPF
(1918–)
*German type designer.
A productive designer with over
30 typefaces to his credit, such as
Palatino, Melior, Optima, Firenze,
Zapf Chancery, and Comenius.
Recent work focuses on
digital type design.*
∾

TrueType fonts were designed to bring scalable type technology to users outside the professional graphics arena. With operating system support of the TrueType interpreter on both platforms and only one font file per typeface to install, this technology simplified typeface installation and use, while improving the quality of type for many computer users working on non-PostScript printers. Today PostScript printer support for TT fonts is as seamless as it is for PST-1 fonts because the TrueType interpreter, too, is built into a printer's ROM.

To display and print TT fonts, the type artist needs only the typeface's outline font file, located in the font suitcase. The required metric data, along with outline information and hints, are located in the outline font. The number of font characters in each font is the same as the PST-1 fonts (256 characters), so each family member (roman, italic, bold, and bold italic) is a separate font file. TrueType fonts use the same keyboard mapping system for activating glyphs as PST-1 fonts.

Most recently released TT fonts are identified by title extensions, such as *.TTF* (Windows TT font) or *.dfont* (Mac TT font) or with the letters *TT* in the title indicating a Mac font. All TT versions work on the Macintosh platform.

For the type artist, the fundamental distinction between TT and PST-1 fonts concerns hinting. While hinting for TT fonts accomplishes the same thing as hinting for PST-1 fonts, the mechanics of it is significantly different and can affect type output quality, type font size, and the long-term viability of the typeface font file. TrueType hints provide more expanded, detailed instructions on the bitmap-pattern level. The TT interpreter follows these directions. PST-1 font hints describe problem areas by characteristic and rely on the PostScript interpreter to determine how that characteristic is optimally rasterized.

This is an important distinction on three levels. First, due to the complexity of TT hinting, the quality of output depends on the hinter's level of expertise and the quality of hinting software used. Second, upgrading the TT interpreter might be problematic with preexisting TT fonts. A third issue concerns how existing hinting techniques interact with newer display or printing technology. The newer LCD font rendering software ignores much of the detailed bitmap-pattern TT hinting instructions. The characteristic-based hinting of PST-1 fonts allows the LCD font rendering software to translate the PST-1 font hints for this output technology.

For type artists whose work does not revolve around the PostScript world of graphics, page-layout, and illustration programs, TT brings the ease and accuracy of well-crafted typefaces into the less-expensive world of non-PostScript printers. The home computer user or the word processing or spreadsheet computer user will enjoy the range of fonts. For professional and semi-professional graphic artists, whose work spends most of its time in a PostScript file format being output to high-quality, high-resolution imagesetters, TrueType does not offer unique capabilities or fonts. For type artists who manipulate the paths and points of letterforms to create typographs, the fewer points of PST-1 fonts are preferable. For professional designers whose work is seen on the Internet, TT fonts have been the font of choice, since the TrueType rasterizer was included in both platforms' operating systems. This software difference

GUDRUN ZAPF VON HESSE
(1918–)
German type designer, bookbinder, and calligrapher. Recipient of the 1991 Frederic W. Goudy Award for book and type design. Her designs include Diotima, Ariadne, and Nofret.

≈

HERBERT LUBALIN
(1918–81)
American graphic designer, typographer, and type designer. Created visuals with type to replace illustrations or photographs. Cofounded International Typeface Corporation. Designed Avant Garde Gothic, Lubalin Graphic, and Serif Gothic.

≈

EPHRAM "ED" BENGUIAT
(1927–)
American type designer and graphic designer. Designs comprise over 500 faces including ITC Souvenir, ITC Bookman, Benguiat, Benguiat Gothic, ITC Korinna, and Panache.

≈

too has changed, but as with print media, individual and service bureau preferences will undoubtedly be maintained. This is why it is important to know the distinctions between font file formats, so the type artist is able to make an informed choice.

OpenType

OpenType fonts (ot), introduced in 1997, were developed by Adobe and Microsoft. OpenType is a cross-platform, multilingual, compressed font format with advanced typographic layout capabilities and a glyph capacity of approximately 65,000. This format is an expansion and enhancement of the tt font format structure to include pst-1 font data and additional font information. Each font file contains outline data, using either a pst-1 or tt mathematical description; bitmap fonts; metric data; and informational tables of font and typographic data. OpenType fonts using pst-1 outlines have the suffix *.otf* and those using tt outlines have a *.ttf, .ttc,* or *.otf* suffix.

OpenType's expanded character set is a result of using the Unicode alpha-numeric encoding system. The Unicode Standard contains code points, or character identification, for characters needed by all the world's written languages. Unlike the extended ascii 8-bit encoding system used by pst-1 and tt fonts that has a maximum character capacity of 256, Unicode uses 8-, 16- or 32-bit encoding to identify a character set of over a million. The ot font format has the capacity to make available approximately 65,000 glyphs in a single font file. Consequently, the ot font format is more suitable for languages with extensive character requirements, such as Japanese or Chinese, which have more than 80,000 modern and historic characters.

Not all ot typefaces provide the extensive language support or glyph array possible with this format. Some manufacturers use demarcations of *Standard* and *Pro* to indicate a font's language capabilities. Those identified as *Pro* include the Latin alphabet enabling multilingual typography in the majority of Eurasian languages, including the Slavic languages, Russian, Portuguese, Turkish, and Polish. Some *Pro* fonts add Greek and Cyrillic language support to that listing. Expanded typographic glyphs, such as those available in expert collection fonts, are available in both *Pro* and *Standard* versions on a font-by-font basis (see Appendix b for ot character access charts). The available individual glyph sets, such as *basic, old style figures, alternates,* and *small caps,* are identified for each ot typeface on the manufacturer's Web site.

Choosing an ot typeface with extended glyph sets and language support, rather than a pst-1 typeface with its expert collection, makes installing and working with typefaces easier. In addition, the size of the single font file is remarkably small. For example, the Minion Pro Regular OT font that provides multilingual support (including Greek and Cyrillic) and enhanced typographic capabilities and glyph sets is 184 kilobytes (KB). The type artist needs only this one font file to print and display. In comparison, to print and display the equivalent glyphs as a PST-1 font on the Mac, for example, the type artist needs six files: the Minion Regular outline font and its bitmap fonts, the Minion Regular Expert outline font and its bitmaps, and the Minion Regular Cyrillic outline font and its bitmaps. A total of approximately 1200 kilobytes is needed. A similar size and number of files is needed for the Windows platform. The PST-1 fonts run on one computer platform (specified at purchase), whereas the same OT font file runs on either.

The OT font format consolidates glyphs previously available from multiple font files and enables programmable implementation of typographic layout features through application support. To access all the available glyphs and typographic features in an OT font, the type artist needs application support in two areas. First, the application must be Unicode-savvy—one that reads the Unicode encoding system providing pathways to thousands of characters. Without this, the application can access only the usual 256 characters. Second, the application must be OpenType-savvy—one that reads the font's informational tables for application-controlled glyph substitution. Without this, the application cannot provide glyph variants for characters, such as swash letters. With both of these capabilities, the type artist can take advantage of an OT font's full complement of typographic features and glyphs.

Adobe's InDesign, for example, is a Unicode- and OpenType-savvy application. A type artist can specify the use of text figures throughout a document, for example, so every time the number-key 3 is depressed, the text figure 3 appears, rather than the default titling figure 3. Instead of switching to the font's expert collection to find the correct ligature or small caps necessary, and then switching back, the type artist checks off the typographic features desired and the application automatically inserts them as the characters are input. With ligatures checked, for example, once the characters *f, f,* and *i* are identified in a left-to-right, contiguous sequence, information from the glyph substitution table in the font instructs the application to replace them with the *ffi*-ligature. If this glyph falls on a line break, the application converts the glyph back to individual characters, if necessary, for hyphenation. The application's spell checker also recognizes the *ffi*-glyph as three individual characters. The

PHILL GRIMSHAW
(1950–1998)
English type designer, calligrapher, and mandolin player. Prolific display type designer. His designs include ITC Rennie Mackintosh, ITC Noovo, ITC Kendo, ITC Kallos, Pristina, Arriba, Gravura, and Oberon.

～

JOVICA VELJOVIĆ
(1954–)
Serbian type designer and calligrapher. Designs include ITC Veljovic, ITC Esprit, Ex Ponto, Silentium, and ITC Gamma.

～

benefits of such a powerful union of type format and application are enormous for a type artist. This type format, with suitably savvy applications, has revolutionized typesetting by providing type artists with a powerful and "intelligent" typographic tool.

An additional level of typographic quality is achieved in a document by using a size-specific category of OT fonts called *Opticals*. The typefaces distinguished by the word *Opticals* in their title continue one of the best features of the multiple master type technology—optical sizing. An optical typeface is designed for use in a specific size range. The four generalized size ranges are: caption (6–8 points), regular (9–13 points), subhead (14–24 points), and display (25–72 points). An example of such a typeface is Adobe's *Minion Pro Semibold Italic Caption*. The optical OpenTypes provide an additional capability to the type artist for setting high-quality type.

Ϸᴓ

TYPOGRAPHIC HISTORY IS FILLED with the intriguing men and women dedicated to furthering the field of typography using their own unique perspective. Punch cutters, merchants, printers, entrepreneurs, type historians, and type designers, with diverse backgrounds as engravers, goldsmiths, diplomats, marionette makers, and graphic designers, all contributed to the field in important ways. They worked in the service of the sacred and profane; for cardinals and kings; as employees of type foundries, advertising agencies, publishing houses, and print shops; as lone entrepreneurs pursuing a passion for typography with elusive financial rewards. Some were lionized, while others were not recognized during their lifetimes.

With all its passionate, outspoken, and reticent participants, this rich history provides the critical foundation, the design history, and the tools for the type artists of today. No matter the tool or technique used to set type, the goal is the same—communication—conveying a message from the author to the reader. No matter what the format, the printed page or the electronic screen, the vehicle is the same—type. Communicating with clarity and style is possible with an understanding and appreciation of the contributions, ideas, and type sense of many individuals. Each stimulates today's type artists toward continuing and extending the typographic heritage.

ROBERT SLIMBACH
(1956–)
*American type designer.
Designs include Giovanni,
Minion, Poetica, Utopia,
Adobe Garamond, Cronos,
Adobe Jenson, Caflisch Script,
and Warnock.*

∾

CAROL TWOMBLY
(1959–)
*American type designer.
First woman to receive the Charles
Peignot Award for type design from
the Association Typographique
Internationale. Designs include
Charlemagne, Trajan, Lithos,
Adobe Caslon, Viva, Nueva,
and Chaparral.*

∾

SPEAKING THE
LANGUAGE
OF
LETTERS

W<small>HEN WORKING WITH TYPE AND THE SUBSEQUENT</small> letters, figures, punctuation marks, and symbols the type produces, the type artist enters a world of new terms, the typographic nomenclature. This collection of terms enables all type professionals at all points in the typographic chain—type designers, graphic artists, service bureau operators, typesetters, and others—to converse about this topic clearly and accurately. The proper use of language in all fields identifies the novice from the expert. The type artist who refers to an ampersand as the "squiggly thing that means *and*" does not engender confidence from an author or supervisor. People do not confidently leave their car with a mechanic who refers to the engine as the "big clunky thing under the hood that goes *rum-rum.*" It is wiser to keep driving. The correct use of language identifies a person's level of knowledge in a given field.

The language of letters breaks into five categories representing specific aspects of type. These categories are type anatomy, type guidelines and measurements, typeface styles, type family members, and type font anatomy. Since digital type artists see type as letters and symbols either on a screen or on a printout, the primary terms of interest to them are those identified in this venue, in other words, that which is seen. Setting digital type is not a mechanical process, as was foundry type. The type artist's primary means of interacting with the individual letters comes either on screen or on a printed page. Typographic success results from the mastery of that digital environment.

The beauty of a letter depends on the harmonious adaptation of each of its parts to every other in a well-proportioned manner, so that their exhibition as a whole shall satisfy our esthetic sense—a result gained only by blending together the fine strokes, stems, and swells in their proper relations.

—————————————Goudy
*The Alphabet and
Elements of Lettering*

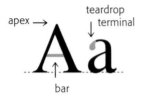

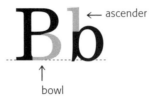

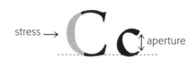

TYPE ANATOMY

Type anatomy refers to the names of the letter's parts—the arm, stroke, spine, swash, and leg, to name a few. "The horizontal thing attached to the top of the vertical thing" is not sufficient here. It is no coincidence that type anatomy adopts many terms from human anatomy. Gutenberg and other early type designers were concerned that the reading public would not accept their type unless the letterforms were familiar to them. It might have been from this concern that the adoption of human body part names originated.

The anatomical elements of type fall into three categories: strokes, endings, and spaces. A *stroke* is a general category that refers to the primary structural components that define the overall appearance of a letterform. Vertical, horizontal, and diagonal marks establish the letter's structural form. An *ending* is a design treatment used to define the beginning and ending of a stroke. An ending completes a stroke in a style complementary to the letterform's overall design style. A *space* refers to the negative area in and around a letterform. This area does not print, but it is visually important for style, legibility, and readability. As a general point of reference that defies all categories, the two terms *head* and *foot* refer respectively to the top and bottom of a letter.

The names of these elements and their definitions are listed by categories in the following sections. Category terms are presented in order of frequency. The most common terms, more frequently seen, are listed first, leading to those less frequently seen.

STROKES

Stroke Besides being the name for this general category of letter components, when lacking a more specific name, the term *stroke* is applicable to any straight or curved line used to define a major

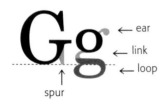

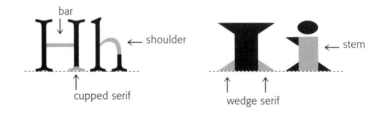

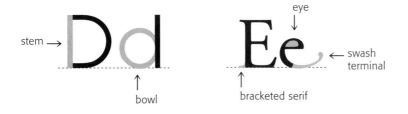

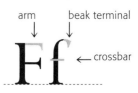

structural portion of a letter. The diagonal line in the middle of the uppercase *N* is a stroke.

Stem A major vertical stroke within a letter, such as in the uppercase *L, E, B, K* and the lowercase *l, d,* and *b.* The stem does not include any serifs or other stroke endings.

Hairline An extremely thin line used as a stroke or a serif.

Ascender A portion of a stroke in a lowercase letter that extends beyond the mean line or above the lowercase *x.* Ascenders are in the lowercase *b, d, f, h, k, l,* and comparable letters.

Descender A portion of a stroke (not limited to lowercase letters) that extends below the baseline, such as in the monocular lowercase *g,* the lowercase *j, p, q,* and *y,* and in some typefaces, the uppercase *J.*

Bar A horizontal stroke that connects two strokes, such as in the lowercase *e* or uppercase *A* and *H.*

Crossbar A horizontal stroke that crosses another stroke, such as in the lowercase *t* and *f,* and the uppercase *T.*

Arm A horizontal or upward diagonal stroke that is attached to the letter on one end and unattached on the other, such as in the uppercase *E, F, L, X, Y, K,* the lowercase *x,* and comparable letters.

Tail A downward diagonal stroke attached to the letter on one end and unattached on the other, such as in the uppercase *K, Q, R, X,* and lowercase *k, x,* and comparable letters. The tail of the uppercase and lowercase *K* is referred to by some as a *leg.*

Spine The main curved stroke in the uppercase and lowercase *S.*

Bowl A curved stroke that creates an enclosed space within a letter, such as in the lowercase *a, b, d, p, q,* uppercase *B, P, R,* and other comparable letters.

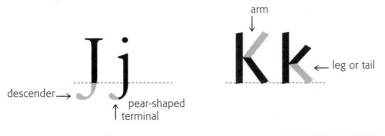

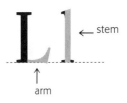

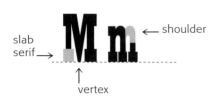

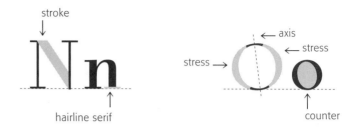

Shoulder The curved portion of a stroke, such as in a lowercase *h, m,* and *n,* that does not create an enclosed space within the letter.

Loop The elliptical stroke at the bottom of the binocular lowercase *g.*

Stress The thickened portion of a curved stroke that determines a direction (vertical, horizontal, or diagonal) in which the letterform appears to lean.

Bracket A curved or sloping shape that smoothly joins a serif to a stroke or stem. Also called a *fillet.*

Link Short stroke that joins the bowl of the binocular lowercase *g* to its loop.

Apex Section of the top of a letter where two straight strokes or stems join and create an angle, such as in the uppercase *A, M,* and *N.*

Vertex Angle created at the bottom of a letter where two straight strokes or stems join, as in the uppercase and lowercase *V* and *W.*

Endings

Serif A cross, or finishing, stroke at the beginning or end of the major strokes of a letterform. Serifs can extend from both sides of a stroke or just one. They enhance readability by facilitating horizontal eye movement. The word *serif* originates from the Dutch word *schreef* (a scratch or flick of the pen). Some serifs are described by their shape, such as *bracketed, cupped, hairline, slab,* and *wedge.*

Terminal Stroke-end treatments, such as tapering or adding a shape, that are not serifs. Some terminals are described by their shape, such as *ball, beak, hooked, pear-shaped,* or *teardrop.*

Swash An extended or decorative flourish that replaces a serif or terminal on a letter.

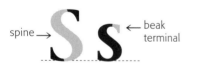

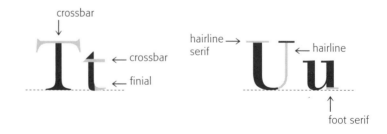

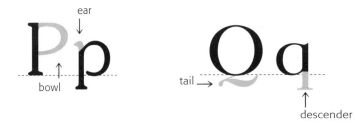

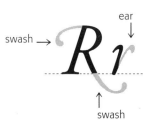

Swash terminal A lowercase letter with a long swash extending from it on the right side. This letter is used at the end of a word or a line.

Finial The tapering end of a stroke, as on the lowercase *e, t,* or *c.*

Ear The short protrusion from the top of the lowercase *g* and *p.* Also applied to the arm of the lowercase *r,* depending upon the typeface.

Spur Small downward extension on some styles of the uppercase *G.*

SPACES

Counter The fully or partially enclosed negative space within or adjacent to a letterform.

Eye The enclosed counter in the upper portion of the lowercase *e.*

Aperture The amount of space between two points in a letter forming an opening into an interior portion of a letterform. An aperture is created by the end of a stroke and its position relative to the rest of the letter. The aperture in the letter *C* is created between the two endpoints of this single, curved stroke. The aperture in the lowercase *e* is created between the right end of its bar and the tip of its finial. Apertures are also in the letter *S,* the uppercase *G,* the lowercase *z,* and the some styles of the lowercase *a.*

TYPE GUIDELINES AND MEASUREMENTS

TYPEFACES AND TYPE FONTS ARE MEASURED using a unit of measure called a *point.* For digital typography, the point is standardized to 1/72 inch (1 point = 1/72 inch) or 72 points equal 1 inch (72 points = 1 inch).

The evolution of the point system for measuring type has had a long and international history involving both individuals and establishments, including the two prominent French typographers Pierre S. Fournier (1712–68) and François-Ambroise Didot (1730–1804); the

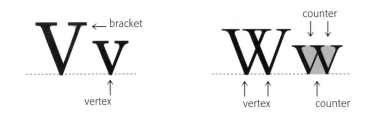

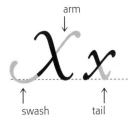

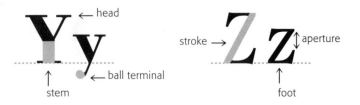

American businessman and printer Nelson C. Hawks (1840–1929); the American printer and inventor Benjamin Franklin (1706–90); the French monarchy of 1723; and the American Type Founders' Association. It was not until 1886 that the American point system, developed by Nelson Hawks, was adopted by the American Type Founders' Association. The British adopted the same measurement system in 1898.

In this Anglo-American point system, a single point measures 0.013837 inches (72 points = 0.996264 inch). In the Didot point system, used in continental Europe, a single point measures 0.0148 inches (72 points = 1.0656 inch). When type was transferred to the digital arena, the point system was converted to even measurements (72 points = 1 inch). The standard Macintosh video screen resolution of 72 dots per inch made this easier.

A type font is not characterized globally as simply big or small. Digital type artists are concerned with the overall height of the type font as well as all the internal points of reference within the font. Enlarging or reducing the overall type font size does not solve all type problems. A problem of decreased readability in a paragraph, for example, may lie with the proportions of x-height to cap height, not the font's overall size.

Measuring a type font involves two categories of information: guidelines and measurements (fig. 2-1). A *guideline* is the location of a specific point of reference from which measurements are calculated. A *measurement* is the distance from one point of reference to another within the type font. The guidelines and measurements are listed by category in the following sections. The terms are presented alphabetically.

GUIDELINES

Baseline The imaginary horizontal line upon which all typeset letters appear to stand or rest.

Cap line The imaginary horizontal line that denotes the top of the uppercase, or capital, letter X. Indicates the tops of the capital letters, although curved uppercase letters, such as the O and C, will extend beyond it slightly.

Mean line The imaginary horizontal line that denotes the top of the lowercase letter x.

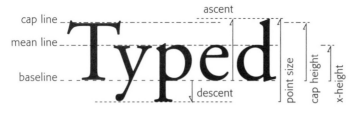

FIGURE 2-1: *Type guidelines and measurements identified*

Ascent The vertical distance from the baseline to the top of the highest glyph in the type font. This location varies from font to font.

Cap height The vertical distance from the baseline to the cap line.

Descent The vertical distance from the baseline to the bottommost point in the type font. This location varies from font to font.

Point size The vertical distance from the bottommost point in the type font to the topmost point in the type font. In foundry type, the depth of the sort's body (see fig. 1-1). In digital type, the height of an equivalent area, called a *glyph window.*

X-height The vertical distance from the baseline to the mean line. This term loosely refers to the height of the lowercase letters, such as *x, a, o,* and *s.* The term *large eye* refers to a typeface with a large *x*-height.

TYPEFACE STYLES REFER TO the ways in which letter parts are designed and connected. Some typeface styles are dramatically different; others are more subtly distinct. Seeing these differences and identifying the major design category to which a typeface belongs is not a goal in itself. The purpose of such distinctions is to help the type artist more easily see the subtle differences between typeface styles, to enhance typeface selection for projects, and to sharpen the eye for proofing documents. Just as the experienced car mechanic can hear the faint, telltale *ping* that identifies a specific car malady, so too can the experienced type artist quickly pick out the wayward italic *a* in a sea of roman letterforms.

AS WITH OTHER ASPECTS OF TYPE, the terminology used to describe typestyle characteristics is unique, although not extensive. These terms describe a typeface's style in the broadest terms. The stylistic terms are presented by frequency of use.

Roman Describes a typeface whose letters stand vertically on, or at right angles to, the baseline. Most continuous-reading text is roman, since it is the easiest to read.

Typeface
Roman

Typeface
Italic

Typeface
Oblique

Typeface
Serif

Typeface
Backslant

Typeface
Sans Serif

Typeface
Script

𝕬𝕭𝕮𝕯𝕰𝕱
abcdefghijklmn
opqrstuvwxyz

The Goudy Text typeface follows the black letter design traditions of the fifteenth century.

Italic Describes a typeface that is structurally redesigned to slant or lean to the right as it rests on the baseline. Effectively used to identify a word(s) having a unique contextual role within roman text.

Oblique Describes a typeface that slants or leans to the right as it rests on the baseline; also referred to as *machine italic.* An oblique typeface is not a redesigned roman typeface, but rather a slanted roman typeface. The angle of oblique can be set, depending upon the typesetting technology used. An oblique typeface is not interchangeable with italic for role identification within roman text because it is structurally too similar to roman.

Serif Describes a typeface that has serifs on the ends of its strokes. Highly suited for continuous-reading text because the serif enhances horizontal eye movement along a type line.

Backslant Describes a typeface that slants or leans to the left as it rests on the baseline. The angle of backslant can be set depending upon the typesetting technology used. Suited for display use only.

Sans serif Describes a typeface whose strokes end bluntly. A sans serif typeface does not have finishing treatments at the ends of its strokes.

Script Describes a typeface that imitates cursive handwriting. Many of the letters are created with a single, continuous stroke. Some typefaces have connecting strokes to join adjacent letters; other scripts have freestanding letters.

AS THE STYLISTIC TERMINOLOGY LISTED SUGGESTS, type artists need a language with which to communicate general type styles and typeface characteristics to one another. They need a typeface classification system as a means to impose order on the thousands of typefaces available. There are multiple existing systems for classifying typefaces that represent the viewpoints of typographers from different parts of the world. For type artists entering the world of typography from varied backgrounds, some of these systems are too specific and detailed. The categories listed here are based in part on these existing typeface systems, but leave out the heavy, condensed, angular letterforms, called *black letter,* used by Gutenberg. Black letter type, also characterized as *gothic* or *barbarous,* was based on the twelfth-century *hand,* or handwriting, used in the northern European countries of England, Germany, and France.

When classifying type, the term *roman* reappears in its second usage. In the context of typeface classification, *roman* refers to the open, round letterform structure of the English alphabet that is based on the well-proportioned, open, curvilinear forms of the 23-letter Roman alphabet. (The letters *U, W,* and *J* were added to the English language by 1400 to make the final 26 letters.) The traditional roman typefaces, introduced by the da Spira brothers and refined in the early 1470s by Nicolas Jenson, were based on the ninth-century Carolingian minuscule (a further refinement of the original Roman alphabet letterforms) and set a path for generations of type designers to follow.

The typefaces that continued and refined this tradition can be divided into eight classifications: humanist, old style, transitional, modern, slab serif, sans serif, script, and decorative. While each category can be subdivided into finer distinctions, these general groupings help today's type artist make stylistic sense of the vast number of available typefaces. Not all typefaces assigned to a category will display every stylistic characteristic of their category. Typeface designers maintained past stylistic influences while incorporating their own style changes. As those new style changes found their way into other typefaces, new classifications were formed. The typefaces responsible for the evolution are assigned to the category they most represent. Type classification is not an exact science, but a blend of colors.

Within these eight classifications, comparing the treatment of four structural components helps the type artist see the distinctions between classifications. These telltale components are vertical and horizontal proportions, stroke weight, stress position, and serif treatment. There are many more ways to make typefaces unique, but by looking first at these four characteristics, the type artist can get a summary snapshot.

ABCDEFGHIJKLMNOPQRSTUVWX
abcdefghijklmnopqrstuvwxyz!?&1234I234

FIGURE 2-2: *Centaur is in the humanist classification*

Humanist. The humanist classification refers to typefaces with wide, squarish proportions; medium- to heavy-weight strokes with little contrast between stroke weights; slanted stress placement; and heavy cupped serifs with a rounded calligraphic quality (fig. 2-2). The head and foot serifs on the lowercase letters are slanted in relation to the baseline. Humanist typefaces are the first-generation roman typefaces diverging from the calligraphic, imitation handwriting of the black letter faces. They continue the uneven page textures of their predecessors,

AefgHkp

Centaur has low stroke contrast, cupped serifs, slanted stress, and a slanted bar in the lowercase *e.*

AefgHkp

Adobe Garamond has medium stroke contrast, a low *x*-height, slanted stress, and ascenders that extend above the cap line.

which is why this classification is not readily sought for use as a text face for continuous reading. These faces are easily identified by a distinctive slant to the bar of the lowercase *e*. This category includes the Centaur, Jenson, and Stempel Schneidler typefaces.

Old Style. The old style typefaces have a taller, more vertical stance since the ascenders extend beyond the cap height (fig. 2-3). This projects a more elegant appearance, but suggests a lower *x*-height. Stroke contrast within a single letter is medium and the stress placement is slanted. Old style typefaces use thinner, bracketed serifs that are more uniformly drawn than their predecessors. The head and foot serifs on the lowercase letters are slanted. The bar of the lowercase *e* is horizontal. The old style category includes the Garamond, Bembo, Caslon, Palatino, and Caxton typefaces.

ABCDEFGHIJKLMNOPQRSTUVWXY
abcdefghijklmnopqrstuvwxyz!?&12341234

FIGURE 2-3: *Adobe Garamond is an old style typeface*

AefgHkp

Baskerville has increased stroke contrast, vertical stress, high legibility, and easy readability.

Transitional. The transitional classification contains narrow typefaces with an increased contrast between stroke weights within letters and a predominantly vertical stress placement (fig. 2-4). The serifs are bracketed and usually, although not always, horizontal for the head and foot of the ascenders. The horizontal serifs and the higher contrast between stroke widths make this category very readable. The legibility and reproduction quality of these typefaces is high, making them prime candidates for use in early reader materials, newspapers, and magazines. The transitional category is the largest of the previously described categories. It includes the New Century Schoolbook, Bookman, Baskerville, Times Roman, Caledonia, and Cheltenham typefaces.

ABCDEFGHIJKLMNOPQRSTUVWX
abcdefghijklmnopqrstuvwxyz!?&123456

FIGURE 2-4: *Baskerville is in the transitional classification*

Modern. The modern classification displays narrow letters with an extreme contrast between stroke widths in letters (fig. 2-5). The vertical stress further enhances the narrow set. Serifs appear as evenly or mechanically drawn hairlines and slightly bracketed, if at all. The head and foot serifs on lowercase ascenders are horizontal. The extreme contrasting stroke weights and the vertical stress placement are distinguishing characteristics of this classification, the most exaggerated of which earned the name *fat face*. Typefaces in this category represent one end of the typeface spectrum, with the calligraphic styles of the humanist typefaces at the other. The extreme thick and thin stroke weights keep some typefaces in this category suitable for display purposes only. At small sizes, text type can look too blotchy. The modern category includes the Didot, Bodoni, Linotype Centennial, and Walbaum typefaces.

ABCDEFGHIJKLMNOPQRSTUVW
abcdefghijklmnopqrstuvwxyz!?&123

FIGURE 2-5: *Bodoni is in the modern classification*

Slab Serif. The slab serif typeface classification is distinguished by its dominant slab serifs and wide, rectangular set (fig. 2-6). The stroke weights match the serif weight, with or without brackets. Contrast between strokes is low with vertical stress placement. Although sometimes referred to as *square serifs,* the slab serifs form thick rectangular pads under each stroke. The term *Egyptian* was given to this type grouping because they were reminiscent of the slab-form of architecture the Egyptians followed when building the pyramids. A second grouping of typefaces from this category first appeared in the early twentieth century. These typefaces were geometric in structure with unbracketed slab serifs at each stroke's end. The slab serif category includes the Antique, Clarendon, Memphis, Rockwell, and Beton typefaces.

ABCDEFGHIJKLMNOPQRSTUVWXYZ
abcdefghijklmnopqrstuvwxyz!?&1234

FIGURE 2-6: *Memphis is a slab serif typeface*

Sans Serif. The sans serif typefaces were first introduced in 1816 to the dismay of many type designers. Type without serifs—*sans* meaning *without*—was so odd looking that it was dubbed *grotesque* (see fig. 2-7). The first grouping of British sans serif typefaces kept the term *grotesque* or *grot*, but the American typefounders preferred the term *gothic* to describe their sans serif types. The grotesque typefaces are narrow in width with an overall rectangular appearance. Curves are achieved by

AefgHkp

Bodoni has extreme stroke contrast, a narrow set width, vertical stress, and hairline serifs.

AefgHkp

Memphis has stroke weights that match the serif weight.

AefgHkp

Frutiger is a highly legible sans serif typeface.

rounded corners rather than true curves. The stroke weight is consistent, but narrows at junctures or curves. This grouping includes the Grotesque, Alternate Gothic, Franklin Gothic, News Gothic, Helvetica, and Univers typefaces. Univers was one of the first typefaces to be designed as a type family—with 21 family members all logically numbered.

As with the slab serif typefaces, there is a geometric grouping of sans serif typefaces based on the same streamlined geometric structures. This grouping includes the Futura, Kabel, Gill Sans, Avant Garde, and Spartan typefaces. The third grouping of sans serif typefaces combines the calligraphic stroke treatment of the humanist typefaces with this serif-less structure. This produced some elegant sans serif typefaces that include the Optima and Bernhard Fashion typefaces.

ABCDEFGHIJKLMNOPQRSTUVWXYZ
abcdefghijklmnopqrstuvwxyz!?&123

FIGURE 2-7: *Frutiger is in the sans serif classification*

Script. The script typeface classification includes those typefaces trying to duplicate the flowing qualities of excellent penmanship. The typefaces in this category range widely with letter width, stroke-weight contrast, and stress placement (fig. 2-8). The two features useful for subdividing this classification are joined letters and unjoined letters. Examples in this category include the Snell Roundhand, Mistral, Brush Script, Bernhard Cursive, Commercial Script, and Bickham Script typefaces.

ABCDEFGHIJKLMNO
abcdefghijklmnopqrstuvwxyz!?&1234567890

FIGURE 2-8: *Boulevard is a script typeface*

Boulevard capitals have a wide set width and an elegant swash that gives a graceful start to a word.

Decorative. The decorative classification contains all the rest. These typefaces are so visually distinct that they are unsuitable for use as continuous-reading text faces (fig. 2-9). These typefaces project a strong appearance and evoke an emotional response from the reader. They seemingly create words from stamp-pad letters, rolled pieces of metal, neon lights, toothpaste, and weathered pieces of wood. They are elaborately illustrated letterforms or stark, structurally incomplete letterforms. They transport the viewer to the Stone Age, the Old West, a music hall, the circus, and the days of the American Revolution with their unique

AefgHkp

Galahad has the calligraphic edge of newly written letterforms.

stroke treatments and adornments. The decorative category is the hardest to define and the easiest to identify. It is where old categories are combined and new ones are created. Typefaces included in this diverse category are Cooper Black, Belwe, Stencil, Playbill, Sapphire, Caslon Antique, Neon, Neuland, Benguiat, Broadway, Prisma, Calypso, and many more.

ABCDEFGHIJKLMNOPQRSTUVWXYZ
abcdefghijklmnopqrstuvwxyz!?&1231234

FIGURE 2-9: *Galahad is a decorative typeface*

A TYPE FAMILY INCLUDES ALL THE STYLISTIC VARIATIONS of a single typeface. Within the Helvetica type family, for example, there are Helvetica Light, Regular, Bold, Condensed, Extended, and combinations of all and more. Type artists learn to recognize the general descriptive characteristics of these terms, but there is no uniform weight that is *light, medium,* or *bold.* Adrian Frutiger was the first type designer to create an entire type family at once. When introduced in 1957, Frutiger's sans serif typeface Univers had 21 variations, distinguished by a system of numbers rather than names. He identified these variants as a *palette* of type. The idea of numbers did not catch on with the typesetting community, but the idea of having logical, extended families, or collections, of typefaces did. Many type artists believe the more family members a typeface has, the more visual distinctions can be made on the page.

When purchasing digital typefaces, the type artist chooses from type families of varying sizes. Some, such as Times, contain the basic set: roman, italic, bold, and bold italic. Other typefaces come with more extended families, such as Frutiger. It comes with nine family members: light, light italic, roman, italic, bold, bold italic, black, black italic, and ultra black. Each is a separate font file, accessed separately in the font menu or in the Frutiger submenu. This single extended type family offers the type artist a greater range of typographic possibilities.

Adding a type family's expert collection to the font menu doubles the typographic possibilities. The PST-1 Minion type family includes four weights. Together with its expert collection, it requires 22 different typeface files to extend this type family to its fullest. In contrast, the Minion Pro in the OT format requires only eight font files to provide all the same glyphs in four different weights with additional multilingual support not available in the 22 PST-1 files. The OpenType Opticals fonts

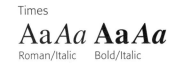

Times

Roman/Italic   Bold/Italic

Frutiger

Light/Italic   Roman/Italic

Bold/Italic   Black/Italic

Ultra Black

Times and Frutiger type families

provide even larger type families by offering four optimized size categories for all the included weights. Access to these extended glyph sets are a must for the thoroughly smitten type artist.

TYPE FONT ANATOMY

WITHIN A SINGLE TYPE FONT, THERE ARE A HOST of different glyphs—all with different purposes. (With PST-1 and TT font formats, the type font spans several font files; with OT, it is just one.) Glyphs in a type font go far beyond the common uppercase letters, lowercase letters, figures, and punctuation marks available on a typewriter keyboard. They include small caps, text figures, titling figures, ligatures, ornaments, and diphthongs (fig. 2-10) to name a few. (When a type family sends out invitations to the annual reunion, all sorts show up.) The glyphs in a type font divide into five categories: letters of the alphabet, figures, punctuation marks, joined characters, and symbols.

ABCDEFGHIJKLMNOPQRSTUVWXYZ
Uppercase letters (majuscules)

abcdefghijklmnopqrstuvwxyz
Lowercase letters (minuscules)

ABCD ABCDEFGHIJKLMNOPQRSTUVWXYZ abcd
Small caps

ABCD 1234567890 abcd 1234567890
Titling figures   Superior figures

abcd 1234567890 ABCD 1234567890
Text figures   Inferior figures

¼ ½ ¾ ⅛ ⅜ ⅝ ⅞ ⅓ ⅔
Case fractions

' ' . , ; : " " - – — / / { } [ ] ( ) Á á É ö Ñ ñ Ü ü
Punctuation marks and diacritics

fi fl ff ffi ffl ſh ft ct ß st & æ Æ œ Œ
Joined characters (ligatures and diphthongs)

\$ ¢ £ ™ © ® ¶ = + ≠ ± ÷ ' " ° ❦ ❧ ❀ ❁
Symbols

FIGURE 2-10: *Font anatomy glyph sampler*

THE LETTERS OF THE ALPHABET, or *graphemes,* include all the capitals, or *uppercase,* and the lowercase letters. Within this seemingly simple category, there are many glyph variants: capital letters, display caps, titling caps, small caps, and lowercase letters. The *capitals,* or majuscules, are the large letters drawn proportionally for use within text. Used as capitals at the beginning of a sentence and with proper nouns in text, these letters draw attention to a location (beginning of a sentence) or a single word (proper noun). The strokes are drawn to optically match the stroke weights of the lowercase letters and serve as companion letters within the text.

The *display caps,* on the other hand, are designed specifically to work in display sizes, 14 points or larger. These caps are not scaled from the uppercase, but are drawn separately, emphasizing subtle and delicate details visible in the larger sizes. They are suitable for use in headings and titles that accompany the other family members of the text type.

Titling caps refer to a type font of capital letters only. They are drawn to the height of the type size (almost) rather than the cap height. They are not meant for use with lowercase letters and do not maintain the same color as the text faces. Some typefaces use the terms *display caps* and *titling caps* interchangeably and conform to the definition of the former.

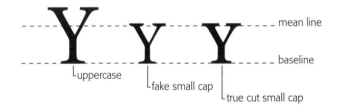

FIGURE 2-11: *Uppercase and small cap stroke comparison*

Small caps are capital letters that are the approximate size of the *x*-height. They are redesigned, or recut, to maintain the stroke weight and proper proportions for use with the lowercase letters. The term *true cut* refers to such redrawn letters. *Fake small caps* are scaled down from capital letters, rather than redesigned. These pseudo–small caps do not maintain proper stroke weights (fig. 2-11) and appear too light on the text page. (See "Titling Caps and Small Caps" in chapter 6.)

The *lowercase letters,* or minuscules (developed from the Carolingian minuscule alphabet of the ninth century), are designed for use in text. Lowercase letters create word-specific shapes that assist readers in

A B C D E F G H I J
K L M N O P Q R S
T U V W X Y Z
Capital letters

A B C D E F G H I J
K L M N O P Q R S
T U V W X Y Z
Display capitals

A B C D E F G H I J
K L M N O P Q R S
T U V W X Y Z
Small capitals

a b c d e f g h i j
k l m n o p q r s
t u v w x y z

Lowercase letters

FIGURES

1 2 3 4 5 6 7 8 9 0

Titling figures

1 2 3 4 5 6 7 8 9 0

Text figures

identifying words more quickly and consequently increasing their reading speed. (See "Readability" in chapter 3.)

In the past when setting books using foundry type, two wooden type cases were needed for a single font's sorts. The typesetter placed the cases, one above the other, on the angled top of the type case cabinet. The top, or upper, case contained majuscules, small caps, case fractions, and symbols. The lower case contained minuscules, spaces, figures, and ligatures. Over time the terms *uppercase* and *lowercase* evolved to represent the letters in each case. A single case, called a *job case,* was used when setting brochures and advertisements—*job work*. This case contained capitals, lowercase, figures, spaces, and a few ligatures and symbols—the digital equivalent of a PST-1 font without its expert collection.

THE FIGURES, OR NUMERALS, IN A FONT fall into five categories. They are titling figures, text figures, superior figures, inferior figures, and fractions. A *true cut figure* is redrawn for its particular size and usage to blend with the weights of the surrounding letters. As with small caps, scaling the titling figures, for example, to create the smaller inferior or superior figures decreases their stroke weight and weakens their color on the page. A true superior figure maintains consistent typographic color and typographic quality.

The *titling figures* are the visual equivalent of uppercase letters. They are the size of the cap height, do not extend below the baseline, and have a uniform height. Titling figures, also referred to as *ranging, lining, capital, aligning,* or *modern figures,* are designed for use with capital letters in headlines or in tabulated materials. In text, these figures are too overpowering and disturb the color and texture of the text. Some OpenType fonts offer tabular lining and proportional lining figures. *Tabular lining figures,* the default figures for many typefaces, are the same width, so they align vertically in columns. *Proportional lining figures* have varying widths and should be used for all other titling figure uses.

The *text figures* are the lowercase letters of the number world. They are the size of the *x*-height with ascenders and descenders extending from some of the figures and they have a stroke weight comparable to a lowercase letter. Definitely harder to access than their bigger counterparts, the text figures are worth finding in a type font. Titling figures call too much attention to a number within a sentence—in a street address, for example. Instead, using a text figure blends the number nicely into the rest of the text, eliminating the unnecessary emphasis. If a number is present with lowercase letters or small caps, that number should be a text figure. Text figures also are referred to as *lowercase, old style, non-ranging,* or *hanging figures.* Some OT fonts offer *tabular old style* and *proportional old style figures* for use in tables and in text, respectively.

While titling figures are easier to access on a keyboard, historically they were the latecomers. Text figures were the primary form used in typographic printing until 1800, giving rise to the term *old style.* In the nineteenth century, a less auspicious typographic time, titling figures were more prominent and were referred to as *modern.* Text figures returned in the twentieth century and their use and access continue to expand with digital typography.

The *superior figures* are smaller than the text figures, but align top and bottom. They are redesigned and resized titling figures. They are positioned to align along the top with the font's ascenders. Superior figures are used as superscript for exponents and footnoting and as numerators in piece fractions.

1 2 3 4 5 6 7 8 9 0
Superior figures

The *inferior figures* are the same size as the superior figures, but they sit on the baseline. In this location, they serve as the denominator in a piece fraction. When the figure is lowered below the baseline, it serves as a subscript for chemical symbols and mathematical equations.

1 2 3 4 5 6 7 8 9 0
Inferior figures

Fractions came as a single character on the old Royal manual typewriters. They were simple to use, limited in quantity (¼ and ½), and fit nicely with the surrounding letters. With all the available figures in a digital typeface, fractions are no longer that simple. There are three types of fractions: case fractions, piece fractions, and level fractions. The single character fraction from the bygone days of the manual typewriter is the equivalent of the *case fraction.* It is a single character—designed and positioned for proper stroke weight and color. (Its name originated from the days of foundry type when it came out of the case as a single sort.) A *piece fraction* is constructed by the type artist using a superior figure for the numerator, a fraction bar (or *solidus*), and an inferior figure for the denominator. The *level fraction* is constructed using titling figures separated by a slash (or *virgule*).

¼ ½ ¾ ⅛ ⅜ ⅓ ⅔
Case fractions

¼ ½ ¾ ⅛ ⅜ ⅓ ⅔
Piece fractions

1/4 1/2 3/4 1/8 3/8
Level fractions

WITH ALL THE LETTERS AND FIGURES AVAILABLE for putting thought to paper, punctuation marks and diacritics are needed to fine-tune those words for emphasis and clarity. Punctuation marks are used alone at the beginning of sentences, in the middle of sentences, and at the end of sentences. For all their many purposes, punctuation marks are typeset characters that must fit within the page's typographic texture. If an em dash, for example, careens into the adjacent letter causing a blotch in the

PUNCTUATION MARKS AND DIACRITICS

. , ; : " " ' ' ! ?
Punctuation marks

– – — – – ~

Hyphen and en, em, threequartersem,
figure, and swung dash

[ ] ⟨ ⟩

Square and angle brackets

{ } ( )

Braces and parentheses

À à É è Ö ö Ñ ñ

Letters with diacritics

Joined Characters

Æ æ Œ œ

Diphthongs (aesc and ethel)

fi fl ff ffi ffl Th fft ffk

Minion ligatures

fi fl ff ffi ffl

Bembo ligatures

texture, its role is weakened. Correct letterspacing around punctuation marks is important, just as it is around letters. If an exclamation point is placed within the quotation marks, when it should have been outside of them, the meaning of the statement is altered. Typographic quality enhances delivery of the written message—it should not confuse it.

Just as the type artist chooses the correct caps for a situation, the correctly sized punctuation for those caps is important as well. There are fewer choices to make in this category, but there are choices. There are at least six dashes available—the hyphen and the en, em, figure, threequartersem, and swung dash. To enclose material in text, there are two brackets available—square and angle—as well as braces and parentheses. Choosing the right punctuation mark for the situation (when a choice is available) is important, but inserting the mark comfortably into the text is equally important and more frequently required.

Diacritics are placed in text at the same time as the letter they accompany. The *a* acute (á), the *e* circumflex (ê), and the *o* with an umlaut (ö) are properly spaced when they are set simultaneously. These marks are essential to the different languages that use them, but each language requires the same level of typographic quality for a seamless delivery of its message.

Joined characters include two (sometimes three) letters set as a single character. They can be physically joined, such as *diphthongs* (æ); precisely aligned, such as the *f-i ligature* in the Bembo typeface (fi); or joined so long ago, that now they are viewed by many as a character by itself, such as the *ampersand* (&).

Diphthongs were born from a need to indicate an unique sound. A *diphthong* is a merging of two vowels to create a particular sound. Several sounds did not carry over well from Latin into the English language. The diphthongs, *aesc* and *ethel,* are found in words making this crossover. Some words, such as *encyclopædia,* have been in the English language so long that the use of the aesc was dropped—*encyclopedia.*

The pursuit of typographic quality necessitated the use of ligatures, also called *tied letters.* The ascender of the lowercase *f* in many type fonts was so effusive that it extended into its neighbor's set width. With some neighbors, such as the lowercase *o,* making the *f*'s ascender a kern on its foundry type body solved the problem. Letters such as the lowercase *i* and *l,* however, would not relinquish any horizontal territory; thus the need for the *f-i* ligature and the *f-l* ligature. (Originally, the term *ligature* referred only to the stroke connecting the two letters.)

The lowercase *f* and all its various English-language forms—*ff, fl, fi, ffl, ffi*—are not the only ligatures. A *T-h* ligature (Th), available in the Minion Pro type family, merges the crossbar of the *T* with the ascender of the lowercase *h* for improved typographic texture. Decorative ligatures are available also on a typeface-by-typeface basis depending upon the type designer's interest. Ligatures for *s-t* and *c-t* are available in the typeface Adobe Garamond and Minion, although they are not essential for consistent text color, since a lowercase *s* does not naturally collide with a lowercase *t*. The *eszett* (ß) is an *s-s* ligature used in German language typesetting, but was used in the past when setting English.

The ampersand is a union of the two lowercase letters *e* and *t* from the Latin word *et* (et per se and). These two joined characters create a recognizable symbol for the word *and* that, if done well, fits within the design parameters of the typeface.

THE REST OF THE MARKS, symbols, signs, and ornaments possible in a type font fall into the general category of *symbols*—characters that represent a word, monetary system, mathematical function, or flourish. Some of these symbols are designed to fit within the design structure of their parent font. Others, such as mathematical symbols, might be in a separate symbol or pi font. Ornaments are not always included, but when they are, these small flowers, flourishes, moons, and leaves add a bit of typographic grace beyond that which the typeface design projects.

✦

UNDERSTANDING TYPE FROM THE INSIDE OUT unlocks its mysteries and capabilities. Being able to identify its components, to talk about its structure, and to distinguish its stylistic differences are as important to a type artist as a car's components, structure, and style are to a professional car mechanic. All the characters in a typeface are the visual tools type artists use to set type. Knowledge of all the characters at the fingertips, as well as of the structure and style of type, lays the foundation for successfully using type on a page. Type that entices its reader into the subject matter is like a high-performance luxury car on the open road.

ct st ct st sp ft ff ffi ffl

Adobe Garamond and
Minion decorative ligatures

& & & *&*

Some ampersands show their
e t heritage better than others.

SYMBOLS

© ™ ® $ ¢ £ ☾ § ℰ
+ = ÷ ‡ † ° # ¶

Assorted symbols

SETTING
TYPE
ON A
PAGE

Communicating information from one person to another employs various formats. People hear news on the radio, see documentaries on television, and read commentaries in the newspaper. People also receive information by "mail"—faxes, e-mail, voice-mail, and the more conventional envelope-with-a-stamp-on-it-mail. Passing along information to one person or to many people occurs between individuals and corporations, amateurs and professionals, as well as families and neighbors. Communicating information to others concerns such diverse groups as medical health service providers and municipal law enforcement agencies. Even the traditional mail carriers want to get the word out about their services, their stamps, their mail trucks, and more.

Print media—words and images on paper—constitute a sizable proportion of these communications. A printed page (in a book, in a booklet, as a direct mailer, or as a single advertisement on a larger page) is a collection of written and pictorial elements placed together for a single purpose—to communicate a particular message. A writer wants to tell the reader something specific. The message can be promotional—the company has a product or service to sell. The message can be informational—a new pet owner receives a booklet on kitten care from the veterinarian.

To design a page is to design a map for the reader's eye to follow. This page map leads the reader to and through all the page elements—the headline, subheads, text, and visuals. Designers are to the page what the auto club is to a road map. The auto club plans the route the motorist takes through the countryside or city. The designer plans the route the reader takes through the visual landscape of the page. Unlike the designer, the auto club cannot relocate states to improve the trip. A designer, on the other hand, can arrange, scale, and select the page elements to communicate the message expeditiously and effectively.

All the visual elements on the page work to enhance a communication—to make the reader's understanding of the message particular and clear rather than general or vague (unless general and vague are the sender's intent). Word for word, the text elements typically outnumber all others on the page. Surprisingly, they can be the elements most often overlooked and least considered.

WELL-EXECUTED PAGE TYPOGRAPHY ENHANCES the act of reading. Typeface selection, type measure, and type alignment are some of the type decisions that enhance readability. On the page, however, the typographic elements are design components as well. Type is not just a designed element but an element of design. The same decisions that affect readability also affect page design. Typeface selection, type block placement, and use of white space integrate the typographic elements into the overall design of the page and expedite the reader's movement around the page. It is not enough to get all the type on the page—using it effectively shows it was worth placing there.

When working with words, it all gets back to reading. How is it done? What is expected? What makes it hard work? A discussion of reading begins with the definition of two words: *legibility* and *readability*. They are not interchangeable. *Legibility* refers to the reader's ability to identify letters. It is a characteristic of typeface design. If the reader is unsure whether a letter is a lowercase *o* or *e,* then the letter is not legible. The reader cannot make a correct identification. *Readability* refers to the reader's ability to identify and comprehend words, sentences, and paragraphs easily. It is a characteristic of typography. Setting a page in a legible typeface enhances the page's readability, but it does not guarantee it. Legibility is a result of the type designer's work. Readability is a result of the type artist's work.

THE PRIMARY DETERMINANT OF LEGIBILITY is typeface design. The design style imposed on the letters of the alphabet by the type designer might distort the letter shapes beyond recognition and thereby decrease legibility; or it might enhance the appearance of the letter shapes and

TYPOGRAPHY AND READING

Legibility and readability control reader interaction with type on the page.

LEGIBILITY

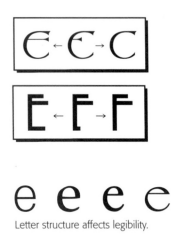

Letter structure affects legibility.

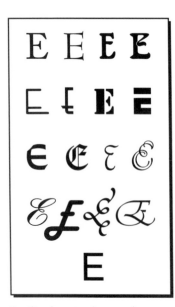

Familiar character shapes enhance legibility.

increase legibility. A type designer's treatment of structural anatomy determines the reader's ability to recognize the letters within a typeface. An uppercase *E* with only two arms can appear to be an *F* or a *C.* The size of the eye in a lowercase *e* controls the ease with which the reader identifies the *e.* If it is too small, it may look like a lowercase *c.*

The human brain works diligently to find patterns in visual elements. If a type designer imposes an unorthodox design style on a typeface, readers can identify the letters once they become accustomed to the style's characteristics—but only if they are applied to strokes, curves, stems, and serifs uniformly. This may be a time-consuming task, but unorthodox design styles applied consistently are decipherable by those willing to take the time to do so.

Concern for typeface legibility is not new. Typographer and type designer Morris Fuller Benton (1872–1948), son of Linn Boyd Benton, the inventor of the Benton matrix cutter for foundry type production, did extensive eyesight and reading comprehension research before designing his Century Schoolbook typeface in 1924. Century Schoolbook became the mainstay for textbook type design as well as the standard for legibility issues in typeface design. Morris Fuller Benton, the most prolific American typeface designer, has been called "the unknown father of American typeface design," due to his vast, diverse contribution of designs—Souvenir, Franklin Gothic, Stymie, Broadway, Clearface, and Hobo, to name a few (Haley 1992).

In his *Essay on Typography,* the typographer Eric Gill (1882–1940) wrote, "Legibility, in practice, amounts simply to what one is accustomed to." Handwriting is a good example of this statement. People can read their own handwriting, but many have difficulty identifying even one or two letters in someone else's. Writers probably can identify all letters in their own handwritten sentences and paragraphs. Writers are accustomed to the shapes and angles of their personal handwriting style. That is not to say because something is legible to a single reader, it is legible to all readers. When choosing a typeface for a page, it should be legible to the widest audience possible.

Typeface features that enhance legibility are familiar character shapes, open counters (*x*-height is one determinant of this), medium stroke contrast, and avoidance of extremes in stroke weight, stroke contrasts, and serifs. Enlarging a typeface cannot make an illegible typeface legible, because the proportional relationship between the counters and strokes remains the same. If a typeface chosen for continuous-reading text is not legible, it is time to select a new one.

ALL DECISIONS MADE BY THE TYPE ARTIST affect readability. Every typographic decision on the page, in a paragraph, and in a sentence dictates the ease with which the reader travels through the type blocks to the message's end. (A *type block* is a shaped area of type [usually rectangular, but not always].) If the reader becomes confused, tired, or discouraged while reading (or thinking about reading) a document, the message is not delivered.

For example, if the type blocks are too wide, the reader can lose the way back to the beginning of the next line and begin rereading the original line. If the lines are too close together, an alluring ascender or a devilish descender can divert the reader into an adjacent line. Reading the first half of one line with the second half of another seldom makes sense. Confusion is caused also if the headline's type style is too informal for its content. In this instance, confusion causes the reader to stop reading and wonder about the veracity of the message. Most typographic decisions influence readability, directly or indirectly.

Letter Case and Readability. Given ideal reading conditions, an experienced reader reads 300 words or more per minute. The faster a word is identified, the sooner the reader proceeds to the next one and so forth throughout the paragraph. There are several well-researched reading models detailing how readers identify words and how their eyes move along the type line.

The oldest model, initially proposed in 1886, purports that readers use the word's shape created by the collective sequence of lowercase letters to identify each word. It is only when readers come upon an unfamiliar word shape that they are forced to sound out the word letter by letter and syllable by syllable. Setting the same word in uppercase removes all the unique visual clues from a word's shape and forces the reader to view each word carefully, decreasing reading speed by a maximum of 10 percent. Some psychologists (and typographers) continue to support this model through a variety of research.

Another group of psychologists supports the parallel letter recognition model. They argue, and their research supports, that readers identify groups of letters in a word simultaneously. The reader's eye moves horizontally across a line of type in a series of small jumps, called *saccades*. Most saccades proceed forward, but a small percentage backtrack before continuing. Saccades vary in length due to word size and function, averaging approximately nine letters. The reader identifies a word's individual letters from their uniquely shaped strokes and then identifies the word through a complex associative process. A reader receives letter

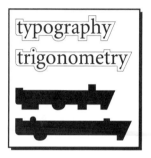

Lowercase letters create identifiable word shapes.

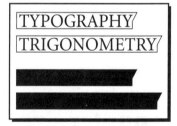

Uppercase letters eliminate word-shape distinctions.

information peripherally to locate the destination of the next saccade
and to provide information for future word identifications.

In both models, lettercase is a factor in varying degrees. The ascenders and descenders of lowercase letterforms create more distinctive
visual structure than the streamlined uppercase, whether individually or
within a word shape. There is general agreement that lowercase letters
foster faster reading speeds than uppercase letters due to readers' greater
familiarity with this lowercase format. Practice will diminish this speed
difference, but for continuous-reading text, the type artist should aim
for the reading preferences of the majority, no matter which reading
model prevails.

When readability issues are not critical, as with short word groupings (headlines and subheads), using all uppercase letters (the visual
equivalent of shouting) can get the reader's attention, give emphasis to a
word, or make type look bigger without changing its point size. Not all
typefaces should be set in all uppercase letters. Script or cursive typefaces, such as Zapf Chancery, have elaborate swash caps designed to call
attention to the beginning of a word. Setting a word with all swash capitals draws attention to every single letter and destroys the word's visual
cohesion. Such an inappropriate use of these beautifully designed swash
letters is a visual nightmare. It is safe to say that almost all script, cursive, and swash typefaces should not be set in all capital letters.

Type Weight and Readability. The nineteenth century was a time of
change and experimentation in printing and type-production techniques, due in part to an increased need to get information to people in
the form of books, posters, and newspapers. It was during this time that
boldface or bold type was introduced, much to the chagrin of some typographers. Bold letterforms are harder to read than book-weight letterforms, because their counters are smaller. The smaller counter diminishes legibility. Typefaces with weight distinctions of *black, ultra, bold,*
and *extra bold* are suitable for headlines. These visually dynamic letters
pop off the page and call attention to their message. In display sizes, the
reduction of counter size does not slow the reader significantly, because
only a few words are affected. Bolding provides needed emphasis, as do
capital letters, when used selectively for subheads and captions. Black or
ultrabold type is suitable only in display sizes, such as 24 points and
above. The increased size maximizes counter size and improves readability. For smaller sizes, the type artist uses semibold type for emphasis.

Heavy stroke weights are unsuitable in text sizes for continuous
text. Here the diminished legibility coupled with the small size tires the

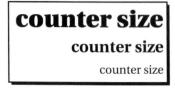

counter size
counter size
counter size

Heavy stroke weights in small sizes
diminish legibility.

counter size
counter size
counter size

Lighten stroke weights as type size
decreases to improve legibility.

reader, slows reading speed and comprehension, and provides ample reason to stop reading. An entire paragraph set in a 12-point bold typeface is difficult to finish.

Point size is directly related to stroke weight. As the point size of a bold typeface increases, so do its stroke weight and counter size. The proportions of stroke to counter remain the same, but the surface area increases. Conversely, as the point size of a bold typeface decreases, so too does the surface area of its stroke and counter. Choosing a lighter-weight typeface, as the point size of text decreases, keeps the counters large enough for easy identification and improves readability. OpenType Optical fonts (see chapter 1) are available to enhance the quality of a digital typeface's design characteristics, such as serifs and stroke weight, in smaller point sizes for improved typographic quality.

Type Style and Readability. Type families include style distinctions, such as *roman, italic,* and *oblique,* for the typographic page. Roman typefaces are the most readable of all since theirs is the most familiar character shape. Consequently, roman type is the best suited for continuous text. Italic and oblique typefaces are variations of the roman style.

Italic typefaces are a structural redesign of the typeface's roman letterforms. These condensed, angled typefaces are the most difficult of the three to read, but they are suited for limited use within a sentence. Setting an entire paragraph in italic is comparable to setting it in boldface type. Readers would struggle and tire with such a type block.

Italicized type is suitable for one or two lines of type, as a subhead, heading, or caption. In limited doses it is extremely effective. Type artists use italics to separate one type line from another. On a business card, for example, the name set in roman is visually distinct from the title set in italics—without a type size change. (See chapter 5.)

Oblique typefaces are a slanting of the original roman and more closely resemble the original roman shape. This visual similarity makes them easier to read in a lengthy block, but less effective than their italic counterparts for specialized use or emphasis within a sentence.

Reading Patterns and Readability. A good type artist respects the studied reading patterns and mechanics of reading. English-language readers read from left to right and from top to bottom, more specifically, from the upper-left corner to the lower-right corner of the page. While that is no surprise, it is a reading characteristic that the type artist should work with, not against. For example, after reading a short, wide column, the reader exits the paragraph on the right side. If the next design element on the page is positioned there, the reader moves easily to

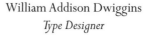

Roman is upright.
Italic is restructured.
Oblique leans.

In a type family, the roman style is the most legible and easiest to read.

William Addison Dwiggins
Type Designer

Changing type style controls emphasis without changing size.

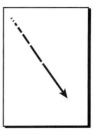

English-language readers move from the upper-left to lower-right corner.

it. A tall, thin paragraph is an excellent way to move the reader vertically downward to the next page stop. Working with the reader's natural inclinations eases the task of moving the reader through a document.

Stock and Readability. The term *stock* refers to printing paper. A designer, for example, chooses an appropriate stock for a client's brochure. The printer uses that stock for the job when the brochure goes to press. A stock's color and *finish* (surface texture) directly affect the legibility and readability of printed type. A stock's finish can be bumpy, smooth, or rough. Stock finish and color add to the viewer's emotional and cognitive response to a printed brochure or page.

High contrast between type color and stock color improves readability.

When choosing stock color, the type artist should maintain a strong contrast between type color and stock color. Printing black type on dark gray paper compromises the readability of the page because the reader has a difficult time distinguishing the letters' edges. They blend with the color of the stock. This is particularly important as it relates to target audience. Some readers can tolerate more work for their reading than others.

When choosing stock finish, the type artist should keep in mind that there is a link between stroke weight and stock finish. As the roughness of a stock's finish increases, so too must the type weight to compensate. The finish determines the quality of the printing surface. If the finish (printing surface) is rough, a lightweight typeface might break apart. The thin strokes cannot make a bold enough mark to visually compete on the bumpy surface. A smooth finish provides a flat printing surface that enables a good reproduction of the type. In this case, the finish does not compete with the delicate stroke weights of the printed typeface. The typographic page appears as the type artist intended.

A stock's finish
affects
typographic quality.

Stock texture influences typeface selection.

Working with type on a page is a form of communication. How the reader interacts with that page and how the stock affects the type elements on the page should influence the type artist's decisions.

PAGE GUIDELINES AND MEASUREMENTS

PAGES AND THEIR COMPONENTS ARE MEASURED using a combination of inches or millimeters, picas, and points. The term *page* is applied to an entire document, such as an 8½-by-11-inch flyer. The front side of the page is called the *recto;* and the back side is called the *verso.* If a document opens like a book with two facing pages, it is a *spread.* The left page is the *verso.* The right page is the *recto.* Page width and depth are measured in inches or millimeters.

The *margin* is the white space surrounding all items that print; it extends to the finished edge of the page, called the *trim.* Margins on a single page are identified by location—top (or head), bottom (or foot), left, and right. On a spread (fig. 3-1), they are identified as the *head margin* (top), *foot margin* (bottom), *fore-edge margin* (outside), and *back margin* (inside). The back margin is also referred to as the *gutter margin,* but the *gutter* also describes the white space between columns on a single page.

Drawing horizontal and vertical lines along the outermost page elements forms a rectangular shape. This area, the *type page,* includes all elements that print—type, illustrations, photographs. Within the type page, the *text page* refers to the primary text area, excluding all smaller type elements such as captions, running heads, and page numbers, as well as graphics.

It is easier to use picas and points for measuring the width and depth of type blocks since typefaces are measured in points. A *pica* equals 12 points (1 pica = 12 points). There are 6 picas to one inch (6 picas = 1 inch). Using the same measurement system enables the type artist to see relationships between measurements more easily.

The area anywhere on the page that does not print is called *white space.* The white space from the top edge of the type page to the topmost ascender of the nearest type block is called the *sink* or *sinkage.* On a multiple-page document the sink on the first page identifies the starting

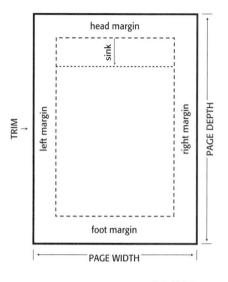

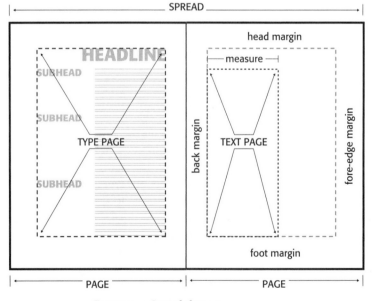

FIGURE 3-1: *Spread elements*

point. If a lengthy document includes chapters or similar major sections, a sink is an effective method for drawing attention to a new section. Points and picas are used to measure white space—the distance between type blocks, for example.

PAGE TYPOGRAPHY PRELIMINARIES

AaBbCcDdEeFfGgH
AaBbCcDdEeFfGg

Adobe Garamond (top)
Souvenir (bottom)

Magic!

MAGIC

MAGIC

Magic!

Copy content influences typeface selection.

Investments

Investments

Investments

Before type appears on the page, the type artist receives the document's copy. The *copy* is the material, the words, the type artist will typeset. With a book, the copy is the typewritten manuscript. For almost everything else—advertisements, newsletters, brochures, or annual reports—the copy is the handwritten or typewritten words to typeset.

Reading the copy is the first step to selecting type for a page. Reading introduces the type artist to the subject matter (product, service, event), to the tone of the material (lighthearted, serious, authoritative), to the context (continuous, discontinuous, technical), to the target audience (grade-school children, retirees, vacationers), and to the format (newsletter, flyer, annual report). This information prepares the type artist for the many type decisions that follow.

For example, the typeface Adobe Garamond is an elegant, old style typeface, but its small *x*-height might make reading difficult for some target audiences. The typeface Souvenir is a readable typeface, but its informal style might be inappropriate for some subject matter. The impact of a message is strengthened or weakened by the appearance of the messenger—the typeface. Knowing what is being said enables the type artist to make appropriate type choices.

The broadest determinant for categorizing copy content is formality. Are the written words informally or formally presented? Is it a flyer about a Saturday-afternoon magic show for five-year-olds or a handout about tax investment services for corporate executives? The tone of the words, the subject matter, and the target audience in this example are dramatically different. The magicians in a magic show want to emphasize fun, excitement, and pizzazz! The tax investment professionals want to emphasize trust, stability, and expertise. The reader evaluates the quality of the service or product based upon the typeset message, because that might be the only item the reader has to appraise this previously unknown organization or service. If the typefaces for these flyers were reversed accidentally, the readers might conclude that the magic show will be low-key and the expertise of the tax professionals suspect.

The second step when preparing copy for typesetting is identifying the different kinds of type blocks required for the material. What is the headline? Are there any subheads? Do the visuals have captions? Is the text copy lengthy or short? What emotional impressions does the text project or did the client request? Even subjective terms, such as stately, classic, or strong, are useful when looking through the available typeface library.

Although it is not part of the page decisions directly, it is helpful to note whether the text copy has any special requirements that would limit the type family selection. For example, if it is technical text filled with figures and symbols, an expert collection, a special pi font, or an OpenType typeface with the appropriate glyph sets is a necessity. If the text contains many foreign words that require italicizing, it is good to note that also. If the text copy is several pages in length, noting the need for a typeface suitable for continuous text is beneficial. The more the type artist knows about the copy, the better the typeset result.

Before page-layout applications were available for use with personal computers, placing type on a page required illustration board, a T square, rubber cement (or wax), type books, a type gauge, scratch paper, and a good head for math. Type was set by professional typesetters who spent the day (hurriedly) setting type according to a designer's written instructions. Before the typesetter received it, however, the designer had counted each letter and space to find out how many characters the text contained; consulted the type book to find out how many characters of the chosen typeface would fit in a single pica; multiplied the number of characters in a pica times the type measure (in picas) required for the layout; and divided the number of characters per type measure into the total number of characters. All this was done to find out how many lines the text block required (fig. 3-2) and, consequently, whether or not it would fit in the allotted space. The wise designer did all these calculations while executing the layout (before the client saw it) to make sure everything fit—in something larger than 4-point type.

Typefaces create a visual environment within which the reader interprets the typeset message.

Copyfitting on the Electronic Page

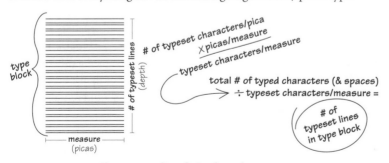

Figure 3-2: *Copyfitting formula*

Electronic copyfitting emphasizes the interaction of typographic elements rather than type fitting.

Few designers long to return to those days of mathematical gymnastics, because the emphasis was on fitting the type into the allotted space. Readability, legibility, and typographic quality sometimes took a backseat to getting it on the page. Computer page-layout applications enable today's type artists to place all the type on the page immediately. Making it fit is achieved by manipulating the type attributes (typeface, size, leading, and style, to name a few). True, these were the factors the designers previously controlled, too, but there were times when the type foundry was closing in 45 minutes and if it was not called in immediately, the client could forget about receiving the finished art at noon the next day. Sometimes the crisis of the moment got the better of the typographic quality.

Now the type artist has the opportunity to make the type choices within the context of the advertisement. The type artist can set the copy in all faces and sizes and can evaluate the results in relation to the other page elements. This is better. The designers, or type artists, have gained the ability to compare different type solutions without buying them from the type foundry. What they also gained is the title *typesetter*. The designer no longer goes home while the foundry's night shift sets the type. Each and every comma, period, and question mark are the sole responsibility of the type artist (who now must know how to type). All the typographic nuances designers should have known, but did not learn in art school, were deposited back in their laps (and the lap of everyone else using type on the computer). Now there is a new cadre of typesetters who spend the day (hurriedly) setting type according to their own instructions, and they do not close until it is done.

PAGE TYPOGRAPHY DECISIONS

When the type is poorly chosen, what the words say linguistically and what the letters imply visually are disharmonious, dishonest, out of tune.

_____Bringhurst
Elements of Typographic Style

TYPE ELEMENTS ON A PAGE ARE A BLEND of written words (content) and visual graphics (typeface). The availability of extended type families provides the type artist with a range of stylistically unified typefaces for headlines, subheads, captions, text, and other type elements. A single type family automatically unifies the design style of all type blocks.

There is a hierarchical structure between page type blocks. The different levels of type (headline, subhead, text) are assigned a different typographic attribute to visually prioritize the weight of their message and establish the visual hierarchy. Type-level treatment should remain consistent throughout the page or document.

The point of this visual hierarchy is not to identify each type block so distinctly that it no longer belongs to the total page. If the subheads are more prominent than the headline, the message makes no sense.

Readers are attracted to the subheads before they read the headline. A page is a single unit, just as a chorus, composed of many vocalists, sings as one unit. The sopranos, altos, tenors, and basses add depth, harmony, and texture, but their voices unite for a single vocal presentation. The typographic elements on a page blend with and support one another for a unified visual presentation. The headline starts it off, the subheads chime in, and the text fills in behind them for body and depth of meaning. The visual distinctions identifying one type block from another should not break the entire page into isolated soloists. If all type blocks project with equal volume, they disrupt the logical blending of elements. As a result, the reader sees chaos and confusion, not a complete, harmonious presentation.

Page type elements create visual distinctions between type levels while maintaining the visual unity of the page.

AFTER READING THE COPY AND UNDERSTANDING its intent and special needs, the type artist decides what type family or families will satisfy the type requirements of the page. The type selection should project the mood, image, or emotional feeling required by the content (see "Page Personality" in chapter 10). If more than one type family is used, choosing the display face is more important initially. Next, after identifying all levels of type blocks required by the text, the type artist needs a type family with enough styles to meet those requirements. Stylistically the text type must visually complement or contrast the display face. In addition, the type families should complement the mood and style of any illustration in the document.

TYPE SELECTION

It is easy to make a distinction between what is a legible typeface and what is not. Deciding what typeface suits the content and emotion of the page involves more than legibility. Besides the obvious style differences of decorative typefaces that suggest scenes from King Arthur's court or script typefaces that elicit thoughts of quill pens or period typefaces reminiscent of manual typewriters, a type artist frequently makes style distinctions based on more subtle design differences.

The projected mood or emotions of a typeface should match the copy it sets.

Deciding to use a serif typeface or a sans serif typeface is a frequent question. Typefaces with serifs project a more formal appearance. The serif finishes the stroke, just like the black top hat on a tuxedo-clad Fred Astaire. Functionally, a serif typeface is easier to read. The serifs form a definite top and bottom, which establishes a horizontal line for a reader to follow across the paragraph. The reader's eye is locked into this typographic channel and moves easily from left to right and back again. In addition, the serifs keep the letters a fixed distance apart. This isolates each letter's shape and enhances legibility.

In broad terms, serif type projects a formal appearance. Sans serif type creates an informal atmosphere.

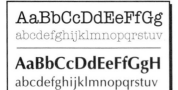

ITC American Typewriter (top) and Optima (bottom)

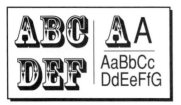

Rosewood (display) and Helvetica Narrow (text) share similar structural proportions.

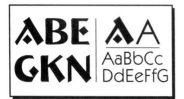

Bremen (display) and ITC Kabel (text) share similar proportions and angled line endings.

Sans serif typefaces have an informal appearance. The finishing touches are missing. Without a serif to hold the reader on each type line, the type artist manipulates the leading (vertical distance between baselines) to isolate the lines and to form a typographic channel equivalent to that created by serif typefaces.

There are many exceptions to this general observation of serif and sans serif typefaces. The typeface ITC American Typewriter has serifs, but the monoweight strokes and the cupped rounded serifs make this anything but formal. This typeface typifies a quick trip to the fast-food restaurant, not dinner out with Mr. Astaire. The typeface Optima is a sans serif typeface, but its variable stroke weights and graceful splayed stroke ends give it an elegance that American Typewriter cannot touch. Even considering the exceptions, the broad generalizations provide a place to start.

Combining Type Families. Combining type families enables type artists to use unique typefaces as attention-getting headlines, and perhaps as subheads, and then to use an easy-to-read typeface to deliver the bulk of the message. Choosing more than two type families in a document places too many competing visual styles on the page. (This does not include the company logotype or a newsletter's nameplate.) Too many type families destroy the visual continuity of the message and the page design. The book *Looking Good in Print* (Parker 1993) characterized the overuse of typefaces in a single document as "the 'ransom note' school of typography." With too many type families the reader is asked repeatedly to identify letters in different shapes, proportions, and styles. All this visual retooling forces the reader to get reacquainted with the visual landscape. This detracts from the purpose of the type—to be read. Using a single type family for a document, on the other hand, provides built-in design unity while still offering the ability to distinguish one level of typography from another through type weight, style, and size differences.

Determining which two type families to pair in a document is challenging, but gets easier (and more fun) with experience. It involves layers of decisions starting with the broadest, progressing to the most detailed. The first decision focuses on function and appearance. Function recognizes the different roles of the display and text type. Appearance focuses on the mood the document should project to the reader through the design features and structural proportions of each typeface. For example, the headline's attention-getting role might dictate the selection of a decorative, structurally extreme (condensed or extended) typeface for maximum impact. A flyer advertising a circus, for example, could use Rosewood or Bremen for mood and impact.

The function of the text typeface, on the other hand, is to deliver the bulk of the details and its selection focuses on legibility and readability issues. Its appearance should be less decorative and more functional, although its visual compatibility with the display face is essential for the document's visual success. It is here that the type artist makes a more detailed set of decisions. These decisions focus on contrast and similarity as applied to the typeface's design features and the structural proportions of its letterforms.

Contrast is the easier place to start. Each of the two previously mentioned display typefaces are dramatically stylized. Selecting a sans serif text type, with its clean lines and lack of stroke endings, contrasts this stylization and clearly identifies display from text as dictated by its function. Contrast also can be applied to structural proportions. A more condensed text type can be used effectively with an extended display type. The extreme width of the letterforms in the headline strengthens its attention-getting role. A more traditionally proportioned text type letterform contrasts the headline, while at the same time functions effectively to aid readability.

The extremes of design style and structural proportions should be restricted to the display type because readability is not a major factor with these short, discontinuous type blocks. Their attention-getting role is more important for the document's effectiveness. With text type, however, the type artist avoids design and structural extremes, since readability is the overriding role of these typefaces.

Decisions regarding similarity further narrow the search for the perfect text typeface. For example, by emphasizing a design feature present in both the display and text typefaces, such as a stroke ending, a unique link is established between the two. Repeating the structural proportions also links the two typefaces. It is this attention to detail that turns a good choice into the best choice when combining type families or typefaces.

Insufficient contrast between the design style of the text and the display face confuses the reader, as when using two similar serif or sans serif type families in the same document. At a quick glance, the reader assumes that they are identical, yet there is a nagging feeling that something is not quite right. That distraction jeopardizes the document's role—to communicate a message without distraction. There are exceptions to this general rule. Some decorative typefaces are so distinctive,

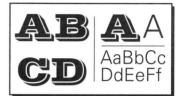

Contrasting structural proportions (wide with narrow) between display and text type is an effective pairing.

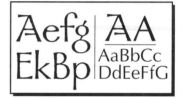

The similarity of flaired line endings makes Galahad and Optima an excellent match.

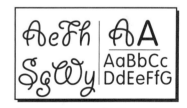

The similarity of rounded line endings makes Giddyup and VAG Rounded an excellent match.

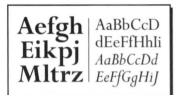

Machine/ɪᴛᴄ Officina Sans

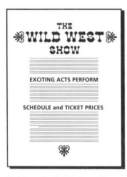

One type family can provide all the visual contrasts and aesthetic enhancements a document needs.

Headlines and Subheads

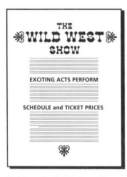

Subheads divide lengthy text into *site*-size pieces.

so unusual, that sans serif or serif is not their major distinguishing feature. The typeface Machine, for example, is a strong, decorative sans serif typeface, straight from the football field with a substantial stroke weight. The strength of this typeface contrasts almost any typeface, sans serif or serif. The objective here is to find a typeface that is structurally similar, condensed, and not too light so it will not be overpowered by the heavyweight Machine. The consistent stroke weight and narrow set width of ɪᴛᴄ Officina Sans can stand up to Machine and compete well on the same visual playing field.

Many type families are so visually distinct that they establish the correct emotional link with the reader all by themselves, while at the same time offering excellent text type choices. Typefaces such as Caxton, Garamond, Caslon, Perpetua, Bembo (the list is endless) are so well designed that using one of them alone is a visual delight. Good typography does not necessitate an endless supply of typefaces (but do not turn any down). It does require a selective palette that includes the timeless beauty of a Perpetua or a Garamond over a faddish, soon-to-be-dated newcomer. The seasoned typefaces, such as Bodoni, have been refined over the years almost to visual perfection. Smart type artists know to reap the benefits of talented type designers who came before them.

Visual page hierarchy recognizes the unique role each type block plays in a typographic message. The headline (the town crier, the attention getter) is at one end of the spectrum and the text (the fine print, the details) is at the other end. The subheads are visually between those two extremes. By position, the subheads are closer in content to the text than the headline. They should have a stronger typographic tie with the text, but not so much so that they pale in comparison to the headline. A quick scan by the reader should include the content of both the headline and the subheads.

Subheads divide the text into *site*-size pieces. A lengthy expanse of text does not look daunting when it appears as three smaller subcomponents of a whole. Subheads also provide a break, a pause in reading, before continuing into the next text section. The surrounding white space, if properly proportioned, indicates that a section ends (more white space) and a new one begins (less white space). Setting type on a page is a visual balancing act. If the type artist remembers the roles of the distinct type levels, it is not difficult to assign correct visual markers.

The display typeface of the headline triggers an emotional response, or establishes a context for the page in the eyes of the reader. If the headline is to be the first page element the reader sees, it must be strong enough to get the reader's attention. If a graphic is the attention getter for the page, then the headline is the first typographic element the reader sees. In both instances, the headline complements the visual—either in style or in subject. For example, a typeface reminiscent of the Old West (fig. 3-3) establishes a context and is aptly placed with photographs of stagecoaches and saloons. A well-chosen headline typeface prepares the reader for what is to come.

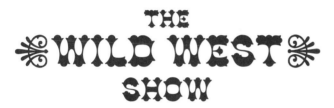

FIGURE 3-3: *Proper type selection establishes a mood*

Headings are phrases, snippets of thought, not lengthy sentences or statements. If a headline or subhead requires more than one line, the type artist should divide it according to logical pauses between word groupings. It should never be hyphenated. Dividing a heading logically (by isolating related word groupings) helps the reader understand its meaning. Letting the software divide the heading according to the line's length can emphasize unimportant words or present a puzzling message. Both occurrences confuse the reader. Delivery of a heading needs proper pacing and enunciation.

RENOVATION REKINDLES ECONOMIC GROWTH

| 0 | 3 | 6 | 9 |

PICAS

Renovation Rekindles Economic Growth

| 0 | 3 | 6 | 9 |

PICAS

FIGURE 3-4: *Uppercase and lowercase letters require different horizontal space*

If there are insufficient words to warrant splitting the heading into two lines, the following techniques can reduce the amount of horizontal space a heading requires: decrease the type size, decrease the type weight, increase the type measure, switch from all uppercase letters to

Headlines set the initial tone of the page.

Headlines and subheads are written concisely and not hyphenated.

SKYSCRAPERS
Modern Urban Vistas

The typeface Kino projects the height and sleek appearance of the subject matter.

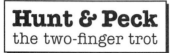

Hunt & Peck
the two-finger trot

ITC American Typewriter prepares the reader for an article on typing speeds and techniques.

A well-placed headline leads the reader to the next page element.

Properly proportioned white space links the heading to its text.

uppercase and lowercase letters (see fig. 3-4), or select a typeface with a narrower set width.

Distinctive typeface design styles, such as decorated letters, inline type, or typefaces with exaggerated features, are well suited for the role of attention getter (as headlines) but are inappropriate for text type. These virtuoso styles are graphic elements by themselves. They would not shrink from view or bow to the message as a text typeface must do. The fact that they are harder to read is not problematic, since a headline contains so few words. The extra effort needed to read headlines is outweighed by the mood, image, or emotion they establish on the page.

The last word of the headline determines the reader's location after reading it. (This is not usually an issue with subheads because they have shorter measures.) The headline should lead or attract the reader to the next page element. The headline may function as the attention-getting element on a page, but it is not a soloist in this visual presentation. It too must hand off to another typographic or graphic element, so the message can continue (fig. 3-5).

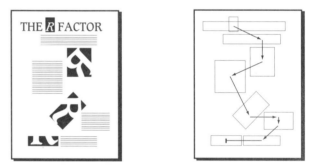

FIGURE 3-5: *Graphic and text elements create a visual path for the reader's eye to follow*

A good type artist sees a type block as individual words (What does it say?); as a graphic (What shape is it?); as a guideline (Where does it take the reader?); and as a design style (What emotion does it project?). Type as a visual element has many important roles for the type artist to orchestrate.

The amount of white space around a headline or subhead also helps to identify the text block it introduces. By placing more white space before a heading than after, the reader associates the subhead with the text block that follows. Floating a subhead evenly between two text blocks stops the reader's momentum. There is no clue as to what happens next (fig. 3-6). By placing more white space after the first text block and in front of the subhead, the reader understands that the first section ended. The white space suggests a pause—exit the text section, coast a bit. After reading the subhead, the small amount of white space that follows serves as a short entrance ramp into the next information highway.

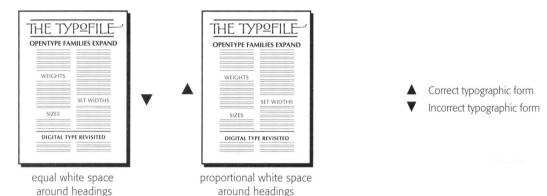

equal white space
around headings

proportional white space
around headings

▲ Correct typographic form
▼ Incorrect typographic form

FIGURE 3-6: *Properly placed white space guides the reader from a heading into its corresponding text*

A triangular cap on a column of text provides an optical transition from the heading above into the wider text block below. If a headline is not as wide as the type artist wants, it should be divided differently. Headings should never be justified. Headlines and subheads are short bits of type. Justifying so few words destroys the rhythm of the letter-spacing and pokes white holes in the heading.

Multiple-line headings benefit from a short top and a long bottom line.

Setting an entire word in capital letters can emphasize its message, if used selectively. Excessive use of uppercase type, however, has the opposite effect. The impact of the capitalized word is lost when all the words are capitalized. The same principle holds true in other venues. For example, if cats were cloaked in feathers rather than fur, the lone feather dangling from a tabby's lips would not automatically link him to the empty bird cage. Type artists should not overuse capitals (remember the feathered cat).

Letter case controls headline emphasis when selectively applied.

With an unavoidable lengthy headline, the type artist could set one or more words in caps and the rest of the headline in upper- and lower-case letters (see fig. 3-7). A change in letter case helps the reader understand the headline's message more easily. This also serves as an effective transition between the headline and the text that follows.

At least two or more text lines follow a subhead.

An embedded subhead serves as a subhead and the first words of the paragraph.

One purpose of a subhead is to call attention to a subsection of text. Starting a subhead at the end of a column or at the bottom of a page without sufficient text lines following it deemphasizes the subhead. An isolated subhead is meaningless. For a single-line subhead, at least two text lines should follow it, providing the block of text lines is taller than the subhead. If it is not, more lines are needed. For a multiline subhead, the depth of the text lines should be more than the depth of the subhead. Just as placing even white space before and after a subhead strands it from the text it introduces, marooning a subhead at the bottom of a column or page results in a similar problem. The relationship between subhead and text is weakened with such placings.

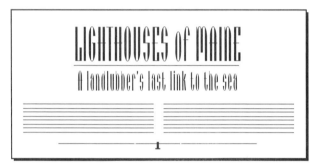

FIGURE 3-7: *Letter case controls emphasis in long headlines*

When designing the type hierarchy for a book, a book designer uses different levels of headings to subdivide the text. A *run-in sidebar* is the lowest-level subhead. It is set in italics, followed by a period, and positioned on the first line of a paragraph with an indent. The same principle (with a twist) is employed with the embedded subhead, but it creates a more prominent division in the text.

When subheads are not designated by the copywriter for lengthy text, the type artist can use the first few words of a paragraph (or a short first sentence) as an *embedded subhead*. With this technique, the type artist increases the point size and changes the typeface style of the first few words of the paragraph. This style and size change calls attention to a new subsection without adding words or using much more vertical space. An embedded subhead needs additional white space before it but does not require a line indention. This subhead technique positions the subhead closer in content to the text than a traditional subhead. Consequently, its typographic treatment is closer to that of the text. If the copy's length requires a stronger subhead, a skilled type artist can

Seafaring captains tell the tallest tales about the Portland Head Light built in 1791 at the mouth of

Seafaring captains tell the tallest tales about the Portland Head Light built in 1791 at the mouth of the

Embedded subhead with type style link to text (above) and type style link to headline (below)

CHAPTER THREE

manipulate type attributes to emphasize the embedded subhead without tearing it from its text foundation.

Not all copy lends itself to this treatment. If the wording does not cooperate, the type artist can insert an ornament in between two sections of type to provide the reader with a well-deserved reading pause. As with everything else, this technique must be applied consistently throughout the document.

CAPTIONS IN A DOCUMENT ARE USED WITH photographs, illustrations, or diagrams to identify or clarify the graphic. Unlike a subhead, a caption's role as a visual is a minor one, but for content and clarification, it is an important one. Its proper placement links it to the graphic it identifies and clarifies (fig. 3-8). If the type artist leaves it off, pairs it with the wrong graphic, or positions it too far away from the graphic, its usefulness is compromised. With appropriate identification in the caption, such as the words *Figure 3,* the type artist can reference the graphic in the text and notify the reader that a visual accompanies that passage.

A caption is the same size or slightly smaller than the text.

Since a caption is discontinuous text, its readability is not as critical as the main text. Nevertheless, it should not be hard to read. Some type artists distinguish the words *Figure 3* with same size bold or italic type as the rest of the caption in order to separate it, but not isolate it, from the caption. The type artist also could set the word *FIGURE* in all caps to distinguish it from the lowercase caption text.

A caption is short and easy to read.

Limiting the number of lines required by a caption makes it easier to position with other page elements. If the caption requires two or more lines, the type artist should divide it logically, just as with a headline or subhead. Although a caption is discontinuous text, there is a logic to its content. Dividing it incorrectly destroys that logic.

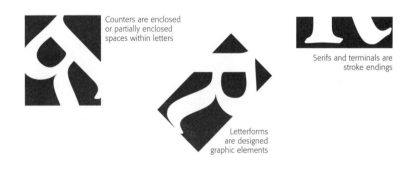

Counters are enclosed or partially enclosed spaces within letters

Serifs and terminals are stroke endings

Letterforms are designed graphic elements

FIGURE 3-8: *Placement visually links captions to graphics*

Correct placement of captions determines whether or not the reader sees them. If the caption is too close to the graphic, it crowds the graphic and is difficult to notice and read. If the caption is too far away from the graphic, the reader might not understand its purpose.

Captions require proper placement to function.

When positioned below a graphic, aligning the left end of the caption with the left edge of the graphic creates a visual link between the two. Captions should not exceed the width of the graphic. When positioned alongside a graphic, the caption should align flush along the graphic's adjacent edge for a cleaner visual placement (see "Type Alignment" later in this chapter). Aligning the caption's cap line with the top edge of the graphic or the baseline of the caption's last line with the bottom edge of the graphic is effective also.

Text

Properly set, legible text typefaces render readable text.

Text type represents the largest amount of characters in a document. It requires the greatest attention to detail. For typography on the page level, the type artist determines type style and type measure. Each type attribute affects readability, although some more significantly than others. (Leading for type style and measure is discussed in chapter 4.)

The amount of reader contact with the text determines the role readability plays in text style and measure choices.

The type of reading, continuous (extended reader contact) or discontinuous (limited reader contact), determines the importance of type style selection and type measure. For example, when selecting type for small, isolated entries in a sales catalogue, the importance of the type style and measure for readability lessens. Since the reader uses the text type only to read four or five product-description lines, it is not critical how the eye responds to the type style and measure over an extended time period. The reader's contact with the text is limited. On the other hand, when selecting text for an annual report that contains lengthy paragraphs of detailed, technical information, the more time the report recipients spend reading, the more informed (and perhaps more supportive) they become. In this situation, eliminating reading fatigue is critically important.

Extreme style characteristics are unsuitable for continuous text typefaces.

Type Style. When selecting text type for continuous reading, readability is of paramount importance. If the readability is too low, the reader tires and stops reading. When choosing continuous text type, the type artist should avoid extremes. Extremely condensed, extended, heavy, or thin faces are not suitable for continuous reading. Style extremes push letters into unfamiliar proportions and configurations. Since legibility depends on ease of recognition, too much style enhancement is detrimental to letter shape. Both serif and sans serif typefaces are suitable for continuous text, but sans serif typefaces need special handling to aid the reader's horizontal eye movement (see "Determining Leading Size" in chapter 4).

Type Measure. During the reading process the reader's eye moves from left to right in a series of small jumps or saccades. Each saccade encompasses spaces as well as letters, approximately 12. A comfortable measure enables the eye to make five or six saccades before beginning another line. The ideal line length of text for continuous reading contains 66 characters (letters plus spaces) or 10 to 12 individual words.

The length of a measure is directly related to readability. If the measure is too long, the increased number of saccades tires the eye, causing the reader's attention to wander. Once the eye reaches the end of a long measure, it must make the long trek back to the left side and start again. The instance of *doubling* (rereading the same line) increases as the measure lengthens. Doubling both tires and annoys the reader. An annoyed reader quickly finds a reason to do something else.

A measure that is too short breaks the rhythm of saccades. The eye is constantly returning to the left side to resume reading. It is similar to listening to a reader who pauses after reading every three or four words. While length of line, or measure, is less important for discontinuous text blocks, the ease with which the reader finds the next line's starting point is always important. If the reader gets lost or distracted after the first line, the content of the rest of the text block is inconsequential.

For a single-column page of text for continuous reading, the type artist should allocate a measure between 60 and 75 characters. (Count characters and spaces by twos for faster results. Place the pen tip after each pair.) For a multiple-column page, a measure between 40 and 50 characters is acceptable (see chapter 4).

Interrelationship of Type Style and Measure. All type decisions in a document are interrelated. A highly legible typeface enhances readability to some degree, just as an illegible typeface does not improve when set on a 66-character measure.

If a text block exceeds the ideal measure and extends to 80 characters (for reasons beyond the type artist's control), using a serif typeface for the text alleviates some of the problems caused by the overage. In this same situation, using a typeface with a larger *x*-height improves readability and keeps the reader from tiring. A type artist delivers more of the message by putting the reader's needs first.

THE POSITIONING OF TYPE LINES WITHIN A TYPE BLOCK or paragraph is called *type alignment.* There are four alignment styles: flush left, flush

A 66-character measure is recommended for continuous text.

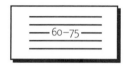

Single-column character count

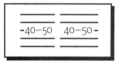

Multiple-column character count

Type style and measure are interrelated attributes— changing one requires reevaluating the other.

TYPE ALIGNMENT

Flush left

Justified

Centered

Flush right

right, centered, and justified. Of the four, flush left and justified are more commonly used in continuous text. Flush left is the easier of the two to read, but not by a significant margin. Flush right and centered, on the other hand, are more commonly used for discontinuous reading, such as small text entries, headlines, subheads, and captions.

Flush left alignment positions the left end of each type line along a common left edge. Since the type lines are different lengths, the right edge of the type block is uneven or *ragged*. Flush left alignment is more informal and contemporary. This alignment style is suitable for continuous and discontinuous text (fig. 3-9).

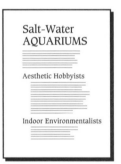
flush left text alignment

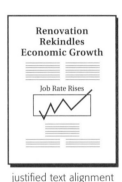
justified text alignment

FIGURE 3-9: *Popular continuous text alignment examples*

Flush left and justified type alignments are suitable for continuous text.

Centered and flush right type alignments are suitable for discontinuous text.

Justified alignment positions the beginning and end of each type line along a common left and right edge, respectively. Each side of the type block is flush and every line is the same length. Since each line contains a different number of characters, the software places additional white space between all words and letters to achieve the exact measure. Some programs provide additional choices regarding the alignment of the justified paragraph's last line. The options include centered, flush left, flush right, or force justified. Justified type is more formal and projects an authoritative, factual air. This alignment style is suitable for continuous text, when set properly.

Centered alignment positions the midpoint of each type line along a common midline. The type block is symmetrical with both edges of the type block ragged. This alignment style is suitable for discontinuous text (fig. 3-10).

Flush right alignment positions the right end of each type line along a common right edge. The left edge of the type block is ragged. This alignment style is suitable for discontinuous text.

CHAPTER THREE

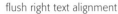

=== AQUARIUMS, Inc. ===

Fulton J. Fishbain
Sales Representative

centered text alignment

Economic Assets

Clayborn Currency
Account Executive

flush right text alignment

FIGURE 3-10: *Discontinuous text alignment examples*

Interrelationship of Type Alignment and Readability. Type alignment directly affects readability by determining where each line stops and starts. During the process of reading, the eye moves to the right across a line of type. At the end of that line, it returns to the left end of the next line and resumes reading. Readability of continuous text is enhanced if this back-and-forth motion is uninterrupted. With discontinuous text (headlines, subheads, and captions, for example) the back-and-forth rhythm might occur only once or, in a single-line headline, not at all. For that reason, discontinuous text alignment is not a major concern.

With flush left type alignment, the eye returns to the same edge with each line change. The common starting point simplifies the task of starting over. There is no question in the reader's mind concerning where the line continues, no pause for logistical reasons. This alignment style is suitable for all kinds of type blocks, both continuous and discontinuous.

With flush right type alignment, on the other hand, the eye returns to a different location with each new line. The reader briefly interrupts the reading rhythm (and train of thought) to locate where the words resume. (This is similar to finding one's dinner plate in a different location after each forkful.) Since a headline might be only two or three lines long, the starting-point issue is inconsequential. For a subhead or headline, the design benefits of a flush right heading outweigh the minor decrease in readability.

With justified type alignment, the eye moves between common points on both the left and right edges. The consistency of edges might sound perfect, but the internal spacing changes necessary to make that alignment possible also adversely affect readability if handled poorly (see chapter 4). For continuous text, justified type (handled well) is easy to read and creates a shaped text block that adds other design options.

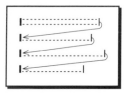

Flush left eye movement

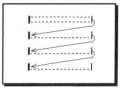

Flush right eye movement

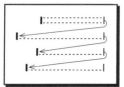

Justified eye movement

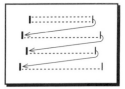

Centered eye movement

Centered type alignment is suitable for discontinuous text only. It has all the problems of flush right type doubled. The starting and ending points vary from line to line. (In this scenario, the dinner plate moves constantly during the meal.) This is not to say that centered type is not perfectly suited to headlines and subheads, because it is. A centered heading is an effective attention-getting device, since it breaks the overall page format. For continuous text, however, it is a headache, both figuratively and literally.

White Space

Adequate page margins welcome the reader into the page.

Insufficient page margins chase away readers by demonstrating that there is too much material on the page.

A DISCUSSION OF PAGE TYPOGRAPHY IS INCOMPLETE without mentioning the use of white space to aid reading. If white space is used correctly, it works to organize, emphasize, and balance page elements. The first decision regarding white space involves page margins. Margins surround the page elements isolating and unifying them for a common purpose. They invite a reader into a document. A well-sized margin gives the reader a place to hold the document without obliterating an important page element.

Margins—External White Space. Margins vary in width according to location and to the document's purpose. On a single-sided page, a large head margin and sink draws attention to a headline and identifies the document's starting point. A large left margin can emphasize small subheads and balance lengthy, adjacent text blocks. The foot margin should be slightly larger than the smaller of the two side margins to balance page contents visually. The optical center of a page is above the measurable horizontal center line. A larger foot margin balances that optical point. Any margin decision made when the page is empty requires review as the page elements appear. A large graphic on the left side might need a wider right margin for balance.

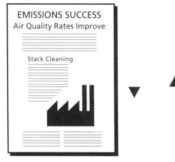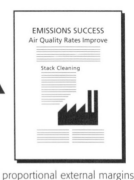

insufficient external margins   proportional external margins

FIGURE 3-11: *External margins invite viewers into the page*

Many page-layout applications provide margin controls along with the initial document size controls. These can be seen only as temporary decisions, since the page is blank. Remember to reevaluate the margins as the page evolves. It is not imperative that all type elements align along the left or right margin. It is easy to feel that they should when the margin guidelines are on a page, but that is not so. If a page element stops short of the margin, it creates white space that can emphasize the edge of a type block or balance a block on the other side of the page. Type artists should use external margins as guidelines to prevent elements from crowding the outside edge of the page, not as magnets that draw everything to them.

A common mistake made by novice type artists is underestimating the visual importance of adequately sized margins. A page with only a sliver of white space around its edge looks like a document that has outgrown its borders (fig. 3-11). Such a monumental quantity of text requires a sizable time commitment to read. Rather than block off next week to read the document, the reader places it aside in a pile labeled "To Read Later." It is more aptly named "To Ignore" because that is what happens. After several weeks the document joins other poorly designed documents in the wastebasket. No one is required to read anything they receive. Most people exercise that option daily.

Internal White Space. White space in and around page elements is the internal white space of a document. This white space is smaller than the margins because its purpose is subordinate to that of the margins. The purpose of internal white space is to set off type blocks or smaller type elements for emphasis, to establish visual links between separate type blocks, such as a subhead and text, and to provide a temporary resting spot for the reader, when a reading pause is warranted. Large areas of internal white space make large holes in a page and destroy the visual unity established by the margins. Excess internal white space should be brought to and lost in the margins.

Additional white space before or around a type block isolates and emphasizes it.

Limited white space between page elements visually links them.

Before leaving this level of typography the type artist should answer two fundamental questions: Are type selection and placement appropriate for the purpose of the page? Is the page hierarchy clear and logically structured?

When readers first look at the page, they should immediately have a sense of the page's intent. If the page is an advertisement, it should look like one. If the page is the front page of a newsletter, it should not look like an advertisement. A newsletter should use type appropriate for

PAGE TYPOGRAPHY EVALUATION

that purpose. An advertisement should use advertisement-appropriate type. Readability, legibility, placement, type style, alignment, measure, and use of white space all come together to create a unique page. A conflict between how the page looks and what the page says is apparent to the reader and casts doubt on the veracity of the information.

During its development, a type artist must look at the page as a whole. The details of typographic decision making should produce a page appropriate for its original intent. The details of type can create a quagmire for the overwhelmed type artist. Climbing out of the alphabet soup to review how the entire page is developing is a necessary skill for a type artist to perfect.

Periodically reviewing the page's overall appearance keeps its development on the right course.

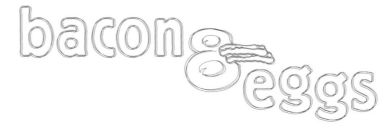

FIGURE 3-12: *Typographs add graphic elements to the page*

After identifying the purpose of the page, the reader scans the headings for a snapshot of its content. A logical page hierarchy creates an accurate snapshot. With a clear arrangement of headings, the reader understands what information is primary—the headline—and what information is secondary, clarifying information—the subheads. The typographic attributes for the headline and subheads establish a visual priority. At the same time, they prioritize the content of those headings. The reader understands the topic (the headline) and what aspects (the subheads) of the topic are discussed. Suitable typographic treatment establishes the headline as the primary heading. Type treatment for the subheads should be visually related to the headline and appropriate for secondary headings. The same logic follows throughout the rest of the type elements on the page or in the document (see chapter 10).

Effective page hierarchy is clear and logically structured.

This is not to say that the arrangement of page elements should be obvious and, as a result, boring. An intriguing, aesthetically pleasing, unique page structure is more appealing to a reader than a commonplace one. An easy-to-navigate page structure is not inherently dull. A reader entering a page is comparable to a shopper opening a door. If the door opens to a crowded hallway filled with placard-waving, clamoring hucksters, the shopper might reconsider entering the chaotic scene. On the other hand, if the door opens to a brightly lit hallway lined with tastefully designed storefronts and welcoming merchants, the shopper continues ahead eagerly.

Elements on a page create a visual terrain through which the reader proceeds (fig. 3-12). If the typographic terrain is strewn with discordant typefaces crowded into seemingly insufficient space, the reader will decide to go elsewhere. A type artist should take a break from working on the storefronts to stand in the doorway and check the hallway.

ℐə

PAGE TYPOGRAPHY INVOLVES DECISIONS on the broadest visual level. The type artist compares groups of words united by function to other word groups with a different function. A type artist might ask, Does the headline work well with the subheads or does it overshadow them? or, Do the subheads provide a smooth transition into the text? Page typography has aesthetic and functional qualities that the type artist controls to deliver a single message. Properly chosen typefaces create a mood; they elicit an emotional response compatible with the message's intent. Properly set type moves the reader's eye between and through type blocks with a minimum of effort. Both typeface style and typographic quality support and enhance the message. It is unwise to rush past these larger decisions on the way to the detailed nuances of paragraph and sentence typography. The finest typeset text goes unread if the reader fails to notice the page itself.

Effective typographic design does not end with the reader noticing the page. It is important to catch the reader's eye, yet even eye-catching design must give way to the importance of communicating the desired information. The use of type in tandem with other page elements must hold the reader's attention and then get out of the way of the message. Page elements establish and maintain the connection between message and reader. This, then, is the test for typographic design. Does the message get through? Does the design connect writer to reader? Type artists need to know how to use type to create visually exciting, functionally successful pages for their target audiences. The page and its elements create the map for the reader's eye to follow—all the way to understanding the message.

SETTING
TYPE
IN A
PARAGRAPH

Grace in typography comes of itself when the compositor brings a certain love to his work. Whoever does not love his work cannot hope that it will please others.

————————Tschichold
*Treasury of
Alphabets and Lettering*

Pᴀʀᴀɢʀᴀᴘʜ ᴛʏᴘᴏɢʀᴀᴘʜʏ ᴀs ᴅᴇꜰɪɴᴇᴅ ɪɴ ᴛʜɪs ᴛᴇxᴛ refers to the use of type characters, white space, typefaces, and type attributes within a typeset paragraph. A discussion of paragraph typography focuses on the effective use of these components to create an even page texture for improved readability. The word *text* in typography originates from the word *texture*. Texture appeals to a viewer's sense of touch. A *tactile texture* is a three-dimensional surface that a person can touch, feel, and experience. An ocean-side beach has a tactile texture. Swimmers and sunbathers feel the sand, the shells, the pebbles, and seaweed as they stroll along the shore. Their feet leave pockmarks in the sand that sculpt the surface and alter its texture.

A *visual texture* is a two-dimensional, visual illusion of a three-dimensional tactile surface. It suggests the desired tactile qualities that viewers cannot feel with their fingers. An artist creates a visual texture on a piece of paper or on a canvas using shapes, colors, proportions, and values to replicate a believable visual frame of reference. When painting the image of a linen napkin as part of a still life, a painter uses small marks of color to create the napkin's textural illusion. To create the illusion of linen, the painter employs short, thin strandlike marks to represent the woven fibers. Applying broad, fat strokes of color to represent the napkin's surface would destroy the illusion of fine linen by ignoring the size relationship of the textural elements to the whole and attracting too much attention to this element.

TYPOGRAPHIC TEXTURE IS AN EVEN, LIGHT GRAY visual texture created by placing type on a page. The type artist controls texture quality through type size, type weight, vertical spacing, and horizontal spacing for every letter, word, and paragraph on the page. Typographic texture is unobtrusive. Its uniformity enables the reader's eye to skim its surface and concentrate on the text's message without distraction from unrelated textural disturbances. Well-executed typographic texture eases reading and facilitates reading speed.

Type size and type weight determine the visual impact of each texture element. An extrabold typeface creates a darker texture than a light typeface from the same type family. A larger type size makes the individual texture elements more noticeable to the reader's eye. It is hard for readers to see a paragraph as an even overall texture when staring at the largest lowercase *a* they have ever seen.

Vertical and horizontal spacing determine the amount of white space between type lines, letters, and words. *Vertical spacing* concerns the distance between baselines of type within a paragraph (*leading*). Evenly spaced lines of type, along with appropriately sized type and measure, create an easy-to-read paragraph. Too much leading in a paragraph isolates each line and destroys the paragraph's visual cohesion. Insufficient leading creates a dense forest of letters that leads the reader's eye in all directions—diagonally, vertically, and horizontally.

Horizontal spacing concerns the distance between letters within words (*letterspacing*) and words within the measure (*word spacing*). Too much letterspacing in a word destroys the visual cohesion that links letters together as a recognizable word shape. Uneven letterspacing forms subgroupings within a word that destroy the word's integrity. Instead of the word *ransom,* the reader sees *ran* and *som.* (Who ran? Isn't *some* spelled with an *e*?) Uneven letterspacing can ruin the logic of a sentence or word. Type size and weight decisions are easy to make. Spacing decisions require a more practiced eye to evaluate the subtle distinctions that enhance or impede reading on this level.

ran som

Incorrect letterspacing changes
one word into two.

PARAGRAPHS AND THEIR COMPONENTS ARE MEASURED using points, picas, ems, ens, leads, and units (see fig. 4-1). Type artists use points to measure typefaces and leading. Leading is measured from the baseline of one type line to the baseline above or below it. The leading includes two items: the typeface size and the remaining white space that separates one line of letters from the next line of letters. Typeface size and leading are written as a level fraction—10/12. The number *10* represents the typeface size (10 points) and the number *12* represents the leading size (12 points). The amount of white space between lines of 10-point type set on 12-point leading is 2 points (12 − 10 = 2).

The distance between paragraphs is measured in points also. Keeping the spacing unit of measure consistent enables the type artist to see proportional relationships of inter- and intraparagraph vertical spacing. Proportional relationships are an important concern when working with type.

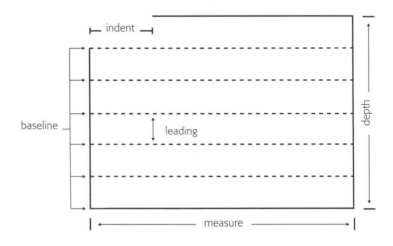

FIGURE 4-1: *Paragraph elements*

A type artist uses picas to measure paragraph width (*measure*) and paragraph depth. Once the character count is established, it is easier to refer to the measure in picas (see chapter 3). The type artist indicates the type family, weight, type size, leading, and measure in the following manner: Centaur Regular 10/12 × 22. The word *Centaur* is the type family; *Regular* indicates the weight; *10* is the type size in points; *12* is the leading in points; and *22* is the measure in picas (fig. 4-2).

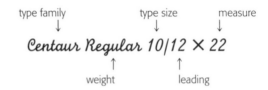

FIGURE 4-2: *Paragraph type notation*

CHAPTER FOUR

Indenting the first line of a paragraph is done with ems, ens, and leads. These three units of measure are important in typography because they are proportional to the paragraph's typeface size. A pica, for example, is a preset unit of measure. A black square with sides of 1 pica looks large alongside the word *pica* set in 8-point type (fig. 4-3). The same 1-pica black square looks small alongside the word *pica* set in 24-point type. The type size tripled, but the square stayed the same. Picas, inches, feet, and miles are all preset units of measure.

1 inch = 6 picas

12 points = 1 pica

■ pica

■ pica

| 1-pica square | 1-pica square |
| with 8-point type | with 24-point type |

FIGURE 4-3: *Picas are preset measurement units*

An *em* is a unit of measure equal to the size of the typeface. Type artists use ems to indent lines, to determine the length of a dash (the em dash), and to add a space (an em space) between words. If the type artist uses an em dash to set off a parenthetical phrase in a sentence typeset in 11-point type, the em dash is 11 points in length. If an em space is between the word and its definition in an 8-point dictionary entry, the em space is 8 points in length. In foundry type, em quads (or *mutton*) were used for spacing type. The *em quad* was a square (quad) with sides equal to 1 em.

Since typeface size determines em size, the em is a proportional unit of measure. Continuing with the previous example (fig. 4-3) with the pica square and the typeset word, placing a black 8-point em quad alongside the words *em quad* set in 8-point type looks proportionally the same as a black 24-point em quad alongside the words *em quad* set in 24-point type (fig. 4-4). The type size tripled, but the proportional relationship stayed the same.

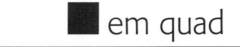

■ em quad

■ em quad

| 8-point em quad | 24-point em quad |
| with 8-point type | with 24-point type |

FIGURE 4-4: *Ems are proportional measurement units*

An *en* is a unit of measure equal to half the size of the typeface. An 8-point en is 4 points in length. In foundry type, an *en quad* (or *nut*) was the width of an en, but the height of the em. Ens are used for indents, dashes, and word spaces also. Type artists also can use a lead as a proportional measurement for indents. The *lead* is equal to the distance from baseline to baseline in a paragraph. Using ems, ens, and leads provides proportional units of measure for working with type.

The horizontal spacing of letters and words is not as clearly specified as spacing for indents and leading. Spacing the letters in a word is an optical placement rather than a measurable calculation. Letters come in all different shapes and sizes. A concave side here and a convex side there create measuring problems. Fortunately for the digital type artist, the type designer provides letterspacing assistance in the font to maintain consistent spacing in many situations.

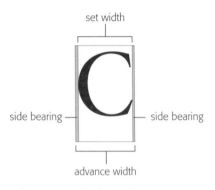

FIGURE 4-5: *Glyph window*

18 units to the em

When designing a digital typeface, the type designer divides the em into proportional, incremental measurements, called *units*. These units serve as the typeface's internal measurement system for horizontal spacing and kerning. In the past, typefaces designed for the Monotype typecasting machine used 18 units per em. Type glyphs in these fonts were limited to 18 possible widths. Digital type designers use more units per em in order to create more customized glyph widths. Frequently 1,000 units per em are used for PST-1 fonts and 2,048 units per em, or more, for TT fonts.

A digital glyph is located within a glyph window the height of the typeface's em, such as 72 points. The width of the actual glyph is called the *set width* and the white space on either side of it is the *side bearing*. Together the side bearings and the set width make the *advance width*—

the amount of horizontal space allocated on a text line for a particular glyph (fig. 4-5). This space enables most, but not all, glyphs in the same typeface to sit comfortably alongside one another in a measure (see "Letterspacing and Word Spacing" later in this chapter).

The size of a glyph's side bearings varies depending upon its shape. Some letters, such as the Minion Pro lowercase *f,* have a positive side bearing on the left and a negative side bearing on the right. The negative space enables the terminal of its ascender to overlap an adjacent glyph window to its right, such as a lowercase *a,* for better letterspacing. In foundry type, this extension beyond the sort's body is called the *kern.* In digital typography, these glyphs are called *kerning characters.* Other glyphs that regularly extend into their neighbor's space, such as a fraction bar, are designed as kerning characters.

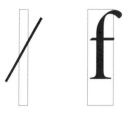

Minion Pro kerning characters

WHEN THE RESPONSIBILITY FOR TYPESETTING moved from the typesetter in a foundry to the type artist in a company, all typesetting instructions remained in-house. They might even stay on the same person's desk. *Proofreaders' marks,* or *proofmarks,* are standardized marks used by type artists for communicating typographic instructions or changes on typeset copy. Proofreading, like typesetting, has evolved with technology. The pros and cons of this evolution can be debated, but it does not change the fact that more and more typographic work is done in its entirety by fewer and fewer pairs of eyes and hands. Type artists rely on spell checkers, dictionaries, proofreaders' methods, and personal techniques to catch errors that their tired eyes no longer see. On the paragraph level, proofing involves checking the texture of the page—type size, weight, letterspacing, word spacing, leading, hyphenation ladders, knotholes, widows, orphans—and the uniform implementation of paragraph attributes in the same hierarchical level—indents, alignment, and space between paragraphs.

Proofreaders' marks, unlike copyeditors' marks, are designed for typeset copy. Because typeset copy uses space measured in points, corrections do not fit between the lines at the point of insertion, as copyeditors' marks do. Instead, proofreaders' marks work in teams within the limited space available. Proofmarks are abbreviations, codes, and symbols that indicate lengthy instructions in minimal space. Type artists use these marks to communicate with themselves as well. Marking a proof to improve typographic quality is the type artist's responsibility. In addition, some type artists are designers also. Proofmarks can indicate type and design changes before anyone else sees the document.

PARAGRAPH PROOFREADERS' MARKS

Type artists use proofreaders' marks to attain typographic quality without altering the author's style and content.

e The brown dog jump̢d

eq ld over the lazy red fox and sent the entire

n chicken house ḭto a

⊙ frenzy Never before had

a | ɟ the fox ḓme so clọe to

⌣ its chosen pr̂ey; and

e nevør before had the

badly dog so ~~poorly~~ bungled

job his ~~obj~~ as barnyard

protector.

Proofreaders' marks come in pairs. Each text mark has a corresponding margin mark.

The word *caret* derives from Classical Latin, meaning *it is missing.*

The extended caret is a precise location indicator within a line of text.

PROOFMARKS COME IN PAIRS. THERE IS A *text mark,* located within the text, and a *margin mark,* located in the margin alongside the edited line. Every mark within the text has a corresponding mark in the margin—*always.* The text mark locates the problem. The margin mark indicates its solution. The margin mark functions also as a flag to catch the type artist's eye. It is easy to miss a small mark buried in typeset text, but not a mark sitting alone in the margin.

There are four categories of proofmarks—additions, deletions, substitutions, and relocations. Type artists and proofreaders make proofmarks with a fine-tipped ballpoint pen with colored ink—red, green, purple, anything but blue or black. The most-used text mark is the *caret.* It indicates an insertion of space, punctuation, letter, glyph, and word into or between lines. The caret intersects a type line from below, with a few logical exceptions, or it intersects a paragraph from the side. A sideways caret identifies an insertion point between lines when adjusting line and paragraph spacing (leading). The margin instructions are written alongside the caret.

To indicate an insertion within a line, the type artist positions the tip of the caret where the missing item belongs, making sure not to cover any letter or word. In extremely tight type (or to prevent confusion), the type artist can extend one side of the caret to pinpoint an insertion. The insertion is written in the left or right margin aligned with the caretted line. If a line requires more than one proofmark, the type artist positions the margin marks in the same order, left to right, as the text marks. A vertical slash between each margin mark separates the insertions to avoid confusion. Keeping insertions in the correct order is important for a properly edited document. The type artist can use the left, right, or both margins for margin marks, as long as the order of text and margin marks is identical. Some margin marks are circled. This draws attention to a small mark, such as a period, or indicates instructions or queries. Margin marks representing words or letters to insert into the text are not circled. In both instances, legible, case-sensitive writing is a must; script handwriting is preferred for letter-case clarity.

A vertical or horizontal strike-through indicates a deletion or a substitution. To delete or replace a single letter within a word, the vertical strike is more visible. To delete or replace two or more letters or a word (or words), the horizontal strike is preferred. It is important not to obliterate a character completely when striking it because the type artist needs to identify the character to delete. An extrafine ballpoint pen makes this easier.

The fundamental purpose of proofmarks is to mark typeset copy clearly with a minimum of clutter. A lengthy note clutters more than clarifies. In other situations replacing an entire word with a new one is clearer than surgically inserting and transposing characters.

WITHIN PARAGRAPH TYPOGRAPHY, WORKING TO improve page texture is a feature of typographic quality. It is fairly easy to get the type on the page. Refining it to do the job well distinguishes the work of a skilled type artist. There are several thoughts to keep in mind while working with paragraph typography.

All typographic page decisions are interconnected; changing one requires reviewing them all. The resizing of one type block might require a proportional resizing of another. Changing one feature, such as stroke weight, changes the relationship of that type block to all other type blocks on the page at that time. There is no point agonizing over the exact point size for a subhead, if the text is not present. If any or all components change, all typographic decisions require review.

A quick way to remember the interrelationship between type elements is by making type attribute selections, such as font, size, leading, and tracking, from a single dialog box or palette. Applications with sophisticated type controls usually have one major type dialog box that lists all type attributes. When a type artist selects a new type size, it is easy to remember to adjust the leading for this change because the leading attribute is listed nearby. A quick scan of the dialog box enables the type artist to compare attributes easily and make all the necessary adjustments. These same attributes are available in single-purpose dialog boxes or submenus, but their isolated display does not remind the type artist of other attributes that may be affected by their change.

The type size and letterspacing appropriate for the 8½-by-11-inch flyer are different from the size and spacing needed for a video presentation. Type is used in so many different visual arenas, yet the type artist designs them from the same viewing distance—artist to monitor. It is useful to stop and think how and where the reader will see the type. The type artist should preview a type sample at its intended viewing distance and in its final form, if possible. The time spent printing a quick sample for preview is beneficial if it avoids an after-hours revision.

Another technique that emphasizes the interaction of type attributes concerns how type artists evaluate their work. When evaluating type elements on a page, it is helpful to describe a type problem in terms of multiple solutions. For example, if the headline on a document, set in

PARAGRAPH TYPOGRAPHY PRELIMINARIES

Type decisions work within the context of the page.

Viewing distance affects all type decisions.

Describing a type problem in terms of a single solution limits ideas for the problem's resolution.

24-point, medium-weight display type, is not satisfactory, the type artist should not describe the headline in terms of a single attribute. Instead of saying that it is not *big* enough or *bold* enough (descriptions with predetermined solutions), the type artist might describe the headline more accurately as *not attracting enough attention.* This opens the door to a variety of solutions. Perhaps isolating the headline with additional white space, changing letter case to capital letters, reducing the size of the surrounding copy, using a larger sink, repositioning the copy below it, italicizing the headline, choosing an extended typeface from the same type family, or selecting a different type family would attract more attention to it. By describing the inadequacy of the visual effect, the type artist sees creative, alternative solutions more easily.

PARAGRAPH TYPOGRAPHY DECISIONS

THE DECISIONS MADE WITHIN A PARAGRAPH CONCERN the elements that control the paragraph's texture. These are the type size, leading, letterspacing, word spacing, hyphenation, and intraparagraph spacing (space between paragraphs). While the units of measure used to adjust texture are small, the end result is obvious to the reader. The importance of these adjustments cannot be overlooked by the type artist.

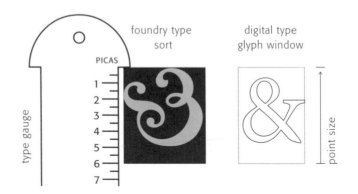

FIGURE 4-6: *Font measuring comparison*

TYPE SIZE

BEFORE THE ADOPTION OF THE AMERICAN POINT SYSTEM by the American Type Founders' Association in 1886, typographers specified type sizes by names, such as *Agate, Minion, English,* and *Nonpareil.* These names, although not standard throughout the industry, did indicate an approximate size for those accustomed to using them. After 1886, the standard unit of measure made size comparisons more reliable and more accurate. Typographers measured the top surface of the sort's body in points by quickly hooking a type gauge to it (fig. 4-6). The letters of the font were smaller than the body itself, but all bodies for a single type font were the same size and easy to measure.

Once typesetting moved away from reproducing letters as impressions from metal type bodies, the tangible, measurable object vanished. Disembodied letters were reproduced from photographic film and later from digital descriptions. Now digital glyphs sit in an area comparable to the top of the sort's body, called a *glyph window* or *bounding box*. The vertical length of the glyph window is the point size of the type font.

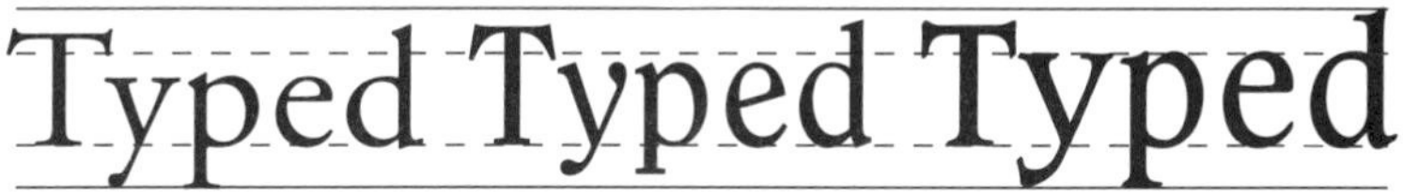

Typed Typed **Typed**

FIGURE 4-7: *Adobe Garamond, Clearface, and Caxton type samples set in the same point size*

Frequently, type artists compare type sizes visually by viewing a printed word, line, or paragraph, never knowing the precise size. When comparing such samples, the type sample of a smaller point size can look larger than the type sample in a larger point size. A type artist can be certain that 16-point type is smaller than 18-point type only when comparing the same typeface.

When categorizing type size, the terms *display* (type 14 points and above) and *text* (type below 14 points) are categories based on generalizations. Display type is for headlines and subheads. (Actual display or titling fonts are designed with proportions, stroke weights, and line endings for larger uses.) Text type is for text copy. These categories provide only a starting point for type size selection, not rigid size ranges.

A reader's perception of type size is influenced by the structural proportions of a typeface. A typeface's x-height and counter size are easier to compare on the page than the actual, measurable type size. The x-height of a typeface represents the torso, or central mass, of each letter. Ascenders and descenders project from it, like arms and legs from a human torso. These appendages do not have the visual weight (or may not be in sufficient quantity) to change the viewer's perception of the typeface's overall size. In the English alphabet 14 of the 26 letters, including 5 of the 6 vowels, do not have ascenders or descenders. A typeface whose x-height represents more of its measurable height appears larger when compared with a typeface whose x-height represents less of its

Typeface structure influences the viewer's perception of type size.

A large *x*-height makes a typeface look larger.

measurable height (see fig. 4-7). It is easier to compare *x*-heights when only a word or a line of lowercase type is available.

For example, an 18-point typeface, such as Adobe Garamond, has a short *x*-height (in comparison to its point size). The elongated ascenders and descenders of this face add to its delicate appearance. Using human colloquial terminology, Adobe Garamond is "small-boned." As a comparison, an 18-point sample of ITC Leawood appears larger than the 18-point Adobe Garamond (fig. 4-8). Leawood has a larger *x*-height to point-size ratio. More of the typeface's point size is devoted to its central mass. Leawood is one of the "large-boned" types. (Human-anatomy terminology is abundant in typography. When a typeface has a large *x*-height, it is said to have a *large eye*.)

Leawood | Garamond
LEAWOOD | GARAMOND

FIGURE 4-8: *Leawood and Garamond type case comparison set in the same point size*

When comparing uppercase samples from these typefaces, the size difference is not as noticeable (fig. 4-8). The cap height of each typeface is proportionally similar. When setting these two faces in a paragraph (uppercase and lowercase letters), the amount of vertical space each line requires is identical because they are the same point size. It is the overall perception of their sizes on a letter-by-letter basis that differs.

Leawood | Caxton
AaBbCcDdEeFf | AaBbCcDdEeFf

FIGURE 4-9: *Leawood and Caxton same-size comparison*

Open counters make typefaces look larger.

The counter size within a typeface also affects the viewer's perception of type size. Using 18-point samples from ITC Leawood and Caxton is a case in point (fig. 4-9). Both typefaces have comparable *x*-heights. Caxton, however, is a more condensed typeface than Leawood. The counter in the Caxton lowercase *o* is egg-shaped. Leawood's counter is more circular. Because of this structural difference, Leawood appears larger than Caxton. As a side note, since the counter-size difference is achieved through character width, the Leawood sample requires more horizontal space than the Caxton sample. These comparisons demonstrate that a type artist cannot rely on point size to determine the visual size relationship between two typefaces. The type artist's eye makes the final decision between *measurable* and *optical* type size.

There is nothing more unsettling than reading a document and all of a sudden realizing that something changed. Once a reader commits to reading several paragraphs of text, he or she becomes familiar with the rhythm created by their type attributes—type size, letterspacing, leading, and measure. Good or bad, the reader is cognizant of the reading rhythm. If one of those attributes suddenly changes—the type size, for example—the reader notices it and the reading rhythm falters. Some readers stop completely until they determine what changed. Then, not only is the reading rhythm interrupted (stopped), but also the delivery of the message.

Some would argue that most people do not notice such nuances. Readers might not know what happened, but they notice *something* happened. People see many things without focusing on them. For example, after a viewer watches several news stories on television, the anchor (who is wearing a navy business suit with a dapper handkerchief in the breast pocket) announces a station break. Once the anchor returns, the viewer realizes something changed. Several news items later, the viewer blurts out, "That's what it is; the handkerchief's gone!" If quizzed, the reader might not recall the stories since the break. The subtle change of the visual landscape was noticed by the viewer and it broke his concentration. Readers must ignore common external distractions when they read. Type artists should not include reader distractions within a document. Changing type sizes between type levels (making the headline bigger than the subhead; the subhead bigger than the text) is good typography. Changing sizes within type levels is not.

Eric Gill wrote in his *Essay on Typography,* "Mere weight and heaviness of letter ceases to be effective in assisting the comprehension of the reader when every poster plays the same shouting game." Gill's reference to the "shouting game" played by posters overusing heavy type also applies to type size. If all type elements on the page are large, the reader receives loud messages from all text blocks. It is impossible for the reader to see page hierarchy through the visual noise. Using type sizes that are too large for the viewing distance is a common mistake made by novice type artists. Reducing the type size for such a paragraph makes the type more welcoming and improves readability. It is difficult

Consistent type size within type levels prevents confusion.

Type size is chosen for reading comfort.

Measure and leading should be checked after a type size change.

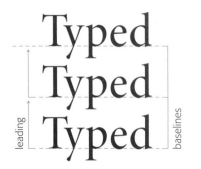 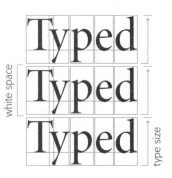

TYPE ON BASELINES   TYPE IN GLYPH WINDOWS

FIGURE 4-10: *Vertical distances, spaces, and guidelines*

to listen when a speaker shouts. (Any adjustment of size requires a review of measure and leading.)

LEADING

CHOOSING LEADING FOLLOWS SPECIFYING TYPE SIZE. Poorly chosen leading can ruin the readability of a well-chosen, legible type font. Leading is the vertical distance (measured in points) between baselines in a type block (fig. 4-10). This distance includes the type size and the additional white space between the lowest point in the first type line and the highest point in the second type line. Increasing or decreasing leading controls the position of the first type line in relation to the second type line. Leading affects page texture by determining the amount of white space between lines of type on the page. As a result, the amount of leading lightens or darkens page texture.

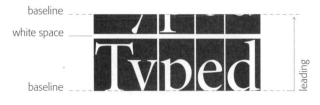

FIGURE 4-11: *Type Size + White Space = Leading*

The term *leading* originated from the days of foundry type when actual strips of lead separated the lines of individual sorts. The height (measured in points) of the lead strip (the leading) determined the size of the white space between the lines of type on the page. Use of this term continued in other typesetting methods, but after type lost its metal body, measuring type size and leading changed. With digital type technology, the vertical baseline-to-baseline measurement became the leading, or *line spacing*. Leading now includes the type size as well as the white space between the lines (fig. 4-11). There are three categories of leading—solid, positive, and negative (fig. 4-12). It is easier to describe these categories by the amount of white space between the type lines.

Solid Leading. The term *solid leading* describes a type block without extra white space between the type lines. The distance from baseline to baseline is the same as the type size. An example of type set solid is 12/12 (12 over 12). Type size is identical to leading. In a set-solid paragraph of continuous text, the bottoms of the glyph windows of the first type line sit atop the tops of the glyph windows of the second type line. If a descender from above is adjacent to an ascender below, the two butt against one another. They do not overlap. Such unfortunate placement creates a hard-to-ignore distraction, and potential detour, for the reader.

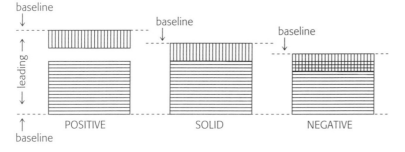

FIGURE 4-12: *Leading categories*

For discontinuous text, a reader's need and the length of the information influence leading decisions. For example, a dictionary entry is a good example of discontinuous text. Readers head for the dictionary when they want a definition, a measurement, an abbreviation—a short burst of data. Using more or less leading for a dictionary entry will not determine whether or not the reader finishes reading the definition. The reader's need for the information and the length of time required to get it override the usual provisions of reading. Set solid works well in this situation with entries separated by bolded words or indentions.

Positive Leading. The term *positive leading* describes type lines separated by white space. The white space keeps the glyph windows of the first type line from butting against the glyph windows of the second line (fig. 4-12). An example of positive leading is 12/16 (12 over 16). Type size

Humpty Dumpty
fell off a wall. ↑
12 pt.

Caxton 12/12—solid leading

Humpty Dumpty
fell off a wall. ↑
16 pt.

Caxton 12/16—positive leading

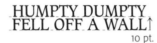

Caxton 12/10—negative leading

HUMPTY DUMPTY
FELL OFF A WALL↑
10 pt.

Caxton 12/10—negative leading
using all capitals

LEADING FUNCTION

is smaller than leading. The amount of white space equals 4 points. With sufficient positive leading, descenders and ascenders cannot form an exit ramp from the first type line into the second.

Positive leading is recommended for continuous text. It isolates lines from one another. With significant text quantity it is impossible to avoid (to catch all instances of) butting descenders and ascenders. Positive leading separates all ascenders and descenders so horizontal eye movement is encouraged over vertical movement.

Negative Leading. The term *negative leading* describes an overlapping of the first line's glyph windows and the second line's glyph windows (fig. 4-12). The distance from baseline to baseline is less than the type size. An example of negative leading is 12/10 (12 over 10). The leading is smaller than the type size. With negative leading, adjacent descenders and ascenders can overlap causing an unsightly blotch in the typographic texture.

WHITE SPACE BETWEEN LINES OF TYPE ISOLATES the lines from one another and facilitates the reader's horizontal eye movement. Easy-to-read text does not force the reader to make procedural decisions, such as, Which way do I go? Up? Down? Right? and does not annoy the reader with frequent distractions, such as, What is that ascender doing in this line? Insufficient white space eliminates the white guidelines that clearly mark the reader's path. Without them, the reader consciously works to stay on the line and to ignore the ascenders and descenders crowding in from adjacent lines. These guidelines serve as guardrails to separate one line of text traffic from another. Doubling and *line skipping* (reading the first half of a sentence with the second half of another) occur more frequently with insufficient leading. In addition, page texture is too dark and often blotchy. Dark page texture signals an overcrowded page and a slow-reading-zone ahead.

Too much white space between type lines also impedes reading. Excessive leading destroys the paragraph's visual cohesion. The reader sees the lines as separate entries without a line-to-line connection. The effortless downward hop from line to line while reading becomes a perilous leap that breaks the reader's rhythm.

Reading a line of text is similar to driving a car along a tree-lined road. If the trees are too close to the road's edge, the driver worries that the car might hit one of them unintentionally. A driver might lean toward the driver's-side door in an unconscious effort to avoid hitting the trees. In this scenario, only a portion of the driver's attention focuses on driving; the rest of it worries about the trees. If the trees are six feet from the road's edge, the driver can concentrate on driving safely. Type artists should provide their readers with distraction-free reading that leaves them attentive to the scope and depth of the document's message.

LEADING SIZE IS DETERMINED BY A COMBINATION of four major factors—type size, type measure, type style, and letter case. Not all of these factors affect leading equally. In some situations one overshadows all the rest. A type artist, however, should consider all four typographic factors initially. Suitable leading size comes from balancing the visual requirements of these factors with the approval of the type artist's eye.

DETERMINING
LEADING SIZE

This does not mean that everything flies out the window if the type artist does not *like* it. Evaluating type has nothing to do with likes and dislikes. An experienced type artist can see if the type in the paragraph *works,* based on type texture, line and paragraph integrity, typeface style, measure, type size, and experience (see chapter 10). Experience includes creating an abundance of effective typographic documents as well as studying the typographic documents of other, more experienced, type artists. Good work is not done in a vacuum. A good eye for type is sustained and nurtured by a diet of good typography.

Type Size and Leading. Type size is the distance from the topmost point to the bottommost point in a font as visually represented by the height of its glyph window. Since structure affects the optical, or perceived, size of a typeface, a type artist cannot base leading decisions solely on point size. For text type (uppercase and lowercase type) the amount of white space between the type lines optically balances the perceived size of the type. A quick squint at a page can show the type artist whether the paragraph consists of multiple horizontal bands or just a sea of unstructured gray.

Type size (measurable or optical) affects the amount of white space needed between lines of upper- and lowercase type.

Many sophisticated type applications provide an autoleading feature. This computes an amount of positive leading as a percentage, 120% for example, of type size. A paragraph of 12-point Adobe Garamond receives the same amount of autoleading—in this case, 14.4 points—as the same paragraph set in 12-point ITC Leawood. Leawood's large x-height, however, makes Leawood appear larger than Adobe Garamond. Using the same amount of leading for each ignores the typefaces' optical size (the only size determinant the reader has). With so much of Leawood's type size devoted to x-height, the ascenders and descenders are not long enough to create a sufficient white zone above and below each type line. The white space included in the leading measurement is responsible for improving readability. Increasing the leading from the autoleading's 14.4 points (2.4 points of white space) to 16 points provides the needed space between lines. Adobe Garamond uses less of its 12 points for the *x*-height, so its ascenders and descenders are longer in comparison. This creates the visual effect of additional, built-in white space that increases the impact of the leading. As a result, the 2.4 points of white space from autoleading is sufficient for Adobe Garamond.

In continuous text or any text block requiring positive leading, 2 points of white space (type size + 2 points = leading size) is a good place to start. While autoleading creates positive leading, some applications do not show the exact amount. Increasing or decreasing the leading from "auto" is impossible until the type artist does the math. Starting with a 2-point add-on to the type size is a more accurate starting point from which to begin adjusting (fig. 4-13).

With text type, the rule of thumb to follow is this: As typeface size increases, so should leading. Switching the type in a leaded paragraph to a typeface with a large *x*-height also requires an increase in leading. With display type sizes in headings, the reverse is true. The larger the headline, the smaller the leading and the resulting white space. The reason for this is simple: As display type size increases, it appears closer to the viewer. In a hand-held document, a proportional increase in leading becomes magnified at such a close distance (18 inches). When increasing the type size of headings, a type artist should leave the leading size at its original setting and evaluate the result. Most times, only the heading size needs to increase.

Type Measure and Leading. A reader makes a significant time commitment when deciding to read an annual report, a novel, a newsletter, or any lengthy text document. The leading works with the measure to maintain a comfortable reading rhythm during that time. Any significant shortening or lengthening of the measure requires a leading adjustment. A longer measure means a longer journey back to the start of the next line. Adding more leading more clearly marks the path to the left edge of the page. As the measure increases, so too must the leading. When the measure decreases from the optimum measure, the leading might decrease, but at a slower rate. Leading increases more rapidly than it decreases in response to measure adjustments.

Type Style and Leading. Type style encompasses different type attributes. The attributes that influence leading are serifs, set width, and stroke weight. A serif provides a visible foundation along the baseline. Since each letter stroke has one, the collective effect is a horizontal band

In continuous text, a significant increase or decrease of measure requires a corresponding increase and possible decrease in leading.

for each type line. When the serif is missing, the vertical strokes in the letters become more visually dominant. In continuous text, sans serif type requires more leading than serif type. The extra white space isolates each line and creates the horizontal banding (inherent in serif type) that makes reading easier.

Condensed typefaces (typefaces with a narrow set width) have a strong vertical appearance. As with sans serif typefaces, condensed faces require extra leading to prevent vertical eye movement between lines. In a lengthy document, if readers must consciously work to stay on the type line, they will tire and eventually stop reading. This is a lesser concern in discontinuous text, because a single-line subhead, for example, is separated from its surrounding by a size increase or style change.

In continuous text, sans serif type requires more leading.

Condensed typefaces and typefaces with heavier stroke weights require more leading.

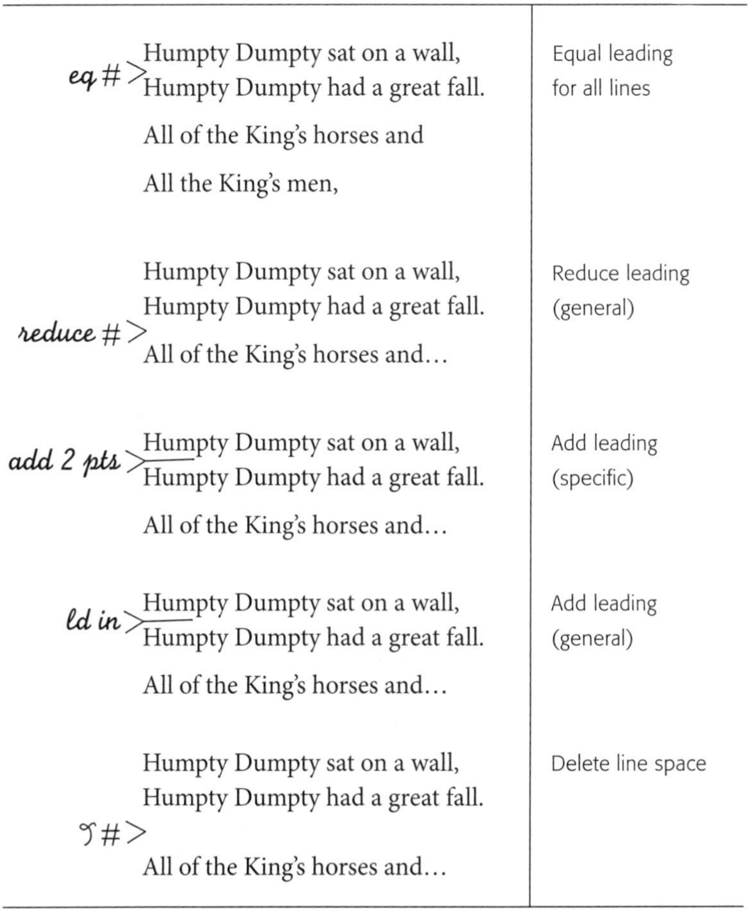

eq # > Humpty Dumpty sat on a wall, Humpty Dumpty had a great fall. All of the King's horses and All the King's men,	Equal leading for all lines
reduce # > Humpty Dumpty sat on a wall, Humpty Dumpty had a great fall. All of the King's horses and…	Reduce leading (general)
add 2 pts > Humpty Dumpty sat on a wall, Humpty Dumpty had a great fall. All of the King's horses and…	Add leading (specific)
ld in > Humpty Dumpty sat on a wall, Humpty Dumpty had a great fall. All of the King's horses and…	Add leading (general)
Humpty Dumpty sat on a wall, Humpty Dumpty had a great fall. ꝃ # > All of the King's horses and…	Delete line space

FIGURE 4-13: *Leading proofmarks*

Type set in all capitals has built-in leading.

TIMES SET IN ALL CAPS.

18/20 Times

TIMES SET IN ALL CAPS.

18/16 Times

LETTERSPACING AND WORD SPACING

Paragraphs set in text faces with heavier strokes benefit by increased leading. The additional white lightens the overall paragraph texture. While bold or semibold type styles are not suitable for continuous text, the humanist typefaces, such as Stempel Schneidler, have medium-to-heavy-weight strokes that darken paragraph texture. Lightening this texture by increasing the leading makes the paragraph more welcoming and easier to read.

Letter Case and Leading. Setting type in all lowercase or all uppercase letters influences the visual effect of leading. Initial capitals and lowercase letters, whether used in a heading or in continuous text, occupy space above and below the baseline. The actual white space between type lines is restricted to the space between the descent and ascent of adjacent lines. Type set in all uppercase letters, in the majority of typefaces, remains above the baseline. The space allocated for the descent is unoccupied. As a result, a two-line, set-solid heading in all caps has white space between the lines. The descent of the first line serves that purpose.

For example, 18-point Times has an ascent of 14 points and a descent of 4 points. With a type block set 18/20, the white space would normally be 2 points. If the type block was set in uppercase letters exclusively, the 4-point descent is unoccupied. The white space separating the type lines increases from 2 points to 6 points. To bring these lines closer together and return to the intended white space size, the type artist uses negative leading. By decreasing the amount of leading from 18/20 to 18/16, the 14-point, ascent-only type lines now have 2 points of white space between them.

It is unusual for a type artist to know a typeface's ascent and descent measurement without access to specialized font utility software. More than likely, the uppercase type lines just look too far apart. It may take a bit of trial-and-error until the right distance is achieved, but negative leading is just what the "type-doctor" ordered.

Negative leading can work with lowercase letters if the first line does not contain descenders or if the ascenders and descenders of both lines interlock, like a well-planned jigsaw puzzle. Both techniques are suitable for headlines only.

TYPE ARTISTS USE LEADING TO PLACE WHITE SPACE vertically between type lines to attain good typographic texture. They use letterspacing and word spacing to place white space horizontally between letters and words for the same goal. Unlike leading, letterspacing is not measurable

Tufa Tufa Tufa

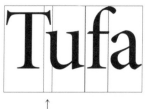

Glyph windows vary in width according to glyph characteristics and spacing needs.

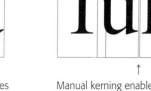

Kerning table information enables automatic overlapping for certain glyph pairs.

Manual kerning enables optical letterspacing adjustments for individual pairs.

FIGURE 4-14: *Letterspacing and kerning with digital type*

in points. Letterspacing has always been described in vague, subjective terms that placed the designer somewhat at the mercy of the typesetter's skills—which has not been necessarily bad. Designers specified letterspacing (and some page-layout applications still do) in the following terms: *loose, normal, tight,* and *tight but not touching.* In the days of foundry type, the letter's face fit on its metal body in such a way that created white space on either side. Normal letterspacing occurred when the individual sorts butted against one another. The kern and the ligature remedied letterspacing for the most troublesome combinations. For word spacing, the typesetter inserted spacers made for that font.

With the liberation of the letter face from its metal type body, the typesetter could position letters on top of each other if the designer requested it. This ability, first possible with phototypesetting, initiated a new era of typographic design, exemplified by the work in the 1960s and 1970s of designers such as Herb Lubalin, Milton Glaser, and others. The development of digital typography provided for the same infinite placement of letters along a baseline.

When designing digital type fonts, type designers use units, a proportional measurement, to define a glyph's advance width (see "Paragraph Guidelines and Measurements" earlier in this chapter). Units enable a nuanced, proportional relationship between a glyph and its side bearings that is applicable in all point sizes. Most glyphs fit nicely together on a baseline using the built-in spacers provided by the side bearings. This designer-created spacing is customized for the design attributes of the typeface—stroke weights, set width, counter, and such.

Some letter combinations, such as *W* and *o* or *Y* and *a,* and certain letter–punctuation mark combinations require letterspacing adjustments because their unique shapes create spacing irregularities when they appear together. The necessary adjustment instructions for these glyph combinations, or *kerning pairs,* are contained in a font's *kerning table.* Once a kerning pair appears, a type-savvy application accesses the kerning table and implements the spacing alterations to maintain consistent letterspacing. A kerning table for a high-quality font contains between 500 and 1,000 different kerning pair instructions. Most often this involves deleting space, but, in some cases, space is added. This form of automatic letterspacing adjustment is called *metric kerning.*

Some type-savvy applications also provide optical kerning to assist type artists with letterspacing. *Optical kerning* uses mathematical algorithms that calculate spacing based on the shapes of two adjacent glyphs. This is useful when combining two type families for a unique display type block or, more commonly, when combining two family members, such as roman and italic, in the same paragraph.

Even after assistance from metric and optical kerning, a type artist can adjust the spacing between any two letters manually. Page-layout applications provide their own system of units per em for the type artist to add and delete spaces between glyphs. *Manual kerning* is more prevalent in display type, where larger type and space size accentuate letterspacing problems (see fig. 4-14). Manual kerning follows the laws of *optical letterspacing* (visually balancing space shapes around and within letters in a single word or group of words). This definition recognizes the visual impact of the counter on letterspacing decisions. For example, in the word *You,* optical letterspacing requires the negative space between the *Y* and the *o* to appear equal to the space between the *o* and the *u,* while recognizing that the counter of the *o* and the *u* affects the space between the *Y* and the *o* also. The type artist's eye is the only tool capable of such delicate balancing.

Experienced typographers recommend visualizing the space between letters filled with drops of ink. Once the space on either side of the same letter holds the same number of drops (in the mind's eye), the spaces are balanced. While this method is not foolproof, it is a place to start. The point of this mental exercise is to force the type artist to see the space rather than the letter. Seeing spaces as shapes is a prerequisite for balancing them.

When Jan Tschichold (1902–74) supervised typographic design at Penguin Books in the 1940s, he became so frustrated editing spacing for capital letters that he had a rubber stamp made. It said, "Equalize Letter Spacing According to Their Optical Value." He then stamped those instructions on every instance of incorrect letterspacing he found. The

① You (no kerning)

② You (tighten *Y* and *o*)

③ You (open *o* and *u*)

(kern)	**Peruvian Proofreader**	Kern letters (close)
ls	**Achieves Profitability!**	Add letterspacing
eq #//	The ✓perfect ✓Peruvian proofreader	Use equal word space
#	parlayed his|perfectionist perusals	Insert word space
less #	and his∧penchant for pencil pushing	Reduce space
⌒	in⁀to a profitable profession.	Close up word space

FIGURE 4-15: *Letterspacing and word spacing proofmarks*

stamping (or slamming) motion of applying stamp to paper probably helped dissipate his continued frustration. Tschichold said, "The rhythm of a well-formed word can never be based on equal linear distances between letters…. This unmeasurable space must always be of equal size. But only the eye can measure it, not the ruler" (Tschichold 1965). This statement still holds true.

Word spacing for a font is determined by the type designer with the inclusion of a *spaceband* (the amount of space [approximately ¼ em] left between letters after a single press of the spacebar). This term is a carryover from linecasting machines where expandable metal wedges (the spacebands) served as word spaces between the matrixes in a single line of justified type.

Setting Letterspacing and Word Spacing. It is impossible to discuss letterspacing separately from word spacing. One is proportional to the other. The space between letters in a paragraph must be smaller than the spaces between the words. If these spaces are equal, the reader faces a page filled with evenly spaced letters that hold no clue as to internal groupings. If the letterspacing is enough to separate the letters comfortably, but the word spacing is extreme, the reader sees a page filled with words with no clue as to line cohesion. Letterspacing and word spacing are the glue holding together the letters and words in a readable, evenly textured paragraph.

Letterspacing and word spacing are proportional.

Letterspacing affects readability by influencing word shapes. If the type artist sets letterspacing too small or too large, word shapes distort

Letterspacing and word spacing
directly affect readability and
page texture.

from their familiar contour. With insufficient letterspacing, letters touch one another and create new letterforms not included in the alphabet's customary 26. Dark blotches appear in the paragraph that distract the viewer with odd patterns. At the other extreme, overabundant letterspacing causes the reader to question whether the space is between two letters or two words. The reader's puzzlement triggers multiple questions, which breaks reader concentration, destroys sentence readability, and jeopardizes reader comprehension and patience.

Word spacing affects page texture and readability by smoothing the breaks between words to carry the reader's eye easily through the sentence. If the type artist sets word spacing too large, white "rivers" form vertically and diagonally between adjacent type lines (fig. 4-16). These rivers carry the reader along a meandering white current through the type and away from the logic of its content. This destroys the page's even texture and distracts the reader with patchy gray text.

For a document to demonstrate carefully crafted spacing, type artists need three key components in addition to a well-trained eye. First, the type artist needs an application that interprets, or reads, the spacing information included in the font. Some graphics applications, for example, cannot access the kerning tables included in a typeface, so customized spacing for troublesome kerning pairs is not available. When using type-savvy applications, setting type is a type-tweaker's delight because all the type controls are there. When using type-clumsy applications, setting type is disappointing, frustrating, and far too time-consuming.

Second, the type artist needs quality typefaces that contain detailed spacing information, such as correctly sized side bearings and complete kerning tables. With the availability of typeface-creation software, all interested comers are invited to design their own typefaces. While the ability to create John Doe Condensed has an appeal for some, the words *You get what you pay for* come to mind. A typeface distributed by a time- and market-tested type manufacturer, while more expensive than some, will include more instructions that improve typographic quality. It is better to have one well-designed, more expensive font than a hundred cheap fonts of inferior quality.

Third, the type artist's printer must interpret and reproduce accurately the information in the typeface and the alterations made by the application. If the spacing on screen fails to materialize on the printer's page, the other two components have limited impact. When all three components are working together effectively, the type artist can produce high-quality typographic documents.

Alignment and Spacing. The type alignments, flush left, flush right, and centered, enable the type artist to maintain even letterspacing and word spacing throughout a paragraph or page. These are the space-friendly formats. The amount of space between letters and the space-bands between words and sentences are consistently maintained. There are no alignment requirements causing the application to override or adjust spacing sizes. With flush left, easy-to-find line-starts combine with uniform letterspacing and word spacing to create an easy-to-read paragraph—with other readability-enhancing attributes assisting also.

The justified alignment forces the application to ignore the designer's spacing preferences and asks the type artist to set an acceptable spacing range. The application increases or decreases letterspacing and word spacing within the range (line-by-line) to justify the text. The goal is to keep the range narrow enough so the reader does not notice the spacing differences between lines, yet wide enough so the application can achieve the desired alignment. If the spacing range appears too narrow for the needs of the text, increasing the measure or reducing the type size can solve the problem by creating more spaces to adjust.

In a page-layout application, there are three settings for word spacing ranges for justified type. Together these settings form an acceptable range with a specific preference when possible. One setting is for the desired or optimum spacing (use this if possible). The second setting defines the minimum spacing (do not go any smaller than this). The third setting defines the maximum spacing (do not go any larger than this). With the desired spacing, the application's default setting uses the type designer's specifications. One popular application assigns word spacing in percentages with the desired spacing as 100%. (Graphic designers should recognize this as the size of the original—what the type designer provided.) A rule of thumb for optimum word spacing is ¼ of an em (M/4). This is equivalent to the width of a lowercase *t*. Since the em is a proportional unit of measure, this spacing is suitable for any size type. Minimum word spacing for justified text is ⅕ of an em (M/5). Maximum word spacing for justified text is ⅓ of an em (M/3).

With 100% representing M/4, a mathematically inclined type artist can start with a sample point size, such as 12 points, determine M/5, M/4, and M/3 (2.4, 3.0, and 4.0 points, respectively), and then work backwards to find the minimum and maximum percentages (80% and 133% respectively). These percentages work for any size type.

Since letterspacing is proportional to word spacing, the logical approach to letterspacing is to use the same proportions as word spacing.

Justified text adjusts letter and word spacing on a line-by-line basis and is not consistent throughout the paragraph.

Recommended word spacing range for justified text:

minimum—M/5
optimum—M/4
maximum—M/3

Assuming the desired or optimum setting is the designer's preferred spacing, a type artist sets a proportional range with the equivalent of an 80% minimum and a 133% maximum. Previewing printed samples of different spacing ranges at the outset of a project saves the type artist hours of adjustment later (see "Paragraph Typography Evaluation" later in this chapter).

When justifying foundry type, the distribution of excess horizontal white space was limited primarily to the spaces between words and sentences and secondarily to the spaces between words and select punctuation marks (fig. 4-16). In those foundry-set texts, larger word spaces are apparent. The result of this was consistent letterspacing from line to line, but uneven paragraph texture since the type was prone to white rivers. The changing visual landscape for each line was restricted primarily to word spacing. Consequently, words maintained their visual integrity and distinct word shape.

> us with a commanding impetuosity, Virgil leads us with an attractive majesty : Homer scatters with a generous profusion, Virgil bestows with a careful magnificence : Homer, like the Nile, pours out his riches with a boundless overflow ; Virgil, like a river in its banks, with a gentle and constant stream. When we behold their battles, methinks the two poets resemble the heroes they celebrate : Homer, boundless and irresistible as Achilles, bears all before him, and shines more and more as the tumult increases ; Virgil, calmly daring like Æneas, appears undisturbed in the midst of the action, disposes all about him, and conquers with tranquillity. And when we look upon their machines, Homer seems like his own Jupiter in his terrors, shaking Olympus,

FIGURE 4-16: *Foundry type sample from the preface of Pope's translation of the* Iliad of Homer *(1867)*

Type artists today can still limit excess white space distribution to word spaces by setting all three letterspacing measurements to the desired or optimum spacing. The type artist then makes line-by-line adjustments as needed, eliminating any texture problems. Longer measures are better suited for this justification technique.

Type Style and Spacing. The type attributes of serifs, set widths, and stroke weight influence horizontal spacing decisions. Fortunately, a well-designed digital typeface has a glyph window sized for its style characteristics. If all the software and hardware requirements are met, the type artist has only a few key spots to check in text type—not each and every word pair. (Chapter 5 identifies the kerning needs of individual typeface characters.) Display-size type for headlines and subheads requires more careful visual scrutiny and more frequent manual kerning due to its size.

Serifs provide a line with built-in letterspacers. The letters cannot get too close to one another without touching. Sans serif typefaces are more challenging because the arm's-length separation provided by the serifs is gone. Sans serif type relies on sufficient letterspacing to keep the letters apart and to prevent oddly shaped mergers from forming. The type artist should carefully check a sample of sans serif type before using it for lengthy text.

Horizontal spacing is proportional to a letter's set width and stroke weight. Using the type designer's preset spacing is the best and easiest option, but if this is overridden due to justified alignment or unsuitable due to a patterned or tinted background, the type artist sets the spacing. Condensed typefaces require less letterspacing than extended typefaces. Reversed type (white type on a black background) benefits by additional spacing. Typefaces with heavy stroke weights cannot be too tightly positioned on the line or word shapes turn into word blobs. Inserting more space between the letters prevents this. Conversely, a thin-weight font needs a bit more glue to hold it together; narrower spacing assists here.

Type Usage and Spacing. Many type artists produce documents, such as advertisements, brochures, and newsletters, that are viewed at a hand-held distance of 18 inches. These high-resolution, printed pieces can demonstrate high typographic quality executed with painstaking care. An initial printout to determine key type sizes, appropriate for this viewing distance and typeface, prevents any surprises at the end. Other type artists work with type for video presentations, billboards, signage, and other larger or smaller final uses. Type for signage and video presentations needs tighter spacing on screen. Otherwise, the horizontal spaces between the letters and words appear exaggerated in their final form. This has to be balanced, however, with output resolution. A low-resolution output needs more letterspacing. Also, type that is reduced after it leaves the type artist's screen needs more letter and word spacing to prevent letters from touching in their reduced versions.

Letter Case and Spacing. Words set in all capital letters are effective as headlines, subheads, titles, and captions. The glyph window for a capital letter is proportioned for use with lowercase letters. All caps set from a font suited for text type requires additional letterspacing to balance the larger letters with larger counters. A typeface with a display or titling font (all capital letters) in the proper weight (regular, semibold, or bold) has a glyph window suited for all-cap usage. This, however, does not eliminate the need for page proof scrutiny. Isolated letter pairs might need manual kerning. Punctuation in an all-cap sequence requires a visual check for kerning also.

Ligatures are a hallmark of classic typographic quality. The *f-i* and *f-l* ligatures are a standard feature of a digital typeface. The *f-f-i*, *f-f-l*, and *f-f* ligatures are more commonplace with the use of expert collections and suitably outfitted OpenType type families. Ligatures have preset spacing, because the two or three letters are designed as a single glyph. Use of the designer-specified letterspacing and word spacing is recommended when using ligatures. Justified type needs sufficient maneuvering room to make ligatures blend into the text.

KERNING AND TRACKING

ISOLATED INSTANCES OF *MANUAL KERNING* (optically adjusting letterspacing between two letters) and *tracking* (uniformly increasing or decreasing letterspacing within a group of letters—word, acronym, headline) might remain after document-wide spacing settings are applied. Well-set letterspacing and word spacing controls should eliminate the need for manual kerning in text type. Kerning text drives the type artist crazy and does not produce a significant improvement in readability. Headlines, primarily, and subheads, depending on type size, are the focus of kerning. The type artist works in an enlarged view (at least 400%) while kerning. A printer or imagesetter capable of reproducing these minute adjustments is a must for high-quality typographic output.

HYPHENATION

HYPHENATION IS ANOTHER FEATURE TYPE ARTISTS USE to control typographic texture. It affects letterspacing and word spacing in justified text (by adding or removing letters from a line) and affects the rag range in unjustified text. *Line-end hyphenation* (hyphenating a word at the end of a line) is suitable in text material, but unsuitable for headlines, subheads, pull quotes, and other examples of display typography. With hyphenation turned off, the application can break lines only after words.

The hyphenation zone determines when word breaks can occur.

In rag text using line-end hyphenation, the type artist sets a hyphenation zone to control the smoothness of the rag. The *hyphenation zone* is a distance measured in from the extreme right edge that determines when hyphenation can occur. Once a word enters this zone, the application begins hyphenating as needed. The longer the zone, the greater the distance between right-side line endings, or the *rag range*. To create a smoother rag, the type artist narrows the hyphenation zone.

Type-savvy applications offer automatic hyphenation. With this feature the type artist continues to enter text while the application breaks the word at preprogrammed hyphenation points. While this increases keyboarding speed, the type artist should check all hyphenated lines on the proof.

There are several guidelines to follow when hyphenating text. The first rule is the anti-ladder rule. It states that no more than three hyphens should be used consecutively in a paragraph (fig. 4-17). Abandoning that precept produces a ladder of hyphens along the right edge of a paragraph that mars typographic quality. Some typographers prefer no more than two consecutive line-end hyphens, since a hyphen disturbs the smooth line of the paragraph's right edge; that can be too limiting, however. Some applications enable the type artist to set the number of consecutive hyphens—a handy feature. The second rule is the two-three rule. It states that a hyphenated word should leave a minimum of two characters before the hyphen (on the first line) and bring a minimum of three characters to the next line.

> A text paragraph should contain no more than three consecutive hyphens.

> Line-end hyphenations leave a minimum of two characters on the first line and bring down a minimum of three characters.

℘ After awaking late, the White Rab/ bit rushed to dress.	Delete line-end hyphen and close up word
although the dic- tionary set thumb- nails on edge; ther- mometers were dis- turbed and simple. *break up*	Too many consecutive hyphens

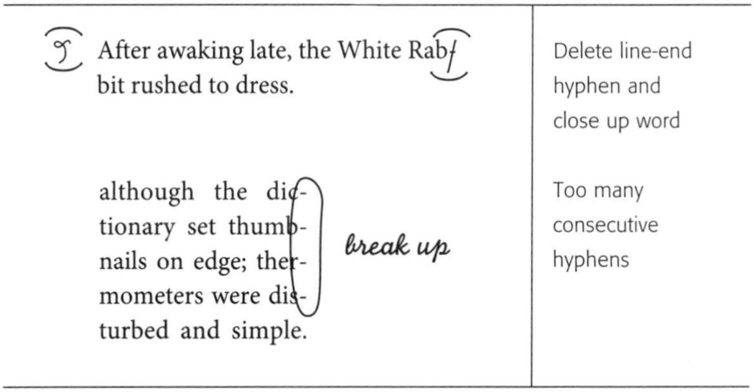

FIGURE 4-17: *Hyphenation proofmarks*

Some typographers prefer to hang the punctuation. Hanging the punctuation is not as gruesome as it sounds and is possible with flush left, flush right, and justified type. When hung, the punctuation, such as quotation marks, are positioned beyond the limit of the left or right margin. This smooths the margins by eliminating the chinking caused by quotation marks, hyphens, commas, and periods. The mark's small size makes its presence beyond the margin unobtrusive.

Another guideline that minimizes message disruption is a variation of an old rule—always hyphenate by syllables. The rule is true, but it does not go far enough. Words should be divided by syllables, but when

> Hyphenating words according to syllables and pronunciation smoothes the flow of words.

there are several syllable breaks available, the updated rule—hyphenate by pronunciation—improves readability. The word *encyclopedia,* for example, has five syllables—en·cy·clo·pe·dia. Breaking the word after the second syllable (ency·clopedia) is confusing. At the end of a long measure the reader reunites the two syllable segments after a two- or three-second delay. The sound the reader forms after seeing the segment *ency* does not flow smoothly into the remaining segment *clopedia.* If the type artist divided the word *encyclopedia* in accordance with its pronunciation—encyclo·pedia—the reader forms the correct sound that flawlessly matches the second segment. Hyphenating by pronunciation maintains the smooth flow of words.

Hyphenating words at the end of a page or at the end of a long column impedes word flow.

The same goal of creating a smooth flow of words holds true when hyphenating the end of a right-hand (*recto*) page or at the end of a column. If the reader must turn a page or scale a lengthy column before reuniting the two parts of a hyphenated word, the type artist should reconsider hyphenation.

Line-end hyphenation belongs between compound words and hyphenated words.

Other common situations requiring hyphenation guidance involve closed compound words, such as *dragonfly;* hyphenated compound words, such as *double-talk;* and words with prefixes, such as *displeased.* A type artist should always divide a closed compound between the two words, such as *dragon·fly,* and a hyphenated compound word at the site of the existing hyphen. Adding a hyphen to a hyphenated word confuses the reader. Hyphenating a word after the prefix is the preferred location.

Indents and Tabs

Indents and tabs position text at precise locations. The type artist sets indents for an entire document or a single paragraph. The application applies the indent automatically as the type artist works. Tabs, on the other hand, are used for a single line or several consecutive lines. The type artist sets the tabs first and then presses the Tab key to activate each tab. In the days of manual typewriters, spacing over with the spacebar worked well because all spacebands and character windows were sized identically. With proportionally spaced type, spacing over is not reliable and is time-consuming to fix.

Indents and tabs align proportionally spaced type more accurately than the spacebar.

Common indents are *indent left* (starting the left side of a text block in from the margin at a specified distance), *indent right* (ending the right side of a text block in from the margin at a specified distance), *indent first* (starting the first line of a paragraph in from the left margin at a specified distance), and *hanging indent* (starting the first line of a paragraph at the margin and indenting left the remainder of the lines). Using indents for relocating a paragraph's edge is preferable to moving

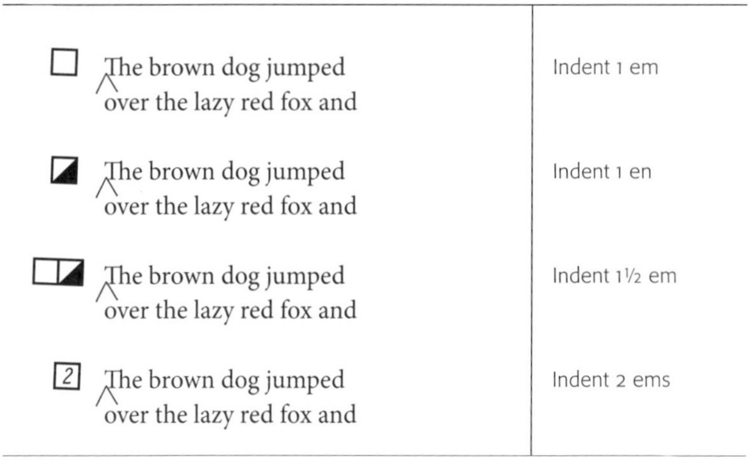

☐	The brown dog jumped over the lazy red fox and	Indent 1 em
◪	The brown dog jumped over the lazy red fox and	Indent 1 en
☐◪	The brown dog jumped over the lazy red fox and	Indent 1½ em
②	The brown dog jumped over the lazy red fox and	Indent 2 ems

FIGURE 4-18: *Indention proofmarks*

and resizing a single paragraph in a multiparagraph document. Indents are more accurate and easier to apply to multiple paragraphs.

Common tabs are *left-aligned tabs* (text lines aligned along the left edge at a specified point), *right-aligned tabs* (text lines aligned along the right edge at a specified point), *centered tabs* (text lines centered at a specified point), and *decimal tabs* (decimal numbers aligned vertically at the decimal point). Tabs are more flexible than indents but just as reliable. They are not restricted to the sides of the text block.

First-Line Indents. First-line indents call attention to the beginning of a new paragraph and provide a small respite for the eye. After a heading, however, the first-line indent is unnecessary because the heading heralded the beginning of the paragraph. If the type artist does not place additional white space between the paragraphs on the page, then the first line of the remaining paragraphs is indented. If the type artist adds additional space between paragraphs, the first-line indent is redundant and should be eliminated.

> A first-line indent does not follow a subhead or headline.

The type artist determines the length of the indent according to the size of the measure and size of the margin. A minimum first-line indent is 1 em or 1 lead. Both the em and the lead are suitable indents because they are proportional measurements and have a visual relationship with the rest of the text. If a paragraph is set 11/14, the indent can be either 11 points (the em) or 14 points (the lead). Increasing the indent is acceptable with a wide margin or long measure. In that case, using 1½ or 2 ems or 2 leads is preferable. There is the rare occasion when a more sizable

> A first-line indent or space between paragraphs identifies a new paragraph. They always work alone.

A 1½-em, 2-em, or 2-lead first-line indent is suitable for wide margins and long measures.

indent works well, but it is a rare case. The problem with longer indents is the large unusual white shape created between paragraphs. It is distracting to the reader.

Hanging indents effectively call attention to a new paragraph by jutting the first line of text into the left margin away from the flush-left edge of the text block. These indents are preceded by additional paragraph space that lightens the texture and emphasizes the indent. Without it, the paragraphs form a single, formidable, mega-paragraph that chases away readers. Initial caps, or versals, are a decorative technique, coupled with first-line indents or hanging indents, that call attention and add graphic emphasis to the beginning of a new section of text. While these initial flourishes (see chapter 7) can enhance a document, they are not suitable for all documents. The job of the type artist is to enhance readability, not design a typographic mine field. Knowing when to stop is an underrated, essential design skill.

Setting Block Quotes. The term *block quote* refers to a quote in running text that exceeds four lines. It is easy for the reader to lose track of the speaker with a quote of that length. Consequently, separating the quote from the text by a typographic change helps the reader recognize the speaker change. Reducing both the type and leading size by 1 point alerts the reader to the shared relationship of the words. Inserting 2 or 3 points of additional white space before and after the block breaks the leading pattern of the text and further supports this subgroup union. (See "Intraparagraph Spacing" later in this chapter.) The block quote has neither a first-line indent, nor quotation marks.

Quotations in excess of four lines are indented, prefaced by additional white space, and not quoted.

If the typographic changes are insufficient, the type artist can use a left and right indent for the block quote. The use of the indent is not required but is helpful if the decrease in type point size, coupled with the decrease in leading, creates a readability problem for the existing measure. The type artist should set the indents in proportion to the first-line indent. For example, with a 2-em first-line indent, a 1- or 2-em block-quote indent makes visual sense. A quote of four lines or less is quoted and included in the running text without typographic changes.

Indents should replace tabs whenever possible.

Using Tabs. Type artists use tabs to organize and to tidy visually a collection of statistics, measurements, facts, and figures in columns. It is difficult for readers to compare statistics when they are racing about the page trying to find them. Tabs position these items into subgroupings that encourage comparison. Many type artists cringe after hearing the word *tab* due to prior bad experiences. Tab-savvy type artists avoid trouble by using indents whenever possible.

CHAPTER FOUR

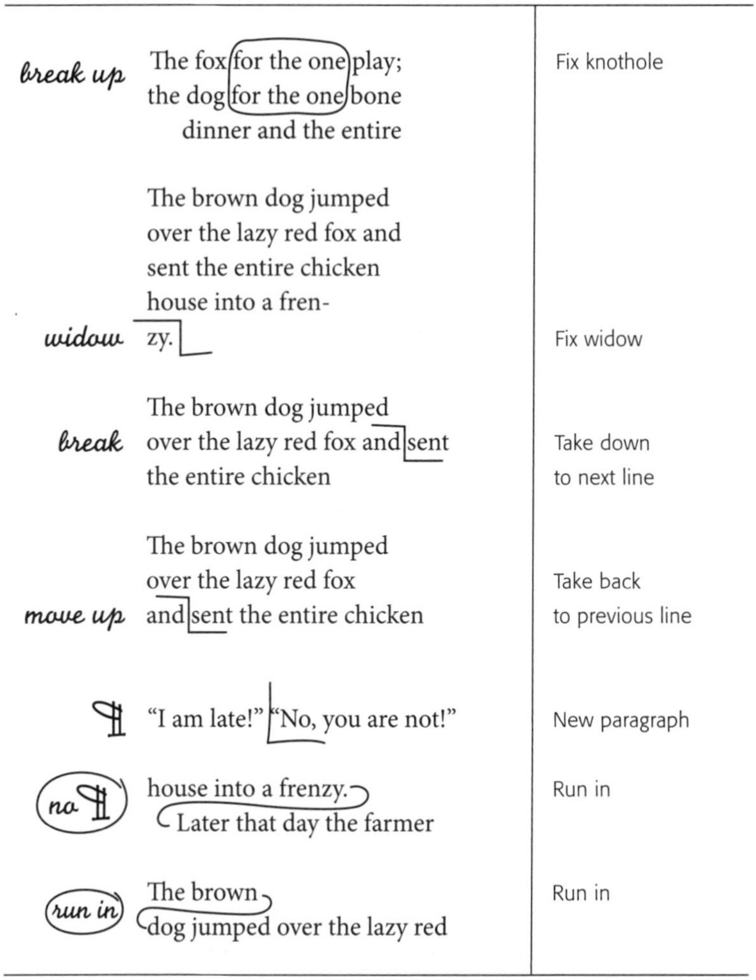

break up	The fox for the one play; the dog for the one bone dinner and the entire	Fix knothole
widow	The brown dog jumped over the lazy red fox and sent the entire chicken house into a fren- zy.	Fix widow
break	The brown dog jumped over the lazy red fox and sent the entire chicken	Take down to next line
move up	The brown dog jumped over the lazy red fox and sent the entire chicken	Take back to previous line
	"I am late!" "No, you are not!"	New paragraph
no	house into a frenzy. Later that day the farmer	Run in
run in	The brown dog jumped over the lazy red	Run in

FIGURE 4-19: *Line-manipulation proofmarks*

Tabs are appropriate when there are multiple alignment points along the same line. To set three adjacent columns of figures, for example, set all the figures first—row by row, abutting one another. With all the material in place, the type artist selects the lines of figures as a single entity, sets the correct tabs, and then (working from left to right) positions the insertion point, and hits the Tab key. Adjustments to column placement can commence after all three columns are aligned. To adjust the columns, the type artist selects all the figures again and drag-edits the tab markers.

Widows and Orphans

A paragraph's last line should not be a whole word of less than four letters or the last half of a hyphenated word of any length.

A PARAGRAPH NEEDS A GOOD BEGINNING—in the form of an indent, additional white space, or an initial cap, to name a few—to draw the reader into the text. Frequently, paragraphs straddle more than one page. The reader starts the paragraph on one page and ends on another. If the type artist could choose, all paragraphs would break in the middle, leaving an ample text block to end the first page and start the second page. Since this is not possible, the type artist tries to maintain the visual integrity of both pages by controlling where the split occurs.

The terms *widow* and *orphan* refer to partial paragraphs residing on a page. The term *widow* refers to the last line of a paragraph positioned at the top of the next page or column. It also refers to a short word (less than four letters) or the tail end of a hyphenated word as the last line of a paragraph. The widowed line (or word) goes forward to the next page (or line) alone. The term *orphan* refers to the first line of a paragraph positioned at the end of a page or column. The orphaned line is left behind while the rest of the paragraph goes forward to the next page without it.

In both cases, an insufficient number of paragraph lines weakens the top or bottom edge of a page. The orphan is the least offensive of the two. How to fix a widow depends upon its length. It could be easier to bring it back to the previous page if it is short. Fixing a widowed word follows the same guidelines as fixing hyphenation problems (see "Hyphenation" earlier in this chapter).

Intraparagraph Spacing

A PAGE OF TEXT TYPE IS FREQUENTLY, AND THANKFULLY, punctuated with type treatments (headlines, subheads, captions, block quotes, and pull quotes, to name a few) as well as illustrations, photographs, or additional white space. These type treatments help the reader by subdividing and organizing the text. They can contribute to page chaos, however, if handled incorrectly. On a multicolumned page, the baselines of the text in the first column should align with the baselines of the other columns. If the page contained nothing but columns of 10/13 text, baseline alignment between columns would be assured. With the addition of subheads, block quotes, pull quotes, and illustrations into columns of text, baseline alignment between columns becomes a challenge.

Size is the key to inserting headings and graphics into a text column while maintaining baseline alignment. The amount of vertical space used by the insertion must be a factor of the leading. For example, if the type artist places a subhead in the middle of a 10/13 continuous-text column, the subhead's total leading should be 13 points (13 × 1), or

26 points (13 × 2), or 39 points (13 × 3), and so forth (a factor of 13). If the subhead is two lines set 12/13 in a semibold typeface, the subhead is larger and bolder, but it still maintains the 13-point leading for a total insertion size of 26 points (a factor of 13, that is, 13 × 2). Because the subhead's leading is a factor of the text leading, the adjacent text baselines realign once they pass the subhead.

Leawood type set in 10-point type with 13-point leading. Leawood type set in 10-point type with 13-point leading for text.	Leawood set in 10-point type and 13-point leading. **Type 13/15** **Type 13/15** Leawood set in 10-point type and 13-point leading for text.	Leawood set in 10-point type and 13-point leading. **Type 13/15** **Type 13/15** Leawood set in 10-point type and 13-point leading.
• Leawood 10/13	• 13/15 two-line subhead • vertical space: 30 points	• 6 points added above/ 3 points below subhead • vertical space: 39 points

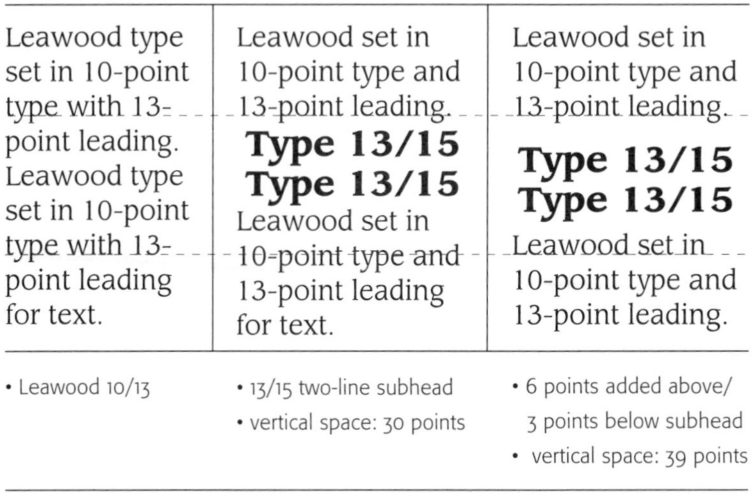

FIGURE 4-20: *Align text baselines in adjacent paragraphs*

Many times, however, a text insertion is not a factor of the leading. In those instances, the type artist adds additional white space before and after the insertion to make its total size a factor of the leading. If the type artist inserts a two-line subhead 13/15 into the same 10/13 text column example (fig. 4-20), the insertion measures 30 points (15 + 15 = 30) vertically. The insertion is 9 points short of the nearest leading factor—39 points (13 × 3). The type artist must distribute a total of 9 points of additional white space before and after the subhead. Placing more of the 9-point white space in front of the subhead positions it closer to the text it introduces, which aids reader comprehension. Although the subhead's baselines will not match adjacent baselines, the text beneath the subhead will align correctly to adjacent text baselines.

Inserting photographs or illustrations into multicolumn pages follows the same principle as typographic insertions. The total vertical insertion size must be a factor of the leading. With graphic insertions of varying heights, the amount of white space varies in size also. If the amount of space around the graphics is too noticeable, the type artist can hide the difference by placing the graphic at the top or bottom of the column. Resizing the graphic is also an option.

With lengthy documents, such as annual reports or newsletters, it is important to establish a baseline-alignment system initially that is easy to maintain as the page numbers increase. For example, many type artists prefer using paragraph indents instead of extra white space between paragraphs because it maintains the leading rhythm while still identifying new paragraphs.

PARAGRAPH TYPOGRAPHY EVALUATION

ONCE THE ELEMENTS ARE ALL ON THE PAGE, it is time to customize. The work is not over by any means. In house-building terms, the house is framed, roofed, and drywalled; now it is time for the carpenters and painters to do the trim and custom work. The type artist's custom work at the paragraph level includes four areas of concern: software spell checking, baseline alignment, consistency, and typographic texture.

The software spelling checker is the broadest means to check spelling and it catches only the most obvious errors. It easily catches the extra letter *t* in the word *litttle* or the additional letter *i* in the word *siilly*. With proportionally sized letters, it is easy to overlook an additional letter or a missing letter when spell checking manually (by eye). There is no reason to spell check manually for this kind of error, because the software does it faster and more reliably. It is the *compliment/complement* errors that await the type artist on the sentence level of typography.

With major spelling errors eliminated, the type artist prints out a proof copy for paragraph-level corrections. It is a waste to use good paper for this because an experienced type artist will cover it with colored ink while editing. Some type artists use a specific paper color for this stage—light yellow, for example—to identify the printout as a proof.

With proof in hand, a good way to check for baseline alignment is to turn the page sideways (similar to holding a cafeteria tray) and tilt upward the page side closest to the type artist. At this angle it is easy to look along the type lines to check baseline alignment. Any insertion (subhead, photograph, and others) breaks the alignment, but baseline alignment should resume below the insertion. If an alignment problem appears, the type artist draws a colored-ink line along the baseline of both offending lines, extends them parallel to one another into the gutter, and writes *align* (circled) above it. If an adjacent text block, such as a caption, uses smaller leading than its neighbor, baselines should come into alignment every three or four lines.

ad a little *(align)* every where t
leece was   Mary went, tl
now, and   was sure to gc

Baseline alignment proofmark

Consistency on the paragraph level concerns uniform treatment of like paragraph elements, such as type size, indentions (see fig. 4-18), alignment, and leading. If the paragraph alignment was to be justified, the type artist checks each and every paragraph for uniformity. The type artist should compare all like paragraph elements individually to confirm consistent treatment.

Typographic texture on the paragraph level also concerns letterspacing and word spacing, knotholes, and hyphenation. Texture is checked with the page turned upside down. By breaking the eye's ability to read the document, it is much easier to see any white rivers or dark blotches in the text. The type artist can circle a white river, add proofreaders' marks for spacing problems (see fig. 4-15), circle a hyphen ladder (more than three consecutive hyphens), check the two-three hyphenation rule, and circle any knotholes.

A *knothole* is an unfortunate placement of two or more identical words (see fig. 4-19) directly below one another in adjacent type lines. Two identical short words directly below one another is not a problem and should be overlooked, but two identical long words will attract reader attention. It is acceptable for two consecutive lines to start with the same word (depending upon length), but three start to look like a list. (See Appendix A for a comprehensive list of proofreaders' marks.)

ℬ

PROOFMARKS ARE SUCCINCT AND EASY TO UNDERSTAND with practice. They indicate a particular remedy without cluttering the page with a lengthy message. A written message can cause more confusion if not worded correctly. With the multitude of items to check on the paragraph level, it is wise to make a prioritized checklist to follow. Trying to catch everything in one look-through is impossible and confusing. Working from the largest infraction to the smallest is a useful order to follow, but an experienced type artist will customize the checklist order to satisfy the specifications of the document or individual work style.

fix spacing

Mary had a little lamb its fleece was white as snow, and every where that Mary went, the lamb was sure to go.

White rivers proofmark

SETTING
TYPE
IN A
SENTENCE

Wʜᴇɴ ᴛʜᴇ ᴘʀᴏʟɪꜰɪᴄ ᴀᴍᴇʀɪᴄᴀɴ ᴛʏᴘᴇ ᴅᴇꜱɪɢɴᴇʀ, Frederic Goudy, started his impressive list of type designs in 1901, the United States railway system serviced almost 200,000 miles of line. Train travel was the primary mode of long-distance travel. Well-appointed trains barreled along well-maintained tracks. Passengers marveled at miles of rugged landscape as the train's wheels glided swiftly along smooth, parallel rails supported by wooden crossties. When the rail lines were maintained properly, the ride was smooth and the mechanics of train travel went unnoticed by the passengers. However, if a rail broke or the track bed eroded or a cow decided to chew while camped in the middle of the track, the train's progress slowed or stopped, and the passengers' ride was bumpy, bone-jarring, or delayed.

In much the same way, lines of type on a page guide a reader's eye past a landscape of printed information. This landscape might contain the intricate twists of a detective mystery, the eloquent metaphors of a soul-searching novel, or the unexpected findings of a research study. A reader's eye flows smoothly from word to word, just as a train glides smoothly past each crosstie. When type lines are constructed properly, reading is smooth, comprehension is high, and type-line mechanics go unnoticed by the reader. Type quality at the sentence level can accelerate or impede the reader's progress through a paragraph. A wayward cow on the tracks will stop the train, just as an errant period in the middle of a sentence will cause the reader to stop and ponder its purpose.

SENTENCE TYPOGRAPHY IS THE USE OF TYPE GLYPHS (letters, figures, punctuation marks, diacritics, joined characters, symbols) and type styles within a sentence to improve reader comprehension. The tools of sentence typography enhance the delivery of the message by giving the words visual clarity and by eliminating visual clutter. On this level, the type artist's role is not to change the writing style or content of the author's words, but to make them easier to discern. The type artist's responsibility is similar to that of an audio technician on a sound stage. The technician adjusts the controls to improve sound quality, so the listener hears the singer's voice or the orator's words clearly without distracting static or booming background noise. These behind-the-scenes professionals enhance, not create, sound quality. The type artist manipulates type controls to improve typographic quality, so the reader reads and comprehends the author's words without distraction.

A well-set sentence displays a high quality of typographic form just as well-written prose displays a high quality of literary form. The experienced writer uses language more adeptly than the novice. The more experienced type artist uses type glyphs more proficiently than the novice. For example, just as the word *there* indicates a place and the word *their* indicates possession, a hyphen (-) indicates noninclusive numbers, as in a telephone number, and an en dash (–) indicates inclusive numbers, as in a range of time.

In the previous *there/their* example, the change in type style from roman to italic identifies the two modifiers as terms for discussion, rather than terms in context. The visual change is subtle enough for the words to remain part of the continuing sentence, but obvious enough to distinguish the term for special consideration. Without the type style change, the reader might misunderstand the author's intent. Hopefully, a second read-through would eliminate the reader's confusion; but good sentence typography should eliminate reader confusion and sentence rereads.

SENTENCE GUIDELINES AND MEASUREMENTS focus on the positioning of glyphs horizontally along the baseline and vertically within the point size. Horizontally the type artist uses incremental spaces to separate glyphs and improve readability. The em and en are the foundations of this measuring system.

Not all applications provide a full range of spaces and their sizes can vary. Some possible options and sizes are thick space (M/3), middle space (M/4), thin space (M/6 or M/8), and hair space (M/12 or M/24). The

TYPOGRAPHY AND TYPOGRAPHIC FORM

SENTENCE GUIDELINES AND MEASUREMENTS

width of some spaces and type glyphs is equal to the width of other glyphs. For example, a figure dash and a figure space is the width of a standard figure or numeral in the typeface. The lowercase *t* is the equivalent of M/4 (almost).

Varying space sizes enable the type artist to adjust letter position when a full spaceband is too much. For example, when setting personal initials, such as in *F. D. Roosevelt,* a spaceband should follow each period. There are times when the space between the *F* and the *D* appears too large, because some typefaces allocate a larger character window to a period than others. In those instances, the type artist might use a thin space (M/6 or M/8) in place of a full spaceband (usually M/4). The smaller space pulls the two letters together and eliminates the oversized, texture-disturbing gap.

Kerning and tracking are another form of horizontal space manipulation. They add or delete space, in the form of units, between glyph pairs or, in the case of tracking, between several selected glyphs. The application sets the unit size: $\frac{1}{1000}$ of an em (M/1000) is a common kern unit. Inserting horizontal space of any size enables the type artist to position letters or words comfortably along the baseline to enhance readability. Sentence kerning, however, is a sinkhole for the type artist's time. Fixing the most egregious errors is more important than improving something that works adequately as is. Setting global word and letter-spacing correctly in a dialog box eliminates 95% of the kerning problems when using a high-quality typeface.

The placement of glyphs within the point size determines how these glyphs align horizontally. The vertical location of a glyph determines whether or not it aligns with or flows easily into the adjacent glyphs. The guidelines within the point size—the mean line, cap line, and baseline, for example—are the points of reference for vertical placement (see fig. 2-1). For example, an en dash (–) sits closer to the baseline than the figure dash (-). The bullet (•) is centered higher than the midpoint (·) within the point size. The type artist relies on an accurate, easy-to-carry measuring tool when evaluating sentence spatial relationships—the human eye.

SENTENCE PROOFREADERS' MARKS

THE FIRST PRINT OF ANY DOCUMENT EMERGING FROM a printer (of any resolution) is a *page proof.* No matter how pristine the letterforms (attributable to a clean printer with abundant toner) or how complete the document (getting all the copy on the page is not the primary goal here), a page proof is a work in progress, a draft—it contains errors. A

the	Inmorning, the dog	Insert word(s)
cat	watched the ~~dog~~ and	Substitute word(s)
℈	the cat watched the ~~the~~ bird.	Delete word
stet	In the ~~afternoon,~~	Let it stand
tr	the (slept) (dog) and	Transpose words
℈	the cat sle∤pt. The bird	Delete letter and close up
wf	(did) lizard impressions.	Set in correct font
al	Things are not ways	Add to beginning of word
y	what theseem.	Add to end of word
tr	(End / The)	Transpose lines
lc ///	Quoted from / Pet And Pal Post For Pets And Pals	Set in lowercase three times

FIGURE 5-1: *Deletion, relocation, insertion, and substitution proofmarks*

The word *stet* (let it stand) comes from the Latin *stare* (to stand). A stetted word should remain in its original form.

reproduction proof (a document ready to be reproduced for distribution) is only pronounced as such after it is scrupulously checked for spelling errors, typographical errors, content-omission errors, consistency errors, printer errors, and all others. Before the document passes through the human error-checker, it is merely a page proof.

Proofmarks on the sentence level are made with surgical precision. Here the type artist uses all categories of proofmarks (fig. 5-1) to fix spelling, add or delete spaces, transpose words, insert or substitute glyphs, standardize glyph usage, change type style (see fig. 5-2), and fix kerning.

The type artist slowly proofreads each text block and carefully inserts text proofmarks to identify the error and neatly positions margin proofmarks to correct the error.

In a heavily edited document, the clutter of margin marks can become confusing. To minimize clutter and conserve space, type artists position a slash (/) after a margin mark to indicate the number of consecutive times they identified the mistake. Each slash indicates a single correction. For example, the letters *lc* followed by three slashes indicates three letter case changes in a row (see fig. 5-1).

A prioritized checklist for proofing reduces confusion and overlooked mistakes as the type artist stares at the same week-old document. Checking for consistent typographic treatment throughout a lengthy document also is easier with a checklist (see "Sentence Typography Evaluation" later in this chapter).

SENTENCE TYPOGRAPHY PRELIMINARIES

Sentence typography employs consistency to communicate effectively.

ONE WAY TO BECOME PROFICIENT TYPESETTING typographically correct sentences is to read (and analyze) well-set type. Publications with lengthy preparation times, such as books and magazines, are good sources. Newspapers have short preparation times and follow a different set of typographic rules. Text set with small caps, text figures, and ligatures are easily identified signs of type likely to be well set.

There are typographic style guidelines for every situation imaginable. For the novice, it is overwhelming at first. The first typographic style rule to remember is consistency. Even in error it is better to be consistently incorrect than to set the same word differently (in the same document) hoping to get it right at least once. To avoid confusion, it is wise to start with a few rules for common situations. The rule *Put one space after a sentence and a colon* is a logical starter rule. Once those rules become second nature, the type artist incorporates more in the repertoire. Keeping a well-marked source book handy (such as this one) is wise as well. It is impossible to remember everything, but type artists should know where to find what they forgot. Many publishers and corporations adopt style manuals, such as the *Chicago Manual of Style,* as their final word on type usage.

Type artists need access to all type glyphs when setting sentences correctly. An expert collection for several often-used typefaces or an OpenType type family with the expert-equivalent glyph sets, and perhaps a specialized pi font, provides the tools of the trade for well-set sentences. For international publishing, OpenType Pro typefaces provide expanded language support (see "OpenType" in chapter 1). The

PST-1 and TT typefaces without their expert collections include a couple of *f*-ligatures, symbols, punctuation marks, and diacritics. They do not provide the additional glyphs that make typesetting a true art form.

THE REMAINDER OF THIS CHAPTER DEALS WITH typographic form as it applies to sentences and the glyphs within them. It notes distinctions between continuous and discontinuous text usage, as well. Each section explains appropriate type glyphs and appropriate punctuation placement for common text situations. Glyphs are listed by frequency of use, not in alphabetical order. (The index lists the individual marks alphabetically.) Text samples, usage rules, and proofmark pairs are included in each section. The arrowheads (▲) and (▼) denote text samples set correctly or incorrectly respectively. Appendix B contains glyph access charts for both Macintosh and Windows platforms.

UPPERCASE, MAJUSCULES, OR CAPITAL LETTERS, as they are known in diverse situations and different times in history, call attention to themselves and their positions on the page. Uppercase letters are more formal, more stately than the lowercase letters. It is the alphabet dressed up in its finest. Type artists use capital letters to identify the beginning of a new sentence, proper names, book titles, personal initials and acronyms, or two-letter state abbreviations (see "Titling Caps and Small Caps" in chapter 6). Personal acronyms, such as *FDR* and *JFK,* use full caps without periods or spaces. In discontinuous text, setting words in capital letters emphasizes or draws attention to them. In continuous text, as a technique for emphasis, they are excessive. They jar the reader, give undo emphasis, and disrupt the smooth flow of the words.

   ▲ Franklin Delano Roosevelt (FDR) was born in Hyde Park, New York.
*caps//*𝒟 Franklin delano roosevelt (FR) was born in Hyde Park, New York.

IN 1501 THE NOTED VENETIAN TYPOGRAPHER Aldus Manutius developed italic letterforms for typesetting books. This condensed typeface increased the number of characters per page, decreased the book's length, and kept printing costs lower. (Initially, italic lowercase letters were used with roman capitals. The design of italic capitals came later.) Italic type gets its name from Italy, its country of origin. It is reminiscent of cursive letterforms with calligraphic terminals and strokes.

    In the early years of the twentieth century when writers and journalists wrote about train travel in the United States, they used manual

CAPITAL LETTERS

- Start sentences and proper nouns with a capital letter.
- Use capital letters for personal initials and two-letter geographic acronyms.

ITALIC TYPE

- Italicize the space before an italicized word to improve word spacing.
- Do not underline a word when italic type is available.
- Italicize the names of books and periodicals.

typewriters (invented by C. L. Sholes in 1868). As their fingers pounded the keys, the typists underlined publication titles (books, periodicals, and newspapers) because italic letterforms were unavailable on their keyboards. Typists also underlined words to emphasize them.

Contemporary type artists should use italics in those situations previously handled by underlining. Underlining is not acceptable typographic form in continuous text because the line beneath the word collides with the letter's descenders creating a texture blot—really. Mixing italic type within running roman text calls attention to individual letters without marring the sentence's texture. Similarly, boldface type also alters the sentence's even texture. Italicized words should enhance the reader's understanding of the content. Italicizing a book title, for example, identifies those words as part of a single unit, the title. Italics as emphasis should be applied with a light touch. Too many italicized words diminish their impact and create textural chaos. Conversely within italicized text, the type artist sets roman a word or words that otherwise would be italicized, such as a book title, in roman text.

bf	The premiere Parisian proofreader	Set in boldface
ital	was not persuaded that	Set in italic
rom	the Peruvian's predominance	Set roman
bf + *ital*	as a precise proofreader was	Set in bold italic
lc	properly and Positively proven	Set in lowercase
lc	to the PERUVIAN's peers.	Set all in lowercase
caps	The end (probably)	Set all in caps

FIGURE 5-2: *Letter case and style proofmarks*

A lone italicized word within a roman sentence creates word-spacing problems. As the italicized letters lean to the right, they lean away from the roman word on their left. This visually increases the word space before the italicized word. At the same time, these letters lean closer to the roman word on their right. To decrease the word spacing preceding an italicized word, the type artist italicizes the space before the word, along with the word. In some instances, this is sufficient. With other letter combinations, kerning the word space tighter is necessary. If the italicized word is crowding its neighbor to the right, the type artist must kern additional word space between the words.

▲ *The Perfect Puppy*, published by W. H. Freeman and Company, helps families choose a puppy based on breed behavioral characteristics.

▼ Although technically categorized as a Golden Retriever, our model of the breed <u>never</u> returns what she finds.

▲ … our model of the breed *never* returns what she finds.

ital … our model of the breed <u>never</u> returns what she finds.

The use of different type styles changes over time, as the 1936 quote from Eric Gill's *Essay on Typography* illustrates. Arthur Eric Rowton Gill (1882–1940) was a noted British type designer, sculptor, wood engraver, and an outspoken social critic of his time—among other things.

THE DEVELOPMENT OF PUNCTUATION FOR TEXT started as far back as 260 B.C., when Aristophanes of Alexandria placed dots between select words to indicate pauses and stops. Since word spaces were not standard until A.D. 600, these dots suggested a relationship between sections of words. In the fourth century A.D., the Romans adapted the use of dots by placing them between all words. Later, when spaces separated words, the dot remained as the equivalent of the current period, comma, and colon. The dot's vertical position within the x-height determined which of these functions it served (Firmage 1993). Aligned at the top of the letters, the dot indicated the end of a sentence. Aligned on the baseline, it functioned as a comma. It is believed that the full system of punctuation marks was not complete until after printing with movable type was invented in the mid–fifteenth century. The foundation for the current system of punctuation is credited to the typographer and printer Aldus Manutius (1450–1515).

Punctuation makes the written message clearer and facilitates its delivery. Distinguishing a question from a statement of fact is important for the reader's overall understanding. A hyphen at the end of a line, for example, differentiates the word *damage* from the two words *dam* and *age*. The hyphen's absence here changes the meaning of the sentence considerably.

The common practice of using italics to emphasise single words might be abandoned in favour of the use of the ordinary lower-case with spaces between the letters (l e t t e r - s p a c e d). The proper use of italics is for quotations & foot-notes, & for books in which it is or seems desirable to use a lighter & less formal style of letter.

—————————Gill
Essay on Typography

PUNCTUATION

◆ All complete text sentences end with a punctuation mark.

◆ Headlines and subheads do not need a terminal punctuation mark.

◆ Set punctuation in the style of the word it follows.

◆ Punctuation following isolated bold words may remain roman to match the rest of the sentence.

◆ Punctuation point size in text matches the text type size.

◆ Punctuation size in display type can be reduced in point size.

A terminating punctuation mark follows a complete sentence. Headlines, subheads, and captions (heading type set apart from other text as a separate type block) do not require a period, however, even if they are complete sentences. If the heading is a question or exclamation, the appropriate mark should follow.

When several punctuation marks are adjacent, each mark's location is important. Frequent questions occur with double or single quotation marks, parentheses, and brackets (see the individual sections later in this chapter).

Type Design and Punctuation. Although punctuation marks are small, they are designed for use with only one typeface. A period in one typeface is a perfect circle, while in another it is an oval or diamond shape. Punctuation clarifies the message and complements the design structure of the typeface. Although small, some punctuation marks require kerning. They cannot crowd or touch the words they clarify. Even a small mark can disturb a paragraph's texture. Question marks and exclamation points are likely to require kerning.

Type Style and Punctuation. Punctuation style—italic, bold, roman—blends the mark into the surrounding text. When type styles change, the mark maintains the style of the preceding word. There are some notable exceptions concerning parentheses and brackets (see "Parentheses and Square Brackets" later in this chapter). When using bold type within a regular-weight sentence (to identify a vocabulary word in a textbook, for example), an exception is made as well. The bolded comma might cause confusion, because the comma is part of the mechanics of the sentence, not part of the vocabulary word.

▼ A Golden Retriever is bred to **retrieve;** a house cat, based on personal observation, is bred to sleep.
▲ A Golden Retriever is bred to **retrieve;** a house cat,…
▲ In human terms, the word *retrieve* means to return or to bring back. In dog terms, it means *gotcha!*

The type artist italicizes small punctuation marks (such as commas, periods, and semicolons) that follow italicized words. It improves the letterspacing. A type artist would italicize an exclamation point or question mark (following an italicized word) only if the mark belonged to the word. This clarifies the message.

Type Size and Punctuation. Punctuation marks in text are the same point size as the body copy. In display type, however, a type artist

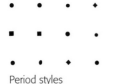

Period styles
from book and regular types

▲ Correct typographic form
▼ Incorrect typographic form

can reduce the point size to maintain the mark's proper visual relationship to the words. The decrease in punctuation size is proportional to the display type's point size. The larger the type, the larger the reduction in point size. When using a large initial cap, or versal, in a quoted sentence, for example, the typesetter can set the opening quotation marks to match the size of the initial cap, the text, or a suitable size in between. The closing quotes would match the text size, because they fall within the text block.

An experienced type artist establishes a personal style for some of the discretionary typographic rules. Consistent application of these distinguishes the work of one type artist from that of another. There is only one basic rule to follow: Apply type rules consistently within a single document.

Periods belong at the end of a sentence, after personal initials, after an abbreviation, and after figures and letters enumerating elements in a vertical list. The typist with a manual typewriter placed two spaces after a sentence-ending period. With monospaced type, the extra white space distinguished sentence breaks by visually overpowering the sentence's generous letterspacing. With proportionally spaced type, a single space between sentences is correct and two spaces is a puzzling excess. One space follows a colon within a sentence as well.

▲ The dog stood guard. The cat prowled. The bird did nothing.
▼ The dog stood guard. The cat prowled. The bird did nothing.
less # The week's shopping list included:ˌdog food, cat food, and bird foodˌ ☉

Within a sequence of personal initials (F. D. Roosevelt), a space follows each period. A thin space is preferred if the spaceband appears excessive. Some typographers prefer to drop the space between personal initials, but this emphasizes them and weakens their link to the last name. Some spacing is recommended.

▲ The speaker, E. M. Gottschall, was scheduled in the green room.
▼ The speaker, E.M. Gottschall, was scheduled in the green room.
#/☉ The speaker, EˌMˌGottschall, was scheduled in the green room.

When a parenthetical statement is a complete sentence and not positioned within a larger sentence, no space separates the period and the closing parenthesis.

Apply type rules consistently within a document.

PERIODS AND COMMAS
— . , —

◆ One space separates typeset sentences.
◆ A period follows complete sentences and personal initials.
◆ Use a period after enumerating figures or letters in a vertical list.

◆ Commas separate elements in an address or location.
◆ Commas separate items in a series.

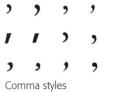

Comma styles
from book and regular types

Commas separate items in a series, offset a direct quote as dialogue, precede conjunctions in compound sentences, and separate elements in an address or location. A single space follows a comma used in text. The design of the comma varies in appearance from a circle with a downward-curving tail to a diagonal line angled into the letterform at the bottom.

▲ The voracious dog lives at 23 First Street, Middletown, Ohio 45042, in a large, well-chewed mansion.
▲ We will visit London, England, during our summer vacation.
We will visit London⌄England⌄during our summer vacation. ⌃/\//

SEMICOLONS AND COLONS

— ; : —

◆ Semicolons join sentences that can stand alone.
◆ Semicolons link elements in a run-in series when complex punctuation is used.

◆ A single space follows a colon.
◆ Colons set off elements in a run-in list.
◆ Colons set off a vertical list after the word *follows* or *following.*

Semicolons and colons are similar in appearance but have different functions. A semicolon joins two related independent clauses that could be written and punctuated as separate sentences. Also, a semicolon links elements in a series when complex punctuation is within one or more of the individual elements. In this situation, the semicolon shows a hierarchy of punctuation that helps to clarify the meaning for the reader. A single space follows a semicolon.

A colon, on the other hand, sets off elements in a run-in list (within the text) or comes after the word *follows* or *following* before a vertical list. A single space follows a colon.

▲ Eating for the dog was an avocation. She practiced (a) nutritional eating (dog food served in a dog bowl at the beginning of the day); (b) recreational eating (shoes, children's toys, and crayons partially consumed, mostly chewed, strictly for sport); and (c) stealth eating (the successful capture and consumption of a bar of bath soap without leaving incriminating evidence—soap crumbs, wet feet, or bubble breath).

She practiced (a) nutritional eating (dog food served in a dog bowl at
;/ the beginning of the day)⌄(b) recreational eating….

▲ The week's shopping list included the following:
    1. dog food
    2. cat food
    3. bird food
:/ The week's shopping list included the following⌄

THE EXCLAMATION POINT AND THE QUESTION MARK clarify the author's intent and indicate how to place emphasis when reading the sentence. These marks differentiate between an imperative shout *Watch out!* and a puzzled inquiry *Watch out?* Both marks can appear at the end of the sentence or within it according to the meaning. If the question or exclamation is not a direct quote, it is not set off by a comma.

▲ Why isn't the cat hungry for his dinner? she speculated silently.
▲ "Is the bird cage empty?" she queried in a quailing quake.
"Is the bird cage empty" she queried in a quailing quake. *?* (set)

Both exclamation points and question marks require careful proofing. They create kerning problems with certain letters—the lowercase letter *f*, for instance. Often an all-cap headline requires kerning when followed by either mark. Display-size type always exaggerates letter-spacing problems as often seen when using exclamation points and question marks. When used with other punctuation, such as quotation marks, parentheses, and brackets, the exclamation and question marks are positioned according to the meaning of the statement. (See chapter 6 for special small cap punctuation.)

▲ "He's in here, dear!" a falsetto voice fluttered in from the foyer. Fortunately for our feathered flapper, his stark sanctuary was the result of scrupulous scrubbing rather than sumptuous snacking.
"He's in here, dear" a falsetto voice fluttered in from the foyer. *!* (set)

THE DASH CATEGORY ENCOMPASSES MARKS OF varying lengths from the hyphen, the shortest, to the three-em dash, the longest. Because dashes vary in length, their effect on paragraph texture and their spacing requirements differ also. Each dash has a different function, ranging from offsetting a break in thought to separating groups of figures. A type artist checks the horizontal spacing around each dash in the text. Some require a whole space on either side and others require gentle kerning. In all cases, the dash should not mar the texture either by opening a large white hole or by colliding with adjacent letterforms.

Learning that there are at least five dashes from which to choose can confuse and daunt the novice type artist; when to set them also can be confusing. Many typeface packages provide three—the hyphen, the en dash, and the em dash. These three are good starter dashes. The expert collections can add at least four more. An easy way to remember

EXCLAMATION POINTS AND QUESTION MARKS
— ! ? —

✦ An exclamation point indicates an interjection or exclamation.
✦ Exclamation points are not limited to end-of-sentence usage.
✦ An exclamation point requires kerning with all caps and some lowercase letters.

✦ A question mark indicates an interrogative.
✦ Question marks are not limited to end-of-sentence usage.
✦ A question mark requires kerning with all caps and some lowercase letters.

DASHES

✦ Check dashes for kerning.
✦ Equate dash length to reading-pause length.

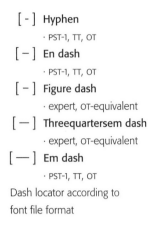

[-] Hyphen
      · PST-1, TT, OT
[–] En dash
      · PST-1, TT, OT
[–] Figure dash
      · expert, OT-equivalent
[—] Threequartersem dash
      · expert, OT-equivalent
[—] Em dash
      · PST-1, TT, OT

Dash locator according to
font file format

— - —

- Hyphens divide words at line breaks.
- Hyphens create compound modifiers.
- Hyphens link noninclusive numbers.
- Do not hyphenate more than two or three consecutive lines.

- - -

Hyphen styles from Adobe Garamond
(left), Adobe Caslon (center), and
Centaur (right) set on the same
baseline

which dash goes where (or at least to provide the means to make an educated guess) is to equate the length of the dash with the length of the pause the author intended in the text.

For example, when reading the hyphenated word *up-to-date,* the reader hears these words as a single word. No pause is required. When hyphenating a word at the end of a line, the reader knows the word is not complete and a pause is not suggested. Some readers unconsciously hold their breath until the last portion of the word comes into view.

An em dash in text, on the other hand, sets off a break in thought—an aside or an explanatory comment. This dash replaces a colon in some situations. In the previous sentence, the length of the dash suggests a long pause before the words *an aside.* Equating the length of dash with the length of pause keeps dash choices less devil-may-care and more matter-of-fact.

Hyphen. The hyphen evolved from a varied ancestry. Some of the hyphen's precursors slanted up on the right side; some paralleled the baseline; some were slanted and doubled (like an equal sign), so they were not confused with commas (Bringhurst 1992). Today's hyphen is ¼ em in length or (approximately) the width of the lowercase letter *t.* In some typefaces, such as Adobe Garamond, the hyphen slants up on the right side, but the majority of hyphens are parallel to the baseline. The type artist employs a hyphen for line breaks, when an entire word does not fit in the measure; for hyphenating words, such as a compound word; and between noninclusive numbers, such as a telephone number or a social security number.

Line-end hyphenation should not disrupt the word flow. Incorrectly hyphenating a line creates confusion and causes doubling. It also can change a sentence's meaning by forming new or questionable words. A line-end hyphen remains with the first part of the hyphenated word. Proper line-end hyphenation dictates leaving a minimum of two characters on the first line and bringing down a minimum of three characters to the next line (see chapter 4 for additional hyphenation information). In headings, line-end hyphens are too noticeable, creating clutter and confusion. In text, the type artist does not hyphenate personal names, unless their number makes this rule impractical or if the name includes a hyphen of its own.

Hyphens in compound words or noninclusive numbers at times need kerning to even the space on either side. The type artist should check punctuation marks for possible kerning when checking a page proof for typographical form. When hyphenating a compound word set in all caps, an en dash can replace a hyphen for a better visual balance between characters.

▲ The shaggy-haired dog is nearing cat-chasing retirement.
▲ The phone number at the kennel is 555-1234.
▲ The student's social security number is 123-45-6789.
=/ The shaggy⌃haired dog is nearing cat⌃chasing retirement. =/

En Dash. The en dash is ½ em in length or the width of the letter *n*. It has several specific uses: between inclusive numbers to indicate a duration for times of day or a range of page numbers or ages; replacing the word *to* for vote tallies and scores; joining hyphenated modifiers; or replacing an em dash for a break in thought (see "Em Dash"). The type artist sets inclusive numbers in running text with the word pairs *between*/*and* or *from*/*to*. The en dash is acceptable in running text when inclusive numbers are abundant. The type artist should not mix word pairs with the en dash. (See "Figure Dash" later in this chapter.)

▲ The baseball scores were 3–2, 2–4, and 3–6.
▼ The baseball scores were 3-2, 2-4, and 3-6.
▼ The office hours are from 9:00 A.M. – 3:00 P.M.
The baseball scores were 3|2, 2⌃4, and 3–6. N̲ //

En dashes also link two hyphenated modifiers before a noun. It alerts the reader that both modifiers describe the same noun. Without the en dash it is difficult to distinguish the nouns from the modifiers in the crush of words.

In a similar situation, if two words are modifying a noun and one or both are open compounds, an en dash separates the two. This holds the lengthy modifiers together and defines each one's place in front of the noun. Finally, if an open compound requires a prefix, an en dash is used instead of the usual hyphen.

▲ The rat-tailed–lop-eared dog won first place.
▲ The dog was a Shetland Sheepdog–Cocker Spaniel mix.
▲ The new breed of dog is reminiscent of a mini–Shetland Sheepdog.

Em Dash. The em dash is the length of an em and comparable to the width of the letter *m*. Typists use two hyphens (--) for this mark. An em dash sets off a phrase due to a break in thought.

— – —

• An en dash joins inclusive numbers.
• An en dash indicates a duration.
• An en dash links open compounds modifying a noun.
• An en dash replaces the words *between*/*and* and *from*/*to*.

▲ Correct typographic form
▼ Incorrect typographic form

— – —

- Em dashes set off parenthetical elements.
- An em dash indicates a break in thought.
- Do not offset an em dash with a full space.

- Use a two-em dash to indicate missing letters in a word.
- Use a three-em dash to represent a missing word in nonquoted text (single space before and after).

Circling two adjacent hyphens in the text to indicate their substitution is easier to see than a horizontal strike.

The em dash does not need additional space on either side. It often needs subtle kerning to prevent it from touching the letters it separates. Some type artists prefer an en dash bracketed by a single space in place of the em dash (fig. 5-3). They think the dash's length and the amount of attention it draws disrupt uniform paragraph texture and create awkward line breaks. (Line breaks occur after an em dash, not before it.) Still others prefer the threequartersem dash with kerning on either side. Whatever choice is made, consistency dictates its implementation.

▲ After the carnivorous curmudgeon careened through the caravan of caramel-colored camels—although hardly a violation of law—he was incarcerated.

▼ After the carnivorous curmudgeon careened through the caravan of caramel-colored camels--although hardly a violation of law--he was incarcerated.

<u>M</u> After ... the caravan of caramel-colored camels⇔although hardly a violation of law⇔he was incarcerated. <u>M</u>

Type artists use multiple em dashes for specific circumstances. Since the em dash fits tightly between letters, consecutive em dashes form a continuous line. Two-em dashes represent missing letters within a word. This mark indicates that the letters are not known or, for an author, have not been determined. In bibliographies, three-em dashes followed by a period represent the repetition of the previous author's name. In text, the three-em dash, bracketed with a single space, represents the omission of an entire word. Neither mark replaces the ellipsis in quoted material.

em dash—length · ¾ em dash—length · en dash – length

<small>FIGURE 5-3: *Proper horizontal spacing makes three dashes interchangeable for some functions*</small>

Figure Dash. The figure dash is the width of a standard numeral and sits higher from the baseline than the en dash. It is longer than the hyphen and shorter than the en dash. Some type artists prefer this shorter length between figures because it makes a smoother visual transition in an inclusive-number sequence. It is certainly an option to consider, but the final decision is a matter of personal preference. The length decision, however, might take a backseat to its vertical position.

$$26\text{–}34 \quad 26\text{–}34 \mid 26\text{–}34 \quad 26\text{–}34$$

FIGURE 5-4: *Titling figures and text figures with en dash (left)
and with figure dash (right)*

The higher vertical position of the figure dash is more suited to titling figures since they are confined to the ascent. The lower vertical position of the en dash is suited to text figures since they have ascenders and descenders (fig. 5-4). The length of the en dash is a bit long for the text figures, but some type artists might not view that as bothersome. Both dashes should be checked for kerning and consistency. (See "Numbers in Text" in chapter 6.)

▲ The groups of children were divided by age as follows: 1-4, 5-10, 11-14, and 15-19. (Titling figures with figure dash)
▲ The groups of children were divided by age as follows: 1-4, 5-10, 11-14, and 15-19. (Text figures with figure dash)
… divided by age as follows: 1,4, 5-10, 11-14, and 15-19.   −/(figure)

Threequartersem Dash. The threequartersem dash is ¾ em in length. It can replace an em dash to set off a phrase as a break in thought. It is shorter than an em dash and longer than an en dash. For those still unhappy about using either an em or an en dash in this situation, the threequartersem dash is the logical solution (fig. 5-3). It does not disrupt texture, as does the em dash, and it does not introduce extra spaces, as does the en dash. The threequartersem dash needs kerning on either side, but a full space is too much. A thin space here may satisfy the discriminating eye.

▲ The dog is two years old—although he looks older.
The dog is two years old—although he looks older. *3/4M*

THE APOSTROPHE IS A FAMILIAR MARK that indicates possession or the absence of a letter or figure. A typesetter's apostrophe (hereafter called an *apostrophe*) looks like a flying comma. It is positioned above the letters and curves toward the letter it follows. Some typefaces slant, rather than curve, their commas and apostrophes. The apostrophe, positioned before or after the letter *s,* indicates possession. In a contraction, such as *couldn't,* it replaces the missing letter *o.* When indicating a year, such as

- ✦ The figure dash replaces an en dash with figures according to the type artist's preference.
- ✦ A figure dash is shorter and sits higher from the baseline than the en dash.

— — —

- ✦ A threequartersem dash replaces an em dash with kerning on either side.
- ✦ A threequartersem dash is not a Unicode character. It is accessed by the application from the glyph substitution table in the OT font file.

**APOSTROPHES
AND PRIMES**
— ' ' —

- ✦ An apostrophe indicates possession.
- ✦ An apostrophe represents an omitted letter or figure.

• A prime is the linear unit-of-measure symbol for feet.

1986 as '86, the apostrophe represents the missing figures 19. If a period or a comma follows a plural possessive, the punctuation mark follows the apostrophe.

The typewriter's apostrophe (hereafter called a *prime*) is incorrect as an apostrophe. A prime is a short vertical stroke positioned along the cap line. It does not curve or slant toward the letter that precedes it. A prime is a symbol for *feet* when it is used as a linear unit of measure. It is appropriate in tables, charts, and technical or informal writing. (See "Abbreviations and Symbols" in chapter 6.)

▲ The dog was the Joneses', although he followed me home.
The dog's bowl wasn't empty.
▲ The board measures 6' in length.
▼ The board measures 6' in length.

QUOTATION MARKS AND DOUBLE PRIMES
— " " ' ' " —

• Double quotation marks indicate quoted material.
• Single quotation marks indicate a quote within a quote.

• A double prime is the linear unit-of-measure symbol for inches.

QUOTATION MARKS, BOTH SINGLE AND DOUBLE, come in pairs. They indicate words attributed to a specific speaker that are run into the text. A quote long enough to be set as a block (more than four lines) does not use quotation marks (see chapter 4).

Double quotes are used more frequently than single quotes, because the latter indicates quoted material *within* quoted material. The mark used for quotations is similar in structure to a comma. It is a wide stroke that curves (or slants) and tapers into a finer stroke. Opening quotes have the wider stroke at the bottom of the mark. Closing quotes have the wider stroke at the top of the mark. Both curve or slant toward the copy they enclose.

It is important to place other punctuation marks correctly when using quotation marks. Commas and periods are included within the closing quotes since the statement is ending. Colons and semicolons are placed outside the closing quotes since the sentence is continuing. Question marks and exclamation points are positioned inside or outside the closing quotes depending upon their use in the sentence. If the quoted statement is a question, the question mark belongs within the quotation marks. If the quoted statement is part of a larger question, the question mark belongs outside the quotation marks. The same considerations apply to exclamation-point placement.

Typesetter's quotation marks (hereafter called *quotation marks*) and quotation marks from a typewriter (hereafter called *double prime*) are interchanged incorrectly in typeset copy, as with the apostrophe and prime mix-up. A double prime is two short vertical strokes positioned along the cap line. It does not curve to enclose the quoted material. A double prime is a symbol for *inches* when used as a linear unit of measure. (Use a *dimension sign* [×] when setting dimensions, not a lowercase *x* from the typeface.) The double prime is appropriate in tables, charts, and in technical or informal writing. (See chapter 6.)

▲ The dog stated, "Woof! Woof!" The cat asked, "Meow?" The bird said nothing.

▼ The dog stated, "Woof! Woof!" The cat asked, "Meow"? The bird said nothing.

˝/˝ The dog stated, ǀWoof! Woof!ǀ The cat asked, "Meowǀ The bird said *tr* nothing.

▲ The rooms were: 12'7" × 10'6"; 11'5" × 12'3"; and 10'4" × 9'6".

▼ The rooms were: 12'7" × 10'6"; 11'5" × 12'3"; and 10'4" × 9'6".

ǁ *(prime)* The rooms were: 12'7" × 10'6"; 11ǀ5ǀ × 12'3"; and 10'4" × 9'6". ǁ *(dbl prime)*

THE VIRGULE AND THE SOLIDUS ARE DIAGONAL LINES that separate different kinds of information. These marks are identical except for their angle. The type artist does not italicize these marks because it would distort their distinguishing angle.

The virgule ['vər-(ˌ)gyü(ə)l] or *slash* is the more upstanding of the two. It separates alternative words, such as *and/or;* calendar years, such as *1986/87* (dropping the apostrophe); alternative spellings of a single word; and numbers in a level fraction, such as *2/3.*

The solidus ['sä-lə-dəs] or *fraction bar* leans farther to the right than its almost-twin, the virgule. The solidus is the key mark for constructing a piece fraction with superior and inferior figures. With its increased angle, the numerator and the denominator tuck securely above and below the solidus, making a compact, single-unit fraction. The solidus is essential when the expert collection does not include the necessary case fraction for a job, such as ¹⁵⁄₆₄. In most Macintosh type formats, the solidus is available with the Shift-Option-1 keystroke.

▲ The academic year of 1990/91 was an eventful one.
▼ The academic year of 1990/91 was an eventful one.
▲ The dog eats 2⅝ cans of food in the morning, 1⁷⁄₁₀ cans in the afternoon, and 1⅖ cans for a bedtime snack.

The academic year of 1990ǀ91 was an eventful one. / *(virgule)*

The dog eats 2⁵⁄₆ cans of food in the morning,... / *(solidus)*

['] Single open quote

['] Single close quote

["] Double open quote

["] Double close quote

Appendix B lists keystrokes for accessing these characters

VIRGULES AND SOLIDI

— / / —

✦ A virgule separates alternative words, calendar years, and figures in a level fraction.

✦ A solidus separates superior and inferior figures in a piece fraction.

The virgule (left) is more upright than the solidus (right).

PARENTHESES AND SQUARE BRACKETS

— ( )　[ ] —

- Parentheses separate major breaks in sentence content for clarification.
- Parentheses set off the definition of a foreign word.
- Parentheses set off figures or letters to itemize text elements.

- Square brackets isolate editorial insertions in quoted material.
- Square brackets enclose a phonetic pronunciation.
- Square brackets are used as parentheses within parentheses.

[[{ ([•]) }]]

Bracket hierarchy for brackets within brackets

PARENTHESES AND SQUARE BRACKETS SET APART material in text. Both marks are used frequently, but not exclusively, in pairs. The choice of mark depends upon the content of the separated material.

Parentheses isolate a word or words that break the continuity of the sentence in a major way. The information could clarify a word in the sentence, for example, but it might confuse the meaning of the entire sentence if not set apart. A minor break in continuity would use a comma. (See "Foreign Terms and Definitions" in chapter 6 for additional uses.)

Type artists use parenthesis pairs to isolate figures or letters when denoting a list or prioritized elements within text. In this instance, the parentheses physically and visually isolate letters or figures that are outside the sentence's context. They organize material within the sentence and eliminate the need for a list as a separate text block.

Square brackets isolate editorial comments or insertions in quoted material. They indicate a special communiqué from the author or editor. For example, the term *sic* used in quoted material indicates an error in spelling or usage in the original material. Since this is an editorial comment about the material, it is set off in square brackets. The Latin term *sic* (this is the way it was) is italicized although the brackets are not.

A type artist also uses square brackets to isolate the phonetic pronunciation of an unusual or technical word presumably unknown to the reader. This functions as editorial assistance. Square brackets replace parentheses when a parenthetical element is within a parenthetical element. As with single and double quotation marks, square brackets within parentheses indicate a hierarchical structure of marks. Other marks, such as angle brackets (⟨ ⟩) and braces ({ }), are also available for structuring text material once the formerly mentioned marks have been employed.

▲ The week's shopping list included: dog food (large chunks [with bits of cheese] in a bag) and cat food (small cans).

The week's shopping list included: dog food large chunks with bits of cheese in a bagand cat food (small cans).

Technically, parentheses and brackets require special handling. The roman version is preferred in text, even if the contents or the surrounding letterforms are italicized. Inserting a parenthetical phrase or an editor's remark interrupts the text intentionally. Italicizing these punctuation marks deemphasizes this break and changes the author's intent.

Additionally, parentheses and brackets do not italicize well. They are odd-looking marks that do not enhance the text's typographic form.

Since these marks curve or angle around letters, they are an obvious place to check for kerning problems. While a word space is not suitable here, kerning is necessary, particularly with italicized contents.

Typographers of the sixteenth and seventeenth centuries used parentheses and square brackets as today's type artists use italic and boldface type—for emphasis (Firmage 1993). Placing type within these marks called attention to it and gave it added punch. Unlike the use of parentheses and brackets today, these marks were not seen as a technique to segregate the enclosed words for a clarifying or modifying role.

AN ELLIPSIS IS A SEQUENCE OF THREE PERIODS that indicates the omission of a word or words from quoted material. It also can indicate the trailing off of a thought. Digital type fonts provide an ellipsis as a single character, so the type artist need not create one.

Since this mark indicates the absence of a word or words, it is spaced as a word. When used within a quote, the type artist leaves a single space before and after the ellipsis. When used at the end of a quote (indicating that the rest of the sentence was eliminated), the type artist places a period immediately after the last word and positions the ellipsis immediately after the period. This is correct if the remainder of the quote is grammatically complete. The type artist eliminates the spaces before and after the ellipsis, when another punctuation mark, such as a comma, is used. The location of the ellipsis—before or after the mark—depends on the location of what was eliminated.

The following quote is from Lewis Carroll's *Through the Looking-Glass* (1872):

> Alice was too much puzzled to say anything, so after a minute Humpty Dumpty began again. "They've a temper, some of them—particularly verbs, they're the proudest—adjectives you can do anything with, but not verbs—however, I can manage the whole lot!"

▲ Alice was too much puzzled…, so after a minute Humpty Dumpty began again. "They've a temper, some of them … adjectives you can do anything with, but not verbs…."

⟆⬤⬤ Alice was too much puzzled ~~to say anything~~, so after a minute
ʃ Humpty Dumpty began again. "They've a temper, some of them+
⬤⬤⬤ ~~particularly verbs, they're the proudest~~—adjectives you can do
⊙ ⬤⬤⬤ anything with, but not verbs ~~—however, I can manage the whole lot!~~"

◆ An ellipsis replaces words intentionally omitted from quoted material.
◆ An ellipsis in the middle of a sentence is proceeded and followed by a space.

LIGATURES

— fi ff —

- Ligatures are characteristic of good typographic form.
- Use the search-and-replace feature of software to insert ligatures if automatic replacement is unavailable.

fi→fi

fl→fl

ffi st ct

Adobe Garamond ligatures

fi→fi

fl→fl

ff→ff

ct st

Adobe Caslon ligatures

ſ ff ſt fl ſh

Historical letterforms for the long-s, double long-s, and other long-s ligatures

ß

The eszett is a long- and short-s ligature

fi fl ff   fi fl ff

Optima (left) and Palatino (right)

A LIGATURE IS TWO OR MORE CHARACTERS designed and set as a single letterform. Gutenberg originally designed ligatures as a means to control letterspacing when justifying type and to duplicate handwritten text more accurately. Ligatures fell victim to mechanized typesetting at the beginning of the twentieth century. They disappeared from fonts. With the advent of phototypesetting they started reappearing and are available in high-quality digital typefaces.

Common ligatures involve the lowercase letter *f*. The *f* likes to take up more horizontal space than other letterforms. It is similar to siblings sitting on a couch. Even though each child has enough room for comfort, they continue to encroach on the other's space (*Mom!...*). Because of this expansionist attitude, the *f* is always crashing into the lowercase *i* and *l*. There are problems also with other *f*s.

In foundry type the *f* actually extended beyond its metal body and overlapped the metal body of adjacent sorts (see chapter 1). Without the correct *f-i* ligature, for example, the typographer would cut off the *i*'s dot to make room for the *f*'s overlap (the *kern*). A carefully designed *f-i* ligature not only removed the dot of the *i* but also aligned its stem to the *f*'s crossbar and terminal. While the letter *f* gives the English language the most problems, other languages require additional ligatures. Danish, for example, requires a ligature for the letters *f* and *j*. As these words, such as *fjord*, enter the English language these additional ligatures are needed.

Ligatures characterize good typography. They are not used simply to solve border skirmishes. They are also designed to add a flourish to certain letter combinations, such as *c* and *t* (ct) and *s* and *t* (st). These ligatures are referred to as *discretionary ligatures* and are suitable in discontinuous type blocks, where such flourishes are appropriate.

When setting type with OpenType typefaces and an OT-savvy application, ligature glyphs are inserted as needed and the spell checker recognizes them as individual characters. With PST-1 expert typefaces, the glyph is mapped to an unrelated character. The word *find* is *Wnd* to the spell checker. This requires a more labor-intensive technique for setting and proofing quality typography. (See "Sentence Typography Evaluation" later in this chapter for ligature-insertion techniques.)

Not all typefaces come with ligatures; others are designed not to need them. The majority of sans serif typefaces do not require ligatures—Optima, for example. (The letter *f* stays on its side of the couch.) Palatino is a serif typeface that works well without ligatures. A ligature has preset letterspacing. Type set with additional letterspacing cannot use them because the ligature letters stand out on the line with their tighter letterspacing. Type artists should use the designer-specified letterspacing (or very close to it) when they use ligatures. This produces consistent document-wide letterspacing. If a job does not warrant the typographic care that ligatures need, the type artist should choose a typeface that does not require them.

THE AMPERSAND IS ONE OF THE MOST POPULAR typographic abbreviations in handwritten usage. Early ampersand sightings reach back to A.D. 79 (Haley 1994). The ampersand evolved from the Latin word *et* (et per se and) and became a ligature of the two letters *e* and *t*— *&*. The word *ampersand* evolved from a consolidation and distortion of the Latin meaning. In the past, the use of the ampersand and the knowledge of its derivation were so widespread, that typographers abbreviated the word *et cetera* using the ligature— *&c.* The ampersands that retain their visual link to this letter heritage blend better with other characters in the same typeface. The simplified ampersand (&) of some typefaces does not have the grace of the original ligature.

The ampersand has limited use in good typographic text today, although this was not always the case. In *An Essay on Typography* (1936), Eric Gill (1882–1940) stated, "The absurd rule that the ampersand (&) should only be used in 'business titles' must be rescinded, & there are many other contractions which a sane typography should encourage." True to his beliefs, Gill used ampersands (along with the word *and*) and contractions (such as the contraction *sh'ld* for the word *should*) liberally in his book.

He felt these variables enhanced readability by controlling the number of words on a line—preferably 12. Gill also advocated equal word spacing in text to improve readability, preferring it over variable word spacing resulting from justified text. According to Gill, typographers who preferred justified text were more concerned with looking at the page than reading what was on it. Gill's opinion on ampersand use did not sway the day. Jan Tschichold (1902–74) recommended ampersands for use in company names only when joining two surnames; a style, if adopted, that can add an elegant flourish to continuous text.

Within the context of text typography, the ampersand is an informal shorthand suitable for personal notes. For discontinuous text, the ampersand is an expressive typographic embellishment for company names and headlines. The range of available ampersands (Slimbach's Poetica has 58) makes choosing an ampersand a design decision unto itself. Roman ampersands appear subdued alongside their chic italic

- Use ampersands with headlines and company names.
- Ampersands are too informal for text typography.

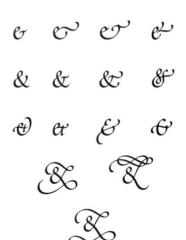

Poetica ampersand sampler (15 out of 58)

counterparts. Type artists should not hesitate to mix an italicized ampersand with roman letterforms for an eye-catching headline. It can produce exciting results. This is one of the rare times when mixing type styles can enhance the typographic quality of a headline rather than detract from it. (See "The Graphic Ampersand" in chapter 8.)

▲ The accounting house of Scrooge & Marley was a creation of Charles Dickens.

The accounting house of Scrooge ~~and~~ Marley was … & (ampersand)

ORNAMENTS AND DINGBATS

— ❦ ☎ —

- Ornaments are designed for one typeface family.
- Carefully size ornaments so they do not overwhelm the text.

- Dingbats are informal, keystroke graphics.
- Carefully size dingbats so they do not overwhelm the text.

Adobe Caslon Ornaments

Adobe Garamond Ornaments

Minion Ornaments

Utopia Ornaments

IT IS FITTING TO END THIS SECTION WITH A DISCUSSION of those elements that can add beauty to a page of type or blemish it. A type artist uses members of a typeface family to communicate the author's message, just as an orator chooses the vocabulary for a persuasive oration. A commanding control of vocabulary distinguishes a rousing address from a disjointed harangue. Selective usage of ornaments and dingbats enhances the flow of text. Overuse creates a jumble of visual characters all shouting for attention. (See chapter 7.)

The difference between ornaments and dingbats is simple. *Ornaments* are visual elements (leaves, fleurons, moons, and others) designed to accompany a specific typeface. The typeface designer applied the design qualities of a typeface—stroke, tone, and structure—to these visual elements. A Minion ornament is distinct from a Utopia ornament. Ornaments serve as typographic flourishes or functional typographic elements. They send subtle typographic signals to the reader. Their careful use is a sign of good typography. Frederic Warde wrote of ornaments in 1928, "… they can be demurely and inoffensively pleasing only because of this family tie." *Dingbats* are designed as separate pictorial elements and have a decorative function. Dingbats are small pictures designed for use with a variety of typefaces. There are dingbat fonts, offering a host of hands, check marks, stars, pencils, scissors, telephones, and others.

Ornaments first appeared when metal type originated in the fifteenth century. They were heavy black shapes, as were the typefaces they enhanced. In an effort to replicate the handwork of the scribes, ornaments served as replacements for the typographic flourishes scribes added to their letters and texts (Haley 1989). While ornaments could never replace the illustrated initial letters that adorned those manuscripts, they were an attempt to bridge the gap between the individual qualities each scribe invested in his handwork and the mechanized, standardized letterforms of the newly invented movable metal type.

CHAPTER FIVE

Ornaments, like other functional characters, clarify the text. Type artists use ornaments to divide text into sections when subheads are not available or appropriate. In a six-page report, for example, the author might make four different points in support of a single position. Subheads might separate these points too much causing the reader to interpret a single position as four separate positions. An ornament suggests a slight pause, rather than the start of a new section. Consequently, the reader views the report as a position paper with four arguments supporting one position. A small ornament (↔) between sections and then a larger one (%) at the end provides the reader with pleasant typographic "signal-ry" along a written path.

Dingbats are fun; they are informal. A dingbat is a miniature graphic that adds information to the text. As a result, it can change the text's content. Selecting the right dingbat face for a typeface requires the same concern as selecting two typefaces for a single document. A poor choice turns serious text into a cartoon.

Some dingbats are more aggressively graphic than others. A *pointer* (the hand with an extended forefinger) draws attention to an item in a list, but also adds an illustrative style to the text that frames the content. In a list of surgical procedures for emergency lifesaving techniques, a cartoon-style pointer is inappropriate. In a list of daycare activities for three-year-olds, it is not. With a typeface such as Tekton, dingbats provide the spark and flash that complement the informal, spontaneous quality of this typeface. An arrow or wide check mark is right at home on a page of this informal typeface. Dingbats, like ornaments, require a light touch for maximum impact.

A type artist can use ornaments instead of bullets to highlight elements in a list. A small ornament (♦) blends better with its typeface than a regular *bullet* (•). In some instance, the bullet is too large and overpowers the text. In those cases, a *midpoint* (·) is a suitable replacement. A midpoint is the little brother of the bullet. It eliminates the need to change the bullet's point size to get a smaller one and the midpoint's vertical placement is more suited to lowercase letters.

Some typeface ornaments include elements that appear more closely allied with dingbats than ornaments. Their style, however, maintains the emotional quality or mood of the typeface, so that while illustrative in nature they still remain typeface-specific. Adobe Caslon, for example, has an hourglass, pointers, and connectable border sections that cross over into dingbats. The typeface Chaparral includes 36 ornaments that evoke images of the southwestern United States.

Pointer samples

→ Tekton
✗ with
✓ Zapf
✏ dingbats

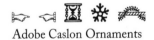

Adobe Caslon Ornaments

Chaparral Ornaments

SENTENCE TYPOGRAPHY EVALUATION

IN DAYS OF OLD WHEN MINUTES PASSED MORE SLOWLY and the personal computer rode atop one's neck, extended proofreading was done in teams. The copy reader held the *dead copy* (the last edited version of the document) and read it carefully aloud to the copy marker. The copy marker corrected the *live copy* (the latest version of the document) with proofreaders' marks. The reader read words, punctuation marks, type style changes, and spelled out proper nouns or easily misinterpreted words (fig. 5-5), using a steady, exaggerated, monotone style. Punctuation marks and unique typographical situations were described aloud with abbreviated words, such as *com* for comma, *stop* for period, *kwes* for question mark, and *bang* for exclamation point. The sentence *The little piggies went to market, stayed home, and had roast beef?* was proofread aloud as *Cap the little p-i-g-g-i-e-s went to market com stayed home com and had roast beef kwes.* An experienced proofreading team caught errors easily using this method.

apostrophe	*pos*	close parenthesis	*close pren*
single capital letter	*cap*	period	*stop*
all capital letters	*caps*	question mark	*kwes*
colon	*cole*	open quotation mark	*quo*
comma	*com*	close quotation mark	*close quo*
ellipsis	*three dots*	semicolon	*sem*
exclamation point	*bang*	slash	*slash*
hyphen	*hyph*	7	*fig seven*
open parenthesis	*pren*	seven	*spell seven*

FIGURE 5-5: *Sample of proofreaders' words for punctuation and type treatment*

Today many type artists proof their own documents. Proofreading a document is difficult, especially after working with it for the past two hours, two days, or two weeks. An adaptation of the team-proofing style coupled with electronic proofing techniques enables today's solo proofreader to produce error-free documents. An effective proofreader is not born with this ability—although some are more predisposed to it than others. Experience, spelling skills, practice, and patience are the keys to developing a critical eye. The local newspaper is a good place to practice. While newspapers follow different typographic and style rules, these differences create a ready practice sheet for fledging proofreaders seeking to hone their skills.

Proofreading on the sentence level focuses on copy accuracy, character usage, spacing, kerning, spelling according to usage, and obvious grammatical bloopers. A type artist is not an editor and does not have the authority to change the style or content of the text; but if the level of responsibility includes catching embarrassing grammatical errors, they will be caught on the sentence level. (Blooper checks, if authorized, are done at the end, when the document is free from proofmarks and the type artist is reading it for almost the last time.)

SOFTWARE DEVELOPERS CONTINUE TO UPGRADE their products with faster, more comprehensive features. Most type-savvy software has a search-and-replace feature (SARF) capable of finding individual characters, words, and spaces quickly and replacing them with alternates. This is an efficient way to insert ligatures, to replace words (including those consistently misspelled), and to delete extra spaces. Once the type artist establishes the parameters of a search, a replace-all feature can implement all substitutions. This is tempting, but it can create other problems unbeknownst to the type artist. By approving each substitution, the type artist can catch problems in the search parameters or identify exceptions in the text. Reviewing each replacement is worth the extra minutes it requires.

Once the obvious spelling errors are eliminated in the paragraph level, it is safe to insert ligatures. Some applications automatically substitute the *f-i* and *f-l* ligatures, while others can substitute any ligature included in the typeface. If manual ligature insertion is required, the type artist works from the longest to the shortest (*f-f-l, f-f-i, f-f, f-l,* to *f-i*). Ligatures replace lowercase letter-groups only and require a case-sensitive search. The SARF feature also replaces titling figures with text figures. The type artist enters the figures *0* through *9* one-by-one and approves each substitution. SARF can replace a word set incorrectly throughout the document. If the client unexpectedly changes the product *Bugaway* to *BugAway,* SARF can find each occurrence and correct them all in a single search. The type artist approves each substitution.

Many type-based applications for word processing and page layout can display word spaces as single, nonprinting dots. It is an optional feature. Checking word spacing on screen is risky because of video resolution. For rookie type artists still sharpening their eyes to see subtle proportional spacing problems, scrutinizing spacing dots on screen is

ELECTRONIC
PROOFING
FEATURES

helpful. A spell checker can identify an absence of word spacing because without word spacing the words *and* and *the* appear as *andthe.* An excess of word spacing or a space between a comma and a word is not flagged by the spell checker.

Fortunately, some SARF programming is space-sensitive. Setting the search parameters to look for two adjacent spaces quickly eliminates those hard-to-see extra proportional spaces. SARF can identify a space-comma combination and replace it with a single comma. If this is a frequent problem, the type artist can set up a search for excess spaces before common punctuation marks. If placing one space after a terminal punctuation mark is still sporadic, the type artist can use this feature to find and fix those also. Seasoned type artists rely on the electronic proofers to minimize the number of remaining errors their tired eyes must identify.

With the document as computer-perfect as possible, the type artist prints it on an inexpensive stock. There is more to do, so using good paper is a waste. While the document prints, the type artist takes a break. This is a good time to go get a drink of water, go get a snack—just *go!* A ten-minute break is better than a five-minute one, and so forth.

Solo Sentence-Level Proofreading Techniques

A SOLO PROOFREADER PARTNERS WITH A LARGE DICTIONARY. The thickest, most up-to-date dictionary is the best proofing partner. The *Webster's Collegiate Dictionary* is revised frequently. The *Webster's Third New International Dictionary* is comprehensive. There are others—the thicker the better. Thin dictionaries have limited vocabularies, they do not show helpful examples, and they never have interesting illustrations. Computer spell checkers do not scratch the surface of the existing word pool. Also, a type artist should not ask a colleague how to spell a word. There are too many opportunities for unintentional error.

In addition to a dictionary, the type artist needs a colored ballpoint pen, the dead copy, a typography resource (this book), a ruler or reading guide, a highlighter, and a comfortable, quiet spot—this takes a while. It is better to keep distractions to a minimum when proofing. A quiet place or headphones connected to silence will keep the dedicated proofreader off-limits to interruptions.

Check one or two errors with each proofing wave.

Proofreading on the sentence level is executed in a series of waves. With so many different errors to find, the type artist should look for one or two of them at a time. It is too easy to forget something. The chance of catching all errors is enhanced markedly by proofing the same document several times.

The first wave checks for doubles and bad page breaks. All parentheses and quotation marks have a beginning and an end. The bottom of a page should not end with a hyphenated word. The proofer's eye skims the surface checking for these pairs and checking page breaks.

The second wave checks kerning. It is easy to be overzealous here. Headline and subhead letterspacing problems are more noticeable and require fixing. Text kerning problems are rare if document-wide letterspacing and word spacing were set properly. There are three rules of thumb for text kerning. If a bus can drive through the space, the type artist should change it; if nothing could squeeze through it, change it; if it is anywhere in between, forget about it. With that in mind, the type artist checks for kerning problems in four key spots—before and after an isolated italicized word, before and after words inside parentheses, around ligatures, and before exclamation points and question marks. These are the most likely offenders.

The third wave checks typographic form and accuracy of content against the dead copy. The type artist places the dead and live copies side by side on a desk or table and uses a finger, ruler, or paper edge to keep position on the dead copy. The pen indicates position on the live copy. The type artist reads aloud in a soft, slow, steady pace and pronounces each word in an exaggerated, syllable-by-syllable style. Enunciating each and every syllable sets up the proper proofreading pace and puts the proofreader eye-to-*i* with every letter in every word. The proofer reads two words from the dead copy, shifts to the live copy and checks the same two words, shifts back to the dead copy to read two more words, and shifts to the live copy, and so forth. Some type artists believe that verbally identifying punctuation marks and typographic style changes (as a team reader does) improves their accuracy.

Every proofreader establishes a comfortable pace. The first proof job is always slower than the second. Speed should keep abreast of accuracy. A speedy proofing job is no proofing job if it leaves errors in its wake. Errors come in groups. All corrected words need rereading to make sure a second error was not overlooked.

Some proofers do not like stopping during the third wave to consult the dictionary or a type resource. It is easy to lose page position and train of thought. It is during this wave, however, that those problems of usage-specific spelling and type glyphs are questioned. If the problem is an isolated one that will not affect the rest of the document, the type artist can highlight or query the word or glyph and return to it later with resource in hand. If the problem reoccurs and becomes a distraction,

Wave One: Check doubles and bad page breaks.

Wave Two: Check kerning.

Wave Three: Check against dead copy.

Like birds of a feather, errors flock together.

Double-check doubt.

The years 1919-25 are ... N̲ (?)
Query proofmark

**Create a style check sheet
for proofing.**

**Proof corrections to check for
unintentional errors.**

The train left the station at 7: (*bb*)
15 A.M. as stated on the sign.
Bad-break proofmark does not
indicate a specific remedy.

the type artist must mark the stop-spot carefully (a double vertical slash
after the last word) and consult the proper resource.

Some type artists also find it helpful to create a style check sheet
while they create a document. This saves them from looking up the
same items repeatedly. They use this sheet during proofing to check
spelling and usage consistency.

Once the live copy is marked, the artist enters the changes, prints
it, and proofs it again. This time proofreading is more focused. The type
artist proofs each *correction*. Using the proofmarked live copy (the new
dead copy), proofmark locations are checked against the corrected locations on the latest printout (the new live copy). The type artist looks to
make sure a new error (extra space, misspelled word) was not introduced and that the kerning adjustments were sufficient. The rest of the
document has remained untouched, so it does not need reproofing. In
all corrected paragraphs, the type artist checks again for bad breaks,
end-of-paragraph widows, and hyphenation problems. If any corrections are made to the live copy, the type artist proofs the newest corrections and checks hyphenation, breaks, and widows once a new live copy
emerges from the printer. This continues until no proofmarks are placed
on the live copy.

Seasoned type artists develop their own proofreading sequence and
style. Some prefer starting with the third wave (typographic form and
accuracy of content) and ending with the first wave (doubles and bad
page breaks). That approach is logical as well. Whatever approach results in an error-free document is the correct one to adopt.

ॐ

ALL TYPE ARTISTS STRIVE FOR GOOD TYPOGRAPHIC FORM through the
correct use of type glyphs. Good typographic form is beautiful to those
who love type and transparent, but functionally necessary, for those
who read it. As Bringhurst said, "Good typography is like bread: ready
to be admired, appraised, and dissected before it is consumed."

SETTING
TYPE
FOR
SPECIAL FUNCTIONS

Within a sentence there are words, figures, and punctuation marks that by their unique appearance identify a special relationship for the elements they represent. These type characters, or glyphs, collectively describe an item or modify a word, such as the name of a book, the age of a child, or the time of day. As a collective, its meaning is complete when all components are read as a whole. Some of these linked words require hyphens to define their common bond; but for others, the type treatment, such as italic type or small caps, identifies this union. The words *entry* and *level,* for example, are linked by a hyphen when they function as a modifier, as in *entry-level typographer.* This is not type treatment for emphasis or accent, but type treatment for clarity. Compound modifiers are joined and released as needed. Some type treatments appear and reappear with such frequency that their appearance becomes second nature to a seasoned type artist. It is these special typographic treatments within a sentence that this chapter explains—those words and numbers that type artists see every day as their fingers dance across the keyboard and as their lines of words pursue the blinking cursor across the screen.

Authors and copywriters create meter and tempo with the syntax of their words. Type artists create typographic form with specialty glyphs and type treatments that communicate the author's message. Many authors are accomplished wordsmiths, aware that the form

Letters in combination may be satisfying and in a well-composed page even beautiful as a whole, but art in letters consists rather in the art of arranging and composing them in an appropriate and pleasing way.

—Goudy
The Alphabet and Elements of Lettering

TYPOGRAPHIC ARTISTRY

their words take clarifies the intended meaning. Most are not typographers and do not know the full range of stylistic subtleties their words can display. This knowledge is the type artist's contribution to the text and the key to typographic form—or typographic artistry—on the page.

Expert typographers talk about letters in terms analogous to music, fine wine, and the fluidity of dance. Just as fine wine swishes across the connoisseur's tongue or ethereal music floats past the aficionado's ear, type to the master typographer is a visual symphony complete with flow, grace, and rhythm. Access to stalwart small caps, graceful text figures, and elegant swash and alternate characters infuses a text page with the nuance and harmony of expert typographic form. For those type artists just discovering these additional glyphs and their uses, it is an area of typography that challenges its practitioners and rewards them with visual artistry when done well.

TYPOGRAPHY AND CONTENT

TEXT FOR A SPECIAL FUNCTION IS BEST UNDERSTOOD in the larger sense of context. A memo to a co-worker looks different than a flyer for a shopper. A short story in a literary magazine filled with dialogue and punctuated with quotation marks looks different than a research article in a mathematics journal filled with equations and theorems. Generally, text falls into several categories—humanistic or technical, continuous or discontinuous, formal or informal, and factual or opinion. As with other things, these categories overlap.

Humanistic text is literary text written for continuous reading concerning broad cultural learning or human experiences. It encompasses diverse topics of general interest and uses a minimum of numbers or statistical data. *Technical* or *scientific text* is written for discontinuous reading due to the complexity of its content. It encompasses topics with particular or practical knowledge about a specialized subject. Examples of statistical or mathematical data, the use of charts and tables, or enumeration to support its conclusions are abundant. The text's complexity forces the reader to reread passages to ascertain the precise meaning.

Formal text is written for presentation to a wide audience, such as a book, magazine, report, or catalogue. *Informal text* is text designed for limited distribution, such as a letter, memo, or note. *Authoritative text* is written to communicate specific knowledge, facts, or documentation, such as newspaper articles, textbooks, or factual reports. *Opinion text* is written as one person's viewpoint, such as editorials, autobiographies, letters, or memos.

The importance of these text classifications for the type artist is their effect on typographic form. Rules that strictly dictate manuscript preparation for a novel (humanist continuous text) are altered when setting copy for a step-by-step repair manual (technical text with discontinuous sections). Rules that require writing out numbers and eliminating all abbreviations in humanist text are modified when setting technical or scientific documents or tabulated lists. The distinction drawn here is one of frequency and the need for clarity.

In humanist text, numbers are infrequent and information is presented in a more relaxed and thoroughly articulated style. The rules for typography in a novel, a book of poems, or a journal article on mythology follow those of humanist text. In this environment, setting numbers as figures and shortening words into abbreviations makes the information appear informal and rushed. An isolated figure or lone abbreviation would jar the otherwise smooth flow of the text and its typography.

In technical text, numbers are frequent and the information is detailed, quantitative, and exact. The text is punctuated with diagrams, tabulated material, equations, and charts. Figures, abbreviations, and symbols are legitimate devices for explicitly communicating complicated statistics, concepts, or theorems within the accepted form of the discipline. Eliminating these devices in technical text denies the author the tools needed to clearly and accurately present the message.

For type artists working with promotional copy that highlights comparative quantities and prices, dimensions and percentages, warranties and component parts, the rules of technical text apply. Clarity of communication is paramount here. This same copy, however, also benefits from some humanist text characteristics. There needs to be a *promotional text* category that emphasizes formality—by eliminating needless abbreviations and inappropriate symbols—and clarity—by relaxing rules that outlaw the use of figures below one hundred. Setting promotional text correctly relies on the type artist's knowledge of context distinctions, typeface glyphs, and typographic form.

Before setting type, a type artist reads the material and determines its appropriate context (humanist, technical/scientific, or promotional). Once the decision is made, the rules for numbers, abbreviations, and other type treatments apply throughout the entire document—not just on one page, or one panel, or one chapter, or one section—but the entire document.

SENTENCE TYPOGRAPHY FOR SPECIAL FUNCTIONS

Titling Caps and Small Caps

- Use small caps in text for abbreviations and acronyms.
- Use small caps for formal-looking subheads.
- Do not use small caps for personal initials and personal acronyms.
- Use small caps for three-letter geographic acronyms.

GG JJ
PPRR

Letter-pair comparisons showing subtle differences between titling caps (left) and uppercase (right)

ABABCabc
ABABCabc

True cut small caps (upper) and fake small caps (lower) comparison for stroke weight

TITLING CAPS AND SMALL CAPS ARE AS DISTINCTLY different as uppercase letters are from lowercase letters. Their use is specific as well. Titling caps are capital letters designed within the entire point size of the font (the ascent and the descent). A typical uppercase or capital letter sits on the baseline and confines itself to the font's ascent. (Occasionally, the cap *J* in a font descends below the baseline, but not always.) A capital letter is designed for use with lowercase letters in text. Titling caps are designed for use as headings, 18 points and larger. Their strokes are proportioned for all-cap headings and are not designed to accompany lowercase letters in a text line. Beside a lowercase letter, a titling cap looks spindly. Titling caps, due to their size, display more design refinements. The detail included in a serif, for example, is appropriate for its viewing size.

Small caps are capital letters designed within the font's *x*-height (approximately) for use in text. Their strokes are proportioned and spaced to fit optically with lowercase letters. Their structure distinguishes the words they display as special, but they do not attract undue attention, as uppercase letters would in the same situation. Some type applications can create *fake small caps* (an uppercase letter scaled to size). The stroke weights of the fake small caps are too thin in comparison to the adjacent lowercase letters. The words they set are too light and create a hole in the text's color.

Small caps are necessary in a typeface with a short *x*-height. The small caps for such a typeface, Adobe Garamond for example, relieves the size differential between the cap height and the *x*-height. Type artists who do not have small caps for their typefaces should choose a typeface with a large *x*-height for documents requiring small caps. By minimizing the contrast between the cap height and the *x*-height, the use of uppercase letters in place of small caps is visually acceptable (fig. 6-1).

TYPO GRA phy · TYPO GRA phy · TYPO GRA phy

- Adobe Garamond
- small *x*-height with small caps

- Clearface
- medium *x*-height with capitals

- ITC Leawood
- large *x*-height with capitals

FIGURE 6-1: *Capitals and small caps with different* x-*heights*

All punctuation marks blend properly with small caps, except for the question mark, the exclamation point, and the ampersand. A small cap typeface includes these resized marks for the rare times they are needed. The ampersand is useful for decorative headlines, because ampersands usually are not appropriate in continuous text.

Type artists use small caps in continuous text for abbreviations, initials, and acronyms. They are not acceptable with personal acronyms, such as *FDR* or *JFK,* personal initials, such as *J. F. Kennedy,* or with two-letter geographic acronyms, such as those used for states—*NY* and *FL.* Abbreviations for academic degrees set in small caps, such as B.A., M.F.A., PH.D., M.D., or D.D.S., blend better when an upper- and lowercase name precedes them, as in *Albert Schweitzer,* M.D. Acronyms, such as NATO, UNICEF, USS, HMS, and OSHA, and three-letter geographic acronyms, such as USA, look better in text as small caps. Acronyms set in uppercase letters in continuous text are reminiscent of roadside billboards—looming large as the reader passes. Set in small caps these acronyms have a typographic distinction that links them visually, identifies them correctly, but does not blow a hole in the type's texture. Small caps require loose tracking to maintain proper text color.

▲ The NATO countries meet this week in Geneva.
▼ The NATO countries meet this week in Geneva.
▲ The USS *Eisenhower* sails later this month.
sc The <u>nato</u> countries meet this week in Geneva.

Caps and small caps, or small caps alone, are appropriate also for elegant subheads. They call attention to a pause in running text and set up a change in thought without creating a sharp break (as would a change of typeface).

When a small cap word or word grouping starts a sentence, the first letter is capitalized and the remainder is set in small caps. For example, if the acronym NATO starts a sentence, the *N* is capitalized—NATO. (See "Time of Day" and "Years, Decades, Centuries, and Eras" later in this chapter and "Initial Letters and Versals" in chapter 7 for other small cap uses.)

THE SIMPLE QUESTION, WHAT ABOUT NUMBERS? can cause a conscientious type artist to groan aloud. It is easier to use a multitude of dashes in a document than it is to answer that seemingly simple question. It does not have to be so. The response to this question is another question: Is the text humanist or technical? Or more precisely, the question is: Is the text filled with numbers?

AB?!& AB?!&

Adobe Caslon punctuation and symbols for uppercase (left) and small caps (right)

▲ Correct typographic form
▼ Incorrect typographic form

NUMBERS IN TEXT

For example, a magazine article discussing the behavioral phases of a toddler and the appropriate sanity-saving strategies for parents is humanist text. It appeals to a general audience and uses numbers infrequently. These numbers are spelled out easily without jeopardizing the reader's comprehension of the material.

A magazine article, discussing the use of lemons in springtime cuisine, that includes several timesaving recipes is technical text. Such an article does not demonstrate a theorem for finding the area of a complex geometric figure, but it is filled with measurements and quantities explaining how to prepare complicated recipes, such as "Stir-Fry Lemon Chicken" or "Linguine with Lemon-Zested Scallops." All struggling neophyte cooks would agree that for them this text is technical, filled with ½ cup of this and ¼ teaspoon of that. Writing out these measurements would lengthen such an article considerably and make the measurements difficult to understand. Within the definition of technical text as text in which "numbers are frequent and the information is detailed, quantitative, and exact," the springtime-cuisine article is at home.

The treatment of numbers in text applies to cardinal as well as ordinal numbers. A *cardinal number* is a number that represents a quantity, such as *25, 43,* or *127.* An *ordinal number* represents an ordering or ranking, such as *25th, 43rd,* or *127th.* A type artist treats both kinds of numbers in text according to the same guidelines.

11　22　33　44　55　66　77　88　99　0o
• Kinesis MM

11　22　33　44　55　66　77　88　99　0o
• Cronos Pro

I1　22　33　44　55　66　77　88　99　0o
• Centaur

FIGURE 6-2: *Titling and text figure comparisons with different regular-weight typefaces*

TITLING FIGURES AND TEXT FIGURES

• Titling figures are used with all capital letters.

• Text figures are suitable in uppercase and lowercase text.

AFTER DETERMINING ITS CONTEXT, THE TYPE ARTIST decides which kinds of figures to use. There are two figures available—*titling figures* and *text figures.* Titling figures, also called *lining figures* and *ranging figures,* are to numbers as uppercase letters are to the alphabet. These figures are confined to the font's ascent. Titling figures are used with uppercase letters. Their size and proportions fit with these ascent-only letterforms. Text figures, also called *hanging figures, lowercase figures,* or *old style figures,* are the lowercase of numbers. The bulk of the figure is positioned in the font's *x*-height with ascenders and descenders protruding outwards. Their size and proportions fit with lowercase letters.

Text figures are the original number symbols used in typography starting in 1540 (Bringhurst 1992). Their grace and elegance produce a document of distinction (fig. 6-2). Titling figures were the latecomers to the page. The precursor of the titling figure (Eason and Rookledge 1991) was introduced in 1788 by the British Letter Foundry of typographer John Bell (1746–1831). By the nineteenth century, true titling figures were the predominant number style.

Today's type artists use titling figures with all capital letters and text figures with upper- and lowercase letters (fig. 6-3). And they can mix them on the page according to their location with respect to either capital letters or uppercase and lowercase letters.

$12 30¢ $12 30¢

Currency symbols with titling figures (left) and old style currency symbols with text figures (right)

He called 555-1234 at 3:00 P.M. from 123 Chester Road. The operator broke in at 3:01 P.M. and said the new telephone number was 555-3456.

• Adobe Garamond with text figures

He called 555-1234 at 3:00 P.M. from 123 Chester Road. The operator broke in at 3:01 P.M. and said the new telephone number was 555-3456.

• Clearface with titling figures

He called 555-1234 at 3:00 P.M. from 123 Chester Road. The operator broke in at 3:01 P.M. and said the new telephone number was 555-3456.

• ITC Leawood with titling figures

FIGURE 6-3: *Text and titling figures with different x-heights*

NUMERIC QUANTITIES, VALUES, AND DENOTATIONS are pervasive in daily communication. From the length and weight of a newborn to the years celebrated at a septuagenarian's birthday party to a street address, people use numbers liberally. Numbers define the magnitude of an experience, such as the length of the one-that-got-away, and they quantify an accomplishment, such as a high Scholastic Aptitude Test (SAT) score for a promising student. Numbers are represented in two different forms—by symbols, such as *1, 2, 3, 4,* and *5* (hereafter called *figures*), and by words, such as *one, two,* and *three* (hereafter called *number-words*).

NUMBER-FORM GUIDELINES

✦ Apply the NONN decision consistently in humanist text.

When determining which form to use, a type artist categorizes numbers by four factors: context, size, specificity, and purpose.

In general, humanist text allows the use of figures on the page according to numeric size. There are a few exceptions determined by specificity and purpose; but as a general rule, size is paramount. Technical text, as a general statement, allows the use of figures for all measurable, quantitative distinctions, wherever they occur. There is a location exception here, but with slight rewording it can appear as a figure too.

There are two schools of thought on representing numbers in humanist text. One school, espoused by the *Chicago Manual of Style,* prefers number-words for all whole numbers through ninety-nine. These number-words represent the numbers *twenty-one* through *twenty-nine, thirty-one* to *thirty-nine,* and so forth through *ninety-nine* and are hyphenated. The other school, espoused by the *New York Public Library Writer's Guide to Style and Usage,* uses number-words for only those whole numbers through nine. The nine-or-ninety-nine (NONN) decision—depending upon which school of thought the type artist adopts—affects a variety of numeric distinctions and is applied consistently throughout a document.

The adverse effect on typographic quality of the NONN decision is diminished if the type artist uses text figures rather than titling figures. The text figure *24* blends more smoothly with the letters in running text than the titling figure *24.* If the type artist only has titling figures for a short–*x*-height typeface, spelling out quantities through ninety-nine is the better typographic choice.

Specialized figure and currency proofreaders' marks

CONTEXT-INDEPENDENT NUMBER GUIDELINES

* Use a number-word, not a figure, if a number starts a sentence.
* Use figures for a decimal or percentage.

·IF THE TYPE ARTIST'S DECISIONS WERE LIMITED to context (humanist or technical) and size (nine or ninety-nine), the choice between figures and number-words would be easy. There are a few general statements regarding form, however, that are context independent.

A number is spelled out when it starts a sentence—always—regardless of context. A figure is not suitable as a visual indicator of a new sentence. It may appear odd if the number is the first in a series, but in this circumstance, inconsistency is accepted. Rewording the sentence can eliminate the problem, but unless the type artist is also the author, the artist rarely has such authority.

▲ Forty-five toddlers were tested for pet preferences.
▼ 99 bottles of beer on the wall …
sp (45) toddlers were tested for pet preferences.

In some instances, a number is set as a figure—regardless of context. A type artist always sets a percentage or a decimal value as a figure. The use of the percent symbol (%) or the word *percent* falls under the rules for context (see "Abbreviations and Symbols" later in this chapter). Type artists use figures for street numbers (although numbered streets are written out according to the NONN decision, such as *123 Fifth Street*); zip codes; phone numbers; social security numbers; interstate, highway, and roadway numbers; years; days; eras; time (when it specifies a precise point in time); and academic grades. If the text refers to a publication's numbered chapter, section, or table, a figure accompanies the word, such as *chapter 3, section 4,* and *figure 7.* (Some of the above categories require additional clarification, which follows later in this chapter.)

THE MAJORITY OF EXCEPTIONS FOR NUMBERS OCCUR in humanist text. They are framed primarily by the need to clarify and less frequently by appearance. Once made, the type artist maintains the exception in treatment throughout the document. For example, if a single sentence in humanist text includes multiple values, the reader might find number-words difficult to compare and awkward to read. In this instance, the type artist uses figures. If the figures represent numbers of voters, for example, every time a number of voters is cited, the type artist continues to set it as a figure. This applies throughout the document—before and after the series occurs.

USAGE-SPECIFIC NUMBER GUIDELINES

- ◆ Treat like number-words and figures consistently.

▼ Of the forty-five toddlers tested for pet preferences, twenty-one preferred dogs; fifteen, cats; eight, birds; and one wanted the bird to do lizard impressions again.

▲ Of the 45 toddlers tested for pet preferences, 21 preferred dogs; 15, cats; 8, birds; and 1 wanted the bird to do lizard impressions again.

IF A WORD, SUCH AS *HUNDRED, THOUSAND, OR MILLION,* follows a number, the NONN decision applies. The type artist writes out the number, such as *fifteen hundred* when using ninety-nine as the number-word cap and *15 hundred* when using nine. The guiding principle is consistency—treat like numbers in a like manner throughout the document.

When punctuating large figures, commas separate groups of three digits (working right to left) in numbers of four or more, such as *1,234* and *15,678.* No space follows this comma, but it often needs kerning.

LARGE NUMBERS

▲ The dog chased 12,345 cats yearly, but only 2,334 mail carriers.

AGE

THE TYPE ARTIST DETERMINES HOW TO TYPESET the age of a person, place, or thing, according to its context and the NONN decision. When the age modifies a noun, it is hyphenated; when it stands alone, it is not.

▲ The 12-year-old camper wanted to bring her dog to camp.
▲ The twelve-year-old camper wanted to bring her dog to camp.
▲ The toddler is two years old.
The camper is ~~twelve~~ years old. *12* (*text fig*)

FRACTIONS

♦ Hyphenate fractions when written as number-words.
♦ Use a case or piece fraction when representing fractions with figures.

WHEN USING COMMON FRACTIONS ALONE, such as *one-half* or *one-fourth*, type artists treat them as they would any other number in the same context. Fractions are hyphenated when spelled out. When mixing whole numbers and fractions in humanist text, type artists use figures to improve clarity and reader comprehension.

Fractions appear frequently when discussing dimensions or portions. The sentence *The paper size, 8½ inches by 11 inches, is suitable for many printing jobs* uses figures to express dimensions because a fraction is included with a whole number. Since this is a humanist-text example, the type artist writes out the words *by* and *inches* within the dimension (see "Abbreviations and Symbols" later in this chapter). In the humanist sentence *The sheet was one-half its original size* the fraction is used alone and written out and hyphenated.

The type artist uses *case fractions* for proper typographic form when setting a fraction as a figure. If a case fraction is unavailable, a *piece fraction,* formed with superior and inferior figures separated by a solidus, is an acceptable alternative. The *level fraction 1/2* is not good typographic form. Type artists should have at least one font with the appropriate figure alternatives when setting figure-frequent text.

▲ The sheet was one-half its original size.
The paper size, 8 inches by 11 inches, is suitable.... *1/2* (*case fraction*)
sp The sheet was ½ its original size.

DOLLARS AND CENTS

♦ Use the currency symbol when the monetary value is a figure.

THE USE OF CURRENCY IN TEXT FALLS UNDER the guidelines of context. If context requires the type artist to spell out the numerical value, then the denomination is spelled out also, as in *fourteen dollars.* Fractional amounts of a dollar fall under the guidelines of decimals and are set as figures, such as *$1.25,* in any context. The dollar symbol ($) or cent symbol (¢) accompany figures in text but are not mixed with comparative figures. Text figures require the old style dollar ($) and cent symbols (¢).

These symbols are included in expert collections and OT typefaces with expanded typographic glyphs. They are proportional to the text figures.

▲ The cost of their pet treats is $1.00, $.50, and $1.10.
▼ The cost of their pet treats is $1, 50¢, and $1.10.
The cost of their pet treats is $1, $.50, and $1.10.   .00 *text fig*/lc

If a whole-dollar amount is used alone in context-appropriate text, the type artist drops the decimal point and the double zeros, as in $5. If the whole-dollar amount is in a series with other dollar-and-cent amounts, the type artist restores the decimal and two zeros (or *ciphers*). Large-dollar amounts can be expressed in figures and words, such as *$4 million,* for ease of reading when the NONN decision dictates figures.

In a promotional brochure or advertisement, the type artist uses figures and symbols for prices. Figures improve reader comprehension and strengthen impact for this kind of document. Consistency with dollar and cent symbols and decimals and zeroes is important here as well.

▲ The cost of dog, cat, and bird food has risen from $4.25 to $5.00, from $1.00 to $1.50, and from $2.39 to $2.50, respectively.
▲ Collar prices begin at $4 and vary according to the animal's size.
▼ The cost of dog, cat, and bird food has risen from $4.25 to $5, from $1 to $1.50, and from $2.39 to $2.50, respectively.
▲ The cost of their collars is still $4, $5, and $1.
The cost of dog, cat, and bird food has risen from 4.25 to $5.00. $C/lc

TYPE ARTISTS SET TIME-OF-DAY NUMBERS ACCORDING TO context. In humanist text, when times are approximate and rounded to the hour, half hour, or quarter hour, the type artist spells out the time, such as *four fifteen* or *quarter past six.* When specifying the hour, the word *o'clock* accompanies it, such as *three o'clock*—but never *3:00 o'clock.* When the author pinpoints a precise moment in time, such as the start of a public event or an airline departure, or when setting time in technical text, the type artist uses figures.

▲ She began practicing the piano at seven o'clock in the evening.
▲ The eleventh runner crossed the finish line at 11:53 A.M.
▲ The train leaves at 7:15 in the morning.
She started her homework at 3 o'clock. *sp*

♦ Spell out the currency when number-words represent the monetary value.
♦ Do not mix the dollar and cent symbols with comparative values.

TIME OF DAY

♦ Use figures to pinpoint a precise moment in time, as for a public event or service.
♦ Use small caps for time-of-day abbreviations with figures only (periods are optional).

The time-of-day abbreviations A.M. and P.M. accompany figures, not number-words. The type artist uses text figures and small caps, such as 7:15 A.M., 12:00 M., or 4:00 P.M. The abbreviation A.M., from the Latin *ante meridiem* (before noon), distinguishes morning hours; M., from the Latin *meridies* (noon), differentiates between noon, 12:00 M., and midnight, 12:00 P.M.; and P.M., from *post meridiem* (after noon), distinguishes the afternoon and evening hours.

A single space separates the figures from the abbreviations. No space occurs within the abbreviation itself. Line breaks should not occur between the figure and the time-of-day abbreviation. It is acceptable to eliminate the periods within the abbreviation, appearing as 10:00 AM. If small caps and text figures are not available, regular caps are acceptable for typefaces with a tall x-height. When using short–x-height typefaces without small caps and text figures, the type artist uses lowercase letters with periods to minimize texture disruption. The combination of text figures and small caps creates a distinctive document.

▲ The lecture will commence in the green room at 10:30 A.M.
▼ The lecture will commence in the green room at 10:30 A. M.
◡ The lecture will commence in the green room at 10:30 A.M.
▲ The New Year's Eve celebration began on Times Square at 12:00 P.M.
▲ The flight to London left at 12:00 M.
_m_ The flight to London left at 12:00 P.

DAYS OF
THE MONTH

◆ Use figures in all contexts.
◆ When both day of the month and year are present, a comma follows each figure.

WHEN USING A DAY OF THE MONTH IN ANY CONTEXT, the type artist uses figures. Although when reading dates, the date sounds like an ordinal, it is written as a cardinal number and no comma follows it. When a year follows the month and day, commas set off the year. With inclusive dates in lists, tabulated material for schedules, or in technical text, the type artist can use an en dash as long as the dates are not preceded with the prepositions *between* or *from* (see "En Dash" and "Figure Dash" in chapter 5). In humanist text, writing out the inclusion is preferred, such as *from May 5 to 13*.

▲ Valentine's Day is on February 14, 1995, and is a Tuesday.
▲ We celebrate Valentine's Day on February 14 every year.
   We celebrate Valentine's Day on February 14 every year.   *lc*
▼ We celebrate Valentine's Day on February 14th.
▲ The experiment was performed May 5–8, June 1–4, and July 3–6.
▼ The experiment was performed from May 5–8, June 1–4, and July 3–6.

A YEAR IS SET AS A FIGURE IN ALL CONTEXTS. If in running text it is set alone or with a month, the year is not set off with commas. When used as part of a specific month and day, it is set off with commas. If an event or time period encompasses part of two calendar years, they are set with a virgule, such as *1994/95*. The type artist drops the century reference in the second year and does not replace it with an apostrophe.

In an informal context when the century is obvious, a calendar year is abbreviated by dropping the century reference and replacing it with a single apostrophe, such as *the blizzard of '93*. Even a calendar year yields its figures and is spelled out when it starts a sentence.

- ✦ Always set a year in figures.
- ✦ Decades are set consistently as number-words or figures.
- ✦ Centuries either follow the NONN decision or are set as number-words.

- ▲ His date of birth was July 4, 1988, not June 24 as his mother predicted.
- ▲ The Valentine's celebration of February 1992 was more festive than usual.
- ▼ 1992 was a joyous year for the family.
- ▲ Nineteen ninety-two was a joyous year for the family.
  The winter of 1992/93 was the coldest on record. / *virgule*

Decades are set as figures or are spelled out, as with *the 1990s, the '90s,* or *the nineties.* With figures, the plural distinction *s* is necessary and no apostrophe precedes it. Centuries are spelled out as ordinals, such as *the fifteenth century.* Those type artists using number-words through nine, spell out centuries below ten and use ordinal numbers with the others, such as *the fifth century* and *the 12th century.* Once again, text figures are preferred here because they do not disturb the texture of the paragraph as titling figures do. Some type artists prefer an exception here and spell out centuries no matter their size.

Eras are distinguished by the appropriate abbreviation, such as A.D., C.E., B.C., or B.C.E. The abbreviations A.D., from the Latin *anno Domini* (in the year of the Lord), and C.E. (of the common era) precede the figure, as in A.D. 600. The abbreviations B.C. (before Christ) and B.C.E. (before the common era) follow the figure, as in *450 B.C.E.*

- ▲ The '60s were tumultuous years.
- ▼ The 60's were tumultuous years.
- ▲ The mid–fifteenth century heralded Gutenberg's invention.
- ▲ Beatrice B. Warde (1900–69) worked in England for Monotype.

- ▲ Correct typographic form
- ▼ Incorrect typographic form

If a type artist cites inclusive years in text they are written with the en dash as long as the words *from* or *between* do not precede the number. If calendar years span two centuries, such as *1887–1902*, all figures are needed. If the years are contained within the same century, the century reference is not repeated, such *1902–4* or *1887–92*. An inclusive era distinction with dates using the abbreviation A.D. or C.E. follows the same guidelines, such as A.D. *43–4* or C.E. *67–78*. Dates using the abbreviation B.C. or B.C.E. are not shortened within an inclusive number grouping because the information might be misinterpreted. The type artist uses full figures for both years, such as *125–123* B.C.

Names in Text

- Italicize names of large publications, such as books and periodicals.
- Capitalize and set in quotation marks the names of the subcomponents of those same publications.
- Capitalize personal names always and names of parks, streets, and buildings when the full name is used.

Identifying names in text uses a system of hierarchical typographic treatments. From personal names to book titles to newspaper articles, a type artist uses different type treatments to alert the viewer that the name is for a person, a large publication, or a landmark. All words in a personal name, for example, are capitalized. This treatment links these words into a single multiword, such as *Giambattista Bodoni* and *William Addison Dwiggins.*

Publications in text receive unique typographic treatment and in doing so identify their role. A type artist italicizes the names of newspapers, periodicals, and books to distinguish a large publication. A small portion of a larger publication, such as a chapter or an article, is capitalized and set off in quotation marks. The use of italics or quotation marks shows the hierarchy between publications and their subdivisions. This same hierarchy is applied to movies and television shows (italicized) and television episodes (capitalized and quoted); symphonies and songs; and cookbooks and recipes.

Quotation marks can cause a visual problem in text if used to extreme. For example, when writing a chronology of character development through a season of television episodes in a single television series, it is acceptable to italicize the episode names rather than quote each one. In such abundance, the open and close quotes appear as annoying bird tracks tap dancing across the page. Switching to italicizing the episode names is a smoother typographic distinction. The quantity dictates a change in typographic treatment. The type artist maintains the same treatment throughout the document.

In running text when the name of an italicized or quoted name starts with the word *The,* it need not be included with the special treatment, if it sounds or looks awkward. If it is not treated specially, it is not capitalized.

There are unusual times when part of a name is italicized and part is not. The name of a ship, such as the USS *Eisenhower* or the

HMS *Ajax,* is set with the name italicized, but the military distinction is set roman in caps or small caps.

Other more common names, such as the name of an office, park, monument, bridge, building, military branch, society, or association, are capitalized when the full name is used, such as *Washington Monument,* but when it is referred to as *the monument,* it is not capitalized.

▲ The bird enjoyed reading the *New York Times* from the perch in his bird cage.

▲ The school children visited the Washington Monument, the Smithsonian Institution, and the Lincoln Memorial. They agreed that the memorial was the most spectacular.

▲ Her favorite dessert recipe in the *Joy of Cooking* was the "Fudge Meringue Cake."

ABBREVIATIONS ARE THE SOURCE OF INTERESTING LORE from the past. It is believed that the exclamation point and the question mark developed from the Latin form of abbreviated writing that positioned letters of short or shortened words on top of one another (Firmage 1993). The exclamation point evolved from the Latin word *Io* (joy). The question mark developed from the Latin word *quaestio* (question). To abbreviate the word *Io* the scribes placed the first letter *I* atop the last letter *o.* The question mark evolved from placing the word's first letter *Q* atop its last letter *o.* The abbreviation for the word *et cetera* appeared as *&c* in some early texts; but unlike the exclamation point and the question mark, it disappeared from use (Haley 1994, 5).

Type artists should avoid using abbreviations in running text. Abbreviations for words that could be spelled out easily appear informal— as if the author did not have time to write the word. The names of states, for example, look hastily written, as with *CA* or *Calif.,* when abbreviated in running text. The type artist should spell out those words, as in *California,* unless they appear in tabulated material, in which case *Calif.* is preferred. This applies to months, *February* rather than *Feb.,* and to days of the week, *Tuesday* rather than *Tues.* Symbols for trademarks and registered names,™ and ®, are not included in running text.

Aside from guidelines for the abbreviations A.M., P.M., B.C., B.C.E., A.D., and C.E. discussed previously (which are exceptions to this rule), other exceptions occur in personal names, as in *John J. Jingleheimer, Jr.* With the full name preceding it, the abbreviation *Jr.* or *III* is an acceptable part of a person's full name. The example, *Mr. Jingleheimer, Jr.,* is

ABBREVIATIONS AND SYMBOLS

✦ Avoid abbreviations in continuous text.

✦ Abbreviations are suitable in lists, tabular material, and notes.

$$\text{I}\atop\text{O} \; \to \; !$$

Abbreviation of the Latin word *Io* is the precursor of the exclamation point.

$$\text{Q}\atop\text{O} \; \to \; ?$$

Abbreviation of the Latin word *quaestio* is the precursor of the question mark.

incorrect because the full name does not precede the abbreviation. The full-name distinction applies to abbreviations at the front of names as well, for example, *Gen. George Washington* or *General Washington.* When writing the names of ships, which are always italicized, the letters preceding them are part of the name and are set in roman small caps, as in RMS *Titanic.*

Abbreviations for academic degrees also are acceptable in text, when they follow a full name. Abbreviating a person's given name in text is not acceptable. Abbreviations such as *Wm.* and *Benj.* should appear as initials or as spelled-out names, *William* and *Benjamin.*

▲ The USS *Enterprise* has been cruising around the galaxy for decades.

Unit-of-measure abbreviations are appropriate only with figures. They are suitable for tabulated material, in lists, or within equations. In some instances a symbol replaces the abbreviation and further streamlines the material for improved reader comprehension. In an equation or dimension, such as $4" \times 9"$, the dimensional symbol (representing the word *by*) is an actual symbol, not the lowercase x of the text font. The symbol for the unit of measure is repeated with each figure.

A common exception occurs with percentages. In any context, a figure represents the percentage quantity and the percent symbol (%) follows in technical text. The word *percent,* however, follows the figure in humanist text.

▲ The cat ate only 75 percent of her breakfast.
✍ The dog ate 100% of her breakfast and 25 percent of the cat's.

When abbreviations are acceptable in running text, the type artist should not allow a line break to separate the abbreviation from its quantity or name. Some applications enable the type artist to insert a nonbreaking space or to join figure-and-word groupings so a line break cannot occur. This shortens proofreading time by eliminating these never-acceptable errors.

Foreign Terms and Definitions

◆ Italicize an unfamiliar foreign-language word or term.

FOREIGN TERMS IN TEXT CAN CONFUSE A READER if they appear unexpectedly. An isolated German word might appear misspelled within English text if it is not identified properly. Italicizing the word alerts the reader that the term (one or more words) is special. The type artist does not set off the word with commas. The change in letter style is sufficient.

Over time some foreign-language words are used so frequently, such as the French term *hors d'œuvre* (outside of the work), that they are accepted into the domestic language and are no longer italicized. These words are then included in English-language dictionaries.

▲ The art opening was exciting and the hors d'œuvres were scrumptious.

If a definition follows the foreign term, the type artist has two alternative treatments. Placing the definition in parentheses after the word clarifies the meaning for the reader immediately. The definition might be critical for understanding the sentence fully; but if it ranks with the same importance as the other words, it might confuse the reader. No additional punctuation marks are needed. This typographic treatment causes the least text disruption. The second type treatment requires inserting four, rather than two, additional punctuation marks. The type artist uses quotation marks around the definition and sets it off with commas.

▲ *Gesundheit* (good health) is heard after someone sneezes in our family.
▲ *Gesundheit,* "good health," is heard after someone sneezes in our family.

WHEN AN AUTHOR USES A WORD OR TERM OUTSIDE ITS functional capacity, the reader needs a visual signal indicating the word's change of purpose. In the following sentence, the words *old style* are identified by a style change so the reader does not misunderstand the sentence:

Some typographers disagree with the term *old style* to describe text figures.

The italicized type signals the reader to view both words as a single entity, just as an italicized book title indicates the name of a single object. Some typographers prefer to set off the word with quotation marks, but this adds too much clutter to a type line, especially when multiple words are cited. Authors also use letters outside their normal functional capacities. By italicizing the letter, the author identifies its role in the sentence as the topic of conversation rather than a component of it—the letter *M*. Many times letters and words used in this capacity are preceded by the words *the letter* or *the word*, respectively.

WORDS AND LETTERS AS WORDS AND LETTERS

◆ Italicize a word or letter used outside its functional capacity.
◆ Set letters used as shapes in sans serif type.

Letters are used also as shapes to describe other objects. Letter shapes are so distinct and visually descriptive that they are an acceptable shorthand in text. These letters are set in a sans serif typeface within the text. This unique typographic treatment identifies their special function, just as italic type identifies the foreign word. If the shape of a slab serif typeface represents the shape more accurately, the type artist can use it.

The use of letters as shapes is infrequent. If on the rare chance there are several in close proximity, the type artist should keep the sentence from looking like a type catalogue by limiting the number of typefaces.

▲ The letter *M* represents one thousand as a Roman numeral.
▲ The A-frame house reminded me of our vacation in Switzerland. The skyscraper used many *I*-beams in its construction. I (*slab serif*)

Web and E-mail Addresses

+ Italicize URL and e-mail addresses.
+ End-of-line divisions occur before all punctuation and symbols, but after the double slash in the protocol tag.
+ Never break using end-of-line hyphenation.

Electronic addresses identify web sites, web pages, and electronic mailboxes for consumers and individuals using unique character combinations. Unlike street addresses that have a familiar arrangement of figure, name, and road type, such as *123 Forest Drive,* a uniform resource locator (URL) or e-mail address is a distinct, run-on collection of case-sensitive letters, punctuation marks, and symbols. Because of their unusual configuration, italicizing the address helps the reader view it in its entirety. The common protocol tag *http://* can be eliminated, but all others must be included. If set parenthetically, only parentheses are used, not angle brackets. The domain name alone in text, however, indicating an organization, such as *moveon.org,* is set in lowercase roman.

Dividing these lengthy addresses at the end of a line without altering them is challenging. They can never be hyphenated. To minimize confusion, the type artist breaks the line at these three locations: *after* the double slashes following the protocol tag, *before* all punctuation and symbols, and *after* whole words or syllables (without adding a hyphen). Normal sentence punctuation follows the address.

ℱ

The outspoken Eric Gill is quoted as saying, "There are now about as many different varieties of letters as there are different kinds of fools" (Gill 1936). An appropriate rewording of this quote fits this chapter. There are now as many special functions requiring specific typographic treatments as there are typefaces. Using these treatments improves the readability and the typographic form of the page.

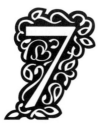

TYPESETTING
AS
DESIGN

For those who love working with type, augmenting and embellishing it is a natural outgrowth of this penchant. Incorporating typographic design elements into a page of text is an age-old practice that has served a variety of purposes. Italian printers Giovani and Alberto Alvise are thought to be the first printers to use *fleurons* (floral foundry ornaments), in the 1478 book *Ars Moriendi*. The fleurons completed short measures of text type for justified alignment and decorated the title page, integrating the fleurons with the display type. Aldus Manutius used ornaments in a 1499 text to complete an inverted triangular-shaped text block when the measures in the tapering shape became too short. These typographic ornaments were suitable design additions to the typeset page because they were designed as characters within a specific type family. Giambattista Bodoni designed many accompanying ornaments for his typefaces in the late eighteenth and early nineteenth centuries. The design features of the ornaments were identical to those of his typeface characters and consequently their visual characteristics supported the mood evoked by the typeface.

Even as typographers actively supported, designed, and used ornaments, they expressed concern that improper use of these elements would detract from the main goal of typographic printing—the communication of content. Typical of their concern was Frederic Warde's 1928 warning that excessive adornment of type would distract the reader with "a dangerous diversion." Warde wrote that ornaments, or printer's

The ornamentation of printing is … charming because of its power to add beauty to the strict simplicity of type; dangerous because all matters of decoration call upon the utmost discretion and sense of fitness for their effective use.

—————————F. Warde
Printers Ornaments
on the 'Monotype'

Through the
Looking Glass

Semibold headline in one point size

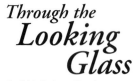

Semibold italic headline in two
point sizes

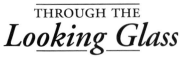

Headline using regular small caps,
semibold italic, and rules

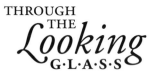

Headline using regular small caps,
italic with swash cap, semibold small
caps, and bullets

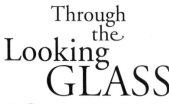

Headline using regular weights with
swash e and titling caps

flowers, were a preferred choice for type ornamentation because of the family resemblance with the corresponding typeface (McLean 1995). Warde's advice to typographers was to use "the utmost discretion and sense of fitness for the effective use" of these ornaments—still good advice today.

In a famous 1932 address to the British Typographers Guild at the St. Bride Institute in London, Beatrice Warde (1900–69), an American typographer, type historian, and eloquent spokesperson for typography, equated the role of a well-set type page to that of a crystal wine goblet. Both the type page and the crystal goblet, she wrote, transport their contents in an elegant and unobtrusive vessel that enhances the recipient's appreciation and understanding. "Everything about it [the crystal goblet] is calculated to reveal rather than to hide the beautiful thing which it was meant to contain." Warde believed that the most important goal of printing was to convey "thought, ideas, images, from one mind to other minds." She went on to state that there was a maze of typographic practices born from excessive enthusiasm that subverted the attainment of that goal, such as inappropriate typeface selection, oversized type, and insufficient word spacing (McLean 1995).

Frederic and Beatrice Warde could only anticipate the mishandling of type possible with the contemporary techniques of the early and mid–twentieth century. They could not begin to imagine the adornment potential for digital typographers at the end of the twentieth century with access to vast type libraries, infinite size and transformation capabilities, and the structure-altering multiple master technology available on desktop computer systems. Even so, Frederic Warde's advice from 1928 still holds true for these technologies, as well as those yet to come. Digitally generated design elements should support and clarify the content by maintaining the "utmost discretion and sense of fitness." If the enhancement of type through inclusion of design elements facilitates the author's link to the reader's mind, then these elements support the author's goal, rather than divert from it. For the type artist seeking to incorporate design elements into display or text type, selecting from a palette of type family styles, sizes, alternate glyphs, and ornaments is a prudent beginning that helps ensure a unified page design. The more expert digital typographer can create effective design additions by combining typefaces, families, and style-appropriate graphics. With the goal clearly in mind—facilitating communication—the type artist's contribution can be both sophisticated and effective—similar in elegance and beauty to a crystal wine goblet.

Adding typographic design elements to a page can begin by controlling the type sizes and styles in the headline. Why is it necessary that all words in a headline be the same size or style? By controlling the type size, type style, and placement of words in a headline, a savvy type artist can introduce a creative, unique, eye-catching typographic design element to the page.

The italic styles of many type families contain elegantly proportioned letters suitable for a unique, graceful headline. The Adobe Caslon, Adobe Garamond, and Minion type families include swash letterforms that add another level of visual interest while conveying a message of sophistication. The italic and roman styles of these typefaces contain alternate glyphs with swash endings suitable for a decorative headline. A complementary script typeface can add the flourish a headline needs for a script-appropriate article. A well-placed ornament with a rule or two can give a headline a more pronounced presentation. Type artists can use all the possibilities a typeface provides, but should keep in mind that too much of a good thing dilutes its impact. Effective type artists must choose and use these type elements judiciously to enhance the visual presentation.

Alice

IN WONDERLAND

Headline using italic word with swash cap, regular small caps, ornament, and rule

Benjamin
Franklin
(1706–1790) writer
inventor &
statesman

FIGURE 7-1: *Caflisch Script headline*

Typefaces have a uniform design structure that moves the eye through the letters and words to the conclusion of a thought. Applying these same fluid movements to a designed headline is a natural application of the design inherent in most typefaces. Calligraphic typefaces, such as Caflisch Script (fig. 7-1), Ex Ponto (see fig. 7-2), Boulevard, Bickham Script (see fig. 7-7), Spring (see fig. 9-25), Aristocrat, Ruling Script Two (the list goes on and on), with their quick, expressive strokes, transform a staid, tightly corseted headline into a symphony of movement and a celebratory display of energy and awe.

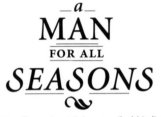

a
MAN
FOR ALL
SEASONS

Headline using Minion semibold italic, caps, small caps, italic caps with swash *S*, ornament, and rules

WORKING WITH ALTERNATE GLYPHS

$\mathcal{A}A$ KK RR SS
ee nn rr tt zz
ct ct st st vv ❧ ♣

Adobe Garamond regular and italic
with selected alternate glyphs,
ornaments, and ligatures

A digital typeface with a 256-character limit has little room for multiple designs of the same letterform. Fortunately, certain type families come with customized branches on their family tree. The Adobe Garamond family has an alternate regular and an alternate italic that add several roman lowercase letters, swashed surrogates for all italic capitals, ornaments, and extra ligatures. With the OpenType format, these separate font files of alternates are united in the same typeface.

Other typefaces differentiate alternate glyphs into use groupings. Ex Ponto has three: beginnings, letters with swashes that extend from the letter's left side, suitable for use at the beginning of a line; endings, letters with swashes that extend from the letter's right side, suitable for use at the end of a line; and alternates, structurally altered substitute letters, suitable for more extensive type customization. When a type artist becomes familiar with these unique typeface glyphs, the number of design enhancements possible increases significantly.

*A thing of beauty
is a joy forever*

Original Ex Ponto typeface

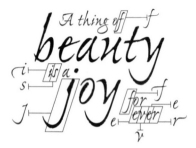

FIGURE 7-2: *Ex Ponto type graphic for quote by Keats*

Ex Ponto (created by Jovica Veljović) is used in the Keats quote about beauty (fig. 7-2). The original letterforms demonstrate the calligraphic beauty and expressive flair inherent in the typeface. After altering word placement and size, the typeface's design characteristics become more actively involved in the delivery of the message, thereby diminishing their role as "transparent" messenger. In the final iteration two beginning alternates, two ending alternates, and four alternate glyphs enhanced the graphic's design and helped determine each word's final location. In its lowered position, the *J* in *joy* was an uppercase letter; the horizontal stroke at its head better defined the word's mean line. All letters were set in the regular weight regardless of point size. This gave visual emphasis to the words *beauty* and *joy* just as a speaker would give audible emphasis when reading the quote aloud. In this instance of

Substituted alternate glyphs for
improved design

type for discontinuous reading, typeface transparency is not an overriding principle; graphic concerns dominate, enhancing the message and also attracting the reader to it.

The typeface Galahad (created by Alan A. Blackman) has an array of alternate glyphs that expand the typographic design possibilities throughout a graphic. The letters in the first version of the Arts *&* Crafts Movement graphic (fig. 7-3) are set in Galahad Regular. After resizing selected words for improved emphasis, ten different alternate glyphs were inserted to improve the visual movement through the words. The *f-t* ligature in the word *Crafts* nestled these two letterforms together so the ascender of the *f* flowed smoothly into the stem of the *t*. A shared crossbar joined the two letterforms. The letters *r* and *t* in the word *Arts* would have benefited from a ligature, because their positioning with regular and alternate glyphs was not satisfactory. Aligning the end of the alternate *r*'s swash ear with the stem of the *t* caused an overlap that darkened the texture and diminished legibility. The solution was a fake ligature. By duplicating the *r,* changing it to white, and using it as a spacer, the two letters aligned nicely, while legibility and typographic texture improved.

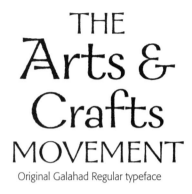

Original Galahad Regular typeface

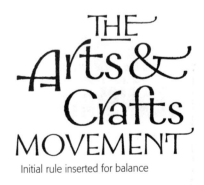

Original letter placement (left); fake ligature solution (right)

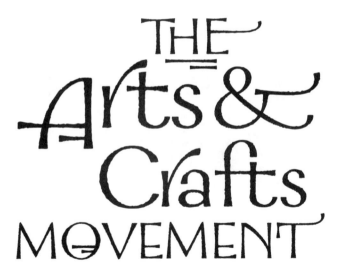

FIGURE 7-3: *Arts & Crafts Movement graphic in Galahad*

With word and letter placement finalized, a rule was inserted beneath the word *THE*. The rule was intended to balance the double horizontal rules inside the alternate *A,* but it was insufficient. In the final

Initial rule inserted for balance

iteration (see fig. 7-3), a double rule (similar to those used in the letter *A*) was positioned under the word *THE* and within the counter of the capital *O* in the word *MOVEMENT*. The Galahad em and en dashes were used as the long and short rules to maintain the typeface design style (rough calligraphic strokes with flaired endings).

WITH THE VOLUME OF TYPEFACES AND FAMILIES available in the digital type environment, it is not uncommon for enthusiastic type artists to overindulge. If more than two type families are being used in a document or on a page, the type artist's internal alarm should sound and a good design case made for this use. Just as setting an important document in all caps to signify its noteworthiness is counterproductive to the point of being unreadable, so too is employing multiple type families merely for their attention-getting characteristics. This visual clash has the same effect as a roomful of arm-waving kindergartners all trying to answer a question simultaneously—visual chaos (without the noise). Design is organization. Too many competing typefaces defy organization, confuse the reader, and do not speak with one voice.

COMBINING TYPEFACES

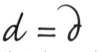

Alternate lowercase *d* suggests sprouting bean

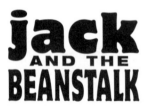

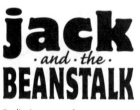

Preliminary typeface treatments for words *and* and *the*

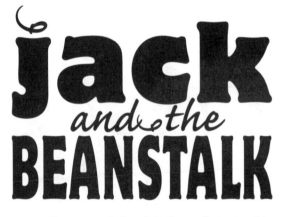

FIGURE 7-4: *Jack and the Beanstalk type graphic*

A well-chosen combination of two typefaces can make an otherwise plain headline into a visually enhanced statement. The key component to a successful visual marriage is contrast. Using two similar typefaces, such as Times and Minion, in a document would have a puzzling effect on the reader. Some readers might not realize they are seeing two different typefaces, but will suspect something is wrong with the type. Once readers start puzzling about the type, they are no longer listening to the author. Contrasting typefaces eliminate the uncertainty; the design difference is obvious. If they are an appropriate selection, both typefaces add or emphasize something about the subject matter.

In the Jack and the Beanstalk graphic (fig. 7-4), the typeface Motter Corpus (designed by Othmar Motter) was used for the words *jack* and *BEANSTALK* to emphasize the giant's size in this well-known tale. The words *and the* were set in Caflisch Script because the script is visually reminiscent of the beanstalk's vining tendrils. The sprouting-bean shape used to dot the lowercase *j* and as ornamentation between the words *and* and *the* was a flipped and rotated alternate character for the letter *d*. Several iterations illustrate the design process for this headline. The final graphic (fig. 7-4) shows a light touch with the design elements that strikes a balance between readability and graphic enhancement.

The use of multiple typefaces on a page was in its heyday with wood type during the period from 1830 to 1870. Wood type was used primarily for display faces in advertisements and posters, because above 144 points, a single metal sort was extremely heavy, awkward to use, and its manufacture was problematic.

Darius Wells was the champion of wood type. He imported English boxwood because of its fine grain for the manufacture of these typefaces. The fine grain was less prone to splintering and enabled the production of intricately designed typefaces, when used in conjunction with his invention, the lateral wood router. The detailed designs of this period were later revived in the 1960s when phototypography proved to be an equally flexible medium for a wide range of typeface designs.

When using the wood type typographic style, design principles still dictate what typefaces work together well. In the example (see fig. 7-5), the words *WOODEN TYPEFACES,* set in Thunderbird and Rosewood respectively, deliver the primary message. Size, intricacy of design, color, and proximity all work to make this the most eye-catching element in the type graphic. The date 1830–70 is set in the heavy black Madrone typeface. It is reminiscent of the color and weight of *WOODEN,* thus linking it visually to the primary type elements. The secondary pieces of information *ENGLISH BOXWOOD* and *DARIUS WELLS* border the piece on top and bottom. They serve as bookends holding the graphic together while relating back to the primary type elements in the interior. The curves of the Juniper typeface, along the top, relate back to the curves in Thunderbird and Madrone, while the shadowed Horndon typeface, along the bottom, balances the white of the Rosewood typeface in the interior.

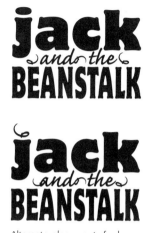

Alternate placements for lowercase *d* ornamentation

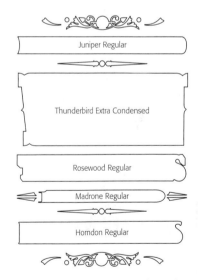

Wooden Typefaces typeface legend

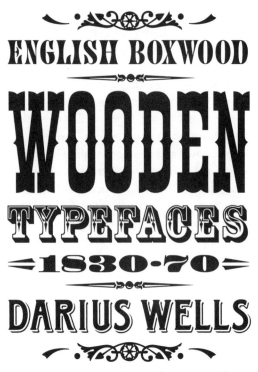

The choice of appropriate ornaments is important also. The ornaments were chosen for their style and mimic the typefaces' heavy, carved design features. The date-line ornaments were put together to create the weight and emphasis required for their location. They relate to the pointed ornament directly below and above the primary type message (fig. 7-5). These tapered diamond shapes are repeated inside the Rosewood typeface. The heavy floral ornaments at the top and bottom are style appropriate and effectively balance the color of the heavy Thunderbird and Madrone typefaces. Two curved, dotted ornaments were added on each side of the floral ornament to extend their width.

Unifying and balancing the style of these visual elements throughout the type graphic emphasizes its overall rectangular shape. In a design variation of the graphic (see margin graphic), the delicate, open style of the ornaments relates to itself, but does not relate strongly to the heavy typefaces. Consequently, ornament areas are lighter in color causing the overall shape of the graphic to be a top-heavy hourglass rather than a rectangle. This affects the delivery of the message. The ornament

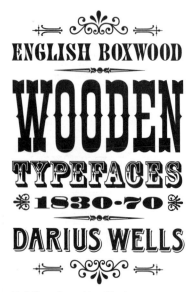

Variation of graphic with alternate ornaments

flourishes accentuate the curves and points of the Thunderbird typeface, increasing its visual impact. The quantity of white added by the ornaments diminishes the impact of the Rosewood word *TYPEFACES,* weakening the link between the two primary type elements *WOODEN* and *TYPEFACES* and jumbling the message. While the graphic is still well designed and visually interesting, this design change alters the message—the primary reason for the typography.

THE USE OF ORNAMENTS FOR GRAPHICALLY ENHANCING display type can emphasize the elegant lines of a well-designed typeface, such as Robert Slimbach's Poetica (1992). In the graphic of the word *fleurons* a host of typeface characters—ornaments, alternates, and punctuation marks—come together to make this unique visual (fig. 7-6). Poetica is a challenging typeface to use because there are so many alternate glyphs from which to chose. For example, there are nine swash capitals available for *each* letter. There are separate groupings for lowercase alternates, lowercase beginnings, lowercase endings, ligatures, ampersands, and ornaments.

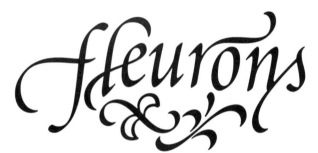

FIGURE 7-6: *Fleurons type graphic in Poetica*

The original word *fleurons* was set in Poetica Chancery III, a heavily swashed chancery cursive typeface with long ascenders and descenders. The increased emphasis on swashes made it the best selection from the Poetica family. When designing a single-word type graphic, the ability to balance the chosen letters is a major concern. Poetica offers many alternate letterforms, but only the ones used at the beginning of the word that can be successfully balanced at the end of the word would be suitable. Several alternatives for the beginning were considered before the final selection was made. The final word used three lowercase beginnings, one lowercase ending, and one lowercase alternate.

Original Poetica typeface

Preliminary alternate beginnings

Curved baseline placement

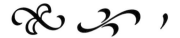

Poetica ornaments (left, center) and apostrophe (right)

The letters in *fleurons* do not share a common baseline. The visual flow between adjacent letter swashes dictated their positions, resulting in a curved baseline. The interior of the curve was the perfect location for the ornaments. From Poetica's 44 available ornaments, two were chosen to best continue the word's visual movement and maintain the swash-heavy style of the graphic. The ornaments were angled and, as with the letters, optically aligned with the swashes in the word. The design's final iteration used an apostrophe as an ornament to complete the movement from the ornaments back into the word.

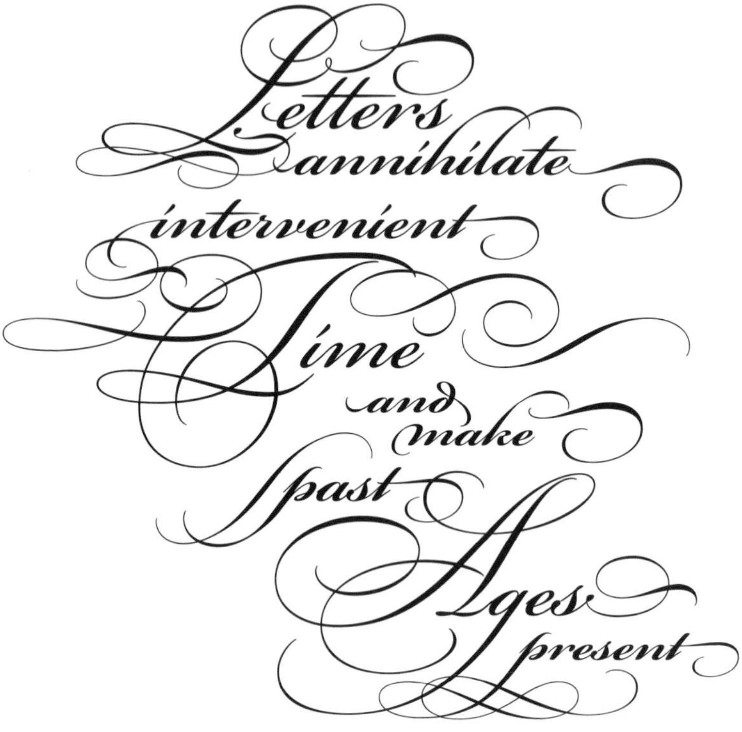

FIGURE 7-7: *Calligraphic type graphic for quote by Bickham*

Letters annihilate
intervenient Time
and make
past Ages present

Original Bickham Script typeface

The typeface Bickham Script (created by Richard Lipton) is based on the calligraphy of George Bickham (Elder), an eighteenth-century calligrapher and engraver, and his contemporaries. Samples from 25 calligraphers of that time period appear in Bickham's book *The Universal Penman* (1743). These writing masters created letters and words of varying sizes using a nibbed pen held at a prescribed angle. By maintaining a consistent nib angle throughout the work, the calligraphers achieved the same stroke endings, stress placement, and stroke weight for all letters regardless of size. If the calligrapher made the first letter of a word larger than the remaining letters, the stroke weight for the word stayed consistent, because the tool and its handling remained the same. The visual result was a medley of consistent thicks and thins regardless of letter size "… performed with boldness and freedom," as Bickham described. In these ornate calligraphic designs, elegant swirls created swash letters and orchestrated the negative space of the page into fluid lines of motion to guide the reader's eye around the page.

Unlike calligraphy, enlarging a digital letterform increases not only the overall size, but the relative stroke weight, as well. The larger letter has a heavier stroke than the rest of the letters in the word. Visually, the first letter dominates. While this is a useful design technique for a versal at the beginning of a paragraph, it may not be appropriate for other typographic situations. To achieve the same visual stroke-weight consistency in a type graphic, for example, the type artist must be more resourceful. The Bickham quote (fig. 7-7) incorporates three different type weights to create this unifying effect with three different type sizes.

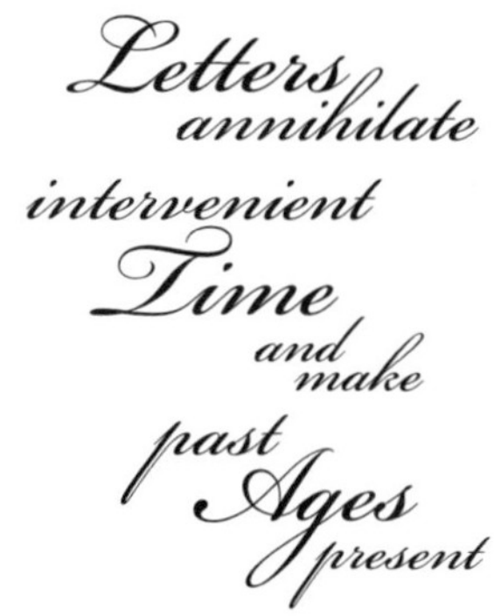

Original Bickham Script Regular typeface resized and repositioned

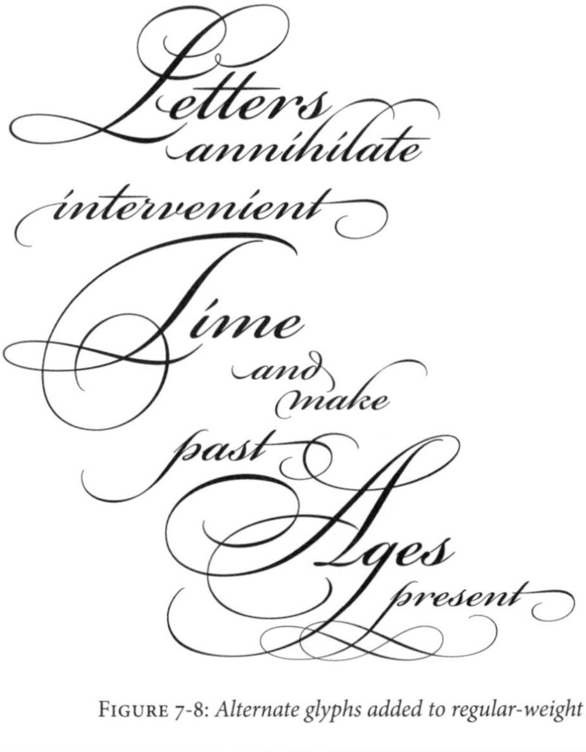

FIGURE 7-8: *Alternate glyphs added to regular-weight script*

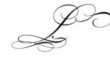

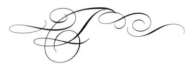

Added ornaments increase emphasis and unify letters with surroundings.

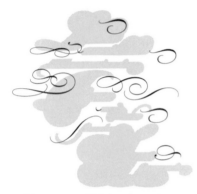

Ornaments and joining elements

TEXT TYPE DESIGN

Bickham Script offers extensive alternate glyphs divided into categories of swash capitals, lowercase (stylistic, beginnings, endings), ornaments, and swash joining elements that are representative of this time period. The quote was originally set in Bickham Script's default capital and lowercase letters, which have the uniform, controlled appearance of disciplined penmanship. After repositioning and resizing the regular-weight words for emphasis and design, swash capitals and stylistic alternatives were substituted to enhance eye movement through the words and word groupings (see fig. 7-8).

The design of the capital *L* and *T* in the words *Letters* and *Time* did not blend as well into the surrounding letters as did the capital *A* in *Ages.* The *L* in particular needed greater emphasis since it was the entry point into the graphic. In a technique reminiscent of the eighteenth-century calligraphers, ornaments were added to the *L* and *T* to give these swash capitals additional emphasis to control readability and to unify them more effectively with their surroundings. Additional ornaments and joining elements were added to orchestrate the negative spaces and unify the entire graphic by repeating elements found in the alternate letters and swash capitals.

To equalize the stroke weights between the three different point sizes used in the quote, the largest point size (120 points) was set in the thinnest weight (regular), the smallest point size (72 points) in the heaviest weight (bold), and the middle point size (90 points) in semibold. All ornaments and joining elements were set in bold to strengthen their hairlines.

FOR THE TYPE ARTIST READY FOR THE NEXT LEVEL OF typographic design, similar opportunities are possible with paragraphs of text. Text design has an increased level of difficulty for creative design, but nothing that care and thought cannot handle. Beyond the text decisions for alignment, measure, type size, and leading, the type artist can integrate text type with other page elements (type or visuals) through the use of text wraps. *Text wrapping* is a text-design technique that embeds a letter, type block, photograph, or illustration into a block of text. The wrapping of text around the element occurs by controlling where lines of text type stop and start. In addition, shaped-text blocks are possible but are more challenging.

Text and headlines usually maintain a polite distance from one another with the headline first, then a band of white, followed by the text paragraphs. It is easier to distinguish these elements one from another with this traditional placement, but it is not the only way to present the information (see chapter 10). When these two mingle, or visually connect, they present a more varied, and more enticing, visual environment within which to move the reader's eye. There are three kinds of text wraps—runarounds, contoured wraps, and shaped-text wraps.

A *runaround* refers to a rectangular shape, such as a photograph, illustration, or initial letter set into a block of text (fig. 7-9). The paragraph's measure is shortened to make room for the rectangle and then lengthened to its original distance beyond the shape. When a graphic is inset into the text, the type artist aligns the bottom of the inset or its caption (if it has one) with the nearest baseline. This alignment unites the text with the graphic.

A *contoured wrap* refers to an organic shape, such as an illustration or type block, set into a paragraph of text (fig. 7-9). In this situation the text lines follow the contour of the shape or create a contrasting white shape within which the organic shape rests. Type artists use contoured wraps with illustrations, shaped photographs, initial letters, pull quotes, and inset headlines and subheads. Baseline alignment with the inset element is important for all text wraps.

The artist must leave sufficient white space between the inset element and the text. Page-layout and graphic applications provide graphic boundaries that the type artist manipulates to form nonprinting text-repellent fences. The fence determines where the text lines stop or start. If the text is too close to the graphic, the page looks crowded and cramped. If the text is too far away from the graphic, the reader might not realize the relationship between the two elements. Shaping the graphic boundary on screen without the text creates a false impression of adequate white space. The text's gray color makes the white space

In kitchens throughout the United States, famil breakfast of eggs each morning. There are as there are chickens—to cannibalize a quote. Sor soft boiled, over easy, sunny-side up, and oth

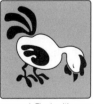 hard boiled, or jus cooking style, the freshest, biggest, the chicken house

Egg producers foll between the farm prevent breakage freshness. First, th Malformed or weak removed. The healthy eggs are packaged amo size. Second, the eggs are chemically stabilize

In kitchens throughout the United States, fami breakfast of eggs each morning. There are as there are chickens—to cannibalize a quote. Sc soft boiled, over easy, sunny-side up, poached, hard boiled, or just fried. style, they all require the freshest, egg from the chicken house.

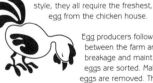 Egg producers follow between the farm an breakage and maint eggs are sorted. Mal eggs are removed. Th packaged among others of similar size. Secon chemically stabilized. A chemical is injected int any further development of the yolk. In the sto

FIGURE 7-9: *Runaround (left) and contoured wrap (right)*

Chickens Prefer B

In kitchens throughout the United
to a breakfast of eggs each morn
egg styles as there are chickens-
Some like scrambled, soft boiled
up, and others prefer poached, h
Whatever the cook
the freshest,
egg from

Egg p
preca
and t
break
freshn
sorted. M
eggs are rem
are packaged amon
Second, the eggs are chemically
injected into the egg to prevent a
of the yolk. In the store, the eggs
display case that keeps the yolk a

Contrasting white egg-shape formed
by contoured wrap

For the
egg-eaters of
the morning world,
there are as many egg
styles for breakfast as there
are chickens. Some like soft
boiled, scrambled, over easy,
sunny-side up, and others prefer
poached, hard boiled, or just
fried. Whatever the cooking
style, they all require the
freshest, biggest, most
perfect egg from the
farmer's chicken
house.

Shaped-text block formed by shaped-
text wrap

INITIAL LETTERS
AND VERSALS

look smaller when viewed with the text. Leaving a generous amount of white space around the graphic actually can prove to be just right once the text is in position on the page.

A *shaped-text wrap* uses the graphic boundaries or an unpainted path to confine a block of text and control its exterior shape. Some applications make this easier to do than others. The type artist uses this technique to create a text block inside a shaped element or as a freestanding text block. A freestanding shaped-text block interacts with other graphic elements on the page, as would any graphic, but includes the additional challenge of maintaining readability.

All three text-wrap alternatives present several text-related problems from which to steer clear. When shortening the measure to make room for an inset element, the type artist needs to monitor the character count so it does not fall below the 40-character minimum. If the measure gets too short, the application may not have the number of options necessary to break lines unobtrusively. In the worst-case scenario, a single word is stretched to fill the space like knots along an elastic thread. Reading comprehension slows to a crawl while the reader quickly assembles the isolated letters. The measure adjacent to the inset element must contain sufficient characters to maintain readability and paragraph texture. If a letter or a type block is inset, the type artist uses the intraparagraph spacing techniques (see chapter 4) to maintain correct vertical rhythm and baseline alignment.

Text wraps enable the type artist to insert a graphic element anywhere in text, including inside a block of text. For example, a type line could begin to the left of the graphic and continue on the right. Just because the application can do something, however, does not mean it is worth doing. All text lines should remain readable as a cohesive unit. If excessive word spacing interrupts a reader's progress along a measure, leaping over an overgrown graphic planted in the middle of a measure can be a real puzzler. In most cases, a single text block should remain to the left or right of the graphic—not both. Positioning text on either side of a graphic requires two columns of text and is a better solution. The graphic is inset into the right side of the left column and into the left side of the right column. The reader easily reads through both columns of text without negotiating the graphic roadblock.

THE SCRIBES OF PRE-GUTENBERG DAYS FUNCTIONED as the "printing presses" of their time. Readers dictated to batteries of scribes who carefully transcribed what they heard. Once the text was complete, there were just as many new copies of the book as there were scribes. It was a slow process and kept the number of available books to a minimum. Despite the shortcomings, there were benefits. The skill of the individual scribe provided subtle style variances to each text. The resulting book was not viewed as one copy out of thousands emerging from an anonymous press, but one unique, handcrafted treasure. The scribes incorporated unique flourishes that distinguished their work from that of others. These hand-drawn documents frequently featured an individualistic focus on the text's first letter.

Initial letters or *versals* evolved from enlarged heavy letters of the sixth century, which called attention to the beginning of the book, into eloquently illustrated letters of the fourteenth century. By the fourteenth century these ornate versals cascaded down the side of the text and extended up and around the top of the page. Religious texts, in particular, received this grand adornment signifying the text's religious importance. Intricate decorations enhanced texts up to and including full-page illustrations. The use of versals in text was such an important page element that Gutenberg left blank space in his printed text for the scribes' artistic embellishments. Some printers printed a small, lower-case typeset letter in the space to identify the specific hand-drawn letter required there. Versals varied from outlined letters to be colored by the *rubricator* (colorist), fifteenth- and sixteenth-century letters surrounded by floral ornamentation, and letters with more pictorial embellishments using animal images (real or mythical) and human forms. (See "Designing Graphic Letters" in chapter 8.)

There are two kinds of initial letters—the drop cap and raised cap. A *drop cap* or *cut-in letter* is embedded within the first few lines of text. The top of the letter aligns with the cap height of the first text line and the drop cap's baseline aligns with the nearest text baseline. The baseline alignment of the drop cap is essential for the letter to be solidly positioned within the text. A *raised cap* or *stick-up letter* sits on the same baseline as the first line of text and towers above the adjacent text block.

Initial letters draw attention to the beginning of a chapter. Not every paragraph merits the attention of the first paragraph. Type artists also use initial letters as typographic section markers and as elements adding visual interest to a page of gray when a document does not contain illustrations, graphic elements, or subheads. Without them the seemingly endless paragraphs might overwhelm the reader.

An initial letter also determines the amount of white space that precedes the paragraph. A drop cap draws attention to the beginning of

W ITH THE ADVENT OF DIGIT
easier to incorporate into
and linecast type. There are two
raised cap. A drop cap or cut-in
few lines of text.
Embedded drop cap with small cap
text transition

W ITH THE ADVENT OF DIGIT
easier to incorporate into text t
linecast type. There are two kin
raised cap. A drop cap or cut-in
few lines of text.
Raised cap with small cap
text transition

W ith the advent of digital
to incorporate into text th
linecast type. There are two kin
raised cap. A drop cap or cut-i
few lines of text.
Isolated drop cap without
text transition

*W*ITH THE ADVENT OF
became easier to incorpor
type and linecast type. There ar
cap or raised cap. A drop cap o
the first few lines of text.

Text transition using regular caps

*W*ith the advent of digita
easier to incorporate into t
linecast type. There are two kin
raised cap. A drop cap or cut-i
few lines of text.

Text transition using larger point size

ROME PROVIDES THE
BACKDROP for a
vacation of spectacular proportions. In the
moonlight the Mediterranean sparkles like

*B*efore the dawn's light
aroused the good people of the
kingdom to another day of toil in the king's
fields, the cows began to rustle in their stalls.

Text transition using initial letter
typeface

the paragraph without adding white space to the page. A stick-up cap inserts additional white space (determined by the initial letter's point size) in front of the paragraph.

Initial letters also aid eye movement around the page. For example, if the headline is embedded in the text (to function as a type graphic when no illustrations are available), it leads the reader's eye away from the first paragraph. An initial letter would attract the reader back to the first paragraph. This technique also works in other situations where the reader enters the page at a point beyond the first paragraph.

Type artists create initial letters with caps, titling caps, lowercase letters, swash letters, script, illustrated letters, or letter and graphic combinations (fig. 7-10). There are many possibilities. Although the letter is a graphic attraction, it also functions as the first letter of the first word or just the first word in the sentence. The size and graphic treatment of this letter require a visual bridge into the text.

If the initial letter is the first letter of the first word, then the first text line should hug the initial letter. The proximity of the two enables the reader to see all the letters of the word together. If the letter is a word by itself, such as *A* or *I,* a larger word space can separate the initial letter from the text line.

UPER HEROES as a group currently find liability insurance a major cause for concern. Ever since a rescue-ee was inadvertently dropped during her rescue, the premiums for the beloved crime fighters have skyrocketed.

FIGURE 7-10: *Initial cap with a few dingbats gives pizzazz to a content-appropriate paragraph*

In either situation, the size difference between the initial letter and the first text line remains a concern. Although not widely practiced, it is necessary to provide a size transition here. Without a transition, an elaborate initial letter functions as an isolated graphic and does not lead the reader into the text. The transition is made by setting the first few words (approximately 12 or more characters) in small caps. Regular caps are an alternative if the typeface does not need or the type artist does not have small caps. Setting these first words in type noticeably larger than the text type (and in a style matching the initial letter) also provides the same transition into the text as the small caps. As with line breaks in a headline, the small caps are applied to a logical collection of words. If the sentence starts with a phrase, it is better to set the entire phrase in small caps. If this technique is used properly, the reader cannot help but read those first few words. Besides adding graphic interest to a page full of text, the initial letter functions as a lure out trolling for readers. Once snagged, they are hauled into the boat (text).

PULL QUOTES ARE SEVERAL LINES OF TYPE USED TO break up large quantities of continuous text. Pull quotes, also called *quote-outs, breakers,* and *grabbers,* serve both a content and a graphic function. They attract the reader to the text's content and provide a visual resting spot. Unlike a subhead that has a precise location in the text, a pull quote's location is not restricted.

Pull quotes range from one to five lines in length. The rules of discontinuous text and headlines apply—lines are divided logically and not hyphenated. The type artist sets pull quotes in a larger type size than the text, coordinates their style with the headline or text, and sets them off with rules, white space, or ornaments. Quotation marks are not needed with excerpted material, but can be effective as a graphic element. Pull quotes, like subheads, break the vertical rhythm of the text. In multiple-column documents, the rules of intraparagraph spacing apply (see "Intraparagraph Spacing" in chapter 4).

For its role in content, the type artist selects a pull quote that reflects the flavor of the article—much like quotes from critics used to advertise a movie or headlines broadcast on television to solicit viewers for the late-night news. The pull quote repeats or paraphrases information contained in the text. Readers quickly skim pull quotes when considering whether to read a document. Arranging these items according to article content is recommended.

A type artist can embed a pull quote into the text and wrap the text around it, as discussed earlier in this chapter. For example, positioning several lines of text within a diamond shape created from two adjacent text columns can add an additional level of visual interest.

With more than one pull quote on a page, the type artist balances and coordinates them with other page elements (see chapter 10). Although some type artists position pull quotes close to the headline for clarification, the pull quote's primary function is breaking up long quantities of text. At the other extreme, locating a pull quote at the bottom of the page may maroon readers unless another graphic entices them back into the page.

PULL QUOTES

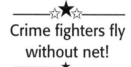

★
**Crime fighters fly
without net!**
★

Subject-appropriate graphic embellishments

"
**There are
as many egg styles
as there are
chickens**
"

Quotation marks as graphic elements

**King's fields
produce royal crop**

Mood-appropriate typeface selection

Shaped-Text Blocks

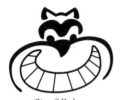

*Alice fell down a
hole at the bottom of a tree.
Many have read her story with
fervor and glee. All the creatures
she met in Wonderland were mad
or ill-bred. A pink Cheshire Cat
told her this as he sat
upon his head.*

Swash capitals identify beginning of
paragraph or line.

SHAPED-TEXT BLOCKS ARE ONE OF THE MOST DIFFICULT type design techniques to use effectively. All the techniques that make it effective graphically make it more difficult to read. When a type artist uses this technique, there is a constant tug-of-war between readability and graphic success. This is definitely an advanced technique that a novice type artist should save for later—much later.

A shaped-text block maintains the integrity of the shape by using justified text alignment. The beginning and ending of each measure creates the shape. The integrity of the whole requires an even texture to prevent holes and rivers from appearing. If the shaped block appears within a graphic, a centered alignment with manually selected line breaks is more successful. The graphic itself maintains the integrity of the shape, and the text functions as a gray fill. Leaving sufficient white space between the block and the graphic's edge prevents the text from appearing cramped.

A stand-alone shaped-text block is the most challenging. This technique involves a large quantity of text, but the paragraph breaks and indents undermine the overall shape. The type artist could solve the problem by running the paragraphs together and eliminating the paragraph breaks. The reader, however, needs the content separation the paragraphs provide. In order to balance the graphic and readability needs, the type artist can use a *pilcrow* (¶), an ornament, or a swash letter at the beginning of every paragraph. This adds white space to the line and indicates a break between each paragraph. (Oswald Cooper used the swash letter technique effectively in the Packard automobile advertisements [see chapter 9].) This technique requires a light touch. Too strong a break riddles the text with graphic elements that detract from the overall shape and distract the reader.

෫ා

TODAY'S DIGITAL TYPE ARTISTS ARE ASKED TO CREATE typographic magic in many environments: electronic media (web pages, video presentations) and traditional print (advertisements, posters, brochures, annual reports). With varying amounts of distractions present in each venue, a resourceful type artist emphasizes different features of the typographic material to improve message delivery on a case-by-case basis. A display-type graphic (fig. 7-11) on a web page or advertisement, for example, can get the reader's attention, before transitioning quickly into the text type where readability is paramount—the same task a graphically enhanced versal performs as the gateway into a lengthy text block.

Visually competitive typographic environments challenge type artists to experiment with new techniques while trying to achieve the same goal from centuries past—successful communication of the message. With all the typographic options available within type families, there is an extensive, well-equipped type palette from which to select.

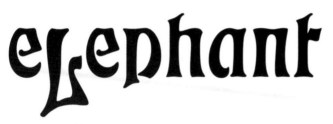

FIGURE 7-11: *Restructured letter functioning as graphic within a word*

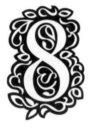

GRAPHICS
AS
TYPE

Often typography is the main or only graphic element in a design. This is a common solution when the subject matter is too broad or complex.... Letterforms are inherently more abstract than pictures, consequently more useful for this kind of problem.

_____Glaser
Milton Glaser Graphic Design

WHEN THE DESIGN COMMUNITY EMBRACED THE USE of phototypography in the 1960s, designers found new ways to express their ideas typographically. Phototypography went beyond the practice of integrating type and visuals as adjacent elements on the page. It also enabled a physical union of letterforms and graphics. Gone were the limitations of typeface, letterspacing, size, and type style that were ever-present with foundry and cast type. Gone too was the strict separation between typesetters and designers. Through the use of lenses, for example, type could be slanted to a designer-specified angle. By the manipulation of film and developing during typesetting, typesetters could superimpose one letter on another. With this new technology, the purview of designer and typesetter began to overlap. Designers depended on typesetters to execute their graphic ideas within the walls of the type foundry.

Designers, such as Milton Glaser, Seymour Chwast, and Herbert Lubalin, to name only a few, embraced this technology and explored its capabilities. Their design work encouraged an explosion of type manipulation and a recognition that type was a graphic as well as a readable element. Illustrations served as letters within words or were interwoven into the letters as if they were three-dimensional, stand-alone elements. Letters and typefaces were created from anything—people, animals, and inanimate objects.

Such type treatment was not invisible. Its goal was twofold—readability and graphic expression, but not necessarily in that order.

Compromises between readability, legibility, and graphic communication were struck on a project-by-project basis. As illustrative or graphic elements, these typographic solutions fell into the category of typography for discontinuous reading. A highly manipulated word or two would not suffer diminished readability because the amount of text was small. The type's attention-getting capabilities far outweighed the effects of a change in word shape for such a limited use. This form of typographic exploration continued into the next generation of typesetting technology—digital typography.

With digital typography, the world of the designer and the typesetter merged. High-resolution output devices, professional-grade graphics programs, and new font technologies enable type artists to impose graphic effects on an existing letterform; use letters as masks for digital photographs; and manipulate the fundamental structure of each letter. An experienced type artist with an eye for the subtle nuances of strokes, endings, and spaces, can create exciting display-type graphics with these capabilities.

SPECIAL TYPE EFFECTS STRENGTHEN A WORD'S IMPACT and at the same time provide a graphic element to the page. Different techniques are possible with various computer-graphic applications or application filters. For example, some applications can take a letter's outline and create a three-dimensional letter. Other applications can place type on a curving, even freeform baseline, so a sentence wanders up and down on an invisible path. Some effects maintain the standard type controls, such as kerning, tracking, and word spacing. Others do not.

If the effect requires converting the type to outlines, the letter or word is transformed into a graphic image shaped as a letterform. The type controls for kerning and such are no longer available. The special effects that require type conversion are the most complicated. Executing them requires drawing, design, and type skills. If there is a chance the type artist might need to edit the converted text, it is wise to keep the file in two forms—one with the text as outlines and one without.

Graphic applications offer many transformation techniques that artists apply to all graphic elements. By converting a type block to outlines (making it a graphic element), the type artist can apply these same transformation techniques to create interesting type effects. The following sections demonstrate some of the many special effects possible with type. As with all graphic effects, a light touch provides a focal point for a page; a heavy touch overwhelms, rather than dazzles, the reader.

SPECIAL TYPE EFFECTS

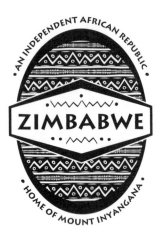

Setting type on a path

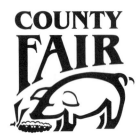

Arcing the word's bottom edge

Shaded emboss

Texture emboss

Arc. There are two ways to approach the arc effect—setting type on a path or arcing the bottom or top edges of a word or words. The first simply places a line of text on a shaped path. The type artist sets it on a circle or on a wavy line with text above and below. All standard type controls remain with text on a path.

The second approach requires converting the word to outlines and manipulating the structure of the letter to arc the bottom or top. In order for a bottom or top arc to succeed, the type artist must maintain the stroke width of the arced strokes. In some letters, the entire stroke curves; in others, it is just the bottom edge.

Embossing. Embossing is an easy technique to use. The type artist controls the fill of the type and its placement on the page to create the embossment illusion. There are two embossed effects—the shaded emboss and the texture emboss.

The *shaded emboss* uses two copies of the same type block. The copy on top (closest to the viewer) has an opaque white fill. The copy in back has a tint fill and defines some of the white type's edges. Neither type block has an outline. The depth of the emboss is determined by adjusting how much of the tinted type block shows on the edge of the white copy.

The *texture emboss* creates a textured surface and then embosses type in it. It requires three copies of the type block on top of an area of texture. This special effect makes a striking initial letter. First, the type artist creates a shaped area of texture. Coarse textures do not work well for this effect. This shaped area of texture functions as the background for the initial letter. Second, the type artist converts the letter to outlines and makes two additional copies. One letter receives a fill of the same texture as the shaped background. Another letter receives an opaque white fill, and the last letter receives a black fill. The type artist places the black letter on the textured background first. Third, the white letter is placed a few points to the left and up from the position of the black letter. Lastly, the textured letter is placed on top of the two, so some of the black letter shows to the bottom right of the textured letter and some of the white letter shows to the top left of the textured letter.

Shadowing. The shadowing effect includes two kinds of shadows—a drop shadow and a cast shadow. A *drop shadow* is a simple effect to achieve. The type maintains its integrity as a type block with all appropriate type controls. The type artist makes a copy of the type in solid black and positions the copy behind the original, but down and to the right of its original location. The type on top receives a different fill or it has an outline with an opaque white fill. The visual result makes the outlined type appear to be floating above the surface of the page; the greater the size of the black drop shadow, the greater distance above the page. (Variations in color and texture may be used also.)

Some typefaces come with a drop shadow. In those cases, the type appears three-dimensional. The shadow is connected to each letter and the viewer sees two sides of it. Other typefaces use a hairline stroke that mirrors the letter's shape on two sides to create the dimensional effect. Some applications provide filters or special effects for creating the shadow as needed.

The *cast shadow* effect requires two copies of the text block. The first remains as a text block and the second is converted to outlines, filled with a gradient, and angled. The position of the angled shadow (in front of the word or behind the word) makes the word appear to be casting a shadow onto an imaginary surface.

Zooming. The zoom effect creates a three-dimensional type block that appears to be coming closer to the viewer and leaves a gradient trail in its wake, extending from its original position to its final position. A type artist creates this effect in a graphic application by creating a blend between a small version of the type block (converted to outlines) and a larger outline version of the type block. Some graphic applications prepackage the effect and essentially talk the artist through the zoom development; others provide the capabilities that the artist applies to the type's outline. In either case, an effective zoom is achieved by controlling the size and color of the two type blocks and the number of blend steps between them.

SPECIAL TYPE EFFECTS EMBELLISH THE APPEARANCE of an existing typeface letterform. Designing graphic letters involves creating a new, one-of-a-kind letterform for use with existing typeface letters. Type and graphic designers have used a host of items representing various objects, animals, vegetables, or minerals to create single letters or entire alphabets. Designing an alphabet from a ballet slipper or a fire hydrant is a challenge of the type designer's design, structure, and style skills (see "Designing Graphic Alphabets" in chapter 9). Designing a single letter for an unusual initial letter or to fit within a single word adds a graphic element to the headline and possibly eliminates the need for an illustration. If the letter is the only one of its kind, as is a graphic versal in text, for example, the type artist is free to design the letter according to any design structure appropriate for the subject matter. If the letter appears

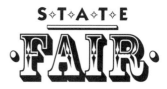

The word *FAIR* set in Rosewood, a true drop shadow typeface

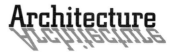

Cast shadow effect on word set in Berthold City type

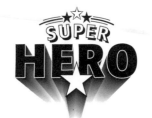

Drop shadow effect on word *SUPER* and zoom effect on *HERO*

DESIGNING GRAPHIC LETTERS

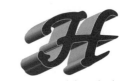

Software-generated drop shadow

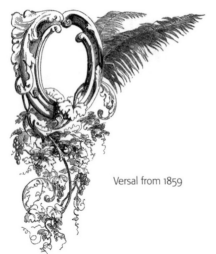

Versal from 1859

within a word set in an existing typeface, the letter must adhere to the design style and structure of the typeface (fig. 8-1).

rabbits

FIGURE 8-1: *The b-rabbits adhere to the Garamond style*

As discussed in chapter 7, the use of versals in text is an age-old practice from before the time of Gutenberg. Designing letters from other objects is not new either. The versal *O* (see margin graphic) comes from the 1859 two-volume set the *Pictorial Field-Book of the Revolution* by Benson J. Lossing (Harper *&* Brothers, New York). This versal is a combination of leaves, grapevines, and feathers. All elements are intricately woven to make this unique letter a dramatic introduction to the first chapter of the second volume. All other chapters of both volumes start with more diminutive versals (fig. 8-2), some incorporating existing letterforms into an illustration, such as a letter displayed on a building, and others created from existing objects, such as the letters *T* and *S* made from malleable tree stumps and branches. Objects from nature are particularly good images for these letters because of their flexibility. As the type artist becomes more familiar with designing letterforms, it is easier to see how virtually anything can be redesigned to make a convincing, legible letterform. The bicycle *S* versal is appropriate for an article on summer cycling, and the stylized oak *A* versal is suitable for an article on the environmental contributions of oak trees.

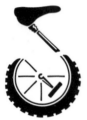

Bicycle versal for letter *S* follows subject-matter design structure

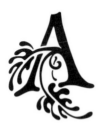

Oak leaf letter *A* versal

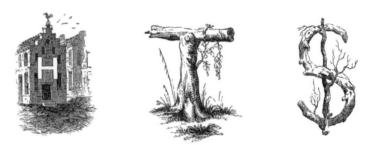

FIGURE 8-2: *Versals from 1859 pictorial field-book*

Use of graphic letters is not restricted to text. Incorporating this form of design into display type, either as first-letter designs or interior-letter designs, can produce a one-of-a-kind graphic that replaces the need for an illustration. In both cases the design style of the letter should adhere to the design style of the typeface. The first priority of such a graphic is readability, but its second goal is graphic. Designing these display-type graphics is a balancing act between the needs of the letterform and the needs of the graphic. It is an exciting challenge, and the rewards are unique and eye-catching design solutions.

The Humpty Dumpty graphic (fig. 8-3) uses eggshell versals for the *H* and *D*. Together they form a single, cracked egg with each half contributing a letter. The typeface Florentine Light is a graceful, delicate typeface with appropriately egg-shaped elliptical bowls and curves.

During the design process, only the letters *H* and *D* were altered. The rest of the letters were letterspaced properly and aligned vertically (the stem of the *p* emphasized vertical movement down to the second word by aligning with the stem of the *m*). Originally the curved stroke of the altered *D* joined its stem on the perpendicular. This produced a harsh join that was out of style for the typeface. By magnifying an unaltered letter, the *p,* it was easy to duplicate the same join and maintain an important style characteristic. The legibility/graphic compromise required for this design problem focused on the question of how much the *D* could tilt and also how close to position the *H* and *D* to form the total egg-graphic.

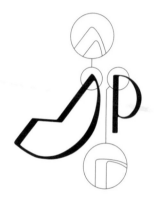

Humpty Dumpty

Original Florentine Light typeface

Maintain all typeface characteristics for a convincing graphic letter

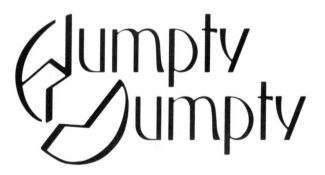

FIGURE 8-3: *Humpty Dumpty graphic with eggshell versals*

The Tempest in a Teapot graphic (see fig. 8-4) is another example of two versals forming a single image while maintaining their role as the first letter of two different words. The Charme typeface (designed by

FIGURE 8-4: *Tempest in a Teapot versals create graphic*

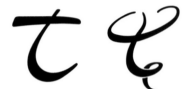

Original Charme *T* (left) and resulting tempest *T* (right)

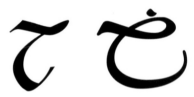

Original Lydian Cursive *T* (left) and resulting teapot *T* (right)

Helmut Matheis in 1958) projects a fluid, informal style perfect for this design. Selecting the right typeface is the single most important part of this unique design technique. A typeface design style that evokes the correct graphic-related images makes the designer's job much easier and the end result more convincing.

This graphic used two different *T* structures to form the single teapot with tumultuous steam. Knowledge of the letter *T*'s structural variations among myriad typefaces made this possible. The tempest *T* was an altered version of the original Charme uppercase *T*. Similar in style to a traditional lowercase *t*, the informal typeface design style was altered easily to be more steam- and tempestlike. The teapot, based on the *T* from the Lydian Cursive typeface, was revised and recreated in the Charme style. The entire display-type graphic was originally planned for the Lydian Cursive typeface. Lydian was more condensed and formal and the swirling tempest was difficult to achieve.

The Garbage graphic (fig. 8-5) is an example of an initial versal designed to further the meaning of the word while drawing attention to its beginning. It is also an example of the design problems that arise when the mix of letters does not blend smoothly. The original typeface Eccentric is a condensed typeface with proportions similar to a metal outdoor garbage can—tall, thin, and rectangular. Eccentric has a high bar and middle arm placement throughout the alphabet that emphasizes its tall, thin appearance. In the word *GARBAGE,* however, the *G*'s horizontal serif placement contrasts with that of its neighboring letters and causes a dip in the visual flow through the word. The design of the versal and an adjustment to the final *G* eliminates this problem.

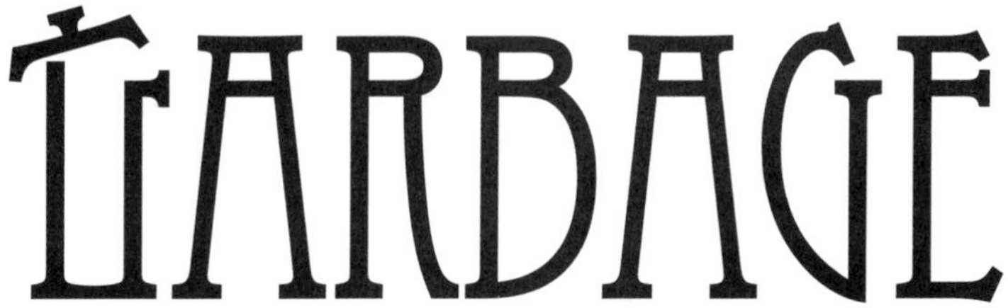

FIGURE 8-5: *Garbage graphic in Eccentric typeface*

Several Eccentric letters, *H, T,* and *E,* contributed letter parts to the garbage-can versal. These letter parts served as the major structural components of the can. Joining the serifs at the foot of the *H* and widening the crossbar of the *T* finalized the versal. Using sections of preexisting letters saved the type artist a significant amount of time by keeping stroke weights and ending treatments consistent. Redrawing would open the door for error. After positioning the versal, the vertical stroke of the second *G* was elongated to align with the middle arm of the *E.*

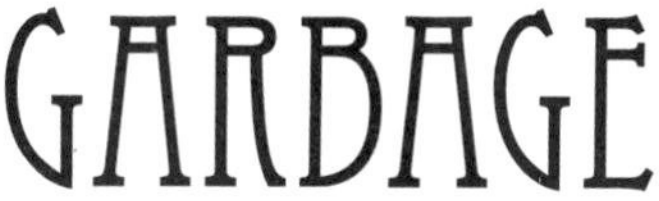

FIGURE 8-6: *Garbage graphic first iteration*

Review of the first design iteration (fig. 8-6) pointed out several design weaknesses. The horizontal strokes in the middle of the letters (bars, arms, serifs, and can handle) did not align. In the design/typeface comparison graphic (fig. 8-7), the differences in stroke location were apparent. The middle strokes of the *R* and *B* shared a common location, with the bars of the *A* higher and the middle arm of the *E* and the garbage can handle lower. This bouncing of adjacent strokes was noticeable at display size and was distracting in a graphic context. Adjustments

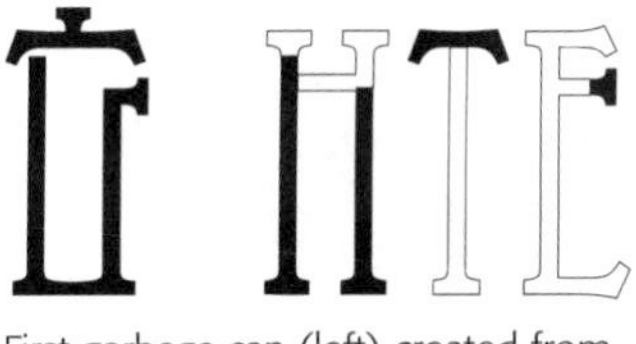

FIGURE 8-7: *Design/typeface (outline) comparison*

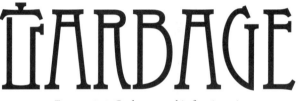

Original Eccentric typeface

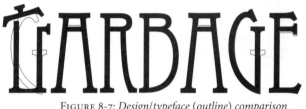

First garbage can (left) created from altered black letter parts (right)

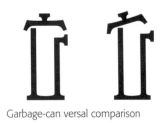

Garbage-can versal comparison

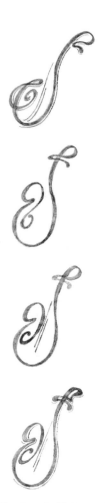

Design iterations for Violin versal with development from top to bottom

brought all horizontal strokes and endings into common alignment with the *R* and *B*. The redesign of the original versal (see fig. 8-5) by angling the lid and elevating the handle solved the handle-alignment problem and increased the versal's attention-getting ability. The angled lid repeated the angles in the head serif of the *E* and second *G,* thus unifying the two ends of the word and strengthening the design.

Subtle letter-structure adjustments are common and necessary when designing display-type graphics. A legible typeset headline, on the other hand, requires only correct line breaks and letterspacing to communicate its message. It is the graphic component of a display-type graphic that changes the type artist's mode of working. This graphic form is a design element subject to the rules and principles of good visual design. The unique mix of letters (highlighting structural differences), the larger point size (making discrepancies more visible), and the word's graphic purpose all make these design adjustments critical for the overall strength and effectiveness of the graphic.

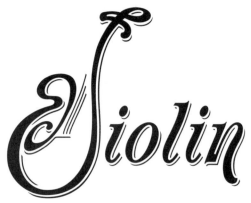

FIGURE 8-8: *Violin graphic from musical instrument series*

Designing a series of display-type graphics presents the additional challenge of maintaining consistency between related designs within a single subject category. The versal graphics in the musical instrument series (fig. 8-8) were drawn freehand, rather than constructed by duplicating existing typeface letter parts.

When designing a series, individual designs are not complete until all are evaluated for consistency. The type artist's work method should reflect this. Instead of finalizing each design individually, the type artist benefits by moving to the next design in the series and revising a previous design when a different treatment or solution suggests itself.

       CHAPTER EIGHT

The Oberon typeface (designed by Phill Grimshaw) is an informal, expressive script harkening back to the 1970s. It has a high stroke contrast and a thin drop shadow line offset to the lower right of the letterforms suggesting dimension. The capital letters depict a flurry of visual movement with expansive swashes and spirals. They are the flamboyant family member at the annual reunion.

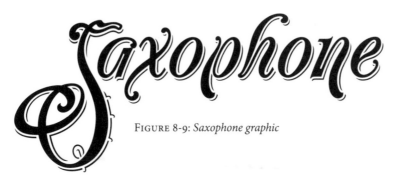

FIGURE 8-9: *Saxophone graphic*

The Saxophone graphic (fig. 8-9) is an example of using typeface style characteristics, such as the drop shadow line, to add subject details to the graphic. The lower end of the spine of the original capital *S* was redrawn to create the illusion of the saxophone's bell, while at the same time creating a plausible ending for the *S*. The bell treatment maintained the elliptical swash from other capitals, such as the *B* and *H,* but placed it at an angle reminiscent of the instrument's bell. The drop shadow line added dimension to the saxophone and defined instrument details, such as a key and rod.

The mouthpiece replicated stroke treatments from the ampersand. This flamboyant, eye-catching depiction of the mouthpiece balanced the large bell at the other end of the spine enabling the viewer to see both ends simultaneously for improved letter legibility. To balance the visual impact of the versal and unify the entire graphic, some of the remaining lowercase letters were altered. An alternate *h* was substituted for the default *h,* and the lowercase letters *a, x, p, n,* and *e* were altered structurally by substituting strokes from other letters and figures.

The Guitar graphic (fig. 8-11) explores the expanded use of subject details without significantly diminishing letter recognition and reenforces the need for maintaining and balancing style attributes for design success. The structure of the guitar versal mimics the capital letter *G* of the cursive handwriting style taught in many American elementary schools.

Oberon typeface sample

Additional Oberon reference letters

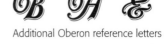

Original Oberon typeface

Cursive handwriting structure for capital *G*

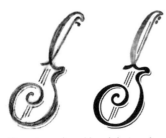

Alternate neck and head designs for
the guitar versal

The original scan for this graphic (fig. 8-10) demonstrated that the letter structure was suitable for an acoustic guitar, but it showed that the versal's style was too subdued for the typeface. Much time and energy went into redesigning tuning keys and strings without demonstrable improvement. By relentlessly tinkering with a detail within the problem rather than reexamining the nature of the problem itself, significant time was wasted. All designers experience this at one point or another. It is comparable to changing a flat tire on a car that has been totaled. Changing the tire is a small detail on a much larger problem. Once the problem is redefined, the details usually fall into place.

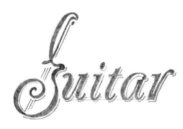

FIGURE 8-10: *First Guitar graphic scan*

With the problem correctly identified, the guitar's neck and head were redrawn (fig. 8-11) using the stroke to identify features calligraphically. The thin drop shadow line was repositioned and segmented to suggest the frets as well as the strings, thus adding more details to balance those in the guitar's body. The top of the body was redrawn to balance the shapes added to the neck. These were all stroke treatments found in the typeface that were altered to serve the needs of the versal.

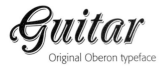

Original Oberon typeface

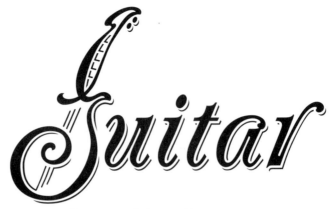

FIGURE 8-11: *Guitar graphic*

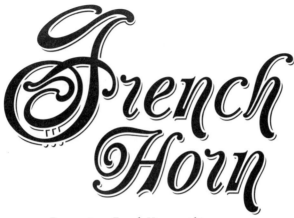

FIGURE 8-12: *French Horn graphic*

The French Horn graphic (fig. 8-12) explores organizing a multitude of overlapping, intertwining curves and swirls to create a dominant structure suggesting a cursive letter *F*. The versal uses the structure of the same cursive handwriting style employed by the guitar graphic. The original Oberon *F* has a simpler structure that was not suitable for the French horn. After exploring myriad structural ideas for looping and curving the horn's tubing, three areas surfaced as key to defining this instrument. The structure of the graphic required a bell, a large circular area composed of intertwining tubing, and a mouthpiece. By starting with the original cursive letter structure and then embellishing it in the style of the typeface, both visual goals for structure and style were met.

The large opening of the bell was created by the top stroke looping back on itself. This created the illusion of a single stroke to define the letter, but a dimensional area to define the bell. The large circular section used intertwining tubes to guide the viewer's eye toward the terminal that suggested the mouthpiece. This terminal also helped define the left stroke of the lowercase *r* that was removed from the alternate letter. The drop shadow line was redrawn to add valves to the bottom of the tube section. Three letters in the rest of the word were altered structurally to improve the design of the entire graphic by balancing the dominate versal. They were the lowercase *r, n,* and *h.*

Learning to draw in the style developed by the original type designer is interesting. Some find it helpful to manually trace the original letterforms to improve their understanding of stylistic details and proportional relationships. This hands-on investigation of typeface nuances is more revealing than a careful visual study. When executing the final

Cursive handwriting structure for capital *F*

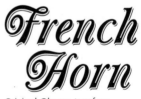

Original Oberon typeface

Lowercase *r* with alternate

THE GRAPHIC AMPERSAND

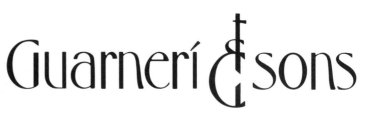

Ampersand sampler

digital art, it is helpful to keep several typeface letters on screen for comparison so appropriate stroke weights and distances are maintained.

FOR TYPE ARTISTS WHO ENJOY THE CHALLENGE of designing graphic letters, the ampersand is an amendable letter to alter and redesign. The ampersand assumes a variety of shapes and structures, from its more evident *e-t* origins to those not as apparent. These variations offer a type artist a satisfying array of structures that accommodates most ideas. As an abbreviation, the ampersand's role is an important one, as well as its design link to the words it joins. Designing the ampersand in a stand-alone illustration style (see fig. 8-15) will disrupt readability by causing confusion or misinterpretation of the message; maintaining the stylistic link to the surrounding typeface eliminates that problem by preserving the visual unity with the words on either side (fig. 8-14).

The Guarneri *&* Sons graphic (fig. 8-13) creates a content-specific ampersand graphic that links the members of the seventeenth-century Italian violin-making family. Andrea Guarneri of Cremona, Italy, started the family business in the mid–seventeenth century. Violin production continued with his two sons and other family members. Andrea's nephew, Giuseppe, became the most noted of the family for his pursuit of tonal quality over form.

This display-type graphic uses the typeface Florentine Light. Its elongated, vertical proportions, strong contrast between stroke weights, and vertical stress placement relate visually to the graceful elegance of a violin's shape. The original typeface shows a figure-8 ampersand—not at all violinlike in structure. This ampersand does not emphasize the tall *x*-height that was important to its selection. With all the variations of ampersands that are in the public consciousness, it is easy to substitute a more suitable structure without diminishing recognition.

Guarneri & sons

FIGURE 8-13: *Guarneri & Sons ampersand graphic*

When designing any letterform to be both a graphic and a typeface character, the type artist seeks to strike a compromise between the two visuals. The violin, for example, cannot be a direct replica of a Guarneri original or it will not read as an ampersand. Conversely, if the ampersand is too faithful to its master design it will not look like a stringed instrument. The challenge to the type artist is to determine which ampersand and violin features are essential and which are not.

Once the correct compromise is reached, the final graphic is rendered in the style of the typeface. Maintaining this style visually links the violin ampersand to the adjacent words, so the text reads as a unified thought, not two words separated by an illustration. Rendering a typeface style accurately requires an eye for subtle detail. Type designers are to be respected for their accuracy of style in letterform after letterform. (Two hundred and fifty-six characters might seem insufficient for a type-hungry type artist, but for their designer it must be more than enough.) The recommended approach for constructing this unique graphic letter is recycling existing strokes and endings from other letters in the type font. The uniform size maintains stroke consistency. The violin ampersand is constructed from the Florentine Light capital *C* and the lowercase letters *s, l,* and *t.* The end result shows its *e-t* roots clearly.

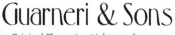

Guarneri & Sons

Original Florentine Light typeface

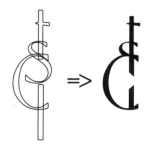

Violin-ampersand construction diagram

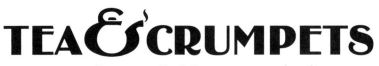

FIGURE 8-14: *Tea & Crumpets ampersand graphic*

The Tea *&* Crumpets graphic (fig. 8-14) is another example of an ampersand graphic created in a specific typeface design style. The design route for type graphics varies—in some instances the typeface triggers an idea and in other cases the opposite is true. The original ampersand for this typeface, Binner, is an easily identified *e-t* combination with tightly curled stroke endings. Within the context of the entire typeface the curled ampersand blends with other similarly designed letters. Within the context of Tea *&* Crumpets, the curled ampersand is too visually distinct to blend with the other letters and is not reminiscent of a teapot.

Tea *&* Crumpets began as an idea in search of a typeface. The teapot was designed originally as an isolated graphic. When incorporated into the display-type graphic (see fig. 8-15), the teapot needed redesigning to match Binner's design style whose high contrasting stroke weights

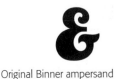

Original Binner ampersand

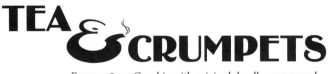

FIGURE 8-15: *Graphic with original doodle ampersand*

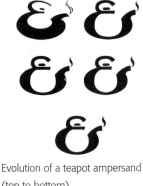

Evolution of a teapot ampersand
(top to bottom)

were similar, but not identical, to the teapot's. The teapot ampersand was a combination of same-point-size letter parts from the *S, E,* and *P.* The steam was the bar from the *H,* narrowed and rotated.

When creating a graphic letter with a beautifully curved typeface, such as Binner, curved sections are redrawn to join letter sections or endings taken from existing letters. These require multiple proofs to check the curve's smoothness as well as structural modifications to strike the right compromise between teapot, typeface style, and ampersand. Any glitch in the bézier outline weakens line quality and diminishes the display-type graphic's overall effectiveness. A typeface with rough edges, such as Berliner Grotesk, is more forgiving.

Hansel & Gretel

FIGURE 8-16: *Hansel & Gretel with gingerbread ampersand*

The Hansel & Gretel graphic (fig. 8-16) uses both a graphic versal and a graphic ampersand. Selecting the typeface Berliner Grotesk set the correct informal, edible tone. Its rounded stroke endings and uneven, rough edges are suited to a gingerbread visual. The graphic versal, the letter *H,* has to read easily with the rest of the word, while simultaneously suggesting the gingerbread house.

The house was achieved by converting the bar of the *H* to a caret shape, indicating the peaked roof, and by elongating the *H*'s right stem, indicating a subtle chimney. These changes introduced just the right amount of graphic without compromising legibility. A wider *H*-house

Hansel & Gretel

Original Berliner Grotesk typeface

was tried, but Berliner Grotesk's condensed proportions made it appear out of place.

As with Binner's ampersand, the original Berliner Grotesk ampersand did not provide a suitable structure for a gingerbread-cookie shape. A straighter, more masculine ampersand was tried, but the ampersand needed curved bottom strokes to relate to the curved top stroke, as well as the curved letters in the names. In the final iteration (fig. 8-16), the alignment was changed so the reader saw the word *Hansel* and the *H*-house before being lead to the gingerbread ampersand and the second name. Due to the uniqueness of the ampersand, it was necessary to tuck it under *Hansel* to assure proper reading order.

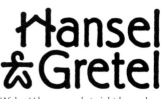

Wider *H*-house and straight-legged ampersand design iteration

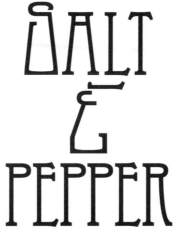

FIGURE 8-17: *Salt & Pepper with pepper-mill ampersand*

The Salt *&* Pepper graphic (fig. 8-17) is another example of both a graphic versal and ampersand. The latter is more pronounced, but the versal is a design of subtleties. The original typeface Eccentric (designed by Gustav F. Schroeder in 1881) is a cap-only, elongated, monoline, bracketed slab serif typeface. It has a high-waisted or long-legged quality achieved by locating the bars of the *A, H,* and the middle arm of the *E* in the upper third of the letter. This design characteristic is ideal for the pepper mill and salt shaker graphics. The typeface's original ampersand is a unique, signature character, exceeding the starkness of the Eccentric face, but giving a mark of distinction that would add pizzazz to a display type block.

SALT & PEPPER

Original Eccentric typeface

SALT & PEPPER

Original graphic design solution

Preliminary salt shaker designs

Salt & Pepper was a graphic that required several iterations before its final form emerged. The original solution, which closely followed the layout, deleted all the typeface's line endings from the two graphics. The starkness of these two graphic letterforms made them unable to blend with the rest of the letters. By using the arm of the *L* and adding the top half of a period (.), the revised crank for the pepper-mill ampersand blended smoothly into the typeface. The salt-shaker versal took many wrong turns while exploring various options for success. The final salt shaker kept the proportions consistent for a letter of its increased size, while maintaining the stroke weight of the smaller letters. This assured even color within the word *SALT*. A long bracketed serif was added to the end of the spine and an altered short serif was added to the top of the spine. Both line endings successfully linked the shaker to the rest of the letters through consistent design treatment. The sans serif shaker could not achieve this.

The Cream & Sugar graphic (fig. 8-18) uses a graphic versal on each word along with a graphic ampersand. The original typeface Tango has a figure-8–style ampersand that triggered the idea for a spoon. With the pitcher as the capital *C* and the sugar bowl for the capital *S,* a stirring spoon was the logical subject for the ampersand.

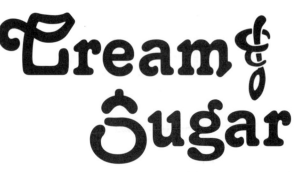

FIGURE 8-18: *Graphic with stirring-spoon ampersand*

The pitcher versal was a study in evolutionary subtlety. Through trial-and-error with dips, points, and angles, the pitcher's spout finally emerged. In the end, several sections from unsuccessful iterations were combined to produce the final, successful pitcher versal. The original pitcher had a pointed spout that never suggested a cream pitcher. The angled spout used in the final solution required a slight reshaping of the pitcher's body. The reshaping blended the right amount of curve with

Cream & Sugar

Original Tango typeface

the right amount of blockiness. The original swash of the *C* served as the pitcher's handle.

The original sugar bowl incorporated the bottom swashed bowl of the *B* as the sugar container and the mirrored loop from the capital *G* for the lid. A shortened hyphen created the handle. The result was a segmented sugar bowl that did not blend as smoothly as expected. Two revisions solved the problem. First, the handle was attached to the lid by using the top vertical stroke from Tango's dollar sign. This eliminated the overly segmented appearance that is not characteristic of Tango. Second, the center horizontal stroke was "dipped" slightly, as it is across the top of swashed capitals. This eliminated the starkness of the precise horizontal mid-stroke of the original design and added a softer, informal quality to the stroke—a characteristic of Tango.

The stirring-spoon ampersand incorporates a spoon with an E-shaped stirring-swirl to create a convincing ampersand in the Tango style. When viewed separately, readers might not see the ampersand immediately, but within the context of a display-type graphic, readers receive clues that lead them to the correct visual association. The spoon's design starts with the leg of the original ampersand and then springboards into the realm of original creation. Using the Tango style as a recipe for line endings, counters, and strokes, the unique stirring-spoon ampersand is convincing.

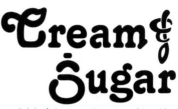

Original Cream & Sugar graphic with pointed-spout pitcher and segmented sugar bowl

Slight dipping of horizontal strokes is characteristic of Tango

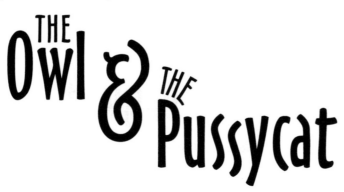

FIGURE 8-19: *Owl & Pussycat graphic with cat ampersand*

The Owl & the Pussycat graphic (fig. 8-19) evolves from the unique ampersand of the Oz Handicraft typeface (based on lettering by Oswald Cooper), which suggests the back view of a sitting feline. The original typeface is a vertically proportioned, lettering-style typeface with low contrast between stroke weights and rounded stroke endings.

The Owl &
The Pussycat

Original Oz Handicraft typeface

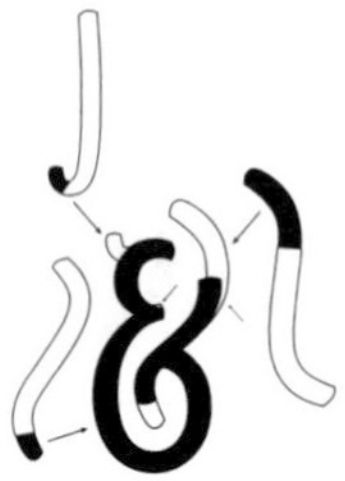

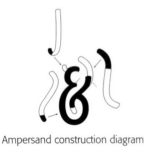

Ampersand construction diagram

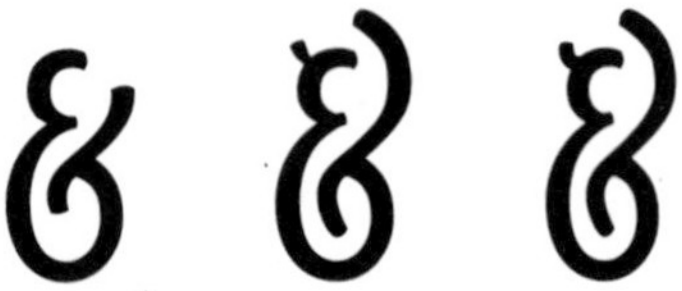

Ampersand evolution from original to final (left to right)

After changing the letter case and size for the words and repositioning them, the alterations began. The sitting-feline image was integrated into the ampersand successfully by using pieces from a capital *S* to extend the cat's tail. The cat's ear came from the curved stroke of the capital *J*, much like an ear on a lowercase *g*. Originally, a comma was used for the ear but the thinning of the stroke at the ear's base appeared stylistically incorrect (see margin graphic).

The second *the* was placed on a path to follow the *P*'s shoulder. The bottom and middle arms of the *E* were curved to blend better with the graphic. In the word *Pussycat,* the baseline of the second lowercase *s* was lowered to form a downward diagonal along the bottom edge of the *s-s-y* letter sequence. The original letters *c* and *a* curved into the *x*-height area forming an enclosed unit. By splicing the bottom of the lowercase *s* to the *c* and the top of the lowercase *s* to the top of the *a,* the angles of the *s* were visually linked back to the rest of the word, thereby unlocking the *c-a* unit present in the original typesetting.

From fairly simple beginnings, this entire design evolves into a medley of letter placement and letter structure alterations for a tightly designed display-type graphic. These alterations employ techniques used in chapter 7 and introduce techniques to be discussed thoroughly in chapter 9. The Owl *&* the Pussycat graphic is complete at this point, but two variations are possible.

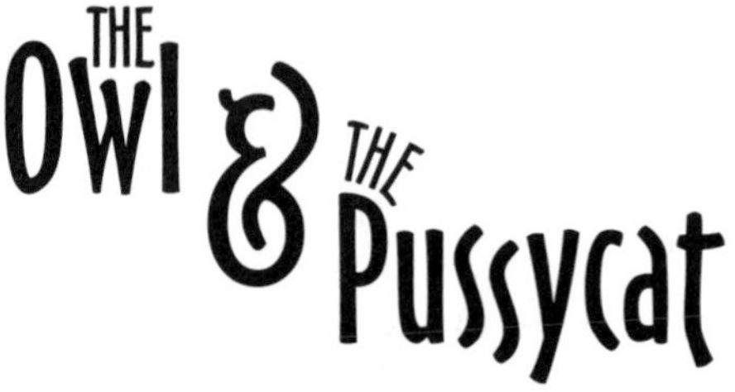

FIGURE 8-20: *First variation of Owl & Pussycat graphic*

In the first variation (fig. 8-20), the descender of the lowercase *y* replaced the terminal of the lowercase *t.* By itself this change worked well within the word *Pussycat,* but weakened the entire graphic by drawing too much attention to the word. Extending the left arm of the lowercase *w* in *Owl* balanced this last alteration and unified the graphic. The second variation (fig. 8-21) added the words *went to Sea* to the end of the original graphic. The words *went* and *to* were stacked vertically aligning the lowercase *t* in each word. The stem of each *t* was elongated upward to suggest a ship's mast. The letter *a* in *Sea* was repeated from *Pussycat* to visually link this new section to the original. The lower half of the spine of the *S* was embellished by adding the lower curved section of the original ampersand and by finishing the stroke with the ending from the original *S*. This made a type graphic for the first line of Edward Lear's famous nursery rhyme *The Owl and the Pussycat*.

ℰⓐ

DESIGNING LETTERS FOR USE AS VERSALS, AMPERSANDS, or others requires the type artist to be very familiar with three design components: (1) the different letter structures available for each letterform, (2) the design characteristics of typefaces, and (3) the thousands of available typefaces. Knowledge of alternate letter structure opens up more design options when fusing letters with graphics. Maintaining typeface design characteristics enables the new graphic letter to function successfully within the typeface. The right typeface propels a design much faster along its evolutionary design path.

Digital typography gives the type artist access to the structural bézier points for altering letterforms and creating new graphic letters. It calls on all of the type artist's understanding of typeface legibility and typesetting readability as well as design and illustration skills. It is a unique area of design that, although technologically possible, has not been fully explored. The 1960s has more examples of this kind of design and the type designs of that decade are a source of inspiration for the type artist new to this design technique. This is an exciting area of design that is both challenging and satisfying when executed successfully—something every type artist should try.

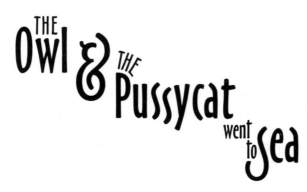

Figure 8-21: Second variation of Owl & Pussycat graphic

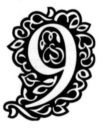

TYPOGRAPHS
AS
TYPOGRAPHIC ART

THE RULES OF TYPOGRAPHY HAVE A SINGLE INTENT—beautiful typography with enhanced readability. In this context, the word *beautiful* connotes a freedom and a creative spark that enlivens a page. The words *enhanced readability* refer to the uniformity and order that enable the reader's eye to move effortlessly along the text lines. Grace, power, elegance, and whimsy are all possible with type. Typographic rules are the underpinning of this creativity. They are the unifying backdrop on which the type appears. Yet, most rules of type usage pertain to continuous text; discontinuous text offers the type artist the freedom to try new things and to push the limits of type.

It is erroneous to conclude that the sheer number of type rules leaves no room for creativity. Such a statement ignores the works of innovative typographers, such as Oswald Cooper (1879–1940) and Herb Lubalin (1918–81), as well as examples of art nouveau and art deco typography. Each of these designers and movements demonstrates the limitless possibilities for designing with type.

Oswald Cooper was a designer, typographer, lettering genius, and a student of Frederic Goudy. Cooper's hand-lettered advertisements, announcements, and posters display his gift for using lettering as the major component of design. His lettering ability became the focal point of his Chicago advertising and typography firm, Bertsch *&* Cooper. Cooper's ads for the Packard Motor Car Company (Haley 1992), for example, show how his lettering style established a mood and projected an elegance associated with this product. (The American Type Founders later developed this lettering into the Packard typeface.) Oswald Cooper also designed the Cooper typefaces from a lettering style he created, starting with Cooper in 1918 and followed by the immensely popular Cooper Black in 1925. Several variations followed, including Cooper Black HiLite, Condensed, and Italic (Eason 1991; Haley 1992).

Herb Lubalin started as a designer in 1939 after graduating from the Cooper Union School of Art and Architecture in New York. By the end of his career he had won hundreds of professional awards including the prestigious American Institute of Graphic Arts (AIGA) Medal (Muller 1981, 5), and he had designed three typefaces—Avant Garde Gothic (1970), Lubalin Graph (1974), and Serif Gothic (1974). His love for typography inspired many designers to take another look at the alphabet's 26 letters. Lubalin took type from the confines of text and headlines and used it to express ideas graphically, as typographic designs or typographs. By merging graphic design and typography, Lubalin demonstrated that in addition to being read, type could represent the meaning of those same words. It could imply a nuance that the reader might not discern from the words alone.

It is not essential to be a master typographer on the scale of Oswald Cooper or Herb Lubalin to add typographic design elements to a page. Additions can start on a small scale, as discussed in chapter 7, with the headline. Design elements can expand to include headline-compatible elements within the text, such as initial letters and pull quotes. Typographic special effects, such as three-dimensional type, text on a path, and graphic letters are next, as discussed in chapter 8. Finally, typographic design can go all out with the restructuring of type to form typographs, logotypes, and graphic alphabets.

The mantra of typographic design is still consistency. For display type, it is consistency of style. Placing multiple conflicting typefaces on a page creates chaos, not beautiful design. Type artists undertaking typographic design for the first time have a tendency to overdo—too many typefaces, too many styles, and too many points (too large). Having a small number of typefaces from which to choose is not always a hardship; it can be a blessing. It forces the type artist to uncover the always-present design possibilities inherent in all type. The possibilities are there, only often overlooked when more flashy faces are available.

A similar problem occurs with ice cream. When faced with a vast array of brightly colored, scrumptious-sounding ice cream flavors, the salivating consumer often overlooks vanilla and chocolate. Chocolate

ABCDEFGHIJK LMNOPQRSTU VWXYZabcdefg hijklmnopqrst uvwxyz1234

Cooper Black

ABCDEFGHIJKL MNOPQRSTUV WXYZabcdefghi jklmnopqrstuvw xyz1234

Cooper Black Italic

ABCDEFGHIJKLM NOPQRSTUVWXYZ abcdefghijklmno pqrstuvwxyz1234

Avant Garde Demi

ABCDEFGHIJKLM NOPQRSTUVWXY Zabcdefghijklmno pqrstuvwxyz1234

Lubalin Graph Bold

connoisseurs, however, argue that there is chocolate and then there is *Chocolate!* Just because a type artist does not have multiple folios of fonts with the expert collections, or the OpenType equivalents, to match does not mean that a tasteful, well-designed document is not possible. A basic typeface with limited style options provides a design safety net for the type artist just entering the typographic design sweetshop.

TYPOGRAPHS

THE WORD *TYPOGRAPH* REFERS TO THE ART OF DESIGNING a graphic using and manipulating typeset letters and words. It requires a thorough understanding of a typeface's design style and structure. A logotype is an example of a typograph. A *logotype* is a single word or words designed to be a cohesive whole in the style of a typeface. It goes beyond being a collection of typeset words, such as a pull quote, subhead, or headline. It becomes an intricate interlocking design achieved by connecting, aligning, and adjusting strokes, serifs, angles, and endings.

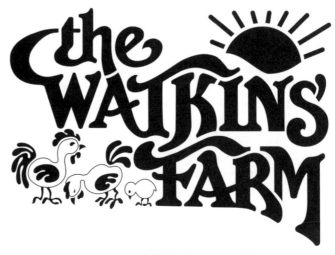

FIGURE 9-1: *Watkins' Farm typograph*

Typographs focus on only those letters involved in the designed unit. The type artist strengthens the design bond between those letters by adjusting the letters' structure according to the principles of design, which include unity, balance, focal point, positive/negative shapes, rhythm, and proportion. Typographs do not abandon the typographic design principles that apply to alphabets and typefaces, but rather they hone them. When incorporated effectively, these underlying principles make the end result appear as a natural union of letters (fig. 9-1). This is the application of typography that is the most fun; it is also the most challenging. The subtleties that make a typograph successful and the nuances that control the reader's eye movements through the typograph appear to require the precise touch of a surgeon and the knowledge of a master typographer.

The result of this work is not unlike watching an athletic performance. A flawless performance by a professional figure skater, for example, appears effortless as the athlete weaves intricate movements in and around a carefully chosen musical accompaniment. Gone from view are the times spent sitting on the ice when the intricacies got the better of the athlete's ability to bend and twist. The outward simplicity of a well-designed typograph belies the stacks of tracing paper layouts littering the floor and the countless false starts and U-turns from dead-end design paths. The end result is fun and beautiful to view, but its development was far from happenstance or luck.

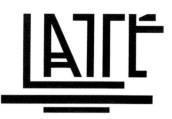

Latté typograph

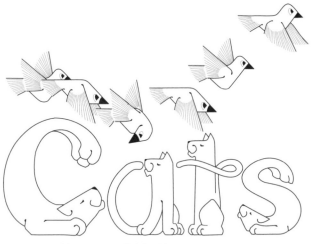

FIGURE 9-2: *Original letters united by style*

DESIGNING A GRAPHIC WORD OR A LOGOTYPE (a designed word-unit functioning as a graphic identity for a product, company, or service) challenges the type artist to visually unify multiple letters as a readable graphic unit. Letters in a single graphic word either adopt a similar style that identifies them as a typeface (fig. 9-2) or are united by subject matter (see fig. 9-3) and/or illustration style. In all cases, the more stylistic, structural, and color similarities shared by the letters, the easier the word is to read.

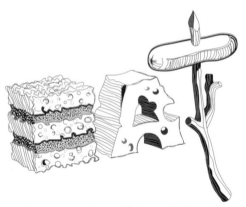

FIGURE 9-3: *Original letters united by subject matter*
(Source: Wheeler, *Pencils to Pixels: Exploring FreeHand Version 3.1,* 1993, William C. Brown Publishers. Reproduced with permission of The McGraw-Hill Companies)

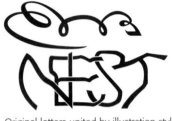

Original letters united by illustration style
(Source: Wheeler, *Pencils to Pixels: Exploring FreeHand Version 3.1,* 1993, William C. Brown Publishers. Reproduced with permission of The McGraw-Hill Companies)

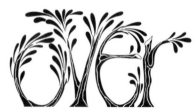

Graphic word integrating text with illustration

Designing a word from original letterforms is comparable to designing a limited-letter alphabet. The graphic word *Over,* designed for the unpublished children's picture book "If Cats" by S. G. Wheeler, serves both as part of the text and as part of the illustration (fig. 9-4). The design of the word is both readable and illustrative—it serves as a clump of trees. Its style, structure, and color are similar throughout the four letters. This consistency strengthens readability and the use of familiar letter structures strengthens legibility.

The graphic word *Under,* designed for the same picture book, also serves as part of the text and illustration (fig. 9-5). The letter shapes are not as traditional, but for such a limited use and within the context of a continuing story, readability is not diminished significantly. What it adds to the story, and to the reader's enjoyment, far outweighs any departure from convention.

A logotype differs from a graphic word because the logotype is a single, intertwined designed unit rather than individual graphic letters.

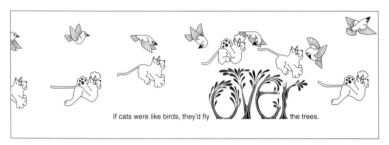

If cats were like birds, they'd fly OVer the trees.

FIGURE 9-4: *Graphic word in children's picture book spread*

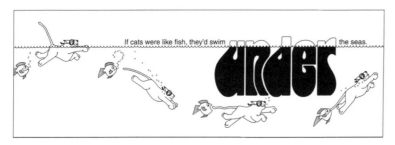

If cats were like fish, they'd swim **under** the seas.

FIGURE 9-5: *Graphic word in children's picture book spread*

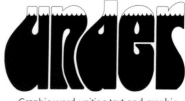

Graphic word uniting text and graphic

These categories are not rigid; consequently, overlap occurs, but for this discussion a distinction is made. When designing a simple logotype, the type artist can start with an existing typeface and add a graphic element that functions as a single letter within the unit. Many logotypes use actual identifiable graphics; many do not. Some *suggest* an image or style and let the viewer's imagination provide the graphic association; the logotype is just the trigger. Through the use of organized curves, for example, the type artist can suggest rolling water, a waterfall, or a riverboat, without ever showing the actual object. Other logotypes are well-designed, nonobjective words that project an appropriate mood, style, or time period suitable for the subject.

JUST SCRATCH

Graphic element as letter within simple logotype

FIGURE 9-6: *Espresso Pot logotype*

The Espresso Pot logotype (fig. 9-6), an example of a simple logotype, had the first two letters of the word restructured to suggest the espresso pot. Originally this idea was a quick sketch in a sketchbook without reference to a particular typeface. Once the idea was ready for finished art, the angled typeface Harvey (designed by Dale Kramer in 1989) was the natural choice for this espresso pot. A major design goal was to unify the angles in the spout of the *S,* the unaltered *P* and *R,* the elongated *S*s, and the restructured *O. The O* was constructed from an

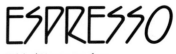

Original Harvey typeface

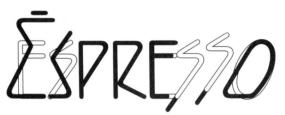

Construction of letter *O* from
combined letters *R* and *C*

upside-down *R* and *C*. The original letter *O* lacked the angles included
in the word's other letters. Its uniqueness made it a soloist rather than a
member of the group. All letter alterations supported and balanced the
graphic so the entire logotype functioned as one designed unit (fig. 9-7).

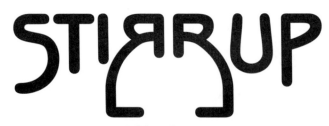

FIGURE 9-7: *Logotype comparison with typeface (outline)*

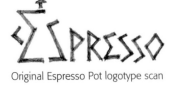

Original Espresso Pot logotype scan

With the right typeface, a logotype's execution goes smoothly. The
type designer should remain open, however, to any design alterations
the actual typeface suggests, as with the selection of Harvey. Without
the right type, executing the logotype is tantamount to teaching a dino-
saur to sing—it is not going to happen.

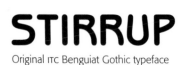

FIGURE 9-8: *Stirrup logotype*

STIRRUP

Original ITC Benguiat Gothic typeface

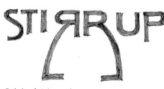

Original Stirrup logotype scan

The Stirrup logotype (fig. 9-8) repeats two letters in the center as
the graphic element and angles the surrounding letters to support and
balance it. The original typeface ITC Benguiat Gothic (designed by Ed
Benguiat in 1979) has a unique capital *R* with an arced tail that suggests
the curve of the stirrup iron beautifully. Shortening the *R*'s stem, extending its tail, and adding the horizontal bar creates the stirrup's right half.
The flipped image creates the stirrup's left half and completes the signature graphic element.

Angling the letters on either side of the graphic required letter restructuring and optical balancing. The letter *S* was restructured to repeat
the elongated look of the graphic. It was created by combining the top of
the *S* with a horizontally flipped capital *C*. Shortening and lengthening

the stems of the *T, I,* and *P* completed the mirrored arc on either side of the graphic. Letterspacing was critical since three letters balanced two. This logotype was not as effective without the correct *R* to suggest the stirrup iron. The original layout was very similar to the completed logotype, but selecting the right typeface added the correct style to the final graphic.

The Aviary logotype (fig. 9-9) and Coffee logotype (see fig. 9-10) increase in complexity by expanding the number of restructured typeface letters. At this point, many type artists question the need to work from an original typeface. They reason that with such extensive letter restructuring, why not create the entire thing from scratch? The consistency of detail in a well-drawn typeface results from time, skill, and experience—from the consistent bracket on every serif to the identical arc of multiple curves. Such consistency is impossible for many type artists to achieve due to time constraints and inexperience. It is much more efficient to relocate an existing swash from one letter to another than it is to redraw that beautifully balanced stroke accurately. The Aviary logotype uses many swashes and arced strokes to suggest feathers. These are all found in the original typeface Poetica. Poetica is a swash-lover's delight with its vast supply of alternate glyphs. For this logotype, swashes are relocated, crossbars commandeered, and stems redistributed for use in the six restructured letters.

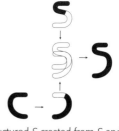

Restructured *S* created from *S* and flipped *C*

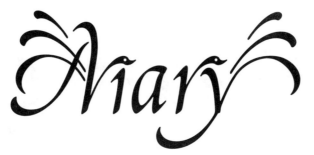

FIGURE 9-9: *Aviary logotype in Poetica*

Original Poetica typeface

The Coffee logotype (see fig. 9-10) suggests graphics throughout the word, from the coffeepot in the *C, O,* and *F* to the coffee mug in the two *E*s. The first priority of this design is to produce a readable, designed unit; the second to suggest graphics that only continued perusal will reveal. This design, which took many wrong turns, proves the you-get-what-you-pay-for adage regarding inexpensive typefaces.

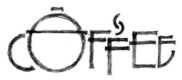

Original Coffee logotype scan

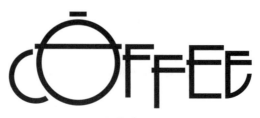

FIGURE 9-10: *Coffee logotype*

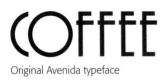

Original Avenida typeface

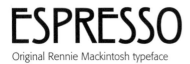

Original Rennie Mackintosh typeface

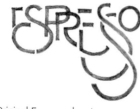

Original Espresso logotype scan

This design used a version of Plaza from an inexpensive typeface collection for the layout. During the design process it became apparent that the width of the letter strokes was not consistent. This was a problem easily solved by buying the correct typeface from the International Typeface Corporation for the finished art. The inexpensive typeface collection provided the typeface for layout purposes only. Once the finished art was needed, it was time to buy the high-quality version. The amount of time saved using quality type made it money well spent and it rewarded the type designer for a job well done. In this case, Plaza (designed by Alan Meeks in 1975) turned out to be too thin for this design and a perusal of ITC's collection uncovered Avenida (designed by John Chippindale in 1994), which was very similar in structure but heavier in weight. The quality of Avenida was excellent—important even when the finished work only displays four different letters. Several other letters were incorporated into the restructuring of the *C, O,* and *E.*

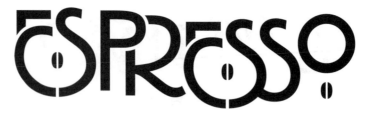

FIGURE 9-11: *Espresso Bean logotype*

The Espresso Bean logotype (fig. 9-11) is a series of letters that creates a nonobjective image and projects a subject-appropriate mood and style using a few coffee-bean graphics for accent. This logotype, executed in ITC Rennie Mackintosh (designed by Phill Grimshaw in 1996), is an uppercase-only typeface with alternative caps in place of the lowercase letters. Rennie Mackintosh is based on the lettering style of Charles

Rennie Mackintosh (1868–1928), a Scottish architect and designer. He used this lettering on his architectural drawings.

The Espresso Bean logotype started out as an idea without a typeface. The first *E* and *S* shared some strokes, but they read as separate letters. The last two *S*s intertwined to form the bottom of a graceful cascade of extended letters. In the production of the design, the crossover of spines never intertwined smoothly as they did in the layout. This snag started an interesting design evolution that demonstrated the merits of another author-embraced design adage: When stuck, repeat something already present in the design.

The *E-S* combination became the centerpiece of the design. It was constructed from the top arm of the *E*, the top of an alternate *G*, and the bottom of the third alternate *S*. The overlapped *P* and *R* are alternate glyphs with the right stroke placement and swashes to help lead the viewer's eye to the repeated *E-S* combination. The final *S* is the second alternate *S* that tucks nicely back into the *ES*. The letter *O* is actually the figure *0* (zero). The original letter *O* was too small, the alternate was oblong, and the zero was just right. With its shorter stature, the zero continues the roller-coaster flow through the word. The three coffee beans were created from an alternate *O*. Here the oblong shape is ideal and the white stroke relates to the white breaks in the *E-S* combination.

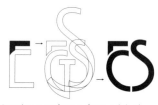

Creating new letters from original letter parts

Letter *O* (left, center) and zero (right)

Four letter *S* alternates

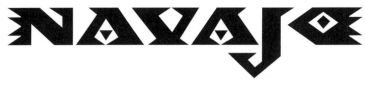

FIGURE 9-12: *Navajo logotype*

The last series of logotypes have style characteristics appropriate for two American Indian tribes. Careful study of tribal artwork, textiles, and pottery suggests these characteristics and makes selecting suitable typefaces relatively easy. Research is a sometimes overlooked precursor to good design. Designing without research is comparable to mountain climbing without ropes—it will be slow-going and without success.

The Navajo logotype (fig. 9-12) develops from the typeface Latin Wide, a heavy, extended typeface with wedge serifs. The wedge serifs are ideally suited to the triangular design characteristics of Navajo rugs. The original idea (see fig. 9-13) is similar to the final iteration, but with one fundamental difference—the Navajo style elements are placed *between*

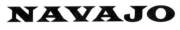

Original Latin Wide typeface

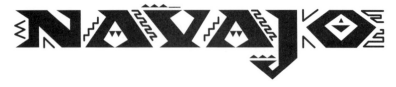

FIGURE 9-13: *Original Navajo logotype*

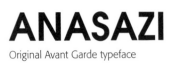

ANASAZI

Original Avant Garde typeface

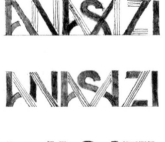

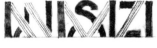

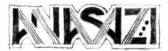

Design evolution (top to bottom)

the letters, rather than incorporated *into* the letters. Reading the first logotype is possible only after seeing through the adornments. In the final iteration, the stylistic elements are decreased, simplified, and incorporated into the letters. The resulting logotype is more readable and more powerful.

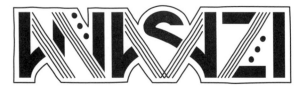

FIGURE 9-14: *Anasazi logotype*

The Anasazi logotype (fig. 9-14) evolves directly from research. Only the basic structure of the typeface, Lubalin's Avant Garde, is used for consistent stroke widths and letter proportions. Tribe style characteristics are manifest in strokes of four hand-drawn parallel lines, two lines of roughly drawn circles, and a freehand outlining of the entire logotype. The restructured *A*s are similar to the alternate *A* in the typeface with the addition of a curved bar. The letter *S* is restructured to function as the centerpiece of this symmetrical design.

The final Anasazi logotype is a successful evolution of a credible initial idea. Many poor designs are actually credible ideas that are halted too soon. A good designer knows when to keep going, when to put it on the back burner to simmer, and when to start again. Every idea follows a unique design path.

DESIGNING NAMEPLATES

ANOTHER APPLICATION OF LOGOTYPE DESIGN IS FOR nameplates. A *nameplate* is a logotype that establishes visual name recognition for a newspaper and is prominently displayed on the front of the publication. The term originally referred to the engraving plate created to print a newspaper's name on letterpress printing presses. This term evolved to represent the design of the name itself. The term *nameplate* here is expanded to include all logotypes used for names of periodical publications, such as newspapers, magazines, and newsletters.

Nameplates follow the same design guidelines as logotypes with an additional size and/or proportion requirement. For maximum effectiveness on a newsletter, many nameplates are designed as a horizontal band across the top of the first page. Besides name identification, these logotypes establish the publication's personality. The target audience for different publications varies. Some hope to attract a wide, general audience. Others target readers within a more narrowly defined group. These groups can be distinguished by age, subject matter, and many other overlapping, identifying factors. Projecting the intended visual personality lets the readership know they have come to the right place.

The Creek Nation nameplate (fig. 9-15) is appropriate for a newsletter for the Creek Indian tribe. This newsletter could contain information regarding current tribal issues, leadership, art, museums, and current affairs. The nameplate is based on the black-and-white, Seminole-style beadwork seen in early nineteenth century tribal handwork. This intricate handwork exhibits zigzagging and interlocking fingers of linear beadwork. The nameplate design emphasizes the parallel repetition of the interlocking bead lines, the consistent line width, angled joins, and rounded endings. The typeface Mercedes had the line weight, joins, and endings necessary for this style. Only the structure of letters *E* and *K* was maintained from the original typeface. The rest of the letters were altered to suit the design.

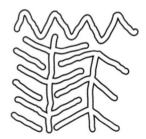

Sample Seminole-style beadwork structure

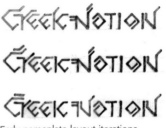

CREEK NATION

Original Mercedes typeface

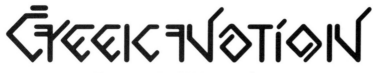

FIGURE 9-15: *Creek Nation nameplate*

The key to the design's development was tilting the *E*. Angling it backwards 45° emphasized the parallel and zigzag lines found in the beadwork. The angle was maintained in the restructuring of the *C, R, N, A,* and *O* and the dot of the *i*. Parallel line treatments were distributed evenly throughout the nameplate to unify the design.

Certain letters required more design attention for emphasis or legibility. The *N*s, for example, used a capital-letter structure and the first *N* received more details than the last. This drew attention to the beginning

Early nameplate layout iterations

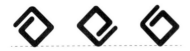

Different break positions suggest
different letters and figures.

of the second word, while maintaining the appearance of a single word through its alignment to the other letters. The *O* was restructured and its outline broken to include another parallel repetition. Correctly determining where to position the break avoided a structure suggestive of a lowercase *a, e,* or figure *6.* Controlling the aperture's size also improved the legibility of the *O.*

FIGURE 9-16: *Wine Aficionado nameplate*

The Wine Aficionado nameplate (fig. 9-16) is intended for a newsletter targeting wine lovers. Its visual personality suggests such descriptors as modern, urban, and bold. The ITC Anna typeface (designed by Daniel Pelavin) combines geometric curves, severe acute angles, and a narrow set width in its letterforms. Its tall, narrow proportions enhance the modern, urban personality desired. The picturesque, hand-tilled, terraced vineyards of the Côtes-du-Rhône region of France do not spring to mind with this design.

The structures of the letters included in this word posed a design problem common to logotype design—how to balance, or better unify, the typeface's contrasting design attributes that are disproportionally represented in the required letters. The *A, F, I,* and *O* are similar in style—narrow, vertical rectangles with tight curves and perpendicular joins. The *C* and *D* share a similar open arc, but the intersection of the *D*'s bowl and stem creates a severe acute angle that extends noticeably beyond the baseline and cap line. The *N* is a cross between the two letter structure styles with the narrow, rectangular appearance of the first group and the acute join of the second. The nameplate design required either balancing these two letter structures throughout the word or letting one of them dominate. Both options required letter restructuring.

Another dominant design characteristic of these particular letters is the parallel, vertical strokes visible in the two *A*s, two *O*s, and the *N*. This is supported by the *F* and *I*s. Since this characteristic was more in

Original ITC Anna typeface

Letters with similar structural attributes

Letters with similar structural attributes

Letter with combination of typeface's
structural attributes

keeping with the publication's intended personality, the angled protruding letterforms were restructured to unify the whole.

A designer can weigh the need for design unification with the design possibilities presented by what Alan Blackman called a "… 'signature' character. It [the character] adds a little visual drama to a piece of typography set in all caps." The letter *C* became the signature character for this nameplate. The gentle arc of the *C* was repeated in the restructured *N* and enabled a better visual balance of that unique characteristic within the word. The *D* was restructured using the *L* and the perpendicular joins of the *T* to blend with the majority of letters.

Another interesting challenge was incorporating the strong parallel lines from the *A* and *O* throughout the other letters (fig. 9-17). This additional design attribute opened letter counters and helped diminish the letterspacing problem created by the open arc of the *C*. This treatment created more unique letterforms taking the nameplate farther away from its original typeface and giving it its own unique identity. The angled line endings of the horizontal strokes were used judiciously to call out the beginning and ending of the word as well as to improve legibility of the *F*. In the interior letters, the parallel horizontal bars were blunt cut to deemphasize this treatment for better blending of the whole.

T + L = D

Letters *T* and *L* created the restructured *D*.

Final layout iterations

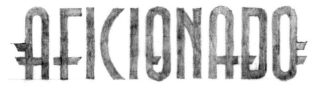

FIGURE 9-17: *Original nameplate layout*

The nameplate incorporated a second word, *WINE,* to clarify the publication's content. The word was incorporated into the whole by using square bullets between letters to visually link it to the dots of the *I*s.

DESIGNING LONG TYPOGRAPHS, SUCH AS TITLES, PHRASES, or quotes, relies on the type artist's accumulated typographic knowledge and experience. Typefaces, type families, alternate glyphs, type weights, type sizes, and graphic letters are the tools on the typographic toolbelt. With these, the type artist leads the reader through the words and sets the proper pace, much like a poet controls the tempo of a verse.

The typograph for the book title *The Little Engine That Could* (see fig. 9-18) uses URW Egyptienne, an extended slab serif typeface with a

DESIGNING
TITLES, PHRASES,
AND QUOTES

The Little
Engine
That Could

Original Egyptienne typeface

The sky is that beautiful old parchment in which the sun and the moon keep their diary

Original Caflisch Script typeface

variety of similar weights and widths. The viewer is attracted first to the left side of the typograph by the large engine graphic in the word *Engine* and the smoke created by the curved word *THE*. This starts the visual movement through the title. The engine-smoke graphic is balanced by the horizontal bar extending through the letters *g, i, n,* and *e,* which is reminiscent of the linked wheels of vintage train engines. Without this balancing element, the design is optically heavy on the left side.

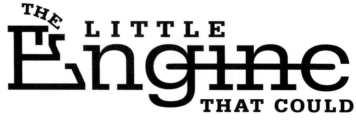

FIGURE 9-18: *Little Engine title typograph*

The Sky quote (fig. 9-19) is set in Caflisch Script. Control of type weights, use of large caps, and selective placement of alternate glyphs aid visual movement through the quote while controlling its pacing.

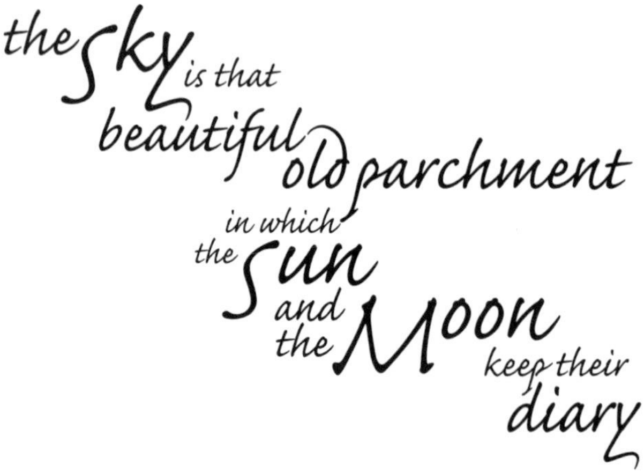

the sky is that beautiful old parchment in which the sun and the moon keep their diary

FIGURE 9-19: *Placement and size pace quote by Kreymborg*

Typefaces including glyphs with alternate endings and beginnings, such as Adobe's Ex Ponto or Poetica, give the type artist even more options for crafting long typographs. By using the type designer's letters, the style of the typeface is maintained while still giving the type artist

the heart of the fool is in his mouth but the mouth of the wise man is in his heart

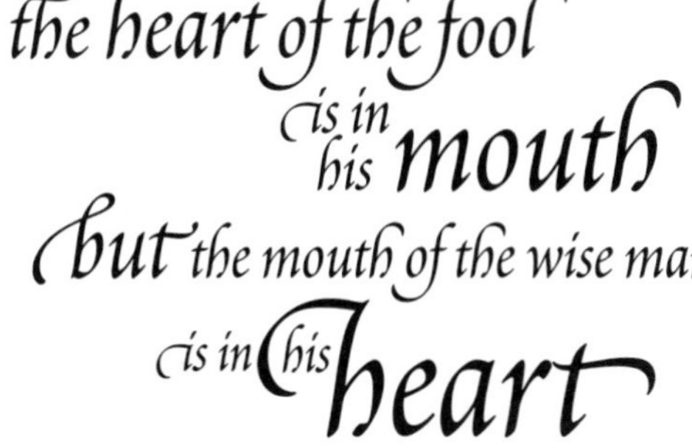

FIGURE 9-20: *Poetica's myriad alternate letters provide flair for a quote by Franklin*

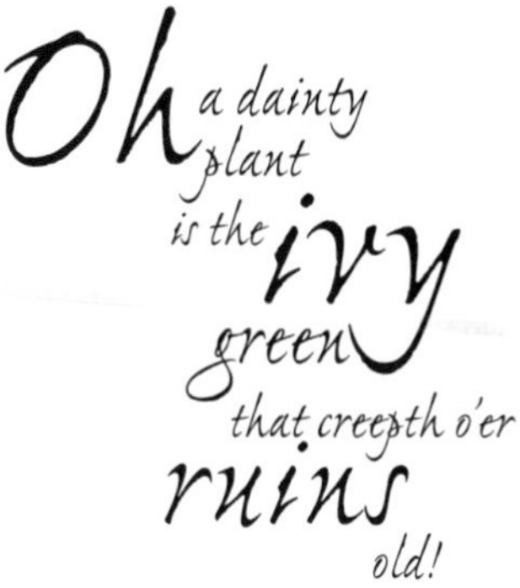

freedom of expression (fig. 9-20). Integrating a style-consistent graphic (fig. 9-21) or a single redesigned letter (see fig. 9-22) into the typograph is another option for the type artist who wants a unique typograph without redesigning an entire alphabet for the occasion.

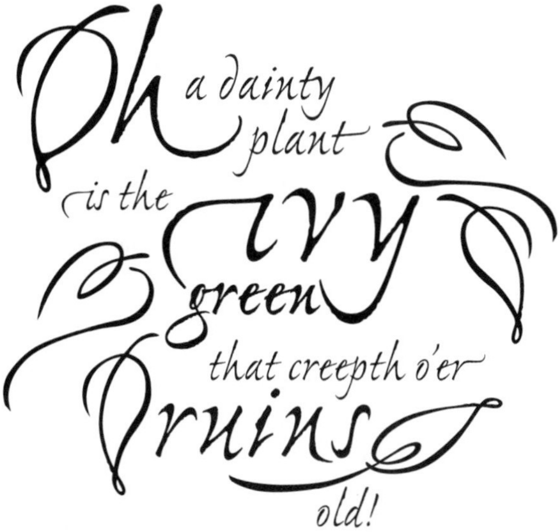

Oh a dainty plant is the ivy green that creepth o'er ruins old!

FIGURE 9-21: *Calligraphic beauty of Ex Ponto creates elegant typograph for a quote by Dickens*

Oh a dainty plant is the ivy green that creepth o'er ruins old!

Original Ex Ponto typeface

Effective use of alternative glyphs as well as all the other available type tools is a mark of typographic quality in typographic art. An eye for detail is a hallmark of high-quality typography and appreciated by

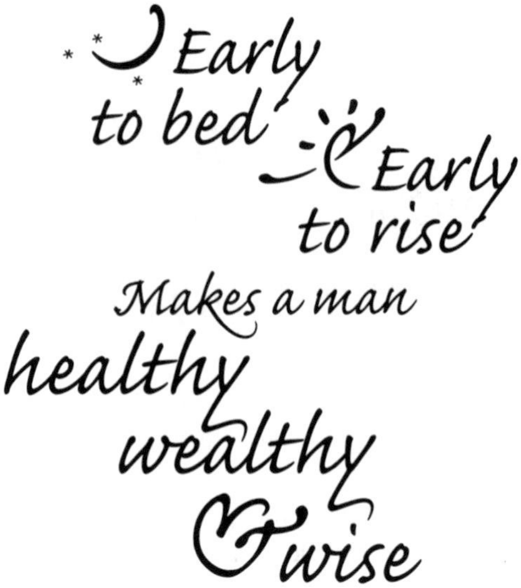

FIGURE 9-22: *Ampersands as contributing graphics*

Early to bed & early to rise
Makes a man healthy,
wealthy, & wise.

Original Caflisch Script typeface

those familiar with it. Each of these options is challenging and fun but requires a knowledge of typography and typefaces that can push the limits of the letterforms without diminishing the letter's role in the word or statement.

Designing Graphic Alphabets

MANY TYPE ENTHUSIASTS EVENTUALLY ENTERTAIN THE IDEA of designing a typeface. Some type artists develop their graphic words into full-fledged graphic alphabets (fig. 9-24). In this chapter, a distinction is made between an original typeface and a graphic alphabet. A typeface is designed for setting words into type, is hinted, designed for proper letter-spacing, is either *unicameral* (a typeface with one letter case, such as a cap-only typeface) or *bicameral* (a typeface with two different cases, usually upper- and lowercase), contains punctuation marks and figures, and is contained within a font file—available with keystrokes. Its style or graphic component does not dominate its appearance because readability is the primary goal. A graphic-alphabet designer restructures the

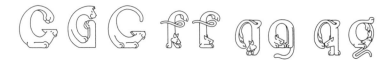

FIGURE 9-23: *Alternates for cap G and lowercase* f, g, *and* q

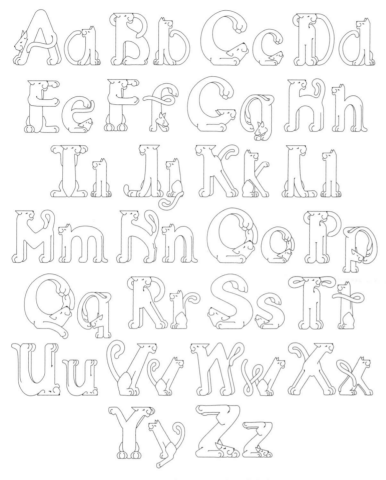

FIGURE 9-24: *Schuster graphic alphabet*
(*designed by S. G. Wheeler in 1999*)

familiar 26 letters according to a dominant graphic style or subject, such as cats. Sometimes graphic alphabets are limited to the capital letters, ignoring completely the lowercase letters, figures, and punctuation marks. Other graphic-alphabet designers create all font characters and produce alternate glyphs (fig. 9-23).

For graphic-alphabet designers, the fun is twisting, restructuring, and reproportioning an existing object into recognizable letters. These alphabets are viewed as graphics and typically are not placed into a font format to be accessed from a keyboard. Their application is limited, such as a single letter or word, because more would be difficult to read.

Many view graphic alphabets as pieces of art and frame them for display. It is a true form of typographic art that is time intensive, but very satisfying when complete—the personal culmination of years of appreciating the typeface designs of others.

ॐ

THE PURSUIT OF LETTERS FROM THE SCRIBE'S CALLIGRAPHY to Gutenberg's invention to phototypography to today's digital typography has intrigued typographers, typesetters, and designers for centuries. Communicating with type for most is a simple, straightforward task—one that does not go beyond the proper use of language, punctuation, and syntax. For a typographer, communicating with type is so much more. It is a form of graphic expression that improves and, therefore, clarifies the message. Manipulating type and integrating type and graphics (fig. 9-25) are avenues of typographic exploration that continue to intrigue typographers. Type is not only the conveyor of the message but a contributor to it as well. In some documents, the type delivers the message smoothly with invisible ease. In other documents, it is expressive and delivers the words with pizzazz and aplomb—invisible it is not. No matter what technology is used to set type in the future, type artists will continue to find new ways to design and influence this powerful, exciting communication language.

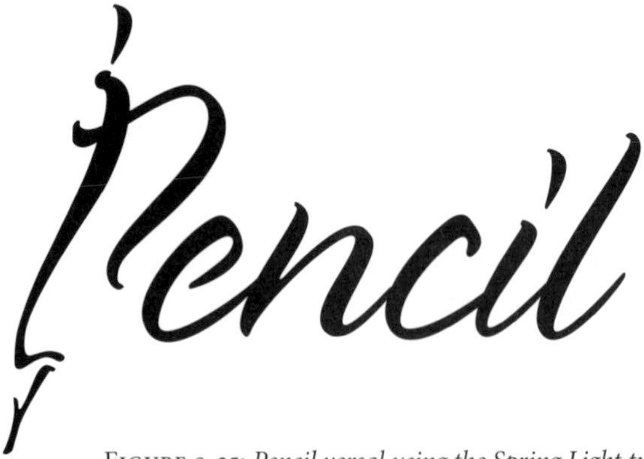

FIGURE 9-25: *Pencil versal using the Spring Light typeface*

INTEGRATING
TYPOGRAPHIC ELEMENTS
ON A
PAGE

BEATRICE WARDE'S 1932 CRYSTAL GOBLET SPEECH is a classic in the annals of typographic writing. In this speech she made an analogy between choosing the perfect wine goblet and creating a beautiful typographic page. Both the goblet and the typography serve as conduits that facilitate the appreciation of wine and the transfer of knowledge, respectively. In her analogy the wine connoisseur had to choose between an exquisitely patterned, solid gold goblet or a long stemmed, thin, crystal-clear glass goblet for sampling his flagon of wine. She wrote, "The first thing he asked of this particular object was not *'How should it look?'* but *'What must it do?'*" It was only when he fully understood the goblet's function, she explained, could he determine its appearance. His goal was not simply beverage transportation—for which a bucket might suffice—but enhanced appreciation of the wine through integrated, multisensory evaluation of bouquet, color, clarity, temperature, and taste. It is not the taste alone that is the culmination of the experience, but the combination of multiple sensory experiences that makes the final tasting even more profound.

Although the crystal-goblet analogy focused primarily on book typography, Warde argued that the same issues were "fifty times more obvious in advertising" and their implementation could have more tangible returns. It was thought that book typography received greater care due to increased production time and loftier content. Typography for advertising had a less revered content, shorter production time, and

Nobody [save other craftsmen] will appreciate half your skill. But you may spend endless years of happy experiment in devising that crystalline goblet which is worthy to hold the vintage of the human mind.

———————————— B. Warde
British Typographers' Guild lecture

209

therefore might exhibit lower quality. She encouraged her audience not to let that happen. The argument is still true today. No matter the length of time available, effective use of type on a page is not a luxury, but a necessity for all forms of typography.

The success of a typographic page is also a cumulative experience of visual sensory input coming from multiple sources, such as the headline, pull quotes, subheads, versals, transition type, and text. All elements contribute their portion of the message at the appropriate time and in the correct order. As with choosing a wine goblet, the first question before creating a typographic page is not How should it look? but What must it do? Once the type artist is clear about the intent of the page, the same question is asked repeatedly in regards to the individual typographic page elements. What must the headline do? What must the versal do? With function clearly established, the type artist determines appearance and integrates the elements into the whole.

PAGE TYPOGRAPHY

A TYPOGRAPHIC PAGE COMES IN MANY FORMS, from a single, noncontinuous page to one of several sequential pages. Some pages are replete with visuals that create a diverse landscape of photographs, illustrations, logotypes, headlines, and text. Other pages are entrusted with dense typographic information for which photographs or illustrations are not available or suitable. These text-dense documents provide the greatest opportunities for typographic treatments. It is here that all the type artist's knowledge regarding type as a readable, directional, and graphic element comes into play. Typographic page elements must accomplish what they are intended to *do*, while being interesting visually and integrated aesthetically on the page.

A newsletter provides an excellent format within which to explore the interrelationship of typographic elements on a text-dense page. Some refer to newsletters as *magapapers* because they combine the design and purpose of a magazine with that of a newspaper. Newsletters present multiple articles on a page, like a newspaper, but can use article-specific design treatments, like a magazine. Due to the quantity of text type and the number of articles on a page, a newsletter can appear either visually monotonous or overwhelming or both. To avoid this, the type artist punctuates the text with typographic treatments that both aid reader comprehension and eliminate the monotony of endless text lines.

To create an effective, complex page, the type artist focuses on several issues concerning the interrelationships of page elements (fig. 10-1) that enhance reader comprehension and page unity. These issues are

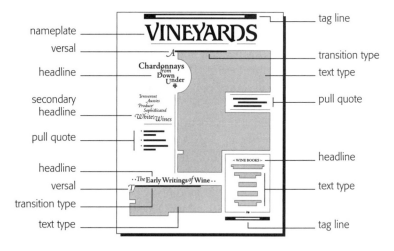

nameplate

versal

headline

secondary
headline

pull quote

headline

versal

transition type

text type

tag line

transition type

text type

pull quote

headline

text type

tag line

FIGURE 10-1: *Common newsletter page elements*

establishing and maintaining a page personality, reinforcing page hierarchy, and maintaining consistency within each typographic level. These
typographic challenges and solutions are explored in this chapter within
the context of three all-type newsletter front pages. While these particular pages use a multitude of typographic treatments, other less dense
text environments benefit from including one or more of them. The decisions made when designing these pages and their individual typographic elements are all prefaced by the question What must it *do*?

BEFORE PLACING A SINGLE GLYPH ON THE PAGE, the type artist needs a
firm understanding of its intended personality. *Page personality* refers to
the use of design treatments that collectively project a distinctive, unified page appearance that is appropriate for the product, service, or publication. Such personalities could suggest a mood, time period, or descriptive adjective to the reader, for example.

Today publishers and designers target their publications and pages
to specific readerships, a target audience, in an effort to successfully
match product to purchaser or information to enthusiast. Many adults
will purchase a car at some point, but certain kinds of people are more
attracted to specific models or manufacturers than others. For example,
a person with children has different vehicle requirements than a person
without children. When an advertisement or page appeals visually to its
intended audience, it is more likely to be read by that audience. This is
one way that subgroups of the greater purchasing public are attracted to

PAGE PERSONALITY

information suited to their needs and interests. It is similar to what happens when people surf the Web at home or scan radio stations in their car. What about this visual or audio stimuli makes them stop to read or to listen? What makes them feel as if they belong or are welcome? Something about the Web page or the radio station is comfortable; it makes a connection.

A visual connection, a sense of belonging, is also made between the reader and the typographic page. A good type artist creates a personality for the text-dense page from the cumulative visual effects of its typographic elements. This personality is attractive and comfortable to its target audience. Identifying the appropriate page personality provides the framework within which all subsequent typographic decisions are made.

The newsletters *Vineyards* (see fig. 10-3), *Wine Aficionado* (see fig. 10-5), and *Fine Bottlings* (see fig. 10-7) are intended for novice wine enthusiasts seeking a regular source of information about their new culinary interest. These newsletters contain articles ranging from the historical to the practical—from a discussion of wines from specific countries to tips for purchasing wine glasses. While the content is the same, the personality of each differs. The terms *sophisticated, modern,* and *elegant* are some of the subjective terms that describe the mood or personality these newsletters project. Such broad descriptors guide the type artist to create a visual landscape that makes the target audience feel welcome.

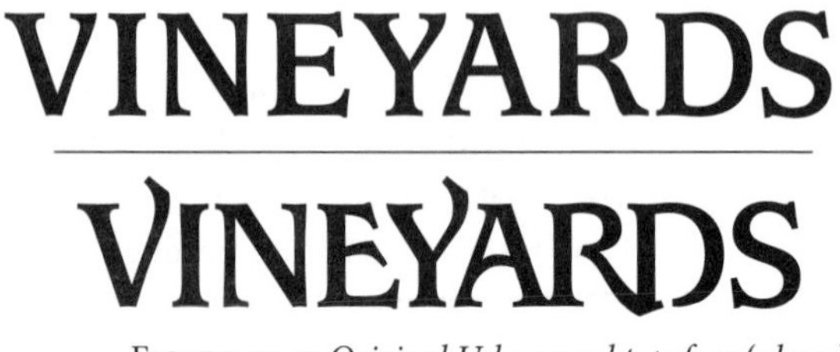

AKMN

Usherwood's asymmetrical serifs

Q

Distinctive tail of Usherwood's Q

VINEYARDS
VINEYARDS

FIGURE 10-2: *Original Usherwood typeface (above)*
for nameplate (below)

A nameplate is the major embodiment of a newsletter's personality. It is the largest typographical element on the page (see "Designing Nameplates" in chapter 9) and that which the reader sees first. A well-designed nameplate communicates the newsletter's personality accurately; it sets the tone. The next decision concerns selecting the typeface for the articles, or the body, of the newsletter. This typeface supports the personality through all other typographic page treatments. Do its design attributes complement or reenforce these personality traits? Will one extended type family unify the page and provide the necessary glyphs for the content? Should the display and text typefaces contrast one another? (See "Type Selection" in chapter 3.) For text-dense documents, particularly those published at regular intervals, such as a newsletter, selection of the typeface takes time, careful study, and many printed samples for comparison. Rushing this selection can lock the designer into a weak, ambiguous type choice that must be maintained for future document continuity. Once the type artist makes these two initial decisions, page design proceeds within this framework.

THE *VINEYARDS* NEWSLETTER HAS A MATURE, sophisticated personality. These terms evoke an elegant dinner party with carefully prepared food and literary discussions around a candle-lit dining table. The nameplate was designed with ITC Usherwood Bold (designed by Leslie Usherwood in 1984). This is an old style typeface with bracketed cupped serifs and a large x-height. Usherwood is intended primarily for display type or discontinuous text type uses. The asymmetrical serif on some of its capital letters, such as the *A, K, M,* and *N,* is a distinguishing feature important to this nameplate. This stroke-ending treatment gives the typeface an organic, rather than a mechanical, appearance making it perfect for suggesting vine-like images. The distinctive tail of the *Q* is a signature stroke that is incorporated into the *V, Y,* and *R* to further support this imagery (fig. 10-2).

 An old-fashioned, detailed typographic page treatment best exemplifies this personality. Consequently, the typeface for the body of the newsletter had to satisfy three requirements. First, it had to complement, rather than contrast, the nameplate. Due to the nameplate's delicacy, the typeface needed to emphasize its more subtle personality traits. Second, because of the prevalence of figures, dates, and foreign language terms in the copy, text figures, small caps, and a well-designed italic were needed. Third, text treatments would include extensive use of type weights and typographic glyphs, such as swash letters, alternate letters, ornaments, symbols, and historical and discretionary ligatures. These requirements suggested an extended type family of historical origins.

 After carefully comparing Adobe's Centaur, Bembo, and Jenson Pro, only Jenson Pro (designed by Robert Slimbach) met all three requirements. Jenson Pro is a humanist typeface with attributes such as bracketed cupped serifs, medium stroke contrast, enhanced typographic capabilities and glyph sets, and a calligraphic stroke that emphasizes the

VINEYARDS

··*The* **Early Writi**

*T*HE GROWING OF GRAPES AND THE MAK 3000 B.C. in the Middle East. Its use and mented. The Hittites in 1500 B.C. referred to of *woinos,* but in classical Greek is became *oi*

 ❡In the *Iliad* and *Odyssey,* Homer wro tance in society. Wine was a product for trad Spain and west to the Black Sea. It was used ceremonies, and for fun. *Kottabos* was an earl in the book *The Deipnosophists.* ❧

Extensive ligature and glyph use creates a detailed page texture.

AefgHjkMnp
AefgHjkMnp
AefgHjkMnp

Centaur Regular, Bembo Regular, and Jenson Pro Light (top to bottom)

nameplate's organic quality. Adobe's Jenson is based on the roman characters of Nicolas Jenson's typeface and its companion italic letterforms are based on Ludovico Arrighi's graceful italic types.

WHEN ESTABLISHING PAGE TYPOGRAPHY FOR a single page with a single message, the type artist determines the path the reader takes to comprehend the message. The information conveys a single train of thought. Newsletters, however, present multiple articles, so two hierarchical levels emerge. The first hierarchy identifies the page as a single entity, a newsletter, composed of individual components, the articles. These articles have varying degrees of importance (primary, secondary, tertiary). The reader understands that these are individual, although related, articles contained within a single document. The second hierarchy exists within each individual article. What path does the reader take to comprehend its content correctly? A newsletter exemplifies the interrelatedness of typographic elements within a single article and within a collection of articles.

The *Vineyards* front page contains three articles. Each conveys a separate identity and communicates its place in the page hierarchy, while maintaining a single page personality and design structure. Secondary and tertiary headlines are not subheads within the same article, but headlines of lesser importance that identify stand-alone articles.

The primary article, "Chardonnays from Down Under," is identified as the most important, not only from the amount of space it occupies and its location on the page, but also by the size and number of type treatments it contains and the amount of introductory white space it uses. Introductory white space, in general, separates the body of the newsletter from the nameplate, while spotlighting the beginning of the first article. If this white space is insufficient, the crush of typography prevents the reader from understanding the page's structure. This hinders the reader's ability to settle in to enjoy the information and the process of reading.

The first article employs an on-the-side headline style. An *on-the-side headline* aligns either at the top, bottom, or middle of the article. It is an excellent style to use when the type artist wants to insert a significant amount of white space into a page. Consequently, it works well for a primary article. The Chardonnay headline functions as a graphic by using the words to create a directional, diagonal shape; by using different type family styles (roman and italic), weights (semibold and regular), sizes, and alternate/swash glyphs; and by placing a grape-leaf–like

Two hierarchical structures exist on this newsletter front page.

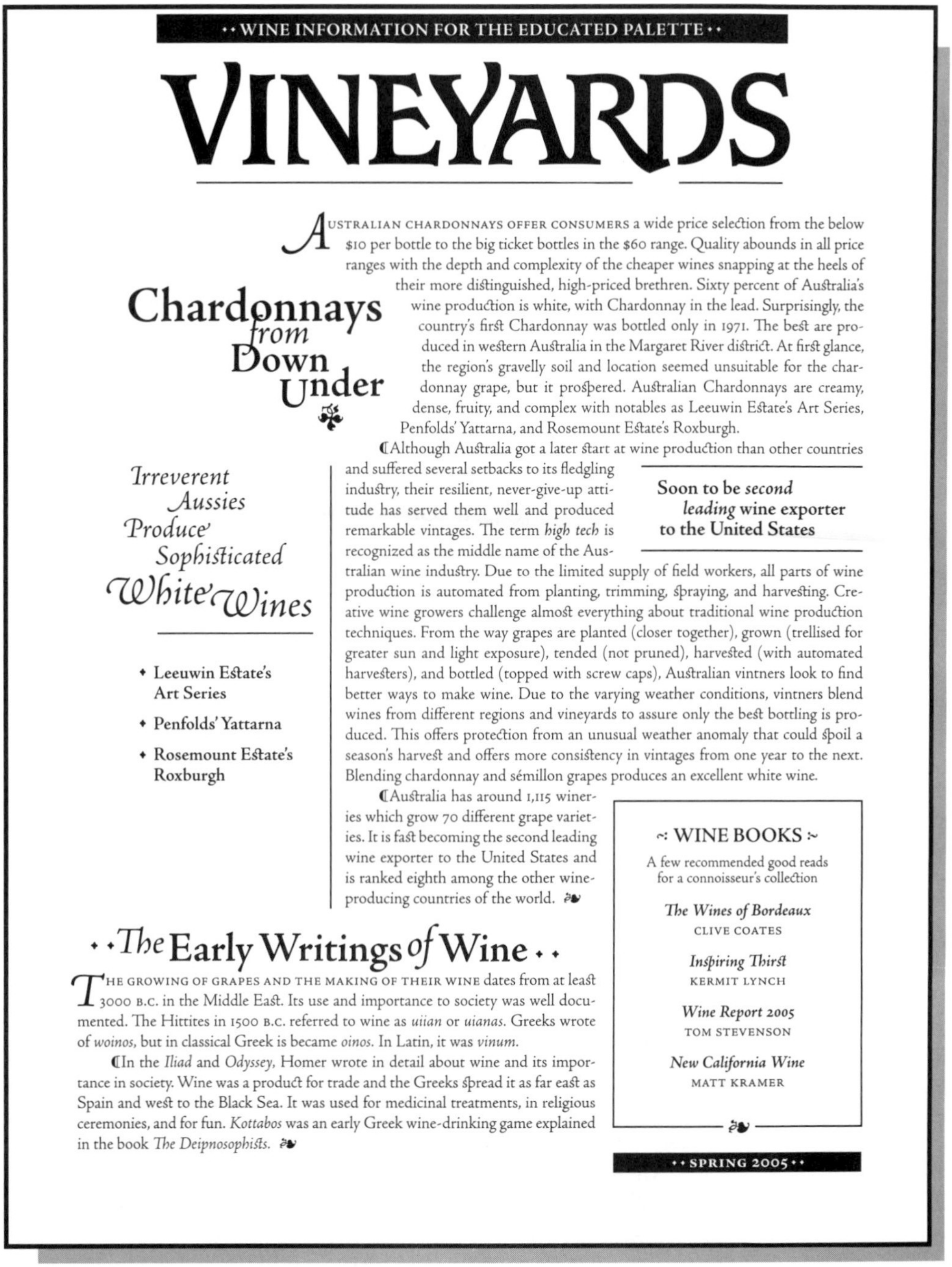

VINEYARDS

Chardonnays *from* Down Under

Irreverent Aussies Produce Sophisticated White Wines

- Leeuwin Estate's Art Series
- Penfolds' Yattarna
- Rosemount Estate's Roxburgh

*A*USTRALIAN CHARDONNAYS OFFER CONSUMERS a wide price selection from the below $10 per bottle to the big ticket bottles in the $60 range. Quality abounds in all price ranges with the depth and complexity of the cheaper wines snapping at the heels of their more distinguished, high-priced brethren. Sixty percent of Australia's wine production is white, with Chardonnay in the lead. Surprisingly, the country's first Chardonnay was bottled only in 1971. The best are produced in western Australia in the Margaret River district. At first glance, the region's gravelly soil and location seemed unsuitable for the chardonnay grape, but it prospered. Australian Chardonnays are creamy, dense, fruity, and complex with notables as Leeuwin Estate's Art Series, Penfolds' Yattarna, and Rosemount Estate's Roxburgh.

Although Australia got a later start at wine production than other countries and suffered several setbacks to its fledgling industry, their resilient, never-give-up attitude has served them well and produced remarkable vintages. The term *high tech* is recognized as the middle name of the Australian wine industry. Due to the limited supply of field workers, all parts of wine production is automated from planting, trimming, spraying, and harvesting. Creative wine growers challenge almost everything about traditional wine production techniques. From the way grapes are planted (closer together), grown (trellised for greater sun and light exposure), tended (not pruned), harvested (with automated harvesters), and bottled (topped with screw caps), Australian vintners look to find better ways to make wine. Due to the varying weather conditions, vintners blend wines from different regions and vineyards to assure only the best bottling is produced. This offers protection from an unusual weather anomaly that could spoil a season's harvest and offers more consistency in vintages from one year to the next. Blending chardonnay and sémillon grapes produces an excellent white wine.

> Soon to be *second leading* wine exporter to the United States

Australia has around 1,115 wineries which grow 70 different grape varieties. It is fast becoming the second leading wine exporter to the United States and is ranked eighth among the other wine-producing countries of the world.

··The Early Writings *of* Wine··

*T*HE GROWING OF GRAPES AND THE MAKING OF THEIR WINE dates from at least 3000 B.C. in the Middle East. Its use and importance to society was well documented. The Hittites in 1500 B.C. referred to wine as *uiian* or *uianas*. Greeks wrote of *woinos*, but in classical Greek is became *oinos*. In Latin, it was *vinum*.

In the *Iliad* and *Odyssey*, Homer wrote in detail about wine and its importance in society. Wine was a product for trade and the Greeks spread it as far east as Spain and west to the Black Sea. It was used for medicinal treatments, in religious ceremonies, and for fun. *Kottabos* was an early Greek wine-drinking game explained in the book *The Deipnosophists*.

> ∾ WINE BOOKS ∿
>
> A few recommended good reads for a connoisseur's collection
>
> *The Wines of Bordeaux*
> CLIVE COATES
>
> *Inspiring Thirst*
> KERMIT LYNCH
>
> *Wine Report 2005*
> TOM STEVENSON
>
> *New California Wine*
> MATT KRAMER

··SPRING 2005··

FIGURE 10-3: Vineyards *newsletter front page*

ornament at its end. Inserting the headline into the text and creating a rounded negative space with the contoured wrap draws additional emphasis to the headline and its role as a graphic attention-getter (see "Text Type Design" in chapter 7).

Once attracted to this article, the reader progresses from the headline into the text along an informative route. The full headline consists of two sections. The main section, "Chardonnays from Down Under," and the secondary section, "Irreverent Aussies Produce Sophisticated White Wines," function similarly to a title and subtitle of a book. This distinction is indicated with the change of type treatment. The divided headline and two pull quotes (one external, one internal) keeps the page from being overwhelming, due to quantity, or monotonous, due to lack of visual diversity. After navigating the display and discontinuous type elements, a large, hanging, swash *A* versal entices the reader into the text with the help of an extended length of small-cap transition type, appropriate for the extended measure.

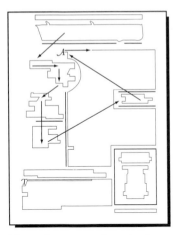

Vineyards page map through primary article

FIGURE 10-4: *Headline placement styles*

The secondary article, "The Early Writings of Wine," employs an umbrella-style headline. An *umbrella headline* extends across the top of an entire article (fig. 10-4). It is effective for establishing the beginning of a new article when it follows another. With this headline style, there is no need to position a rule at the end of the preceding article, because the change in typography, as well as its location, signals a new beginning. The Early headline also receives graphic treatment by incorporating regular italic with the semibold roman for visual interest. The two bullet-like ornaments on either side of the headline are enlarged periods. Jenson Pro includes beautiful, plus-shaped periods. Their inclusion is reminiscent of the dots used to separate words in early writings before the adoption of word spaces. They provide another graphic touch.

The article "Wine Books" is not intended as a stand-alone article, but as a supporting article of discontinuous information. Positioning, or *packaging*, two related articles together helps the reader easily find additional information on a single topic. An outlining rectangle separates it from the adjacent text. Unlike page hierarchy that establishes the route through a page to improve reader comprehension, packaging information organizes tangential information that is read at any time. Its page location is adjacent to, or embedded in, the related article.

CONSISTENCY WITHIN THE DISPLAY TYPE focused on the controlled use of type treatments to maintain hierarchy and attract attention. With the text type, size and weight consistency is maintained more stringently to define hierarchical placement and establish a comfortable reading environment. Text type is not an attention-getting element. In the two longer articles, the text type is Jenson Pro Light 11/13 × 28. This produces 80 characters per measure and slightly exceeds the optimum character range (60–75) for a single type column. The longer measure is useful because the pull quote and packaged article inserted into the primary text block narrows its measure to 45 characters—a comfortable length for multicolumn text. This provided enough characters and spaces to prevent white rivers within the narrowed measures.

Historical and discretionary ligatures support the personality by creating a more detailed page texture. In addition, pilcrows identify paragraph beginnings. This was particularly useful when the rounded contoured wrap coincided with, and eliminated, the 2-em indent of the second paragraph. This symbol is maintained in the other continuous-text articles for continuity and consistency.

The third article is a listing of related information—discontinuous text. Change in type treatment identifies this change of purpose. The individual book titles are set in upper- and lowercase Jenson Pro Semibold Italic 11/12 and the corresponding authors' names are set in small-cap Jenson Pro Light 11/12. By manipulating the space after each listing, the baselines align four times. The headline, as the most prominent element,

~: WINE BOOKS :~

A few recommended good reads
for a connoisseur's collection

The Wines of Bordeaux
CLIVE COATES

Inspiring Thirst
KERMIT LYNCH

Wine Report 2005
TOM STEVENSON

New California Wine
MATT KRAMER

— 🐝 —

PARAGRAPH AND SENTENCE TYPOGRAPHY

A USTRALIAN CHARDO
$10 per bottle to t
ranges with the d
their mor

Chardonnays wine p
from count
Down duced
the r
Under donn
🍀 dense,
Penfolds'

Irreverent ¶Although
Aussies and suffered sever
Produce industry, their res
Sophisticated tude has served
remarkable vintag
recognized as the
White Wines tralian wine indu
production is aut
ative wine growel
techniques. From

On-the-side headline with contoured wrap creates a spotlight effect.

the second text line that follows it, and the second and fourth authors' names align with adjacent baselines. Aligning baselines is necessary for visual organization (see "Intraparagraph Spacing" in chapter 4). Unaligned adjacent baselines bounce around, or vibrate, in the reader's range of vision. The aligned baselines visually link, or anchor, the text elements together, thus unifying, organizing, and quieting the page to the reader's benefit.

Baselines of the primary article's display type blocks align with the adjacent article at least once. The word *Down* in the headline, the word *Wines* in the secondary headline, and all lines of each pull quote (set 12/13 and 13/13) align with an adjacent baseline. This provides a strong visual relationship between these corresponding type blocks.

WINE AFICIONADO

THE *WINE AFICIONADO* NEWSLETTER (see fig. 10-5) has a modern, bold, and urban personality. The hustle and bustle of city life comes to mind. The nameplate (see fig. 9-16) projects this personality through the bold, elongated letters of ITC Anna. This design's development was discussed in chapter 9 (See "Designing Nameplates").

slowly. Sauvignon blanc grapes prosper in this climate and sible for putting New Zealand wineries into the world's *sauvignon* is from the French word *sauvage* (wild). These es produce wines with flavors of green limes, green melons, es, and passion fruit.

flavors produces the ———— most noted for
tful vintages true to **Sauvignon Blanc**
rapes are handpicked
n lyre trellises that open them to sunlight and airflow. This eeps them dry and ripening. Frost is another one of Mother The crops of 2001 and 2003 were reduced significantly due rly frost. To combat frost, wine growers employ overhead

Chaparral Pro's serifs and clean lines create a modern, easy-to-read page.

The page design chosen to support this personality is sleek and streamlined. It requires a clean, simple typeface—nothing delicate or fussy. The article lengths limit the amount of available white space for leading and intraparagraph spacing, suggesting the need for a serif typeface to maintain readability. The content requires text figures for typesetting several dates, quantities, and a numerical listing. In addition, a variety of weights is necessary for diverse type treatments and graphic headlines. Chaparral Pro (designed by Carol Twombly) satisfies all those needs. It is a slab serif typeface with four different weights, corresponding italics, and extensive glyph sets and typographic capabilities. Chaparral is promoted as a "hybrid slab serif" due to its narrower letter proportions, unlike traditional geometric slab serif designs. This smaller width makes it suitable for a long document with restricted measures, while providing the clean, modern look of a slab serif.

PAGE HIERARCHY

THE FRONT PAGE CONTAINS THREE ARTICLES. The primary article is a lengthy discussion of New Zealand wines, the secondary article is an enumerated list of tips for purchasing wine glasses, and the tertiary article is a discontinuous article of brief facts about four prominent wine glass manufacturers. This last article is packaged with the secondary article to provide related information. Page hierarchy emphasizes the primary article and unifies the two other articles into a horizontal band along the bottom through the use of rules and tints. Balancing boldness with easy-to-comprehend page hierarchy is the primary challenge here.

The primary article, "Battling the Elements," employs a wrap-style headline. A *wrap headline* is useful on tight, multicolumn pages where white space is at a premium. There are two styles of wrap headlines—Dutch and U-shape. The *Dutch wrap* positions the headline atop the first column and aligns the top of the remaining columns either with the headline's highest cap line or extends the text above it, as is done here. The first alignment option minimizes the amount of white space used to spotlight the headline. This is more typical for an article other than the first. A rule is necessary across all columns without a headline to alert the reader of the new article's upper boundaries. Without it, a reader from the story above could easily enter the text columns not capped with a headline, thus causing confusion. The second alignment option adds more white space before the headline as sinkage. A rule is not needed here because the article follows the nameplate and, with prudent white space, the demarcation between the two is clear. A *U-shape wrap* positions the headline above an interior column. The columns on either side align with the headline's highest cap line (see fig. 10-4). Both wrap techniques require capping rules to prevent confusion.

This newsletter's primary article has an extended headline divided into two sections. The first section is set in 28 point, with the words *BATTLING* and *ELEMENTS* in bold caps and *THE* in semibold small caps. Rules and midpoints add more graphic elements that visually connect the headline with the versal and pull quote. The secondary headline is set in 18-point, regular upper- and lowercase. The controlled use of white space within and after the headline connects the sections while introducing the text. The reader follows a simple, vertical route from headline to text.

Unlike the *Vineyards* newsletter that uses a versal to lure the reader from the pull quote into the text, the *O* versal performs a slightly different task. It is more informative than directional. With the graphic headline and the large transition type all converging in the same spot, it is easy for the reader to get confused. The versal announces the start of the text type, making clear the role of the large transition type that follows. If the reader went from the headline to the pull quote, the role of the versal is more directional. The pull quote's flush right alignment and horizontal rules propel the reader to the left and into the versal's waiting grasp. The challenge of graphic headlines and large transition type in close proximity to one another is that with all the attention-getters in

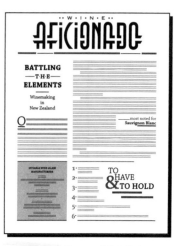

Graphic headlines and tints help define page hierarchy.

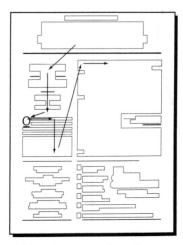

Aficionado page map through primary article

·· W · I · N · E ··

ALICIONADO

SPRING 2004 ———— WINE INFORMATION FOR THE EDUCATED PALETTE ———— VOLUME IV

BATTLING

—T·H·E—

ELEMENTS

Winemaking
in
New Zealand

O NE CANNOT BE faint of heart and tie their long term economic livelihood to winemaking in New Zealand. The climate condition unique to this part of the world, approximately midway between the equator and the South Pole, necessitate tenacious wine growers. Discovered in 1642 by the Dutch sea captain Abel Tasman, New Zealand is a country composed of multiple islands; the largest are North Island

and South Island. Auckland, the capital and the birthplace of its wine industry, is located on the northern end of North Island. To the Māori, New Zealand's indigenous people, home is *Aetearoa* (Land of the Long White Cloud).

New Zealand's climate is cool and windy, the terrain is rugged, and the soil is clay and high in acid. During the day the vines are subjected to intense sunlight and at night the cool sea breezes prevail. In addition, the weather in Auckland is wet. Here average rainfall is 3.9 inches a month compared to much smaller amounts (.39–.78 inches) in areas to the south. The clay soil actually is beneficial because it repels much of the rain, while at the same time holding moisture during dry periods.

Grapes here are chosen for their climate suitability. They must be hardy and be able to ripen slowly. Sauvignon blanc grapes prosper in this climate and initially were responsible for putting New Zealand wineries into the world's spotlight. The word *sauvignon* is from the French word *sauvage* (wild). These New Zealand varieties produce wines with flavors of green limes, green melons, gooseberries, mangoes, and passion fruit.

This combination of flavors produces the ——— most noted for untamed and delightful vintages true to **Sauvignon Blanc** the name's origins. Grapes are handpicked

and the vines grow on lyre trellises that open them to sunlight and airflow. This growing technique keeps them dry and ripening. Frost is another one of Mother Nature's challenges. The crops of 2001 and 2003 were reduced significantly due to an unexpected early frost. To combat frost, wine growers employ overhead sprinklers, wind machines, and even helicopters to keep it from settling on the delicate fruit.

New Zealand largest winery is Brancott, owned by the Montana company. Their Sauvignon Blanc Marlborough 2003 is an excellent vintage. ❖

**NOTABLE WINE GLASS
MANUFACTURERS**

RIEDEL
*Family-owned, 300-year-old Austrian company.
Pioneered wine glasses shaped
for specific wines*
·
SPIEGELAU
*Bavarian manufacturer since 1521
of leaded and lead-free crystal*
·
SCHOTT ZWIESEL
*German glassworks since 1872. Created
dishwasher-safe, lead-free Tritan crystal*
·
RAVENSCROFT
Specializes in lead-free crystal

1 · Reasonably priced to encourage use

2 · Thin rim for steady flow of wine into mouth

3 · Tapered opening to concentrate bouquet

4 · Generous bowl for adequate aeration of wine

5 · Clear, smooth glass for uninhibited view of wine's color and clarity

6 · Adequate stem-to-bowl proportions for stability when drinking ❖

TO
&HAVE
TO HOLD

Six Tips to Choosing
the Perfect Wine Glass

FIGURE 10-5: Wine Aficionado *newsletter front page*

one spot the reader can become confused. The type artist prioritizes these type blocks through size, weight, and sometimes, more significantly, through control of white space. Subtle, rather than overt, changes usually do the trick.

The secondary article, "To Have & To Hold," is a listing of purchasing tips for wine glasses. The graphic treatments for this headline serve as an excellent visual change since it follows such a lengthy article. The 30-point words in both regular and semibold surround a large, 72-point, tinted ampersand. Placing a headline on the right side of an article usually requires a strong versal and transition type to lure the reader to the correct text entry point. With this listing, large tinted figures attract the reader to the listing. Tinting both the ampersand and the figures maintains both the page and the article hierarchy effectively without competing with the primary article's headline.

The tertiary article, "Notable Wine Glass Manufacturers," is a packaged, discontinuous-text article that relates to the wine-glass purchasing article. The information is set within a tinted block lowering the contrast between text and background, thus intentionally diminishing the article's impact on the page. Unlike the *Vineyards'* packaged article that sits within articles, the common use of rules and tints visually links this article with its companion.

THE PARAGRAPH AND SENTENCE TYPOGRAPHY in this newsletter addresses typographic situations in keeping with its personality and enhanced readability. The text type in the primary article is Chaparral Pro Light 10/13 with a 2-lead, first-line indent. Chaparral is a highly legible typeface with a medium to large *x*-height and a medium set width. It produced a 49-character measure for the first, narrow column and an 80-character measure for the second, wider column. The 48-point Chaparral semibold versal leads into multiple lines of 13-point transition type. The first three words are set in regular small caps and the remainder in upper- and lowercase light. The size of the versal warrants the additional transitional element.

When using narrow columns, large-size transition type benefits from multiple lines. With only one line, the visual impact of the transition is short and, therefore, the size distinction between the transition and text type must be extreme. With four lines of short-measure text, the size difference can be smaller because the size difference is easier to distinguish with a larger sample. Baseline alignment becomes an issue here because the larger transition type is adjacent to a text column. Only

NOTABLE WINE GLASS MANUFACTURERS

RIEDEL
*ly-owned, 300-year-old Austrian com
Pioneered wine glasses shaped
for specific wines*
•

SPIEGELAU
*Bavarian manufacturer since 1521
of leaded and lead-free crystal*
•

Regular and semibold increase contrast on tinted background.

PARAGRAPH AND
SENTENCE TYPOGRAPHY

AefgHjkMnp
Chapparal Pro Light

BATTLING
—T·H·E—
ELEMENTS

Winemaking
in
New Zealand

O NE CANNOT BE faint of heart and tie their long term economic livelihood to winemaking in New Zealand. The climate condition unique to this part of the world, approximately midway between the equator and the South Pole, necessitate tenacious wine growers. Discovered in 1642 by the Dutch sea captain Abel Tasman, New Zealand is a country composed of multiple islands; the largest are North Island

and Sou
is locate
indigen
                          N
soil is c
sunligh
Aucklar
smaller
benefici
moistur
                          c
and be i
initially
spotligh
New Ze
goosebe
This com
untame
the nam
and the
growing
Nature'.
to an ur
sprinkle
delicate
                          N
pany. Th

Baseline alignment anchors type elements together.

FINE BOTTLINGS

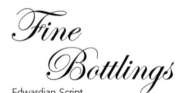

Edwardian Script

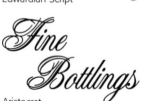

Aristocrat

the first and last lines of the transition type are aligned, as these are the most noticeable. To achieve this, transition type is set 13/17.34. Within the display type, the words *BATTLING* and *ELEMENTS* align with adjacent baselines to anchor it.

Within the third paragraph, the pull quote narrows four measures to 41 characters, but the length and number of words within those measures are such that the narrowing does not produce any white rivers. Within the sentences, text figures are used for annual rainfall amounts and dates. Italics identify foreign language words, whose definitions followed in parentheses, and a word discussed as a word (see chapter 6).

The secondary article uses Chaparral Pro Light 10/13 with 8-points of white space following each enumerated tip. A modified contoured wrap is created by breaking (rather than hyphenating) the text lines after words. Hyphenation would be too distracting. The last line of the secondary headline aligns with an adjacent baseline.

The tertiary article, "Notable Wine Glass Manufacturers," employs type style differences to make easy visual distinctions between the four discontinuous-text elements. The headline is set in 10/13 semibold, manufacturer names in 11/10 caps and small caps, and descriptive text blocks in 9/10 regular italic. Space following each entry is controlled so the first line of the headline and the last line of the article aligns with adjacent baselines to anchor the article with its surroundings. The change to regular and semibold weights provide sufficient contrast between text and background (see "Stock and Readability" in chapter 3).

THE *FINE BOTTLINGS* NEWSLETTER PROJECTS a florid, ornate personality (see fig. 10-7). The hand-tended, terraced vineyards of France and slower pace of the countryside characterize the intended mood. Vining imagery is suggested by the twisting, intertwining strokes of the nameplate (fig. 10-6). The Phyllis typeface (designed by Heinrich Wieynck in 1911) with its multistroke, decorative initials and simple lowercase captures this well. Other typefaces, such as ITC Edwardian Script (designed by Ed Benguiat) and Aristocrat (designed by Donald Stevens), were considered, but the complexity and elegance of Phyllis prevailed. The nameplate's design presented two interesting challenges: first, orchestrating the complexity of strokes in the letters while maintaining the nameplate's readability and, second, using an asymmetrical placement on the page without confusing the nameplate's purpose. Not all newsletter nameplates are centered above the body, as on a newspaper. Those that employ a nontraditional placement must maintain their dominance and identity, so the reader understands their role.

Phyllis is a calligraphic typeface with angled finials, slanted line endings, and pear-shaped terminals. The combination of thins and thicks in the decorative initials creates an interesting interplay between the strokes that define letter structure and those that augment it. Only two initials appear in the nameplate, but the additional strokes and extended swashes added to several lowercase and restructured letters integrate them into the design. The most troublesome section of the nameplate was the *o-t-t-l* letter sequence. Multiple ideas were explored—some too complex for comprehension; others too exaggerated for letter integrity. The final iteration achieves a balance between complexity and readability, while maintaining the desired personality. The tag line is set in semibold small caps in the text typeface. A large brace from a different typeface serves as a transitional link between the simple type of the tag line and the elaborate typography of the nameplate.

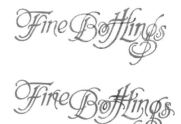

Iterations for *o-t-t-l* sequence

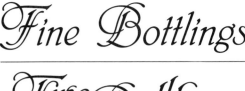

FIGURE 10-6: *Original Phyllis typeface (above)*
for nameplate (below)

Page design supports this ornate personality by emphasizing the oblique angle and intricacies of Phyllis through select and prominent use of italics and swash letters. These treatments are used judiciously within headlines and pull quotes to avoid the page becoming busy and disorganized and for alleviating text monotony. Text typeface selection focused on old style typefaces—those with low *x*-heights and elegant ascenders extending beyond the cap height. The content requires text figures for large quantities, percentages, dates, and others, as well as italics

AefgHjkMnp
A K M S

Adobe Garamond Pro Regular with swash italic glyphs

and small caps. Adobe Garamond Pro meets all those qualifications along with having pear-shaped terminals that match those of Phyllis.

Page Hierarchy

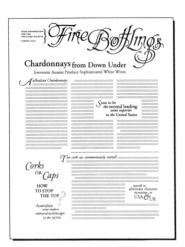

Scannable page map conveys content.

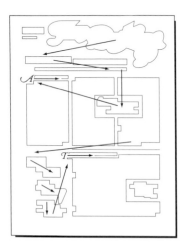

Fine Bottlings page map

Effective page hierarchy enables a reader to easily scan a page and receive an accurate snapshot of its content. This increases the likelihood that the reader is intrigued by the subject matter and decides to continue reading in more detail. On the *Fine Bottlings* front page, the scan route progresses diagonally downward in a left-to-right route from headline to pull quote to headline to pull quotes. By solely reading the discontinuous elements, the reader identifies the two topics, receives clarification as to the articles' focus, and makes an informed decision as to whether or not to continue reading. Unlike the previous newsletter fronts, this one contains only two articles. Consequently, each has a greater volume of continuous-reading text. With fewer articles, avoiding text monotony is a major concern. Graphic headlines, multiple pull quotes, eye-catching versals, and unique transition type are the various techniques that avoid this as well as provide the scannable snapshot.

"Chardonnay from Down Under" displays a formidable amount of text. The three equal-measure columns give it a dense appearance, more so than other measure combinations. The long, two-part, umbrella-style headline separates the primary article from the nameplate. Control of white space before the headline provides sufficient introduction for the body of the publication and smaller white space after the headline links it with the article. The headline divides into three sections. Through control of point size, type weight, and baselines, the headline works in tandem with the versal and italic transition type to provide both an interesting article introduction and transition into the text. The pear-shaped terminal on the swash *A* versal links the body of the newsletter with the terminals in the nameplate, particularly with the loop of the lowercase *g*.

The secondary article, "Corks or Caps—How to Stop the Top?," provides another introductory graphic headline. This on-the-side headline adds much-needed white space to the dense page and spotlights the headline. The strong vertical direction through this headline, accentuated by the external pull quote below it, requires a prominent versal to pull the reader back up to the beginning of the article. For additional emphasis beyond the versal's swash, the versal and second line of text type hang into the white space. An additional connection is made by rotating the 80-point question mark to match the versal's angle. This catches the reader's eye and contributes to the directional pull of the

Fine Bottlings

Chardonnays from Down Under

Irreverent Aussies Produce Sophisticated White Wines

Australian Chardonnays offer consumers a wide price selection from the below $10 per bottle to the big ticket bottles in the $60 range. Quality abounds in all price ranges with the depth and complexity of the cheaper wines snapping at the heels of their more distinguished and high-priced brethren. Sixty percent of Australia's wine production is white. Chardonnay takes the lead. Surprisingly, the country's first Chardonnay was bottled only in 1971. The best are produced in the Margaret River district of western Australia. At first glance, however, the region's gravelly soil and location seemed unsuitable for the chardonnay grape, but it did prosper. Australian Chardonnays are creamy, dense, fruity, and complex with notables as Leeuwin Estates's Art Series, Penfolds' Yattarna, and Rosemount Estate's Roxburgh.

Although Australia got a later start at wine production than other countries and suffered several setbacks to its fledgling industry, their resilient, never-give-up attitude has served them well and has produced remarkable vintages. The term *high tech* is recognized as the middle name of Australia's wine industry. Due to the limited supply of field workers, all parts of wine production is automated from planting, trimming, spraying, and harvesting. Creative wine growers challenge almost everything about traditional wine production techniques. From the way grapes are planted (closer together), grown (trellised for greater sun and light exposure), tended (not pruned), harvested (with automated harvesters), and bottled (topped with screwcaps), Australian vintners look to find better ways to make wine. Due to the varying weather conditions, vintners blend wines from different regions and vineyards to assure only the best bottling is produced. This offers added protection from the unusual weather anomaly that can spoil the season's one harvest and provides more consistency in vintages from one year to the next. Blending both chardonnay and sémillon grapes produces an excellent white wine.

Soon to be the second leading wine exporter to the United States

Australia has approximately 1,115 wineries, growing 70 grape varieties. It is fast becoming the second leading wine exporter to the USA. It is currently ranked eighth among the world's leading wine-producing countries. ✿

Corks OR Caps

HOW TO STOP THE TOP ?

Australian *wine makers* *embraced* screwcaps *in the* 1970S

The cork we ceremoniously extract from the narrow neck of a wine bottle started life as the bark of the cork oak tree (*Quercus suber*), most likely in southern Portugal. Cork oaks live from 150 to 250 years old and are protected under Portuguese law. In the late 1900s Portugal produced 13 billion wine corks per year and currently sells £630 million annually. Corks are suitable wine stoppers because they are impervious to air, do not decompose, and conform snuggly to any given space.

Corks have been used for centuries as wine stoppers, but synthetic closures, such as plastic corks and screwcaps, currently make up 7 to 9 percent of wine closures. Switzerland, Australia, and New Zealand are more accepting of the screwcap closure. Some experts in comparative testings found white wines were fresher and more vibrant than their corked competitors and reds surprisingly smooth, soft, and complex. In the 2003 International Wine Challenge, almost 5 percent of the corks in the competition's 11,033 submissions failed. Either the wine was spoiled or its flavor was flattened.

interest in alternate closures increasing in USA & UK

Not surprisingly wine buyers' preferences or prejudices must be considered. In a 2003 survey, 75 percent of participants felt uncomfortable serving them socially. Consumer's views cannot be ignored, but the wine itself does not appear to suffer. ✿

FIGURE 10-7: Fine Bottlings *newsletter front page*

versal. The outlined question mark diminishes its presence on the page, so the reader is not enticed to it out of turn.

Type sizes for all headlines and typographic elements in these articles are carefully chosen. Since all typographic elements are relative, all sizes work in conjunction with one another. Change one attribute and the type artist must reevaluate the rest with a fresh eye. Not only is the role of all typographic elements within their own article important, but their role and dominance on the page is important as well.

PARAGRAPH AND SENTENCE TYPOGRAPHY

BOTH ARTICLES USE ADOBE GARAMOND PRO 10/12 with a 1-lead indent. An ornament signals the end of each article. Justification settings are 80%, 100%, and 133% for minimum, desired, and maximum word spacing, respectively. Letterspacing is set on 0% (zero) for all three. The primary article has a 39-character measure and the secondary article has an 82-character measure. Discretionary ligatures enhance the ornate look of the page.

Sentence and special functions typography are of particular interest with this newsletter. The text contains large quantities, percentages, dates, monetary values, a diacritic mark, genus and species, a word used as a word, and large ornate transition type. These situations require extensive use of text figures and italics. Choosing an appropriate text typeface is key to accurately conveying the type of information contained in these two articles, in addition to maintaining page personality. Select baselines in the pull quotes and secondary article's headline are aligned to anchor these type blocks with the text.

TYPE LEVEL CONSISTENCY

CHOOSING TYPEFACES, DETERMINING PAGE PERSONALITY, and designing page structure are some of the more visible decisions a type artist makes. The behind-the-scenes production decisions determine how successful and enjoyable implementing them are. Production decisions focus on choosing the best tools for the job—software and font format. The software decision comes first. Page-layout applications are the preferred software for executing a complex typographic page or multipage document. With a Unicode- and OpenType-savvy application, there are three font format choices possible. Without such an application, the type artist's choices are more limited.

When creating a well-set typographic page whose copy requires a variety of glyphs, such as small caps, text figures, case fractions, alternates, swash characters, or expanded ligatures, the type artist without a Unicode- and OpenType-savvy application uses a PST-1 or TT typeface with a corresponding expert collection (see "PostScript Type 1" in chapter 1). A typeface, such as Minion Regular, and its expert collection, Minion Expert Regular, are separate files and appear on the application's type menu as two individual family members. Every time an expert regular glyph is needed, the type artist switches typefaces (regular to expert regular) and uses a prescribed sequence of keystrokes to access it. Some applications offer a glyph palette that displays all the available typeface glyphs for by-sight selection.

Kerning issues can be a problem when selecting glyphs from two different typefaces and placing them side by side. With high-quality font files, it is not a major concern, but these glyphs do require scrutiny once printed. Inserting a swash capital, case fraction, or line-ending alternate glyph requires the same procedure. In addition, hyphenation controls and spell checkers do not recognize some multiface words, so they are either not hyphenated or identified as misspelled. There are techniques available that make working with expert collections less labor-intensive (see "Electronic Proofing Features" in chapter 5). An additional font file or files is required, if multilingual support is needed.

For typesetting and producing the same page with a suitably savvy application, the type artist has one additional font format choice—Open-Type. An OpenType typeface with the required glyph sets and enhanced typographic capabilities (see "OpenType" in chapter 1) provides access to the same glyphs previously discussed, but from a single font file, such as Minion Regular. The difference in ease of use is dramatic. Document-wide substitution from specific glyph sets, such as discretionary ligatures and text figures, is available using settings within the software. For example, after typing the characters *f-f-i* in a left-to-right sequence, the software immediately replaces it with the *ffi*-ligature. If hyphenation is necessary, the software can un-substitute the ligature glyph and hyphenate the word appropriately. If the formatting situation changes yet again, the software resubstitutes the ligature. The type artist is not involved in these actions, but can override any automatic substitution, if necessary.

After making the broad production decisions of software and font format, maintaining consistency within the three levels of typography is more enjoyable and the results more successful by taking advantage of other powerful software support. Most page-layout applications offer styles that the type artist creates and easily assigns to an entire paragraph, character, or range of characters. For example, paragraph styles impose a set of type block attributes to an entire paragraph (a type block bracketed by hard returns). These attributes include typeface, type size,

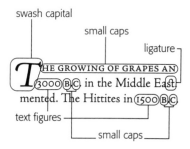

Substituted glyphs inserted by type artist using a PST-1 or TT typeface with its expert collection

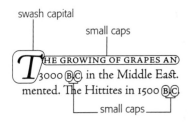

Automatically substituted glyphs possible when using OT font with OpenType- and Unicode-savvy application

swash capital
small caps

Substituted glyphs inserted by type artist using OT font with OpenType- and Unicode-savvy application.

leading, alignment, indents, hyphenation, and space before and after. Using paragraph styles is a must for consistent paragraph typography. Since the text for most articles shares the same attributes, the ability to apply them globally assures consistency. If multiple secondary articles share the same headline attributes, using a paragraph style for them is helpful also for consistent page typography. If the type artist decides later to increase the text type leading, for example, all changes to the original style are applied automatically to all text blocks assigned with that style. This saves time and guarantees consistency.

Although sentence and special functions typography is not as global beyond what an OpenType- and Unicode-savvy application offers, creating character styles for italics, small caps, expert characters, and other frequently used glyphs makes executing this detail work much easier with either font format choice. Character styles affect only type attributes, such as typeface, size and weight. The paragraph format is unaffected when applying this kind of style within a paragraph.

℘

SUCCESSFULLY DESIGNING AND EXECUTING A COMPLEX, typographic page, such as the ones detailed in this chapter, is challenging and extremely rewarding. Type artists tasked with such pages on a regular basis develop a special type sense or passion about these details. They become advocates, as was Beatrice Warde, for the creation of beautiful typographic pages and they develop an appreciation for typefaces that provide the glyphs needed for this form of typographic expression.

Developing this sense takes time, patience, and support strategies to assist with orchestrating these myriad details. There is always more to learn and other design structures to explore with each new page. Some might say that this is where the type artist throws out the rules—that in the crush to create the perfect page, those arbitrary dictates are impossible to employ. On the contrary, by understanding what the rules are intended to *do,* the type artist knows which to emphasize and which to deemphasize in any situation. It is not a matter of ignoring them, but understanding their purpose. The first question a type artist asks is not How should it *look*? but What must it *do*?

INTEGRATING
TYPOGRAPHIC ELEMENTS
IN A
PUBLICATION

A PUBLICATION CREATES AN EXTENDED typographic environment
into which readers are drawn. A story is told or information conveyed
through the skilled writing of the author and the expertise of the type
artist. The term *publication,* as defined in this chapter, refers to multipage documents, such as newsletters, magazines, or books. All are typographic environments within which readers spend prolonged periods of
time viewing information. A half-hour to two-hour read, for example, is
not uncommon. It is here that readers get comfortable and lose themselves in the subject matter.

The interrelationship of typographic elements must be even stronger in a publication than on a page, because the relationship is maintained across several consecutive spreads. By maintaining an effective,
functional, typographic hierarchy, the type artist strengthens readers'
understanding of publication structure as they turn each page. The type
artist's role is not to change the information, but to facilitate its delivery;
to enable readers to forget the surroundings and proceed along an enjoyable, informative trail to its conclusion. It is not that the typography
is forgettable, but that it is so well-executed, so suited to the subject matter, that it reenforces the message rather than detracts from it.

Stanley Morison (1889–1967) was a type historian, typographer,
and eloquent proponent of well-crafted typography, whether referring
to the design of a typeface or its placement on a page. Morison wrote
about the nuances of typography with conviction and passion. In his

*The typographer is apt to be more
keen even than the theologian or
the lawyer in ferreting out
precedent.*

———————————S. Morison
The Fleuron

1930 article, "The First Principles of Typography," published in the seventh edition of *The Fleuron,* he wrote, "Typography may be defined as … arranging the letters, distributing the space and controlling the type as to aid to the maximum the reader's comprehension of the text." Morison's view on book typography decried nontraditional approaches, or "'bright' typography." He believed that books should employ the prevailing typographic traditions of society, so readers were able to slip comfortably into a new book and not be distracted by unfamiliar typographic treatments.

While he adamantly supported adherence to established typographic convention for books, he did admonish his fellow typographers for an insufficient amount of typographic experimentation. "It is always desirable that experiments be made, and it is a pity that such 'laboratory' pieces are so limited in number and in courage. Typography to-day does not so much need Inspiration or Revival as Investigation." Even though he pressed to maintain the traditions of type, his love of typography also spoke to its capacity for exploration and imagination.

Typographic traditions evolve over time and society broadens its acceptance of treatments that were once considered new. Just as leading is now an acceptable attribute in paragraph typography, rather than the "evil" some thought it to be in the 1930s, publication typography too has expanded to include new conventions and treatments. The environments within which today's readers view type, and type artists interact with type, have expanded beyond that which Morison imagined. As current type artists determine the prevailing traditions for different typographic venues, the underlying goal of publication typography continues to be as Morison stated, "… to aid to the maximum the reader's comprehension of the text."

TYPOGRAPHIC CONTINUITY

WITHIN PUBLICATIONS, CONTINUITY IS A GOAL for both authors and type artists. How rigidly typographic continuity is maintained is determined by the diversity of the publication's content, the structure of its format, and its anticipated shelf life. Depending upon the publication, its personality, and its purpose, the role of some type blocks is more visually aggressive than others.

Generally speaking, a book presents a single topic or story. Each chapter contributes another dimension to the subject matter. Typographic structure is identical from chapter to chapter to aid comprehension throughout the one hundred– to three hundred–page publication and reestablish hierarchy after breaks between reading sessions. A book has a target audience, whether narrow or broad, and projects the appropriate personality for it (see "Page Personality" in chapter 10). Because books have a longer shelf life than periodicals, their designs are more timeless or classic.

A magazine targets a specific audience identified by characteristics, such as age, gender, interest, or a mixture of several. Magazines have a shorter shelf life than books and are redesigned periodically to reflect changes in target audience or to project a more contemporary appearance. Each article targets a narrower slice of the magazine's audience and projects an article-appropriate personality in keeping with the whole. Once readers enter an article, they enter a closed, visually contained environment; the other articles are not visible. The intended effect is to create an area within the publication that supports the article's mood effectively and enhances reader experience.

A newsletter fits in between these extremes. The entire publication projects a personality suitable for its target audience, but its articles display a narrower range of personality variations due to the length of the publication and the reader's ability to view multiple articles simultaneously. Some newsletters contain lengthier articles that investigate issues in more detail. Consequently, these are more book-like in their layout and use of type. Similarly to magazines, newsletters are disposable publications, subject to periodic redesign.

Typographic continuity within publications is important in the delivery of the message. It can be publication-wide or article-wide according to the role and format of the individual publication. No matter how long the publication's shelf life, the type artist must address the readers' immediate needs—facilitating their ability to comprehend the information accurately.

THE *CREEK NATION* NEWSLETTER IS INTENDED as a quarterly newsletter for members of the Creek (Muskogee) Indian tribe (see fig. 11-1). The tribe is concentrated in several states of the American Southeast. This newsletter presents and explores information in three broad subject categories—education, health, and culture. Each one serves, on a rotating basis, as the category for an issue's primary article. The primary article in this case, an abridged version of a scholarly paper, explores the subject of tribal colleges in depth, and covers approximately two and a half pages. A focus section follows with a specific tribal college example. The format, content, and personality here are more like an academic journal or magazine than an event-oriented newspaper.

NEWSLETTERS

The nameplate is based on tribal beadwork examples from the early nineteenth century (see "Designing Nameplates" in chapter 9). It establishes a culturally based, tradition-oriented personality. It is bold, modern, and suggests this tribal handcraft style through its parallel-line details, angled joins, and single-width strokes with rounded endings. These attributes are repeated throughout the publication and reinforce the personality, while maintaining design continuity.

Page Typography

THE PAGE TYPOGRAPHY EMPLOYS SIX LEVELS of page elements in the newsletter's body—section heads, headlines, secondary headlines, sub-heads, pull quotes, and text type. Through type selection and repetition of nameplate attributes, this typographic hierarchy supports its personality, visually unifies the page, and structures the information logically. Repeating nameplate attributes is not always necessary or warranted. In an all-typographic publication, however, repeating these elements in a structurally sustainable manner adds another graphic element that helps eliminate typographic monotony.

Adobe's Cronos Pro is the newsletter's dominant type family. Varying weights and styles represent different levels of page elements, typeset almost exclusively in upper- and lowercase. Cronos Pro (designed by Robert Slimbach) is a sans serif type that blends old style characteristics, such as ascenders that extend beyond the cap height, with calligraphic and chancery attributes, particularly noticeable in stroke endings, italics, and swash caps. Its calligraphic qualities give the page a lively feel that helps visually support the nameplate's inspiration from handcrafted beadwork, while at the same time energizing the page.

The section heads are the only page elements that use a typeface in addition to Cronos Pro. These headings begin with the word *In,* created from two nameplate letters, and combine with Cronos Pro semibold all caps. The main article's section head is reduced in size to identify the subject category but not overwhelm the headline. The remaining section heads are larger but tinted and positioned consistently to identify each new section, while providing a design link back to the nameplate.

A wide left margin on the first page serves as a design element to spotlight the section head, headline, secondary headline, and several pull quotes. The margin draws attention to the article's two-part headline and author's name, while providing the reader with a snapshot of its content through multiple pull quotes. Changes in style, size, and weight establish a clear hierarchy. Ornaments reminiscent of the nameplate anchor the typography in the left margin and separate the pull quotes.

AdEgmyt
ABZwfxe

Cronos Pro roman, swash, and italic glyphs demonstrate calligraphic and chancery attributes.

INFOCUS
INHEALTH
INCULTURE
INEDUCATION

Creek Nation section heads

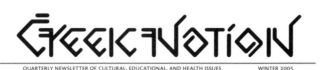

CREEK NATION

QUARTERLY NEWSLETTER OF CULTURAL, EDUCATIONAL, AND HEALTH ISSUES   WINTER 2005

IN EDUCATION

*Emergence,
Alliances and
Vision ...*

Tribal Colleges
and Beyond

by Gary S. Wheeler

*Focus on local
economic needs*

//

*Offer 350 degrees
and 180 programs*

//

*Enroll over
32,000 students*

//

*Predominantly
female student
population*

THE INDIGENOUS PEOPLES OF AMERICA have long viewed education as a key component of being healthy as a people. For the most part they viewed education pragmatically and philosophically, seeing it as a mechanism for cultural survival and as a natural means by which power is understood, communicated, and gained. From the colonial period forward, tribes also have recognized the transformative power of higher education and its practical connection to leadership in the non-Indian world. Despite concerns that this transformative power changed their young people in ways that made them less fit for living as Indians, and despite the regularly dismal results of American higher education for American Indian people, tribes continued to support and encourage the enrollment of their children in colleges and universities.

Tribal colleges were established to provide a nurturing atmosphere on the reservation that Indian students were not receiving when they left to go to state and private schools. According to the 2000 White House Initiative on Tribal Colleges and Universities Report,

> Tribal Colleges are culturally based; they focus on local economic needs and address the whole person: mind, body, spirit, and family. More than 26,000 students from 250 federally recognized tribes now attend these institutions created by American Indians for American Indians. Tribal Colleges offer more than 350 degrees and 180 vocational programs. While all give students the opportunity to earn two-year degrees, 75 to 85 percent of Tribal College graduates go on to earn a four-year degree or become employed in the local community.

Demographic and Enrollment Patterns

Today, the number of tribal colleges is stable or growing, consistent with the increasing population base of those attending tribal colleges. While the constant threat of low funding levels is stressful, tribal colleges have survived and begun to thrive. In 2003, 88 percent of all U.S. high school students completed high school, with about 60 percent of those going on to college. In the same year, only 51 percent of American Indians graduated from high school, and 17 percent of them are attempting college. This low percentage of American Indian high school graduates continuing on to college comes despite the overall success story of having 34 U.S. tribal colleges and universities enrolling over 32,000 students (80 percent of whom are Indian). This number of tribal college and university enrolled college students is an all-time high and compares to 2,100 American Indians enrolled in tribal colleges 20 years ago.

In most tribal colleges, enrollments are growing rapidly, although remain relatively small—from a high of about 2,000 students at Diné College to a low of around 100 at several colleges, with an average enrollment of about 850 students. This relatively small number makes it financially and academically challenging to offer the breadth of student services and academic programs needed by tribal communities.

FIGURE 11-1: Creek Nation *newsletter front page*

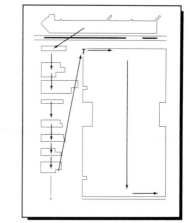

Page map with a strong vertical orientation

Throughout all the newsletter articles, type weight, style differences, and alignment variations continue to maintain the typographic hierarchy established on the first page. These distinctions establish a contrast between elements that help differentiate and prioritize their role. For example, the bold roman of the headline contrasts with the regular italic of the secondary headline; the regular italic pull quotes and the semibold italic subheads contrast the regular weight of the text type; and the headlines and secondary headlines contrast the pull quotes and subheads. These elements work together to communicate

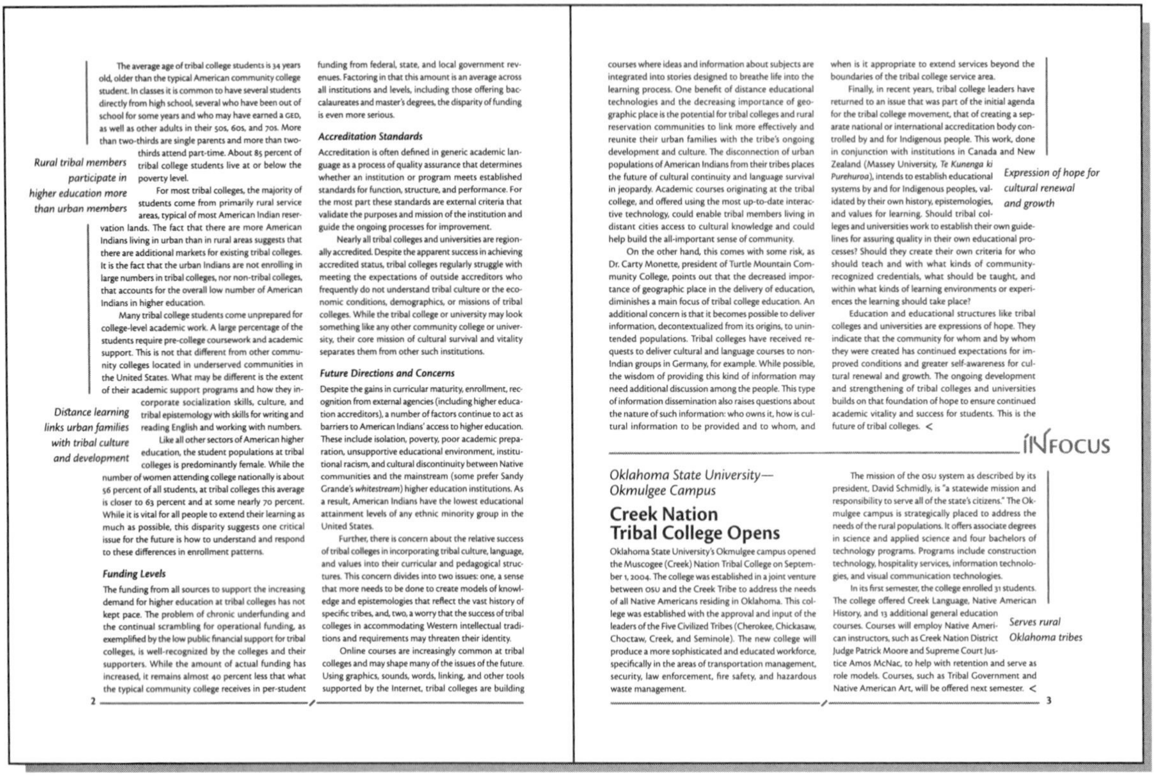

The average age of tribal college students is 34 years old, older than the typical American community college student. In classes it is common to have several students directly from high school, several who have been out of school for some years and who may have earned a GED, as well as other adults in their 50s, 60s, and 70s. More than two-thirds are single parents and more than two-thirds attend part-time. About 85 percent of tribal college students live at or below the poverty level.

For most tribal colleges, the majority of students come from primarily rural service areas, typical of most American Indian reservation lands. The fact that there are more American Indians living in urban than in rural areas suggests that there are additional markets for existing tribal colleges. It is the fact that the urban Indians are not enrolling in large numbers in tribal colleges, nor non-tribal colleges, that accounts for the overall low number of American Indians in higher education.

Rural tribal members participate in higher education more than urban members

Many tribal college students come unprepared for college-level academic work. A large percentage of the students require pre-college coursework and academic support. This is not that different from other community colleges located in underserved communities in the United States. What may be different is the extent of their academic support programs and how they incorporate socialization skills, culture, and tribal epistemology with skills for writing and reading English and working with numbers.

Like all other sectors of American higher education, the student populations at tribal colleges is predominantly female. While the number of women attending college nationally is about 56 percent of all students, at tribal colleges this average is closer to 63 percent and at some nearly 70 percent. While it is vital for all people to extend their learning as much as possible, this disparity suggests one critical issue for the future is how to understand and respond to these differences in enrollment patterns.

Distance learning links urban families with tribal culture and development

Funding Levels

The funding from all sources to support the increasing demand for higher education at tribal colleges has not kept pace. The problem of chronic underfunding and the continual scrambling for operational funding, as exemplified by the low public financial support for tribal colleges, is well-recognized by the colleges and their supporters. While the amount of actual funding has increased, it remains almost 40 percent less that what the typical community college receives in per-student

funding from federal, state, and local government revenues. Factoring in that this amount is an average across all institutions and levels, including those offering baccalaureates and master's degrees, the disparity of funding is even more serious.

Accreditation Standards

Accreditation is often defined in generic academic language as a process of quality assurance that determines whether an institution or program meets established standards for function, structure, and performance. For the most part these standards are external criteria that validate the purposes and mission of the institution and guide the ongoing processes for improvement.

Nearly all tribal colleges and universities are regionally accredited. Despite the apparent success in achieving accredited status, tribal colleges regularly struggle with meeting the expectations of outside accreditors who frequently do not understand tribal culture or the economic conditions, demographics, or missions of tribal colleges. While the tribal college or university may look something like any other community college or university, their core mission of cultural survival and vitality separates them from other such institutions.

Future Directions and Concerns

Despite the gains in curricular maturity, enrollment, recognition from external agencies (including higher education accreditors), a number of factors continue to act as barriers to American Indians' access to higher education. These include isolation, poverty, poor academic preparation, unsupportive educational environment, institutional racism, and cultural discontinuity between Native communities and the mainstream (some prefer Sandy Grande's *whitestream*) higher education institutions. As a result, American Indians have the lowest educational attainment levels of any ethnic minority group in the United States.

Further, there is concern about the relative success of tribal colleges in incorporating tribal culture, language, and values into their curricular and pedagogical structures. This concern divides into two issues: one, a sense that more needs to be done to create models of knowledge and epistemologies that reflect the vast history of specific tribes, and two, a worry that the success of tribal colleges in accommodating Western intellectual traditions and requirements may threaten their identity.

Online courses are increasingly common at tribal colleges and may shape many of the issues of the future. Using graphics, sounds, words, linking, and other tools supported by the Internet, tribal colleges are building

courses where ideas and information about subjects are integrated into stories designed to breathe life into the learning process. One benefit of distance educational technologies and the decreasing importance of geographic place is the potential for tribal colleges and rural reservation communities to link more effectively and reunite their urban families with the tribe's ongoing development and culture. The disconnection of urban populations of American Indians from their tribes places the future of cultural continuity and language survival in jeopardy. Academic courses originating at the tribal college, and offered using the most up-to-date interactive technology, could enable tribal members living in distant cities access to cultural knowledge and could help build the all-important sense of community.

On the other hand, this comes with some risk, as Dr. Carty Monette, president of Turtle Mountain Community College, points out that the decreased importance of geographic place in the delivery of education, diminishes a main focus of tribal college education. An additional concern is that it becomes possible to deliver information, decontextualized from its origins, to unintended populations. Tribal colleges have received requests to deliver cultural and language courses to non-Indian groups in Germany, for example. While possible, the wisdom of providing this kind of information may need additional discussion among the people. This type of information dissemination also raises questions about the nature of such information: who owns it, how is cultural information to be provided and to whom, and

when is it appropriate to extend services beyond the boundaries of the tribal college service area.

Finally, in recent years, tribal college leaders have returned to an issue that was part of the initial agenda for the tribal college movement, that of creating a separate national or international accreditation body controlled by and for Indigenous people. This work, done in conjunction with institutions in Canada and New Zealand (Massey University, Te Kunenga ki Purehuroa), intends to establish educational systems by and for Indigenous peoples, validated by their own history, epistemologies, and values for learning. Should tribal colleges and universities work to establish their own guidelines for assuring quality in their own educational processes? Should they create their own criteria for who should teach and with what kinds of community-recognized credentials, what should be taught, and within what kinds of learning environments or experiences the learning should take place?

Expression of hope for cultural renewal and growth

Education and educational structures like tribal colleges and universities are expressions of hope. They indicate that the community for whom and by whom they were created has continued expectations for improved conditions and greater self-awareness for cultural renewal and growth. The ongoing development and strengthening of tribal colleges and universities builds on that foundation of hope to ensure continued academic vitality and success for students. This is the future of tribal colleges. <

INFOCUS

Oklahoma State University— Okmulgee Campus

Creek Nation Tribal College Opens

Oklahoma State University's Okmulgee campus opened the Muscogee (Creek) Nation Tribal College on September 1, 2004. The college was established in a joint venture between OSU and the Creek Tribe to address the needs of all Native Americans residing in Oklahoma. This college was established with the approval and input of the leaders of the Five Civilized Tribes (Cherokee, Chickasaw, Choctaw, Creek, and Seminole). The new college will produce a more sophisticated and educated workforce, specifically in the areas of transportation management, security, law enforcement, fire safety, and hazardous waste management.

The mission of the OSU system as described by its president, David Schmidly, is "a statewide mission and responsibility to serve all of the state's citizens." The Okmulgee campus is strategically placed to address the needs of the rural populations. It offers associate degrees in science and applied science and four bachelors of technology programs. Programs include construction technology, hospitality services, information technologies, and visual communication technologies.

In its first semester, the college enrolled 31 students. The college offered Creek Language, Native American History, and 13 additional general education courses. Courses will employ Native American instructors, such as Creek Nation District Judge Patrick Moore and Supreme Court Justice Amos McNac, to help with retention and serve as role models. Courses, such as Tribal Government and Native American Art, will be offered next semester. <

Serves rural Oklahoma tribes

2 · · 3

FIGURE 11-2: Creek Nation *inside spread*

and structure the content. Their uniformity at each hierarchical level provides the reader with a familiar pattern between articles.

The left-margin type blocks on the front page contrast the single column of justified text type. A 32-point semibold italic versal with an all cap, roman, regular-weight transition type provides a visual link between these margin elements and the text type. The interior spread contains the bulk of the tribal college article and is typeset to enhance continuous reading (fig. 11-2). Having gotten the reader's attention on the first page, this spread uses two justified text type columns with a proportionally sized gutter. Pull quotes in regular italic extend into the columns as graphic breaks for the lengthy text.

Paragraph and Sentence Typography

On the more detailed level of paragraph and sentence typography, type size, leading, indents, intraparagraph spacing, white space, and glyph usage all come into play. The text type is set in 10.5/13 regular with

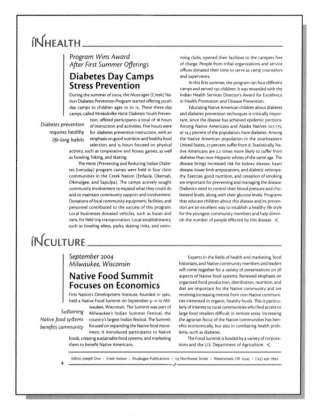

FIGURE 11-3: Creek Nation *back page with masthead*

a 19-point indent (approximately 1.5 lead). The measure of the text column on the first page contains 78 characters and each double column contains 51 characters. An angle bracket in the Mercedes typeface serves as an ornament signaling the end of each article.

Subheads set in 12/13 semibold italic use 10 points of white space before and 3 points of white space after to link visually with the paragraphs they introduce. With the inserted white space equal to the leading (10 + 3 = 13), intraparagraph spacing maintains baseline alignment in adjacent columns below the subheads.

The pull quotes on the first page are larger than the others. Set in 14/14 regular italic, they serve a more aggressive role of enticing the reader into the article, while at the same time remaining subordinate to the 24/26 bold roman headline and the 18/19.5 regular italic secondary headline. Once in the newsletter's interior, the pull quotes are reduced to 12.5/16 and extended into the columns as graphic breaks for the lengthy

Correct intraparagraph spacing around subheads maintains baseline alignment of text lines below them.

support. This is not that different from other
nity colleges located in underserved commu
the United States. What may be different is th
of their academic support programs and how
corporate socialization skills, cult
tribal epistemology with skills for wr
reading English and working with n
Like all other sectors of Americ:
education, the student population:
colleges is predominantly female. V
number of women attending college nationally
56 percent of all students, at tribal colleges thi
is closer to 63 percent and at some nearly 70
While it is vital for all people to extend their le

*Distance learning
links urban families
with tribal culture
and development*

Aligning one or more pull quote
baselines anchors the type block
to the text.

MAGAZINES

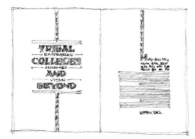

Proportionally accurate thumbnails
(2½ inches high) are a productive
first step in publication design.

text. The second line of each pull quote is aligned to an adjacent text
baseline. Adequate white space around them prevents visual congestion.

The size reduction of the interior pull quotes is warranted because
of their different role (What must it *do*?). The point size of all discontinuous typography (headline, secondary headline, and pull quotes) on the
pages other than the first (see fig. 11-3) is reduced by two points. In addition, headline type weight is reduced to semibold. Their role is to identify new articles within a text-abundant landscape, rather than work in
conjunction with the first-page headlines to entice readers into the entire publication. Maintaining the same size for these elements on all
pages would have made them disproportionally dominant.

A block quote is used on the first page. It is set in 9.5/12 regular
with a 38-point left indent (twice the first-line indent) with 4 points of
white space before and after. The quote uses eight lines of 12-point leading ($8 \times 12 = 96$). The additional 8 points of white space ($96 + 8 = 104$)
keeps intraparagraph spacing a factor of the text leading ($104 \div 13 = 8$),
so the baselines of text on pages printed front to back will align and not
create ghosting in the white space between the baselines.

Sentence typography focuses on setting many comparative enrollment totals, percentages, and dates that require text figures. Cronos Pro
is an OpenType typeface. Working in a page-layout application that supports its features makes these figures easy to set globally throughout the
publication. Instances of italics and a diacritic mark are present also.

A MAGAZINE IS FILLED WITH ARTICLES, COLUMNS, advertisements,
and structural necessities, such as a table of contents and masthead. In
comparison to a newsletter, a magazine is visually more active, because
its components play more diverse roles. There are competing items for
the reader to identify, hopefully read, and possibly ignore. Evaluating
magazine components is done quickly. Standing in front of a newsstand
or sitting in a doctor's waiting room, magazine readers quickly leaf
through the pages making countless snap decisions regarding their interest in the material presented. The type of magazine determines the
environment within which it is typically evaluated.

Within this environment of competing visuals, feature articles offer
readers an extended time period to learn new or more in-depth information about a topic of interest. Feature articles can be divided into two
sections—the opening spread and all those that follow. The challenge for
the type artist concerns the different role each section plays. The opening spread functions like a headline; it must get the reader's attention

and project a content-appropriate personality that offers an accurate impression of what is to follow. This impression communicates both the broad subject area, as well as its specific focus. An article about education, for example, can be narrowed by grade level, such as elementary, secondary, post-secondary, and then focused by a specific teaching technique, such as working with visual learners. A general sense of all of this must be communicated immediately, in a few seconds. Sometimes an article starts on a recto page, sharing the spread with an advertisement. This gives the type artist less space to accomplish all the same goals. If the opening spread or page is vague, projecting an unclear snapshot, the reader will not spend the time to determine its intent; it is not the reader's responsibility. There are too many other options within the magazine that can entertain or inform.

The second section, the remaining spreads, serves a different role. These spreads contain pages of text for continuous reading. The type artist uses more subdued page elements, such as pull quotes, subheads, and smaller graphics to divide and structure them for enhanced comprehension. Designing these pages is similar to organizing a book or an extended newsletter article.

Magazine articles offer a different typographic challenge with each and every article due to their unique personalities. This enables the type artist to experiment and explore. If articles do not project an accurate personality, readers can miss out on items of interest and develop the impression that the magazine's target audience does not include them. This would be unfortunate for both reader and publication.

An opening magazine spread often contains a headline, graphic, pull quote, and a portion of the text type. These elements intertwine and serve to get the reader's attention, define personality, suggest content and focus, and get the continuous-text reading started. How much text type is included on this spread varies. Treatment of the text type on this spread can be more nontraditional, according to how much of it is presented. If it is just a paragraph or two, the type artist can have some fun with its measures and alignment, knowing that the serious reading commences on the next spread.

The two opening spreads discussed in this section introduce the unabridged article on tribal college traditions and opportunities. The spreads do not contain photographs or illustrations, so the type creates both a content-appropriate visual and entices the reader into the first few paragraphs of text.

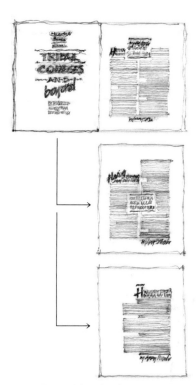

Small pencil thumbnails enable valuable exploration with a limited investment of time.

Page and Paragraph Typography

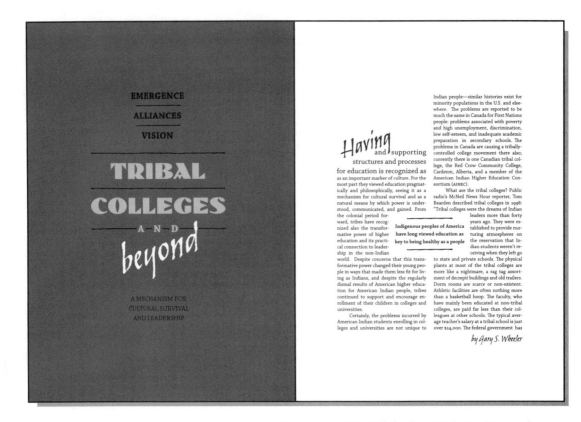

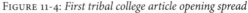

FIGURE 11-4: *First tribal college article opening spread*

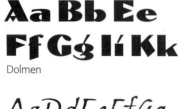

Dolmen

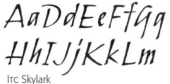

ITC Skylark

The first opening spread (fig. 11-4) creates a graphic headline by contrasting the hard-edged, geometric Dolmen display typeface with the rough-hewn script typeface ITC Skylark (designed by Patty King). Dolmen's triangular shapes and Skylark's rough edges all project visual characteristics and prevalent shapes from tribal handcrafts. The rules between the words are created from Skylark's em dashes to maintain line quality. Different weights of Chaparral Pro serve as the pull quote, secondary headline, and the word *AND* on the verso page.

Chaparral serves as the text type on the spread's recto page. In this instance, the entire Skylark word *Having* performs the function of a versal, attracting viewer attention to the large Chaparral transition type leading into the Chaparral text type. The two columns of text are broken up by a semibold pull quote that straddles the gutter. The author's byline, set flush right, links the Skylark type blocks together and entices the reader to turn the page.

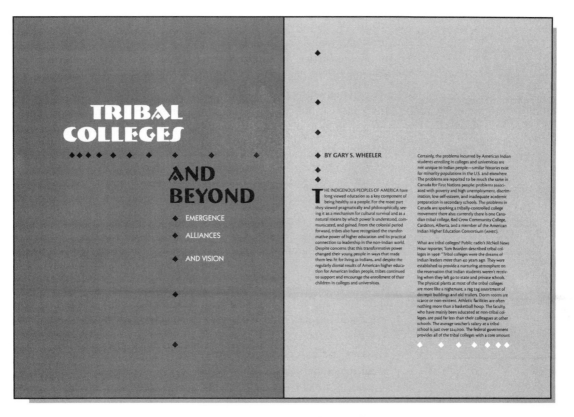

FIGURE 11-5: *Second tribal college article opening spread*

The second opening spread (fig. 11-5) uses the display typeface Bremen (designed by Richard Lipton) in two different weights, black and bold, for the headline and the typeface Cronos Pro for the secondary headline. The placement of type blocks and repetition of diamond-shaped bullets, created from the bar of the capital *A,* move the reader horizontally through the entire spread. Diamond shapes are prevalent in many forms of tribal handcrafts, so Bremen's extensive use of them makes it an appropriate typeface selection.

The Bremen versal on the recto page draws the reader from the end of the headline into the text type using typeface repetition and baseline alignment. The text type is flush left and set below the implied horizontal line established by the row of diamonds leading into the author's name. Baseline alignment is maintained between the columns by using a lead between nonindented paragraphs. The diamond row at the base of the second column propels the reader into the remaining spreads.

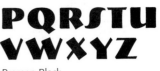

Bremen Bold

Bremen Black

BOOKS

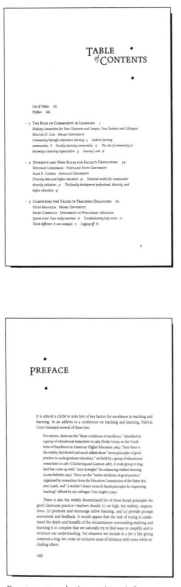

Front matter design unity reinforces
publication-wide hierarchy.

Book typography, as stanley morison described, contained narrow typographic variations dictated by tradition. In the decades since his *Fleuron* article appeared, book typography and design have diversified due to broadened subject matter, expanded formats, and the increased marketing importance of target-audience preferences. In addition to classic literature, biographies, reference books, and prose, there are now coffee-table books, how-to books, self-help books, textbooks, pop-up books, published-on-demand books, e-books, and more. With all these formats and audiences, there is no single way to approach their design and typography. The guiding principle is still "… to aid to the maximum the reader's comprehension of the text." These typographic decisions begin with the following questions: What must it do? Who is its target audience? What is its personality?

Book typography functions on two levels. The first is publication wide. This focuses on consistency throughout its three major components: front matter, text, and back matter. *Front matter* contains divisions, such as the table of contents, list of illustrations, preface, foreword, and introduction. The text component encompasses the chapters. The *back matter* contains divisions, such as appendices, a bibliography, glossary, and index. The amount of both front and back matter varies according to the subject matter and the book's purpose. All of these components must be typographically consistent to accurately communicate their role in the book's overall structure. While this hierarchy is important for a reader's understanding of the book's organization—What chapter is this? Where is the index?—this form of reading is discontinuous.

The second level of book typography is chapter wide. Consistent and effective hierarchy *within* chapters is important to the reader during extended contact (continuous reading). Chapter hierarchy organizes content for improved comprehension, as the reader navigates through the sea of text type, one page at a time. Good chapter typography establishes a logical hierarchy between all page elements from the headline (chapter title) to the subheads to the text type down to the page numbers in the running feet (fig. 11-6). *Running feet* and *running heads* refer to a line of type placed across the bottom or top of the page, respectively, containing the page number, chapter title, chapter number, or book title. The reader references all of these elements at some point and must comprehend their message accurately.

This section explores two different books. Each has its own target audience and personality, which are expressed in its typography. The first is directed to college faculty; the second to design students. While

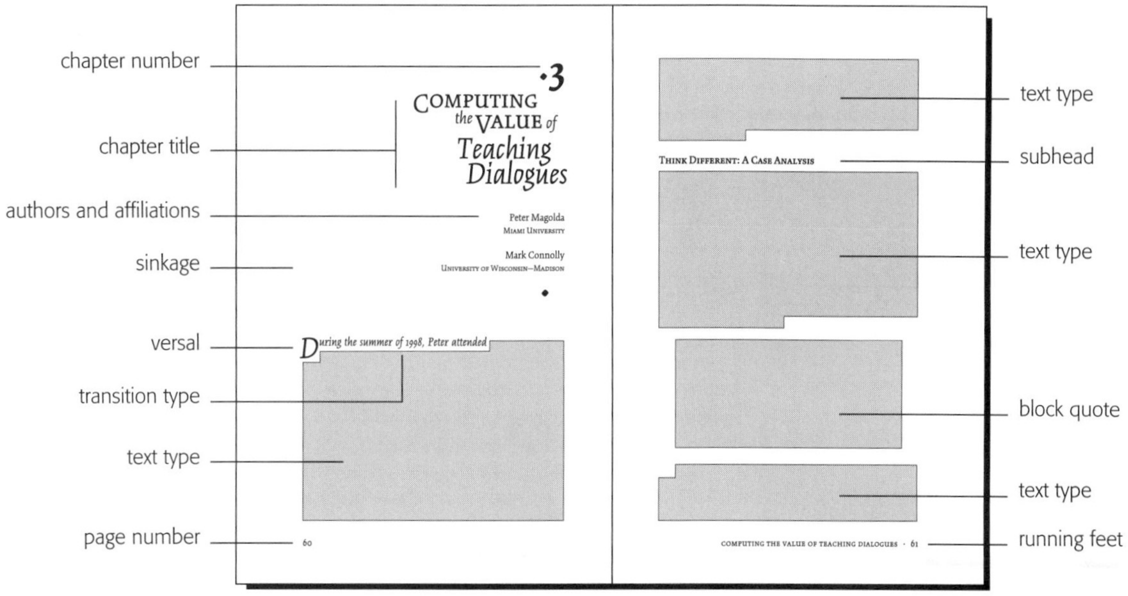
chapter number
chapter title
authors and affiliations
sinkage
versal
transition type
text type
page number
•3
COMPUTING the VALUE of Teaching Dialogues
Peter Magolda
Miami University
Mark Connolly
University of Wisconsin–Madison
During the summer of 1998, Peter attended
60
text type
subhead
text type
block quote
text type
running feet
Think Different: A Case Analysis
COMPUTING THE VALUE OF TEACHING DIALOGUES · 61

FIGURE 11-6: *Common book page elements*

both books use the same type family as their primary type, the type treatments for most page elements vary and, consequently, create two different publication personalities aptly suited to the material they present. One is traditional with few surprises; the other is nontraditional with typographic pages designed in accordance with chapter content. Both enhance the subject matter, while strengthening readability.

Traditional Book Design

THE FOURTH EDITION OF *TEACHING AND LEARNING IN COLLEGE: A Resource for Educators* (Info-Tec 2002) is written for higher education faculty, administrators, or researchers interested in the instructional framework called *learning communities.* Although each chapter explores a different type of learning community, either on an institutional or classroom level, the diversity of content is narrow. Each chapter is written by a different author, or author group, affiliated with different educational institutions. The writing style is formal and the book's structure is traditional. This 211-page book has six footnoted chapters, appropriate front and back matter (table of contents, list of tables, preface, and index), and limited graphics in the form of 13 all-text tables.

The book's personality is authoritative, scholarly, and factual. Readers prefer to read an entire chapter (averaging 32 pages) in one sitting

48-point bold; text figure ———————————————— •6

32-point regular; caps/small caps ——————————— M**ORE**
20-point italic; lowercase ———————————— *than a*

32-point regular; caps/small caps —— THERMOMETER

20-point italic; caps/lowercase ———— *Using* Assessment

36-point regular; caps/lowercase ——— Effectively

12-point regular; caps/lowercase ———————————— Catherine Wehlburg
10-point regular; caps/small caps ———————————— T EXAS C HRISTIAN U NIVERSITY

•

F IGURE 11-7: *Graphic headline type-size diagram*

and then reread portions for improved understanding or when citing and implementing its content. This is not a casual read, but a detailed study replete with statistics. The book's design challenge is to project its scholarly personality, to support the content; to maintain consistent hierarchy between chapters, to aid reader comprehension; and to create interesting typographic treatments, to keep the publication from being visually monotonous. (Book pages reprinted by publisher's permission.)

PAGE TYPOGRAPHY

AaBbCcDdEeFf GgHhIiJjKkLlM

Kinesis Regular and Italic

I N THIS BOOK , THE TYPE FAMILY KINESIS IS USED exclusively. Different weights and styles clearly distinguish typographic elements and establish an effective page hierarchy. Kinesis (designed by Mark Jamra) is a slightly condensed, serif type with unusual, calligraphic letterforms. The italic lowercase *g* is an excellent example of its unique letterforms. Kinesis is a highly legible typeface and, with its ascenders extending above the cap line, provides built-in leading, making it suitable for use in continuous-reading text with minimal leading. The energetic appearance of this type enlivens the page, while supporting its factual content. The letterforms create graphically interesting chapter titles that provide visual breaks to the text-only content (fig. 11-7).

On the first page of every chapter, page typography creates an effective page map for moving the reader successfully into the new material (fig. 11-8). A large versal and italic transition type bridge the gap between chapter title typography and the detail-strewn paragraph and

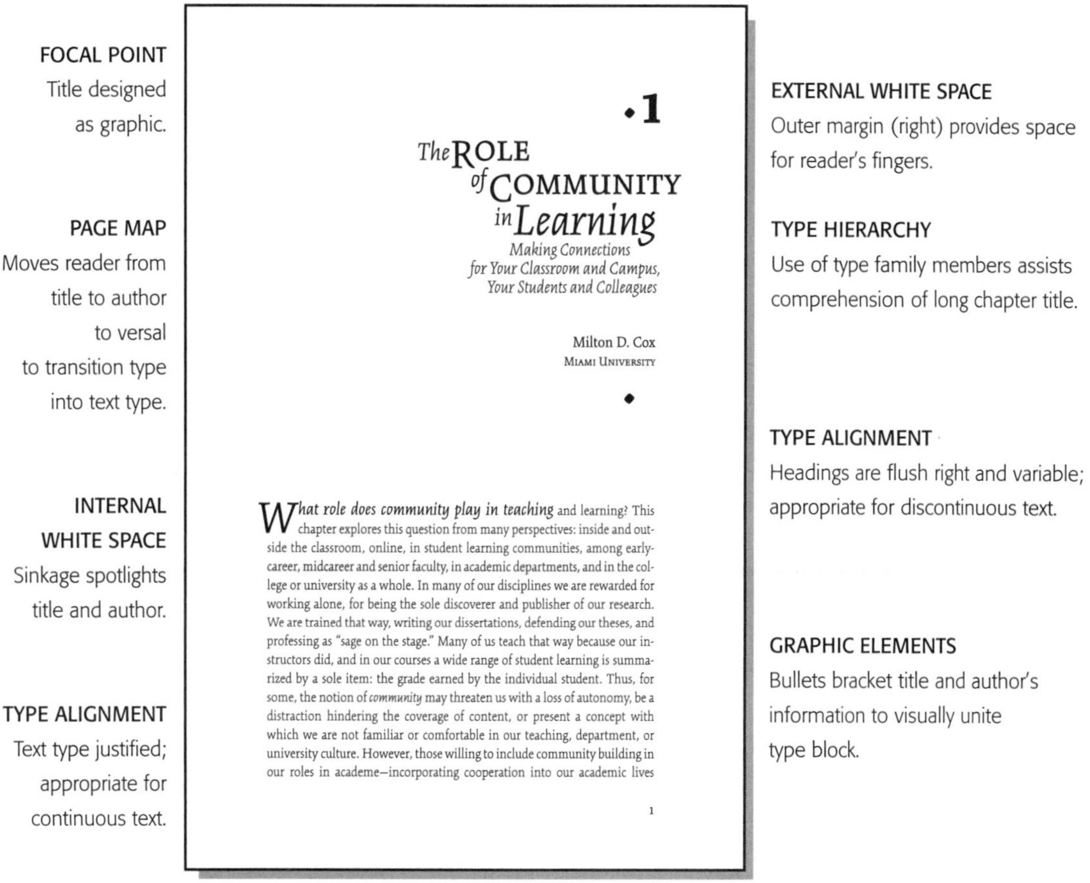

FOCAL POINT
Title designed
as graphic.

PAGE MAP
Moves reader from
title to author
to versal
to transition type
into text type.

**INTERNAL
WHITE SPACE**
Sinkage spotlights
title and author.

TYPE ALIGNMENT
Text type justified;
appropriate for
continuous text.

EXTERNAL WHITE SPACE
Outer margin (right) provides space
for reader's fingers.

TYPE HIERARCHY
Use of type family members assists
comprehension of long chapter title.

TYPE ALIGNMENT
Headings are flush right and variable;
appropriate for discontinuous text.

GRAPHIC ELEMENTS
Bullets bracket title and author's
information to visually unite
type block.

(Figure contains sample chapter opening page)

•1

The ROLE
of COMMUNITY
in Learning
*Making Connections
for Your Classroom and Campus,
Your Students and Colleagues*

Milton D. Cox
MIAMI UNIVERSITY

♦

W*hat role does community play in teaching* and learning? This chapter explores this question from many perspectives: inside and outside the classroom, online, in student learning communities, among early-career, midcareer and senior faculty, in academic departments, and in the college or university as a whole. In many of our disciplines we are rewarded for working alone, for being the sole discoverer and publisher of our research. We are trained that way, writing our dissertations, defending our theses, and professing as "sage on the stage." Many of us teach that way because our instructors did, and in our courses a wide range of student learning is summarized by a sole item: the grade earned by the individual student. Thus, for some, the notion of *community* may threaten us with a loss of autonomy, be a distraction hindering the coverage of content, or present a concept with which we are not familiar or comfortable in our teaching, department, or university culture. However, those willing to include community building in our roles in academe—incorporating cooperation into our academic lives

1

FIGURE 11-8: *Interaction and function of page elements*

sentence typography. All these page elements work to clearly structure the content for improved comprehension.

ONCE IN THE TEXT TYPE, THE READER NAVIGATES a variety of hierarchical levels, including three types of subheads, block quotes, bulleted and enumerated lists, and *endnotes,* a comprehensive listing of all chapter footnotes found at the end of a chapter or book. These typographic variations occur within a continuous landscape of 11/14 Kinesis Light text type (see fig. 11-9). It is there that their effectiveness is gauged. All inserted white space is a factor of the 14-point leading, so baseline alignment across each spread is maintained and no ghosting between lines occurs from type printed on the backside of a page (see fig. 11-10).

**PARAGRAPH AND
SENTENCE TYPOGRAPHY**

VERSAL

Regular italic *O* drop cap creates link with title and indicates start of text type.

TRANSITION TYPE

Lowercase, 14-point, regular italic connects versal and text type.

TEXT TYPE SELECTION

Condensed typeface is suitable for narrow page; 11/14 Kinesis MM Light.

INDENT

First-line indent is 17 points (almost 1½ em).

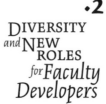

•**2**

DIVERSITY
and NEW
ROLES
for Faculty
Developers

Devorah Lieberman
PORTLAND STATE UNIVERSITY

Alan E. Guskin
ANTIOCH UNIVERSITY

◆

*O*ne of the most important pressures for reform facing higher education today is a direct result of the demographic changes that have been occurring in the United States for some time. Confronted with sharp increases in domestic, international and immigrant peoples of color, as well as older adult learners, and a growing expectation that nearly everyone should go to college, colleges and universities have had to face the reality that their academic and nonacademic programs need to undergo significant changes. These reforms need to respond to new educational needs and be appropriate for both majority as well as minority students.

At the same time that colleges and universities are responding to the needs of a more diverse student population, they also are facing great financial pressures and the need to undertake significant changes in how technology is used in all aspects of college life. These forces for reform will create new and powerful demands on the nature of the curriculum and faculty work. Success in these reform efforts will depend on members of the academic

39

INTERNAL WHITE SPACE

Larger space after author information links it with title rather than text.

TYPE HIERARCHY

Lettercase and size differences contrast author names to institutions.

MEASURE

Text measure has 71 characters for ease of reading.

FIGURE 11-9: *Interaction and role of paragraph typography*

Block quotes are reduced in size to 10/14 with 7 points of white space before and after. Bulleted and enumerated lists maintain the 11/14 text and leading sizes and use significant left indents that allow for hanging bullets and figures.

Changes in type size, weight, letter case, and a careful distribution of internal white space convey the relative importance of the three subhead levels by controlling how much of a break in the text they create. The most important of the three is set in 13/14 semibold using caps and small caps. An introductory 12-point white space precedes the heavier, larger type and signals a substantial break in content. A smaller 2-point white space follows and links the subhead to the content section it introduces. This subhead creates the most significant text break.

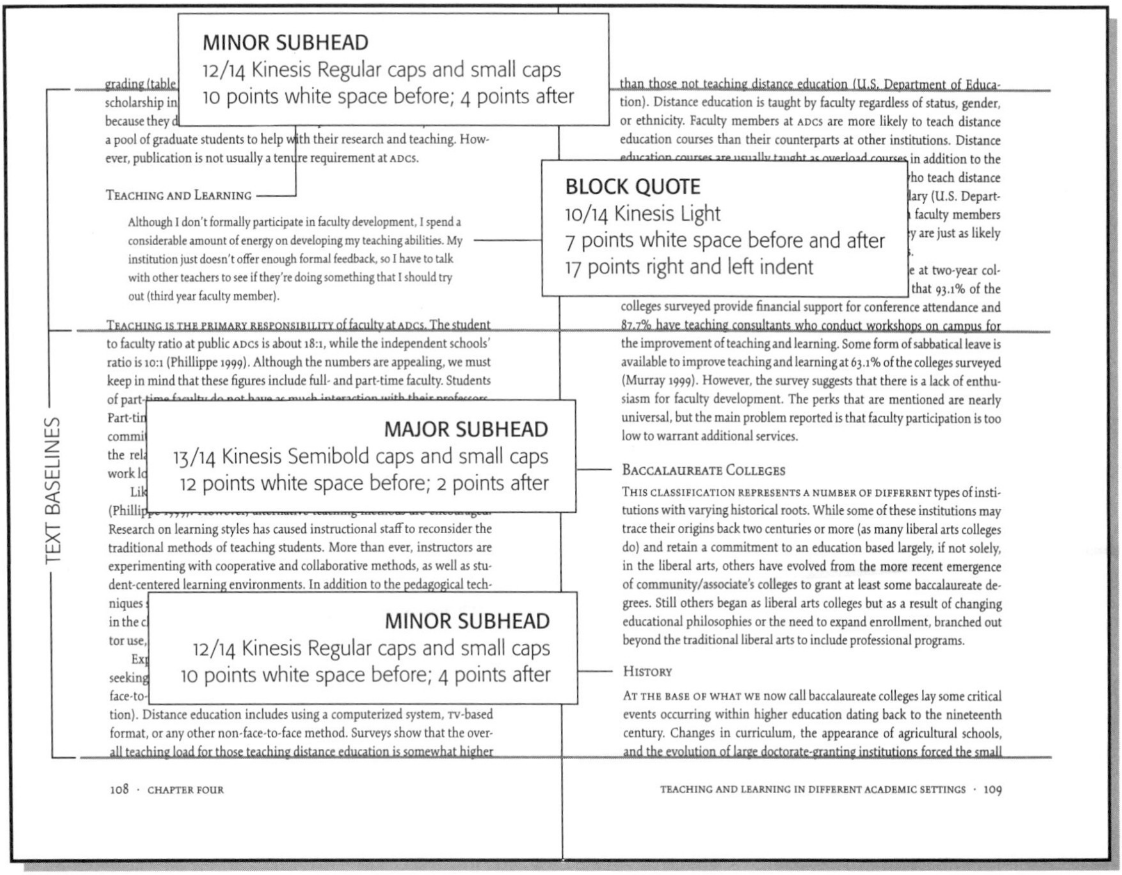

Within the figure, the callout boxes and text read:

MINOR SUBHEAD
12/14 Kinesis Regular caps and small caps
10 points white space before; 4 points after

BLOCK QUOTE
10/14 Kinesis Light
7 points white space before and after
17 points right and left indent

MAJOR SUBHEAD
13/14 Kinesis Semibold caps and small caps
12 points white space before; 2 points after

MINOR SUBHEAD
12/14 Kinesis Regular caps and small caps
10 points white space before; 4 points after

TEXT BASELINES

Left column body text:

grading (table
scholarship in
because they d
a pool of graduate students to help with their research and teaching. However, publication is not usually a tenure requirement at ADCs.

TEACHING AND LEARNING

Although I don't formally participate in faculty development, I spend a
considerable amount of energy on developing my teaching abilities. My
institution just doesn't offer enough formal feedback, so I have to talk
with other teachers to see if they're doing something that I should try
out (third year faculty member).

TEACHING IS THE PRIMARY RESPONSIBILITY of faculty at ADCs. The student
to faculty ratio at public ADCs is about 18:1, while the independent schools'
ratio is 10:1 (Phillippe 1999). Although the numbers are appealing, we must
keep in mind that these figures include full- and part-time faculty. Students
of part-time faculty do not have as much interaction with their professors.
Part-tim
commit
the rela
work lo

Lik
(Phillipp
Research on learning styles has caused instructional staff to reconsider the
traditional methods of teaching students. More than ever, instructors are
experimenting with cooperative and collaborative methods, as well as stu-
dent-centered learning environments. In addition to the pedagogical techniques
in the c
tor use,
Exp
seeking
face-to-
tion). Distance education includes using a computerized system, TV-based
format, or any other non-face-to-face method. Surveys show that the overall teaching load for those teaching distance education is somewhat higher

108 · CHAPTER FOUR

Right column body text:

than those not teaching distance education (U.S. Department of Education). Distance education is taught by faculty regardless of status, gender,
or ethnicity. Faculty members at ADCs are more likely to teach distance
education courses than their counterparts at other institutions. Distance
education courses are usually taught as overload courses in addition to the
 who teach distance
lary (U.S. Depart-
faculty members
y are just as likely

e at two-year col-
that 93.1% of the
colleges surveyed provide financial support for conference attendance and
87.7% have teaching consultants who conduct workshops on campus for
the improvement of teaching and learning. Some form of sabbatical leave is
available to improve teaching and learning at 63.1% of the colleges surveyed
(Murray 1999). However, the survey suggests that there is a lack of enthusiasm for faculty development. The perks that are mentioned are nearly
universal, but the main problem reported is that faculty participation is too
low to warrant additional services.

BACCALAUREATE COLLEGES

THIS CLASSIFICATION REPRESENTS A NUMBER OF DIFFERENT types of institutions with varying historical roots. While some of these institutions may
trace their origins back two centuries or more (as many liberal arts colleges
do) and retain a commitment to an education based largely, if not solely,
in the liberal arts, others have evolved from the more recent emergence
of community/associate's colleges to grant at least some baccalaureate degrees. Still others began as liberal arts colleges but as a result of changing
educational philosophies or the need to expand enrollment, branched out
beyond the traditional liberal arts to include professional programs.

HISTORY

AT THE BASE OF WHAT WE now call baccalaureate colleges lay some critical
events occurring within higher education dating back to the nineteenth
century. Changes in curriculum, the appearance of agricultural schools,
and the evolution of large doctorate-granting institutions forced the small

TEACHING AND LEARNING IN DIFFERENT ACADEMIC SETTINGS · 109

FIGURE 11-10: *Intraparagraph spacing within a spread*

The second subhead level is set in 12/14 regular using caps and
small caps. The white space is distributed more evenly, 10 points before
and 4 points after. In comparison to the first subhead, the smaller size,
lighter weight, and less intrusive white space signal a less significant
content change or text break. With a more diminutive typographic
change, the reader continues quickly into the next section. The third
subhead level uses the same white space distribution as the second, but
the type is less dominant, 11/14 regular set in upper- and lowercase.

Sentence typography is treated as technical text due to the abundance of comparative and statistical data. Percentage symbols (%) and
text figures above the number-word *nine* or for comparative purposes
are used extensively.

Nontraditional Book Design

The visual design primer (Prentice Hall 2002) is written for post-secondary and secondary students enrolled in introductory design courses. This publication is a small format, 120-page book containing short chapters grouped into five thematic sections. An informal style characterizes its presentation, intended to encourage, not intimidate, first-time design students. The book offers a snapshot of the field from a brief history through design and production basics to applying for a job. Individual chapters explore the highlights of each topic and present the material in a customized design format suitable for the content. Chapter lengths range from a single page to 10 pages. Many page elements remain consistent from chapter to chapter, others do not; but each chapter fits within the book's overall personality. The personality is informal, dynamic, and nontraditional.

Because chapters are relatively short, reading time is short. An instructor uses a chapter as a springboard to a larger discussion, demonstration, or project. To reinforce this informal quality, the book employs a variety of typographic structuring techniques. For example, when a chapter does not contain graphics, the typography is visually aggressive. The type creates its own unique visual landscape. When a chapter does contain graphics, the typography is subdued sharing the spotlight with illustrations or photographs. These varying typographic treatments and chapter formats complement the book's informal personality, the needs of its target audience, and the brevity of its content.

PAGE TYPOGRAPHY

The kinesis and caflisch script type families are used throughout the book. Kinesis is the predominant type family, chosen for several reasons. First, the book is only 5½ inches wide, so measures are narrow. In order to include a comfortable number of characters in each measure for enhanced readability, a condensed typeface is the best choice. Second, the energetic personality of Kinesis, along with its unique letterforms, enhances the book's informal personality while providing opportunities for interesting, eye-catching chapter and section headings.

Caflisch Script (designed by Robert Slimbach) is based on the actual handwriting of the graphic designer, Max Caflisch. It has the look of fluid, controlled, handwritten printing. Some letters naturally connect, like script, and others, like printing, do not. The typeface projects a casual quality, but its obvious control suggests a more experienced hand. This condensed, simple, informal script is highly legible with open counters and an ample *x*-height. Its condensed proportions, letter structure, and informal personality complement Kinesis. Caflisch Script is

AaBbCcDdEeFfGg
AaBbCcDdEeFfGg
HhIiJjKkLlMmNn
HhIiJjKkLlMmNn

Kinesis and Caflisch Script comparison

used throughout the book for informal, note-like entries that identify diagram details and contribute design development notes. These suggest something handwritten by the reader (fig. 11-11).

A hierarchy exists between both type families that helps the reader navigate through the abundance of typographic information. Kinesis roman and italic in different type weights work well with the single-weight Caflisch Script to organize the multiple type blocks for improved reader comprehension.

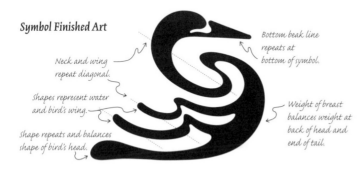

Symbol Finished Art

Neck and wing repeat diagonal.

Shapes represent water and bird's wing.

Shape repeats and balances shape of bird's head.

Bottom beak line repeats at bottom of symbol.

Weight of breast balances weight at back of head and end of tail.

FIGURE 11-11: *Caflisch Script suggests handwritten notes*

Each of the five thematic sections is introduced by a single page. All section pages conform to the same type structure. Section headings in Kinesis combine two weights, black and regular, and two styles, roman and italic, to create a graphic headline (see fig. 11-13). A summary of the section's content follows each heading and is typeset in two staggered text blocks of different type sizes and measures. The use of significant white space and the visually aggressive nature of the typesetting enable these section pages to stand out as the reader leafs through the book. This distinction creates the visual break needed to identify sections when competing with the typography of the other chapters.

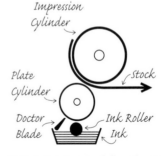

Impression Cylinder

Plate Cylinder

Stock

Doctor Blade

Ink Roller

Ink

Caflisch Script creates informal, note-like entries for diagram identification.

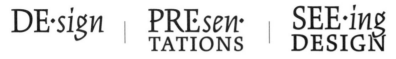

FIGURE 11-12: *One- and two-word chapter title treatments*

Due to the book's small size, chapter numbers and titles are placed in the upper-left corner of a chapter's first page in a space 9 picas wide.

DesignPRE·*liminaries*

DesignCOM·*ponents*

DesignPRO·*duction*

DesignPRO·*fession*

Typographic consistency throughout section headings

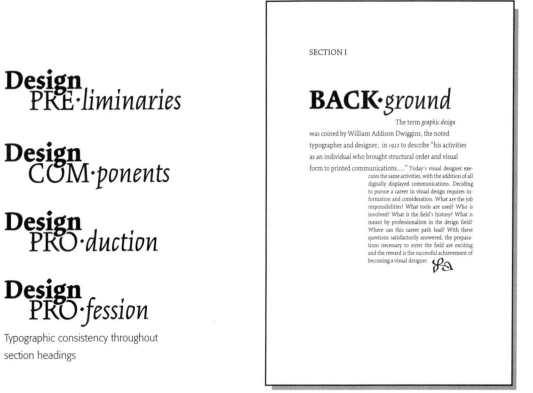

SECTION I

BACK·*ground*

The term *graphic design* was coined by William Addison Dwiggins, the noted typographer and designer, in 1922 to describe "his activities as an individual who brought structural order and visual form to printed communications...." Today's visual designer executes the same activities, with the addition of all digitally displayed communications. Deciding to pursue a career in visual design requires information and consideration. What are the job responsibilities? What tools are used? Who is involved? What is the field's history? What is meant by professionalism in the design field? Where can this career path lead? With these questions satisfactorily answered, the preparations necessary to enter the field are exciting and the reward is the successful achievement of becoming a visual designer.

FIGURE 11-13: *Section page identifies major topic break*

TYPE

COL·*or*

BRO·*chures*

PROOF·*ing*

DE·*sign*PROCESS

Typographic consistency throughout chapter headings

The placement and narrow measure do not allow for substantial sinkage, which traditionally serves to isolate the title and enhance its impact (see fig. 11-15). A major sinkage break is not necessary, because each chapter is so visually distinct and helps the reader recognize a chapter change. Almost all chapter headings, or titles, are one or two words in length. The headings are divided according to syllables to accommodate the narrow measure. This provides an opportunity for an interesting typographic treatment. Kinesis roman and italic are combined for situations of multiple syllables and words (see fig. 11-12). A few instances of small caps occur in longer chapter headings.

The chapter headings create a visual relationship with the section headings by repeating the use of roman and italic type style combinations. Contrasting the black and regular weights of the more dominant section headings against the regular weight of the more diminuitive chapter headings establishes the correct hierarchy between the two.

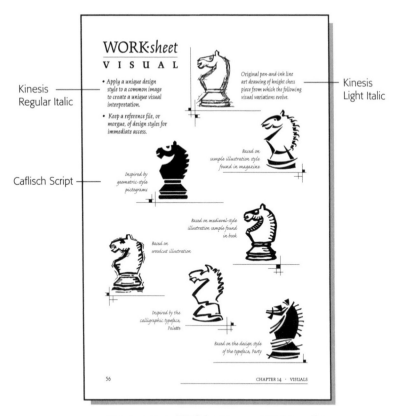

Kinesis Regular Italic

Kinesis Light Italic

Caflisch Script

FIGURE 11-14: *Worksheet typographic hierarchy*

Approximately one-quarter of all chapters have a subsection, called a worksheet. These multiple page sequences demonstrate the development process for a chapter-related design issue. For example, the chapter "Visuals" has a worksheet that depicts various stylistically unique illustrations and describes their style reference. The typography for the worksheet headings is smaller than the chapter headings (fig. 11-14), but it is coordinated with them by matching type style and weight. This strengthens design unity and continues the existing typographic hierarchy. The worksheet's text type uses different type styles and weights from the two type families to define the purpose of each text block, thus enhancing reader comprehension.

The Visual Design Primer includes chapters with graphics and without. The design challenge for the chapters without graphics is to make them visually interesting, while conveying the content accurately. The chapter "Historic Milestones" presents a typographic chronology of

Design
COM·ponents

VISU·
als

WORK·sheet
VISUAL

Type weights, styles, and sizes create hierarchy between heading levels.

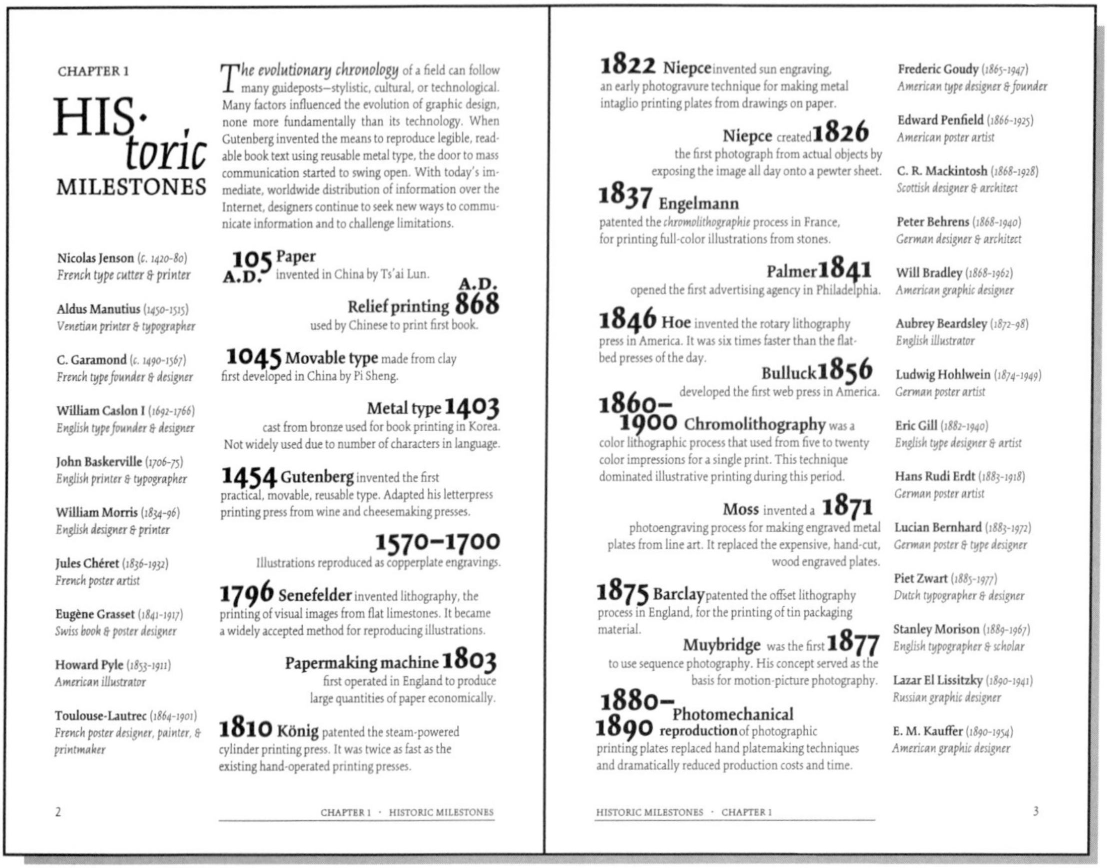

The figure content (the two-page spread shown as Figure 11-15):

CHAPTER 1

HIS·
toric
MILESTONES

The evolutionary chronology of a field can follow many guideposts—stylistic, cultural, or technological. Many factors influenced the evolution of graphic design, none more fundamentally than its technology. When Gutenberg invented the means to reproduce legible, readable book text using reusable metal type, the door to mass communication started to swing open. With today's immediate, worldwide distribution of information over the Internet, designers continue to seek new ways to communicate information and to challenge limitations.

Nicolas Jenson (c. 1420-80)
French type cutter & printer

Aldus Manutius (1450-1515)
Venetian printer & typographer

C. Garamond (c. 1490-1561)
French type founder & designer

William Caslon I (1692-1766)
English type founder & designer

John Baskerville (1706-75)
English printer & typographer

William Morris (1834-96)
English designer & printer

Jules Chéret (1836-1932)
French poster artist

Eugène Grasset (1841-1917)
Swiss book & poster designer

Howard Pyle (1853-1911)
American illustrator

Toulouse-Lautrec (1864-1901)
French poster designer, painter, & printmaker

105 Paper
A.D. invented in China by Ts'ai Lun.

Relief printing 868
A.D.
used by Chinese to print first book.

1045 Movable type made from clay first developed in China by Pi Sheng.

Metal type 1403
cast from bronze used for book printing in Korea. Not widely used due to number of characters in language.

1454 Gutenberg invented the first practical, movable, reusable type. Adapted his letterpress printing press from wine and cheesemaking presses.

1570–1700
Illustrations reproduced as copperplate engravings.

1796 Senefelder invented lithography, the printing of visual images from flat limestones. It became a widely used method for reproducing illustrations.

Papermaking machine 1803
first operated in England to produce large quantities of paper economically.

1810 König patented the steam-powered cylinder printing press. It was twice as fast as the existing hand-operated printing presses.

1822 Niepce invented sun engraving, an early photogravure technique for making metal intaglio printing plates from drawings on paper.

Niepce created **1826**
the first photograph from actual objects by exposing the image all day onto a pewter sheet.

1837 Engelmann
patented the *chromolithographie* process in France, for printing full-color illustrations from stones.

Palmer 1841
opened the first advertising agency in Philadelphia.

1846 Hoe invented the rotary lithography press in America. It was six times faster than the flatbed presses of the day.

Bulluck 1856
developed the first web press in America.

1860–1900 Chromolithography was a color lithographic process that used from five to twenty color impressions for a single print. This technique dominated illustrative printing during this period.

Moss invented a **1871**
photoengraving process for making engraved metal plates from line art. It replaced the expensive, hand-cut, wood engraved plates.

1875 Barclay patented the offset lithography process in England, for the printing of tin packaging material.

Muybridge was the first **1877**
to use sequence photography. His concept served as the basis for motion-picture photography.

1880–1890 Photomechanical reproduction of photographic printing plates replaced hand platemaking techniques and dramatically reduced production costs and time.

Frederic Goudy (1865-1947)
American type designer & founder

Edward Penfield (1866-1925)
American poster artist

C. R. Mackintosh (1868-1928)
Scottish designer & architect

Peter Behrens (1868-1940)
German designer & architect

Will Bradley (1868-1962)
American graphic designer

Aubrey Beardsley (1872-98)
English illustrator

Ludwig Hohlwein (1874-1949)
German poster artist

Eric Gill (1882-1940)
English type designer & artist

Hans Rudi Erdt (1883-1918)
German poster artist

Lucian Bernhard (1883-1972)
German poster & type designer

Piet Zwart (1885-1977)
Dutch typographer & designer

Stanley Morison (1889-1967)
English typographer & scholar

Lazar El Lissitzky (1890-1941)
Russian graphic designer

E. M. Kauffer (1890-1954)
American graphic designer

important art-related events and a list of notable people in the field. Each date and corresponding event, or name, included in the chronology is differentiated by type weight and size. This creates a unique graphic type block for each historical event (fig. 11-15). The text type explaining the event returns to the 10/12 Kinesis Light, the text type used throughout all book chapters. The vertical list of people is located next to the fore-edge margins. Contrasting type treatment separates the list from the chronology and prioritizes the spread's information.

The chapter "Creative Process" presents this topic along two different tracks by interspersing typographic, enumerated steps between justified, continuous-text type blocks. First, the reader follows the enumerated steps of the creative process and learns from the italicized text what is accomplished in each step. Second, the roman text type blocks around

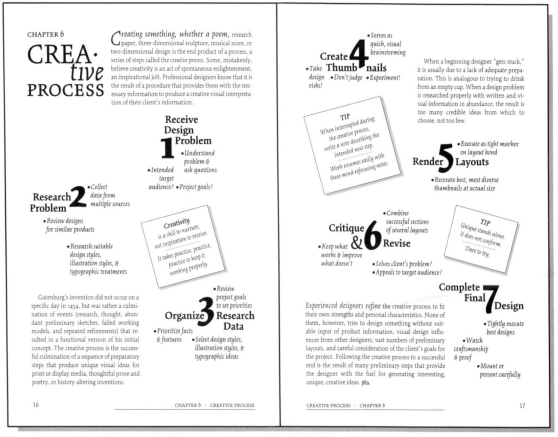

FIGURE 11-16: *Type treatments identify related information*

the steps present a generalized discussion of the process as a whole. By controlling type styles, italic or roman, the reader follows each type style separately to learn one specific kind of information (fig. 11-16). Even though the two type formats share the same page, their visual differences create cohesion between like-appearing blocks for the reader to follow easily.

The last chapter of each section (see fig. 11-17) is a single, all-text page. Each of these pages uses interlocking text blocks of varying measures to create an unusual typographic landscape. This page typography was inspired by Herb Lubalin's typographic design work for *U&lc*, the international journal of typographics published by the International Typeface Corporation. The first line of each paragraph employs transition type, although only the first paragraph uses a versal. This atypical

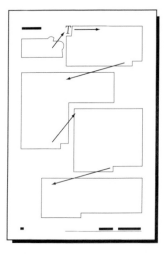

Readers require typographic clues to guide them along an intricate page map.

FIGURE 11-17: *Interlocking text blocks inspired by Lubalin*

use of transition type helps the reader navigate the page map correctly to find the beginning of each paragraph.

The book's more traditional chapters combine continuous-text blocks with graphics. Many of these employ text-block positioning strategies with variable-length measures to create a distinct look for each chapter while working in tandem with the graphics. The chapter "Visuals" staggers the placement of text blocks to move the reader around the page (fig. 11-18). Reading to the end of each paragraph positions the reader close to the beginning of the next paragraph. This is a simple technique that creates an interesting arrangement of page elements, while serving a straightforward, functional role.

The spread for the chapter "Design Process" uses the verso page for all the chapter text and the recto page for the graphic (see fig. 11-19). Text type blocks differ in length, creating a funnel effect leading to the full-page graphic.

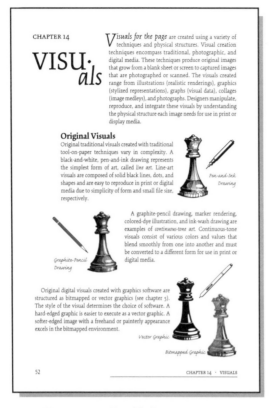

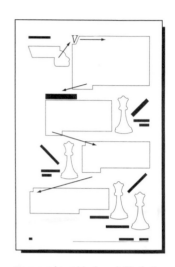

Staggered text blocks solidify their
relationship to their corresponding
visuals and guide the reader.

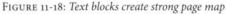

FIGURE 11-18: *Text blocks create strong page map*

The final paragraph of each chapter begins with 12-point, light
italic transition type. This is necessary because the text blocks in all
chapters are arranged differently. The type signifies the importance of
the paragraph, but positions it lower in the hierarchy than the 13-point,
regular italic transition type of the first paragraph. A 32-point, light
italic versal lures the reader from the chapter heading to the first paragraph. The lighter weight establishes its visual priority after the heading.

THE CHALLENGE FOR THESE TWO TYPOGRAPHIC LEVELS focuses on
layout differences in each chapter. Size consistencies within both type
families keep the content understandable and the page maps discernable
when reading each visually distinct chapter. All continuous-reading text
is set in 10/12 Kinesis Light. Text type is justified with word spacing set
to 80% (minimum), 100% (optimum), and 133% (maximum). The letterspacing is set at 0% for all, so the type artist implements solutions for

**PARAGRAPH AND
SENTENCE TYPOGRAPHY**

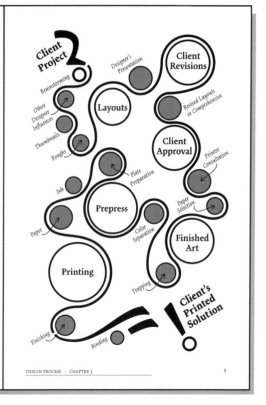

FIGURE 11-19: *Text block placement leads to graphic*

spacing problems line by line. These settings keep letterspacing uniform. When this approach is not successful for all text blocks, the type artist can increase the letterspacing range by a small amount, such as −2%, 0%, and 2%, to fix a paragraph-specific problem. If a single troublesome line still persists, a per-line treatment is applied, such as hyphenating words differently in surrounding lines or applying controlled tracking. Hyphenation settings in this book follow the rules defined in chapter 4. Sentence typography employs italics and bold type for glossary terms appropriate for a textbook. Text figures are used extensively in many chapters for dates, values, and measurements.

TYPE LEVEL CONSISTENCY

MAINTAINING TYPE LEVEL CONSISTENCY FOR publications is increasingly challenging as the page numbers mount. Decisions made quickly on page 3 are long forgotten by page 106. Decisions easily maintained on a mental list while working on a single page are too numerous and complex to remember while working on a publication. Clarity and lack of clutter are not just goals to reach on behalf of the reader, but a way of working for the type artist as well. That is why keeping a record of decisions—Humanist type? Technical type? Figures or number-words? Above nine or ninety-nine?—helps the type artist consistently apply all the rules and formatting details on all pages.

The type artist can enter some of these type-related decisions into the page-layout software in the form of styles. Creating styles for the text type, subheads, and so forth, enables the type artist to uniformly apply them to a selected type block. While styles are essential techniques for maintaining typographic consistency, creating a list of styles elsewhere is useful for comparative purposes, for example, as the number of subhead levels increases. By comparing type attributes, ideas for hierarchical differentiations appear. Even maintaining a list of word treatments, such as hyphenating (or not) words beginning with specific prefixes, can save the type artist time when it occurs again in later chapters.

Choosing typefaces with the glyphs required for the job, along with the correct software to access them, is all part and parcel of working with type. Harnessing the power and features of the page-layout software chosen is essential for executing long publications efficiently and successfully.

℻

PUBLICATION DESIGN IS A REWARDING, EXCITING endeavor. There is much to remember, enough details to make a type artist's head hurt, but the process is challenging and the results eminently satisfying. Whether maintaining the traditions of typography in a formal publication, to satisfy Stanley Morison's ideal, or exploring new ideas and possibily future traditions, in an informal publication, the type artist's role is to aid the reader's comprehension within a beautiful typographic environment. A completed publication that is comfortable to read, easy to comprehend, and aesthetically pleasing is a testament to the functional and visual importance of type. Both are necessary for the publication's overall success, when an appropriate balance is maintained.

APPENDIX A—PROOFREADERS' MARKS

▶ PARAGRAPH-WIDE PROOFMARKS	*set in Times Regular 11/15 × 25* The brown dog jumped over the lazy red fox and sent the entire chicken house into a frenzy.	Set text block in specified typeface, size, leading, and measure
▶ PARAGRAPH-ALIGNMENT PROOFMARKS	*fl* The brown dog jumped over the lazy red fox and sent the entire chicken house into a frenzy.	Flush left
	The brown dog jumped over the lazy red fox and sent the entire chicken house into a frenzy. *fr*	Flush right
	justify The brown dog jumped over the lazy red fox and sent the entire chicken house into a frenzy.	Justify
	ctr The brown dog jumped over the lazy red fox and sent the entire chicken house into a frenzy.	Center
	align The brown dog jumped over the lazy red fox and	Align text
▶ LINE-PLACEMENT PROOFMARKS	[The brown dog jumped over the lazy red fox and	Move left to location indicated
	] The brown dog jumped over the lazy red fox and	Move right to location indicated

eq # > Humpty Dumpty sat on a wall, Humpty Dumpty had a great fall. All of the King's horses and All the King's men,	Equal leading for all lines	LEADING PROOFMARKS ◄
Humpty Dumpty sat on a wall, Humpty Dumpty had a great fall. reduce # > All of the King's horses and…	Reduce leading (general)	
add 2 pts > Humpty Dumpty sat on a wall, Humpty Dumpty had a great fall. All of the King's horses and…	Add leading (specific)	
ld in > Humpty Dumpty sat on a wall, Humpty Dumpty had a great fall. All of the King's horses and…	Add leading (general)	
Humpty Dumpty sat on a wall, Humpty Dumpty had a great fall. ꝺ# > All of the King's horses and…	Delete line space	
ꝺ After awaking late, the White Rab/ bit rushed to dress.	Delete line-end hyphen and close up word	HYPHENATION PROOFMARKS ◄
although the dic- tionary set thumb- nails on edge; ther- mometers were dis- turbed and simple. break up	Too many consecutive hyphens	
The newly hired ~~typ- ographer~~ ty-pog-ra-pher needed help.	Bad break (shows alternatives)	

▶ INDENTION PROOFMARKS	☐	⋏The brown dog jumped over the lazy red fox and	Indent 1 em
	◪	⋏The brown dog jumped over the lazy red fox and	Indent 1 en
	☐◪	⋏The brown dog jumped over the lazy red fox and	Indent 1½ em
	2	⋏The brown dog jumped over the lazy red fox and	Indent 2 ems

▶ LINE-MANIPULATION PROOFMARKS	*break up*	The fox for the one field; the dog for the one bone dinner and the entire	Fix knothole
	widow	The brown dog jumped over the lazy red fox and sent the entire chicken house into a fren- zy.	Fix widow
	break	The brown dog jumped over the lazy red fox and sent the entire chicken	Take down to next line
	move up	The brown dog jumped over the lazy red fox and sent the entire chicken	Take back to previous line
	¶	"I am late!" "No, you are not!"	New paragraph
	no ¶	house into a frenzy. Later that day the farmer	Run in
	run in	The brown dog jumped over the lazy red	Run in

bf	The premiere Parisian proofreader	Set in boldface
ital	was not persuaded that	Set in italic
rom	the Peruvian's (predominance)	Set roman
bf + ital	as a precise proofreader was	Set in bold italic
lc	properly and Positively proven	Set in lowercase
lc	to the PERUVIAN's peers.	Set all in lowercase
caps	The end (probably)	Set all in caps
sc	p.s. The probe was not perfunctory.	Set in small caps
P.P.S.	And perfectly practical!	Insert small caps
caps (titling)	The END! (positively)	Set in titling caps
J	(ust in time!)	Insert cap (uncertain)
D	(efinitely!)	Insert cap (obvious)

(out, see copy)	Mary had a little lamb the lamb was sure to go.	Large omission of copy
N (?)	The mid-fourteenth century is …	Query to check later
(fix spacing)	Mary had a little lamb its fleece was white as snow, and every where that Mary went, the lamb was sure to go.	White rivers in text
(score)	Newsweek arrives at my house on Tuesday.	Delete underscore (or underline)
	ad a little (align) every where t leece was Mary went, th	Align baselines of adjacent type blocks

► Letterspacing and Word Spacing Proofmarks	*kern* Peruvian Proofreader	Kern letters (close)
	ls **Achieves Profitability!**	Add letterspacing
	eq #// The ˅perfect ˅Peruvian proofreader	Use equal word space
	# parlayed his⏐perfectionist perusals	Insert word space
	less # and hisʌpenchant for	Reduce word space
	⌣ pencil pushing in⁀to a practical	Close up word space
	hr # and (profitable) profession.ʌ	Insert hair space
► Deletion, Relocation, Insertion, and Substitution Proofmarks	*the* Inʌmorning, the dog	Insert word(s)
	cat watched the ~~dog~~ and	Substitute word(s)
	ℐ the cat watched the ~~the~~ bird.	Delete word
	stet In the ~~afternoon,~~	Let it stand
	h ⏐te dog slept andʌ	Insert letter
	ℐ the cat sle⏐ept. The bird	Delete letter and close up
	wf (did)lizard impressions.	Set in correct font
	al Things are notʌways	Add to beginning of word
	⌣y what theʌseem.	Add to end of word
	tr (End/The)	Transpose lines
	tr (fromQuoted)	Transpose words
	lc/// Pet /And Pal Post /For Pets /And Pals	Set in lowercase three times
	ℐ (used with⏐ permission)	Delete letter

PUNCTUATION ◄
MARGIN PROOFMARKS
(*Use with standard insertion
or substitution text marks.*)

Apostrophe	$\overset{\vee}{\cdot}$	$\overset{\vee}{\cdot}$	Quote, closed single
Brace, open	{ *(brace)*	;/	Semicolon
Brace, closed	} *(brace)*	/*(solidus)*	Solidus
Bullet	• *(bullet)*	⧸ *(sq bracket)*	Square bracket, open
Colon	:/	⧹ *(sq bracket)*	Square bracket, closed
Comma	/,\	/ *(virgule)*	Virgule
Dash, em	M̲		
Dash, en	N̲		
Dash, figure	—/ *(figure)*		
Dash, threequartersem	3/4M		
Ellipsis	*(•••)*		
Exclamation point	! *(set)*		
Hyphen	=/		
Midpoint	⊙ *(midpoint)*		
Parenthesis, open	⧹		
Parenthesis, closed	⧸		
Period	⊙		
Prime	√ *(prime)*		
Prime, double	√ *(dbl prime)*		
Question mark	? *(set)*		
Quotes, open double	√″		
Quotes, closed double	√″		
Quote, open single	√′		

lc	John Baskerville (1706–75)	Set as text figures
1706 (text fig)	John Baskerville (born︿)	Insert text figures
caps	BASKERVILLE (1706–75)	Set as titling figures
1706	BASKERVILLE BORN︿	Insert titling figures
sp	The (18th) century …	Spell out
$\overset{2}{V}$	The first answer: 14V	Insert superscript
$\overset{2}{V}$	The first answer: 142/	Make superscript
$\underset{2}{\wedge}$	The answer is CO|	Insert subscript
$\underset{2}{\wedge}$	The answer is CO2|	Make subscript
⅓ (case fraction)	Take 1/3 cup of butter,…	Substitute case fraction

& (ampersand)	Deberny and Peignot	Substitute ampersand
¢	75︿SALE	Insert cent sign
¢	The cost of 75︿…	Insert old style cent
✷ (starburst)	✷ 75¢ SALE /	Substitute dingbat
Æ	A‖Elfric, or Grammaticus,…	Create *A-E* diphthong
$	︿.75 SALE	Insert dollar sign
$	The cost of︿3.75 …	Insert old style dollar
ﬁ	The ﬁrst-place winner …	Create *f-i* ligature
ﬁ	ﬁ r s t p l a c e	Set as separate letters
❦ (fleuron)	︿The End ❦	Insert ornament
%	25︿SALE	Insert percent sign
sp	The 25% revenues …	Spell out

key cap	char	shift char	option char	shift option char	key cap	char	shift char	option char	shift option char	char	key sequence	name
A	a	A	å	Å	1	1	!	¡	/	Áá	option-e + A or a	Aacute
B	b	B	∫	ı	2	2	@	™	€	Àà	option-` + A or a	Agrave
C	c	C	ç	Ç	3	3	#	£	‹	Ââ	option-i + A or a	Acircumflex
D	d	D	∂	Î	4	4	$	¢	›	Ää	option-u + A or a	Adieresis
E	e	E	´		5	5	%	∞	fi	Ãã	option-n + A or a	Atilde
F	f	F	ƒ	Ï	6	6	∧	§	fl	Éé	option-e + E or e	Eacute
G	g	G	©	˝	7	7	&	¶	‡	Èè	option-` + E or e	Egrave
H	h	H	·	Ó	8	8	★	•	°	Êê	option-i + E or e	Ecircumflex
I	i	I	^		9	9	(	a	·	Ëë	option-u + E or e	Edieresis
J	j	J	Δ	Ô	0	0	)	o	‚	Íí	option-e + I or i	Iacute
K	k	K	°		`	`	~		`	Ìì	option-` + I or i	Igrave
L	l	L	¬	Ò	-	-	_	–	—	Îî	option-i + I or i	Icircumflex
M	m	M	µ	Â	=	=	+	≠	±	Ïï	option-u + I or i	Idieresis
N	n	N		˜	[	[	{	"	"	Ññ	option-n + N or n	Ntilde
O	o	O	ø	Ø	]	]	}	'	'	Óó	option-e + O or o	Oacute
P	p	P	π	∏	\	\	|	«	»	Òò	option-` + O or o	Ograve
Q	q	Q	œ	Œ	;	;	:	…	Ú	Ôô	option-i + O or o	Ocircumflex
R	r	R	®	‰	'	'	"	æ	Æ	Öö	option-u + O or o	Odieresis
S	s	S	ß	Í	,	,	<	≤	¯	Õõ	option-n + O or o	Otilde
T	t	T	†	ˇ	.	.	>	≥	˘	Úú	option-e + U or u	Uacute
U	u	U		¨	/	/	?	÷	¿	Ùù	option-` + U or u	Ugrave
V	v	V	√	◊	space bar					Ûû	option-i + U or u	Ucircumflex
W	w	W	∑	„						Üü	option-u + U or u	Udieresis
X	x	X	≈	‹						Ÿÿ	option-u + Y or y	Ydieresis
Y	y	Y	¥	Á						´	shift-option-e	acute
Z	z	Z	Ω	‚						`	shift-option-`	grave
										¨	shift-option-u	dieresis
										ˇ	shift-option-t	caron
										¸	shift-option-z	cedilla
										˛	shift-opion-x	ogonek
										^	shift-option-i	circumflex
										∧	shift-6	asciicircum
										˜	shift-option-n	tilde
										~	shift-`	asciitilde
										˘	shift-option-.	breve
										¯	shift-option-,	macron
										·	option-h	dotaccent
										°	option-k	ring
										˝	shift-option-g	hungarumlaut

key cap	char	shift char	option char	shift option char
A	A		Å	a
B	B			b
C	C		Ç	¢
D	D	Ð	$	d
E	E			
F	F			
G	G	¼	¢	
H	H	½	·	
I	I	¾		n
J	J	⅛		
K	K	⅜	°	
L	L	⅝	Ł	l
M	M	⅞		r
N	N	⅓		m
O	O	⅔	Ø	o
P	P		Þ	
Q	Q		Œ	
R	R			e
S	S		Š	s
T	T			
U	U		··	··
V	v	ff		
W	w	fi		
X	x	fl		
Y	Y	ffi	Ý	
Z	z	ffl	ž	

key cap	char	shift char	option char	shift option char
1	1	!	1	1
2	2		2	2
3	3	¢	3	3
4	4	$	4	4
5	5	$	5	5
6	6	^	6	6
7	7	&	7	7
8	8	..	8	8
9	9	(	9	9
0	0	)	0	0
`	`	~	`	`
-	-	-	-	-
=	—	·		
[	(	₵		
]	)	Rp		
\		1		
;	;	:	,	‚
'	'	"	Æ	ˇ
,	,	›	,	,
.	.		.	.
/	/	?	¡	¿
space bar				

char	key sequence	name
$	shift-4	dollaroldstyle
$	shift-5	dollarsuperior
$	option-d	dollarinferior
¢	shift-3	centoldstyle
¢	shift-option-c	centsuperior
¢	option-g	centinferior
(	shift-9	parenleftsuperior
)	shift-0	parenrightsuperior
(	bracket left	parenleftinferior
)	bracket right	parenrightinferior
-	hyphen	hyphen
-	shift-option-hyphen	hyphensuperior
-	shift-hyphen	hypheninferior
-	option-hyphen	figuredash
—	equal sign	threequartersemdash
.	period	period
·	shift-option-period	periodsuperior
.	option-period	periodinferior
.	shift-equal sign	onedotleader
..	shift-8	twodotleader
·	option-h	Dotaccentsmall
,	comma	comma
,	shift-option-comma	superiorcomma
,	option-comma	inferiorcomma
/	slash	fraction
t	option-i + shift-e	tsuperior
i	option-` + shift-e	isuperior

key cap	char	shift char	key cap	char	shift char	char	ASCII char code	char	ASCII char code	char	ASCII char code	char	ASCII char code
A	a	A	1	1	!	€	128	¦	166	Ä	196	â	226
B	b	B	2	2	@	‚	130	§	167	Å	197	ã	227
C	c	C	3	3	#	ƒ	131	¨	168	Æ	198	ä	228
D	d	D	4	4	$	„	132	©	169	Ç	199	å	229
E	e	E	5	5	%	…	133	ª	170	È	200	æ	230
F	f	F	6	6	^	†	134	«	171	É	201	ç	231
G	g	G	7	7	&	‡	135	¬	172	Ê	202	è	232
H	h	H	8	8	*	^	136	-	173	Ë	203	é	233
I	i	I	9	9	(	‰	137	®	174	Ì	204	ê	234
J	j	J	0	0	)	Š	138	¯	175	Í	205	ë	235
K	k	K	`	`	~	‹	139	°	176	Î	206	ì	236
L	l	L	-	-	_	Œ	140	±	177	Ï	207	í	237
M	m	M	=	=	+	'	145	²	178	Ð	208	î	238
N	n	N	[	[	{	'	146	³	179	Ñ	209	ï	239
O	o	O	]	]	}	"	147	´	180	Ò	210	ð	240
P	p	P	\	\	|	"	148	µ	181	Ó	211	ñ	241
Q	q	Q	;	;	:	•	149	¶	182	Ô	212	ò	242
R	r	R	'	'	"	–	150	·	183	Õ	213	ó	243
S	s	S	,	,	<	—	151	¸	184	Ö	214	ô	244
T	t	T	.	.	>	˜	152	¹	185	×	215	õ	245
U	u	U	/	/	?	™	153	º	186	Ø	216	ö	246
V	v	V	space bar			š	154	»	187	Ù	217	÷	247
W	w	W				›	155	¼	188	Ú	218	ø	248
X	x	X				œ	156	½	189	Û	219	ù	249
Y	y	Y				Ÿ	159	¾	190	Ü	220	ú	250
Z	z	Z				¡	161	¿	191	Ý	221	û	251
						¢	162	À	192	Þ	222	ü	252
						£	163	Á	193	ß	223	ý	253
						¤	164	Â	194	à	224	þ	254
						¥	165	Ã	195	á	225	ÿ	255

► *To access the characters in the columns to the right, hold down the Alt key and use the numeric keypad to type a zero followed by the ASCII Character Code.*

key cap	char	shift char	key cap	char	shift char	char	ASCII char code	char	ASCII char code	char	ASCII char code
A	A	a	1	1	!	¡	161	5	205	Ë	235
B	B	b	2	2		¢	162	6	206	Ì	236
C	C	¢	3	3	¢	Ł	163	7	207	Í	237
D	D	d	4	4	$	Š	166	8	208	Î	238
E	E	e	5	5	$	Ž	167	9	209	Ï	239
F	F		6	6	ˆ	¨	168	0	210	Ð	240
G	G		7	7	&	˘	169	1	211	Ñ	241
H	H		8	8	..	ˇ	170	2	212	Ò	242
I	I	i	9	9	(	.	172	3	213	Ó	243
J	J		0	O	)	¯	175	4	214	Õ	245
K	K		`	`	~	¯	178	5	215	Ö	246
L	L	l	-	-	-	¯	179	6	216	Œ	247
M	M	m	=	—	.	'	182	7	217	Ø	248
N	N	n	[	(	₡	°	183	8	218	Ù	249
O	O	o	]	)	Rp		184	9	219	Ú	250
P	P		\		1	¼	188	¢	220	Û	251
Q	Q		;	;	:	½	189	$	221	Ü	252
R	R	r	'	'	"	¾	190	.	222	Ý	253
S	S	s	,	,	'	¿	191	,	223	Þ	254
T	T	t	.	.	.	⅛	192	À	224	Ÿ	255
U	U		/	/	?	⅜	193	Á	225		
V	V	ff	space			⅝	194	Â	226		
W	W	fi				⅞	195	Ã	227		
X	X	fl				⅓	196	Ä	228		
Y	Y	ffi				⅔	197	Å	229		
Z	z	ffl				0	200	Æ	230		
						1	201	Ç	231		
						2	202	È	232		
						3	203	É	233		
						4	204	Ê	234		

▶ *To access the characters in the columns to the right, hold down the Alt key and use the numeric keypad to type a zero followed by the* ASCII *Character Code.*

Character Name and Glyph Sample		Unicode	Windows U.S. Keyboard	Macintosh U.S. Keyboard	Character Name and Glyph Sample		Unicode	Windows U.S. Keyboard	Macintosh U.S. Keyboard
.notdef	⊠	N/A	N/A	N/A	F	F	0046	Shift+f	Shift+f
space		0020	space bar	space bar	G	G	0047	Shift+g	Shift+g
exclam	!	0021	Shift+1	Shift+1	H	H	0048	Shift+h	Shift+h
quotedbl	"	0022	Shift+'	Shift+'	I	I	0049	Shift+i	Shift+i
numbersign	#	0023	Shift+3	Shift+3	J	J	004A	Shift+j	Shift+j
dollar	$	0024	Shift+4	Shift+4	K	K	004B	Shift+k	Shift+k
percent	%	0025	Shift+5	Shift+5	L	L	004C	Shift+l	Shift+l
ampersand	&	0026	Shift+7	Shift+7	M	M	004D	Shift+m	Shift+m
quoteright	'	2019	Alt+0146	Shift+Option+]	N	N	004E	Shift+n	Shift+n
parenleft	(	0028	Shift+9	Shift+9	O	O	004F	Shift+o	Shift+o
parenright	)	0029	Shift+0	Shift+0	P	P	0050	Shift+p	Shift+p
asterisk	*	002A	Shift+8	Shift+8	Q	Q	0051	Shift+q	Shift+q
plus	+	002B	Shift+=	Shift+=	R	R	0052	Shift+r	Shift+r
comma	,	002C	,	,	S	S	0053	Shift+s	Shift+s
hyphen	-	002D	-	-	T	T	0054	Shift+t	Shift+t
period	.	002E	.	.	U	U	0055	Shift+u	Shift+u
slash	/	002F	/	/	V	V	0056	Shift+v	Shift+v
zero	0	0030	0	0	W	W	0057	Shift+w	Shift+w
one	1	0031	1	1	X	X	0058	Shift+x	Shift+x
two	2	0032	2	2	Y	Y	0059	Shift+y	Shift+y
three	3	0033	3	3	Z	Z	005A	Shift+z	Shift+z
four	4	0034	4	4	bracketleft	[	005B	[	[
five	5	0035	5	5	backslash	\	005C	\	\
six	6	0036	6	6	bracketright	]	005D	]	]
seven	7	0037	7	7	asciicircum	^	005E	Shift+6	Shift+6
eight	8	0038	8	8	underscore	_	005F	Shift+-	Shift+-
nine	9	0039	9	9	quoteleft	'	2018	Alt+0145	Option+]
colon	:	003A	Shift+;	Shift+;	a	a	0061	a	a
semicolon	;	003B	;	;	b	b	0062	b	b
less	<	003C	Shift+,	Shift+,	c	c	0063	c	c
equal	=	003D	=	=	d	d	0064	d	d
greater	>	003E	Shift+.	Shift+.	e	e	0065	e	e
question	?	003F	?	?	f	f	0066	f	f
at	@	0040	Shift+2	Shift+2	g	g	0067	g	g
A	A	0041	Shift+a	Shift+a	h	h	0068	h	h
B	B	0042	Shift+b	Shift+b	i	i	0069	i	i
C	C	0043	Shift+c	Shift+c	j	j	006A	j	j
D	D	0044	Shift+d	Shift+d	k	k	006B	k	k
E	E	0045	Shift+e	Shift+e	l	l	006C	l	l

Character Name and Glyph Sample		Unicode	Windows U.S. Keyboard	Macintosh U.S. Keyboard	Character Name and Glyph Sample		Unicode	Windows U.S. Keyboard	Macintosh U.S. Keyboard
m	m	006D	m	m	quotedblbase	„	201E	Alt+0132	Shift+Option+w
n	n	006E	n	n	quotedblright	"	201D	Alt+0148	Shift+Option+[
o	o	006F	o	o	guillemotright	»	00BB	Alt+0187	Shift+Option+\
p	p	0070	p	p	ellipsis	…	2026	Alt+0133	Option+;
q	q	0071	q	q	perthousand	‰	2030	Alt+0137	Shift+Option+r
r	r	0072	r	r	questiondown	¿	00BF	Alt+0191	Shift+Option+/
s	s	0073	s	s	grave	`	0060	`	` (or) Shift+Option+`
t	t	0074	t	t	acute	´	00B4	Alt+0180	Shift+Option+e
u	u	0075	u	u	circumflex	^	02C6	Alt+0136	Shift+Option+i
v	v	0076	v	v	tilde	~	02DC	Alt+0152	Shift+Option+n
w	w	0077	w	w	macron	¯	00AF	Alt+0175	Shift+Option+,
x	x	0078	x	x	breve	˘	02D8	Char. Map, Spacing Mod. Letters	Shift+Option+.
y	y	0079	y	y					
z	z	007A	z	z	dotaccent	˙	02D9	Char. Map, Spacing Mod. Letters	Option+h
braceleft	{	007B	Shift+[	Shift+[					
bar	|	007C	Shift+\	Shift+\	dieresis	¨	00A8	Alt+0168	Shift+Option+u
braceright	}	007D	Shift+]	Shift+]	ring	˚	02DA	Char. Map, Spacing Mod. Letters	Option+k
asciitilde	~	007E	Shift+`	Shift+`					
exclamdown	¡	00A1	Alt+0161	Option+1	cedilla	¸	00B8	Alt+0184	Shift+Option+z
cent	¢	00A2	Alt+0162	Option+4	hungarumlaut	˝	02DD	Char. Map, Spacing Mod. Letters	Shift+Option+g
sterling	£	00A3	Alt+0163	Option+3					
fraction	⁄	2044	Char. Map, General Punct.	Shift+Option+1	ogonek	˛	02DB	Char. Map, Spacing Mod. Letters	Shift+Option+x
					caron	ˇ	02C7	Char. Map, Spacing Mod. Letters	Shift+Option+t
yen	¥	00A5	Alt+0165	Option+y					
florin	ƒ	0192	Alt+0131	Option+f	emdash	—	2014	Alt+0151	Shift+Option+-
section	§	00A7	Alt+0167	Option+6	AE	Æ	00C6	Alt+0198	Shift+Option+'
currency	¤	00A4	Alt+0164	Char. Palette	ordfeminine	ª	00AA	Alt+0170	Option+9
quotesingle	'	0027	'	'	Lslash	Ł	0141	Char. Map, Latin	Char. Palette
quotedblleft	"	201C	Alt+0147	Option+[					
guillemotleft	«	00AB	Alt+0171	Option+\	Oslash	Ø	00D8	Alt+0216	Shift+Option+o
guilsinglleft	‹	2039	Alt+0139	Shift+Option+3	OE	Œ	0152	Alt+0140	Shift+Option+q
guilsinglright	›	203A	Alt+0155	Shift+Option+4	ordmasculine	º	00BA	Alt+0186	Option+0
endash	–	2013	Alt+0150	Option+-	ae	æ	00E6	Alt+0230	Option+'
dagger	†	2020	Alt+0133	Option+t	dotlessi	ı	0131	Char. Map, Latin	Shift+Option+b
daggerdbl	‡	2021	Alt+0135	Shift+Option+7					
periodcentered	·	00B7	Alt+0183	Shift+Option+9	lslash	ł	0142	Char. Map, Latin	Char. Palette
paragraph	¶	00B6	Alt+0182	Option+7					
bullet	•	2022	Alt+0149	Option+8	oslash	ø	00F8	Alt+0248	Option+o
quotesinglbase	‚	201A	Alt+0130	Shift+Option+0	oe	œ	0153	Alt+0156	Option+q
					germandbls	ß	00DF	Alt+0223	Option+s

Character Name and Glyph Sample		Unicode	Windows U.S. Keyboard	Macintosh U.S. Keyboard	Character Name and Glyph Sample		Unicode	Windows U.S. Keyboard	Macintosh U.S. Keyboard
logicalnot	¬	00AC	Alt+0172	Option+l	Otilde	Õ	00D5	Alt+0213	(Option+n)+(Shift+o)
uni00B5	µ	00B5	Alt+0181	Option+m	Scaron	Š	0160	Alt+0138	Char. Palette
trademark	™	2122	Alt+0153	Option+2	Uacute	Ú	00DA	Alt+0218	(Option+e)+(Shift+u)
Eth	Ð	00D0	Alt+0208	Char. Palette	Ucircumflex	Û	00DB	Alt+0219	(Option+i)+(Shift+u)
onehalf	½	00BD	Alt+0189	Char. Palette	Udieresis	Ü	00DC	Alt+0220	(Option+u)+(Shift+u)
plusminus	±	00B1	Alt+0177	Shift+Option+=	Ugrave	Ù	00D9	Alt+0217	(Option+`)+(Shift+u)
Thorn	Þ	00DE	Alt+0222	Char. Palette	Yacute	Ý	00DD	Alt+0221	Char. Palette
onequarter	¼	00BC	Alt+0188	Char. Palette	Ydieresis	Ÿ	0178	Alt+0159	(Option+u)+(Shift+y)
divide	÷	00F7	Alt+0247	Option+/	Zcaron	Ž	017D	Alt+0142	Char. Palette
brokenbar	¦	00A6	Alt+0166	Char. Palette	aacute	á	00E1	Alt+0225	(Option+e)+a
degree	°	00B0	Alt+0176	Shift+Option+8	acircumflex	â	00E2	Alt+0226	(Option+i)+a
thorn	þ	00FE	Alt+0254	Char. Palette	adieresis	ä	00E4	Alt+0228	(Option+u)+a
threequarters	¾	00BE	Alt+0190	Char. Palette	agrave	à	00E0	Alt+0224	(Option+`)+a
registered	®	00AE	Alt+0174	Option+r	aring	å	00E5	Alt+0229	Option+a
minus	−	2212	Char. Map, Math. Operators	Char. Palette	atilde	ã	00E3	Alt+0227	(Option+n)+a
					ccedilla	ç	00E7	Alt+0231	Option+c
eth	ð	00F0	Alt+0240	Char. Palette	eacute	é	00E9	Alt+0233	(Option+e)+e
multiply	×	00D7	Alt+0215	Char. Palette	ecircumflex	ê	00EA	Alt+0234	(Option+i)+e
copyright	©	00A9	Alt+0169	Option+g	edieresis	ë	00EB	Alt+0235	(Option+u)+e
Aacute	Á	00C1	Alt+0193	(Option+e)+(Shift+a)	egrave	è	00E8	Alt+0232	(Option+`)+e
Acircumflex	Â	00C2	Alt+0194	(Option+i)+(Shift+a)	iacute	í	00ED	Alt+0237	(Option+e)+i
Adieresis	Ä	00C4	Alt+0196	(Option+u)+(Shift+a)	icircumflex	î	00EE	Alt+0238	(Option+i)+i
Agrave	À	00C0	Alt+0192	(Option+`)+(Shift+a)	idieresis	ï	00EF	Alt+0239	(Option+u)+i
Aring	Å	00C5	Alt+0197	Shift+Option+a	igrave	ì	00EC	Alt+0236	(Option+`)+i
Atilde	Ã	00C3	Alt+0195	(Option+n)+(Shift+a)	ntilde	ñ	00F1	Alt+0241	(Option+n)+n
Ccedilla	Ç	00C7	Alt+0199	Shift+Option+c	oacute	ó	00F3	Alt+0243	(Option+e)+o
Eacute	É	00C9	Alt+0201	(Option+e)+(Shift+e)	ocircumflex	ô	00F4	Alt+0244	(Option+i)+o
Ecircumflex	Ê	00CA	Alt+0202	(Option+i)+(Shift+e)	odieresis	ö	00F6	Alt+0246	(Option+u)+o
Edieresis	Ë	00CB	Alt+0203	(Option+u)+(Shift+e)	ograve	ò	00F2	Alt+0242	(Option+`)+o
Egrave	È	00C8	Alt+0200	(Option+`)+(Shift+e)	otilde	õ	00F5	Alt+0245	(Option+n)+o
Iacute	Í	00CD	Alt+0205	(Option+e)+(Shift+i)	scaron	š	0161	Alt+0154	Char. Palette
Icircumflex	Î	00CE	Alt+0206	(Option+i)+(Shift+i)	uacute	ú	00FA	Alt+0250	(Option+e)+u
Idieresis	Ï	00CF	Alt+0207	(Option+u)+(Shift+i)	ucircumflex	û	00FB	Alt+0251	(Option+i)+u
Igrave	Ì	00CC	Alt+0204	(Option+`)+(Shift+i)	udieresis	ü	00FC	Alt+0252	(Option+u)+u
Ntilde	Ñ	00D1	Alt+0209	(Option+n)+(Shift+n)	ugrave	ù	00F9	Alt+0249	(Option+`)+u
Oacute	Ó	00D3	Alt+0211	(Option+e)+(Shift+o)	yacute	ý	00FD	Alt+0253	Char. Palette
Ocircumflex	Ô	00D4	Alt+0212	(Option+i)+(Shift+o)	ydieresis	ÿ	00FF	Alt+0255	(Option+u)+y
Odieresis	Ö	00D6	Alt+0214	(Option+u)+(Shift+o)	zcaron	ž	017E	Alt+0158	Char. Palette
Ograve	Ò	00D2	Alt+0210	(Option+`)+(Shift+o)					

Character Name and Glyph Sample		Unicode	Windows U.S. Keyboard	Macintosh U.S. Keyboard
f_i	fi	FB01	Char. Map, Latin	Shift+Option+5
f_l	fl	FB02	Char. Map, Latin	Shift+Option+6
one.superior	1	00B9	Alt+0185	Char. Palette
two.superior	2	00B2	Alt+0178	Char. Palette
three.superior	3	00B3	Alt+0179	Char. Palette
uni2126	Ω	2126	Char. Map, Letterlike Symbols	Option+z
pi	π	03C0	Char. Map, Greek	Option+p
Euro	€	20AC	Alt+0128	Shift+Option+2
afii61289	ℓ	2113	Char. Map, Letterlike Symbols	Char. Palette
estimated	e	212E	Char. Map, Letterlike Symbols	Char. Palette
partialdiff	∂	2202	Char. Map, Math. Operators	Option+d
uni2206	Δ	2206	Char. Map, Math. Operators	Option+j
product	Π	220F	Char. Map, Math. Operators	Shift+Option+p
summation	Σ	2211	Char. Map, Math. Operators	Option+w
radical	√	221A	Char. Map, Math. Operators	Option+v
infinity	∞	221E	Char. Map, Math. Operators	Option+5
integral	∫	222B	Char. Map, Math. Operators	Option+b
approxequal	≈	2248	Char. Map, Math. Operators	Option+x
notequal	≠	2260	Char. Map, Math. Operators	Option+=
lessequal	≤	2264	Char. Map, Math. Operators	Option+,
greaterequal	≥	2265	Char. Map, Math. Operators	Option+.
lozenge	◊	25CA	Char. Map, Block Elem. & Geo.	Shift+Option+v

The above keyboard descriptions are based on the U.S. English keyboard. All characters in the Adobe Western 2 character set can be entered into any Adobe application with a "Glyph Palette," such as Adobe InDesign.

Windows For Windows, the (Alt key+number) combination is typed by holding down the Alt key while typing the number using the number keys found on the numeric keypad (it does not work with the number keys on the top horizontal row of the main keyboard). For Windows laptop computer users, a virtual numeric keypad can usually be activated by turning on the "num lock" key and using the following keys (7, 8, 9, U, I, O, J, K, L, M).

On Windows, the (Alt key+number) combination does not access every character in Adobe Western 2. However on Windows 2000 and XP, the additional characters can still be found and entered into a document through the "Character Map" utility found under Windows' Start menu Programs Accessories System Tools Character Map. After launching the Character Map utility, choose "Unicode Subrange" under the "Group by:" pop-up window. For example, under the "Greek" sub-range, the pi (π) glyph can be found.

In Microsoft Word, another method to enter glyphs is to type in a character's 4-digit hexadecimal Unicode value followed by the 2 keys: (Alt+x).

Mac OS For Macintosh, when a character's keyboard entry is listed above in the form of "(Option+e)+(Shift+a)," this indicates the need to: while holding the Option key down, press the "e" key, release both keys, press and keep holding down the Shift key, press the "a" key, then release both keys. The resulting "Aacute" (Á) character will be entered into the document.

Not all Adobe Western 2 characters can be entered through standard Macintosh keyboard key combinations. However, they can be accessed through the new Macintosh OS X's "Character Palette." The Character Palette is not turned on by default. To turn it on, select the System Preferences -> International -> Input Menu tab and click on "Character Palette." The Character Palette icon will then appear towards the top right of the active application's menu bar. Click on the icon's menu and select "Show Character Palette." Click on the "Unicode Table" tab and scroll to find the Unicode hexadecimal value corresponding to the desired glyph. Once the glyph is found, click on it and then click on the "Insert" button. The glyph should now be entered into an open editable document. (Note: it may be necessary to first change the currently selected font in your application to match the font that you intend to use for the inserted character.)

Alphabet A set of letters or other characters (arranged in a customary order) with which one or more languages are written.

Alternate glyphs Design variations of letterforms included in a typeface family to provide typographic design options.

Ampersand A character used to symbolize the word *and;* ligature formed by the union of the lowercase letters *e* and *t*.

_&- &- Ampersand

Angle bracket A type of bracket, commonly found in pi fonts, used to separate text.

Aperture The amount of space between two points in a letter forming an opening into an interior portion of a letterform.

Apex Section of the top of a letter where two straight strokes or stems join and create an angle.

Arm A horizontal or upward diagonal stroke that is attached to the letter on one end and unattached on the other.

Ascender A portion of a stroke in a lowercase letter that extends beyond the mean line.

Ascent The vertical distance from the baseline to the top of the highest character in a type font. This location varies from font to font.

Back margin The inside margin of a spread; also called *gutter margin*.

Back matter Book sections of reference information that follow the chapters, such as appendix, glossary, bibliography, and index.

Backslant A typeface that slants or leans to the left as it rests on the baseline.

Bar A horizontal stroke that connects two strokes.

Baseline The imaginary horizontal line upon which all typeset letters appear to stand or rest.

Bicameral A typeface with two different cases, usually upper- and lowercase.

Bitmapped font Digital letterforms created by groups of dots (with a fixed, low resolution) arranged on a grid with *x,y* coordinates; also called *screen font*.

Black letter Heavy, condensed gothic letterforms used by Gutenberg and other typographers in his time period.

_m_ Black letter

Block quote A quote in running text that exceeds four lines and is set as a separate text block.

Bowl A curved stroke that creates an enclosed space within a letter.

Brace One of a pair of marks used to enclose text; also used in mathematical equations.

_{} {}_ Braces

Brackets _[ ] [ ]_

Bullet __ • __

Caret — ∧ —

Case fraction __ ½ __

Bracket A curved or sloping shape that smoothly joins a serif to a stroke or stem; also called *fillet;* one of a pair of marks used to enclose text identifying it as a single unit.

Bullet A large dot included in a typeface used to separate text or identify items on a list.

Cap height The vertical distance from the baseline to the cap line.

Cap line The imaginary horizontal line that denotes the top of the uppercase, or capital, letter *X*. Indicates the tops of the capital letters, although curved uppercase letters, such as the *o* and *c*, will extend beyond it slightly.

Cardinal number Number that represents a quantity.

Caret An upside-down–V-shaped proofreaders' mark used to identify the location of additional text or space; from the Latin meaning *it is missing.*

Case fraction A fraction drawn as a single character in a typeface that maintains typographic quality within the text block.

Character A basic, minimal, readable structure used to identify a letter, figure, punctuation mark, or symbol that serves as a component of written language.

Character encoding The digital identity that enables the computer to locate and display the correct glyph.

Character window See *glyph window.*

Chase A large type tray for holding a page of foundry type sorts.

Composing stick A typesetter's shallow hand-held, adjustable-width metal tray for holding several lines of foundry type sorts during typesetting.

Contoured wrap An organic shape set into a block of text.

Copy Typewritten or handwritten material to be typeset.

Copyfitting Process to determine how much space a block of typeset type will occupy on a page.

Counter The fully or partially enclosed negative space within or adjacent to a letterform.

Crossbar A horizontal stroke that crosses another stroke, such as in the lowercase *t* and *f.*

.dfont Font file title extension identifying a Macintosh TrueType font.

Dead copy The last edited version of a document.

Descender A portion of a stroke (not limited to lowercase letters) that extends below the baseline.

Descent The vertical distance from the baseline to the bottommost point in a type font. This location varies from font to font.

Diacritic An accent mark or symbol that accompanies a letter to indicate its particular phonetic value.

Dimension sign Sans serif, lowercase *x* used for typesetting the length and width of an area or object or in multiplication equations.

Dingbat Small, informal keystroke graphic.

Diphthong A single, joined character made from two vowels to indicate a particular sound.

Display capital Capital letter designed and drawn separately to emphasize subtle design details for use as display type or initial letters.

Display type Type set in 14 points or larger, used for headlines, titles, and similar attention-getting situations.

Double prime Linear unit-of-measure symbol for inches.

Doubling The rereading of the same line in a type block due to poor typographic quality.

Drop cap An initial letter embedded within the first few lines of text; also called *cut-in letter.*

Dutch wrap A headline located atop the first column of a multicolumn article that does not extend above the article's remaining text columns.

Ear The short protrusion from the top of the lowercase *g* (and *p*). Also applied to the arm of the lowercase *r,* depending upon the typeface.

Ellipsis A sequence of three periods, set as a single character, that indicates the omission of a word or words from quoted material or the trailing off of a thought.

Em Unit of measure equal to the size of the typeface.

Em quad In foundry type, a spacing sort whose width and height are an em; also called *mutton.*

En Unit of measure equal to half the size of the typeface.

En quad In foundry type, a spacing sort whose width is an en and whose height is an em; also called *nut.*

Encoding system A prescribed method for identifying, cataloging, and accessing individual characters; see *character encoding.*

Ending Design treatment used to define the beginning and ending of a stroke.

Endnotes A comprehensive listing of footnotes located at the end of a single chapter or a compilation of all chapter footnotes located after the appendix.

Eszett An *s-s* ligature used when typesetting the German language; formerly used in English-language typesetting.

_ é ü _ Diacritics

_ ✓ ●◗_ Dingbats

_ æ Æ _ Diphthongs

_ " _ Double prime

_ ••• _ Ellipsis

_ ß _ Eszett

Eye The enclosed counter in the upper portion of the lowercase *e*.

Fake small cap An uppercase letter scaled to the type's *x*-height; displays a thinner stroke weight than surrounding letter strokes.

Finial The tapering end of a stroke.

Fleuron _ 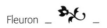 _

Fleuron Floral (or leaf-shaped) type ornaments. They could be used to indicate the end of a section within a lengthy document, such as a book chapter.

Font Originally defined in foundry type as all the sorts needed to produce the letters, numbers, and punctuation marks of one size of one specific typeface, for example, 12-point Minion Semibold. Evolved to mean the entity, such as the matrices, film, or digital file, necessary to create all the glyphs of a typeface, regardless of size.

Foot The bottom of a letter.

Foot margin Margin at the bottom of a page.

Fore-edge margin Right and left margins of a spread.

Formal text Text written for presentation to a wide audience, such as a book and magazine.

Foundry type Pieces of hard, durable metal type used to set pages of type; primary means of setting type from 1454 through 1890.

Fraction bar See *solidus*.

Front matter Book sections, located before the chapters, that provide an overview of organizational structure and content.

Galley A slanted tray for holding a single column of Linotype slugs, similar to a foundry type chase.

Glyph A stylized visual representation of a character or combination of characters.

Glyph window A rectangular shape within which a digital letterform is designed. The height is equal to the typeface's em. The width is the amount of horizontal space allocated to the glyph along a baseline.

Graphemes The letters of the alphabet.

Graphic alphabet A dominant graphic style or subject restructured to serve as letters of the alphabet. May possibly include only the uppercase letters or all the letter cases plus punctuation marks and numbers.

Grotesque Term originally used to describe a sans serif typeface; also referred to as *grot* (England), *grotesk* (Germany), and *gothic* (United States).

Gutter margin The back margin on a page within a spread.

Gutter The white space between columns on a page.

Hair space A space the size of $\frac{1}{12}$ or $\frac{1}{24}$ em.

Hairline An extremely thin line used as a stroke or a serif.

Hanging indent Starting the first line of a paragraph at the margin and indenting left the remainder of the lines.

Head The top of a letter.

Head margin Margin at the top of a page.

Hints Special instructions programmed into the font file that maintain the quality of a typeface's typographic features for point size and printer resolution. Hints include information concerning character alignment, curves and strokes, and other visual subtleties in a typeface design.

Humanist text Literary text written for continuous reading concerning broad cultural learning or human experiences.

Inferior figures Figures of consistent height, smaller than the font's x-height, positioned on the baseline for use as the denominator of a piece fraction; used as subscript, when positioned below baseline.

Informal text Text written for limited distribution, such as a memo.

Initial letter An enlarged, first letter of the first word in the first sentence of a chapter or book section. Some are graphic letters or ornately illustrated letters; also called *versals*.

Italic A letterform that is structurally redesigned from its roman original to slant to the right at varying angles as it rests on the baseline.

$- f -$ Italic

Job case A single type case containing all the sorts required for *job work* (i.e., advertisements and brochures) when setting foundry type.

Kern [*n*] The portion of a letter that extends beyond its foundry type body; [*v*] to incrementally delete or add space between letters or words to improve typographic texture.

Kerning Optically adjusting the letterspacing between two letters; the individual adjustment of spacing between two letters or letter pair.

Kerning pair Two typeface characters whose unique shapes create a letterspacing inequity that requires a decrease, or sometimes an increase, in the space between them, such as *W* and *o* or *T* and *a*.

Kerning table List of kerning pairs and their required spacing adjustments contained in a font file.

Keyboard mapping A prescribed sequence of keystrokes used when retrieving individual characters from the type font for display.

Leading Vertical space between lines within and between paragraphs measured from baseline to baseline; in foundry type, the white

---

space between lines of type created by the placement of thin strips of lead (measured in points) between lines of metal sorts.

Leg The tail of the uppercase and lowercase *K*.

Legibility The reader's ability to correctly identify individual letters.

Letterspacing Horizontal space between letters in a word or a line.

Level fraction _ 1/2 _

Level fraction A fraction constructed by the type artist from titling figures and a virgule.

Ligature _ ffi _

Ligature A single character (and a single sort) created from the physical union or the designed alteration of two or three separate letters to improve typographic quality.

Line skipping Reading the first half of a sentence with the second half of another.

Line spacing Vertical space between lines within and between paragraphs.

Binocular lowercase *G* _ g _

Link Short stroke that joins the bowl of the binocular lowercase *g* to its loop.

Monocular lowercase *G* _ g _

Live copy The latest version of a document.

Logotype A single word or words designed to be a cohesive, readable visual whole that usually functions as a graphic identity for a product, company, or service.

Loop The elliptical stroke at the bottom of the binocular lowercase *g*.

Lowline Short, horizontal line positioned on the baseline or slightly lower, when used as an underscore.

Magazine Compartment of matrices in a Linotype linecaster.

Majuscules Uppercase letters in a typeface; also called *capital letters*.

Margin The white space surrounding all items that print on a page.

Masthead Area in a newspaper, newsletter, or magazine that lists information relevant to the periodical's publication, such as the publisher's name and address, editor's name, and so forth.

Mat A lightweight, reusable letter matrix used in a Linotype linecaster.

Mean line The imaginary horizontal line that denotes the top of the lowercase letter *x*.

Measure The width of a paragraph; also called *line length*.

Metric data In digital typography, information that controls character spacing, style linking, and accessing typeface menu names. Located in the bitmapped font for Macintosh typefaces and in the .pfm file for Windows typefaces.

Middle space A space the size of ¼ em.

Midpoint _ • _

Midpoint A small dot used to separate text or identify items on a list. It is smaller and sits closer to the baseline than the larger bullet.

Minuscules Lowercase letters in a typeface.

Mutton See *em quad*.

Nameplate A logotype designed to establish visual name recognition for a periodical, such as a newspaper, magazine, or newsletter; usually located prominently at the top of the front cover or page.

Nut See *en quad*.

Oblique A roman typeface that slants or leans to the right as it rests on the baseline; also referred to as *machine italic*.

Optical kerning Technique for determining letterspacing using mathematical algorithms to calculate spacing based on shape.

Optical letterspacing Visually balancing space shapes around and within letters in a single word or group of words.

Ordinal number Number that represents an ordering or ranking.

Ornament Typographic symbol or flourish designed to accompany a specific typeface.

Orphan The first line of a paragraph positioned at the end of a page or column.

Outline font Digital letterforms defined as objects using a mathematical formula containing point locations and shaped, connecting line segments; also called *printer font* or *scalable font*.

Page Term applied to a single sheet document or one side of the leaf of a book.

Pi font A typeface consisting of special-usage characters, such as mathematical symbols.

Pica Unit of measure used to measure the depth and measure of a type block; one pica equals 12 points; six picas equal one inch.

Piece fraction A fraction constructed by the type artist from true-cut superior and inferior figures and a solidus.

Pilcrow A symbol used to identify the beginning of a new paragraph; also called *paragraph mark*.

Point Unit of measure used to identify typeface size, indents, and leading. In digital typography, one point is $1/72$ of an inch.

Point size The vertical distance from the bottommost point in the type font to the topmost point in the type font. In foundry type, this is the depth of the sort's body. In digital type, this is the height of an equivalent area, called a *glyph window*.

PostScript A page-description computer language developed by Adobe Systems, Inc., in the early 1980s.

Prime Linear unit-of-measure symbol for feet.

Printer font See *outline font*.

_ *a* _	One-story lowercase *A*
_ a _	Two-story lowercase *A*
_ ❦ ❧ _	Ornaments
_ *μ* ≅ _	Pi font
_ ¹⁄₋2 _	Piece fraction
_ ❡ ¶ _	Pilcrow
_ ′ _	Prime

Proof Copy of foundry type made on a proofing press by running an inked roller across the face of the type; a printout of an in-progress digital document.

Proofmarks See *proofreaders' marks.*

Proofreaders' marks Standardized marks used in pairs (one in text, one in margin) by type artists for communicating typographic instructions or changes on typeset copy; also called *proofmarks.*

Pull quote Several lines of text used to break up large quantities of continuous text; also called a *quote-out, breaker,* or *grabber.*

Raised cap An initial letter that shares the same baseline with the first sentence in the paragraph causing the letter to tower above the first sentence; also called *stick-up letter.*

Readability The reader's ability to identify and comprehend words, sentences, and paragraphs easily.

Recto The front side of a page or the right page of a spread.

Roman A typeface style whose letterforms are at right angles to the baseline; the open, round letterform structure of the English alphabet based on the 23-letter Roman alphabet.

Runaround A rectangular shape set into a block of text.

Run-in sidebar The lowest-level subhead.

Running feet A line of type, placed across the bottom of a book page, containing information such as, the page number, chapter title, chapter number, and book title.

Running head A line of type, placed across the top of a book page, containing information such as, the page number, chapter title, chapter number, and book title.

Saccades Small horizontal jumps a reader's eye makes along a line of type while reading. Encompassing approximately 12 characters (letters and spaces).

Sans serif 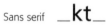 **Sans serif** A typeface whose strokes end bluntly, without a decorative finishing treatment, such as a serif.

Scalable font See *outline font.*

Screen font See *bitmapped font.*

Script **Script** A typeface that imitates cursive handwriting.

Serif A cross, or finishing, stroke at the beginning or end of the major strokes of a letterform. Originates from the Dutch word *schreef* (a scratch or flick of the pen). Some serifs are described by their shape, such as *bracketed, cupped, hairline, slab,* and *wedge.*

Set solid Type set without any white space between type lines.

Set width The width of an actual typeface letter; also called *set.*

Shoulder The curved portion of a stroke that does not create an enclosed space within the letter.

Side bearing The amount of white space on the left and right side of a letter determined by the type designer.

Sink The white space from the top edge of the type page to the topmost ascender of the nearest type block; also called *sinkage*.

Slash See *virgule*.

_ / / _ Slash and solidus

Slug A single sort containing all the characters and spaces for a single line of type set on a Linotype linecaster.

Small caps Capital letters that are redesigned and recut to the approximate size of the typeface's *x*-height; also called *true cut*.

Solidus A right-leaning diagonal line used to create piece fractions; angles farther to the right than a virgule.

Sort A single piece of metal foundry type.

Space The negative, nonprinting area in and around a letterform.

Spaceband The amount of space (approximately ¼ em) between letters after a single press of the spacebar; size is determined for the typeface by the type designer.

Spine The main curved stroke in the uppercase and lowercase S.

Spread Two adjacent verso and recto pages of a book.

Spur Small downward extension on some styles of an uppercase G.

Stem A major vertical stroke within a letter.

Stet Word used in proofreading indicating to leave the typeset word as it is; originated from the Latin *stare* (to stand).

Stress The thickened portion of a curved stroke that determines a direction (vertical, horizontal, or diagonal) in which the letterform appears to lean.

Stroke General category referring to primary structural components that define the overall appearance of a letterform; any straight or curved line used to define a major structural portion of a letter.

Superior figures Figures of consistent height, smaller than the font's *x*-height, positioned to align along the top with the font's ascenders for use as the numerator of a piece fraction; used as superscript for exponents and footnotes, when positioned slightly higher.

Swash An extended or decorative flourish that replaces a serif or terminal on a letter.

_ $\mathcal{A}$ _ Swash

Swash terminal A lowercase letter with a long swash extending from it on the right side. This letter is used at the end of a word or line.

_ e _ Swash terminal

Tag line A line of type adjacent to a newsletter's nameplate describing the publication's focus or audience, as well as date and/or volume.

Tail A downward diagonal stroke attached to the letter on one end and unattached on the other.

Technical text Scientific text; text written for discontinuous reading due to the complexity of its content.

Terminal — *f* —

Terminal Stroke-end treatments, such as tapering or adding a shape, that are not serifs.

Text figures — 4567 —

Text figures Figures positioned primarily in the font's *x*-height with ascenders and descenders for use with text type; also called *lowercase, old style, nonranging,* or *hanging figures.*

Text page An area within the type page that contains the primary text area.

Text type Type set below 14 point, suited for type in advertisements, books, newsletters, and other continuous-reading situations.

Thick space A space the size of ⅓ em.

Thin space A space the size of ⅙ or ⅛ em.

Tied letter See *ligature.*

Titling capital A unicameral typeface of capital letters drawn to the full height of the type size; not meant for use with lowercase letters.

Titling figures — 123 —

Titling figures Figures of consistent height usually confined to the font's cap height for use with display type and in tabulated material; also called *aligning, lining, modern, ranging,* or *capital figures.*

Tracking Uniformly increasing or decreasing the amount of letterspacing within a group of letters, such as a word, headline, or paragraph.

Trim The finished edge of a printed document or page.

Type alignment The positioning of type lines within a type block or paragraph.

Type block A shaped area of display or text type.

Type case A shallow drawer for storing a single font of foundry type. Housed in a vertical cabinet with a slanted top for type case access. Two cases, an upper and lower, were needed to hold all the sorts necessary for book typography.

Type family All stylistic variations of a single typeface, such as light, medium, bold, extra bold, and italic.

Type page The area of a page, usually rectangular, that includes all items that print.

Typeface The distinctive, visually unifying design of an alphabet and its accompanying punctuation marks and numbers. It includes all point sizes of that typeface.

Typograph The art of designing a graphic by using and manipulating typeset letters and words.

U-shape wrap A headline located atop an interior column of a multicolumn article that does not extend above the columns to its right or left.

Umbrella headline A headline that extends across the top of an entire article.

Unicameral A typeface with one letter case, such as an uppercase-only typeface.

Unicode An alpha-numeric encoding system used by the OpenType font format that contains code points, or character identification, for characters needed by all the world's written languages; also called the *Unicode Standard.*

Versal See *initial letter.*

Verso The backside of a page or the left page of a spread.

Vertex Section of the bottom of a letter where two straight strokes or stems join and create an angle.

Virgule A right-leaning diagonal line used to separate alternate words, such as *and/or*; also called *slash.*

— / — Virgule

Widow The last line of a paragraph positioned at the top of the next page or column; a short word (less than four letters) or the tail end of a hyphenated word as the last line of a paragraph.

Word spacing The distance between words on a line of type.

X-height The vertical distance from the baseline to the mean line.

SELECT BIBLIOGRAPHY

Berry, John D., ed. *Language Culture Type: International Type Design in the Age of Unicode.* New York: Association Typographique Internationale; Graphis, Inc., 2002.

Bickham, George. *George Bickham's Penmanship Made Easy or The Young Clerk's Assistant.* c. 1733. Reprint, Mineola, NY: Dover Publications, Inc., 1997.

———. *The Universal Penman.* c. 1740–1741. Reprint, with an introductory essay by Philip Hofer, New York: Dover Publications, Inc., 1954.

Brady, Philip. *Using Type Right.* Cincinnati, OH: Northlight Books, 1988.

Bringhurst, Robert. *The Elements of Typographic Style.* Vancouver, BC: Hartley & Marks, 1992.

Carter, Harry. *A View of Early Typography.* London: Hyphen Press, 2002.

Dowding, Geoffrey. *Finer Points in the Spacing and Arrangement of Type.* Vancouver, BC: Hartley & Marks, 1995.

Eason, Ron, and Sarah Rookledge. *Rookledge's International Handbook of Type Designers: A Biographical Directory.* Surrey, England: Sarema Press, 1991.

Eckersley, Richard, and others. *Glossary of Typesetting Terms.* Chicago: The University of Chicago Press, 1994.

Fairbank, Alfred. *A Book of Scripts.* Middlesex, England: Pelican Books, 1968.

Felici, James. *The Complete Manual of Typography: A Guide to Setting Perfect Type.* Berkeley, CA: Peachpit Press, 2003.

Firmage, Richard A. *The Alphabet Abecedarium.* Boston: David R. Godine, 1993.

Gill, Eric. *An Essay of Typography.* 1936. Reprint, with an introduction by Christopher Skeleton, Boston: David R. Godine, 1993.

Glaser, Milton. *Milton Glaser Graphic Design.* Woodstock, NY: The Overlook Press, 1983.

Gottschall, Edward M. *Typographic Communications Today.* Cambridge, MA: The MIT Press, 1989.

Goudy, Frederic W. *The Alphabet and Elements of Lettering.* Rev. ed. New York: Dorset Press, 1989.

Haley, Allan. "Bullets, Boxes and Dingbats," *Upper and Lower Case* 16, no. 2 (Spring 1989), 16–7.

———. *Hot Designers Make Cool Fonts.* Gloucester, MA: Rockport Publishers, Inc., 1998.

———. "Parts of a Character," *Upper and Lower Case* 11, no. 4 (February 1985), 20–1.

———. "Serif vs Sans," *Upper and Lower Case* 12, no. 1 (May 1985), 28–9.

———. *Typographic Milestones.* New York: Van Nostrand Reinhold, 1992.

———. "'&perseand," *X-height* 3, no. 2 (1994), 5.

Johnson, A. F., and Stanley Morison. "The Chancery Types of Italy and France." *The Fleuron* 3 (1924): 23–51.

Jury, David. *About Face: Reviving the Rules of Typography.* Switzerland: RotoVision SA, 2004.

Larson, Kevin. "The Science of Word Recognition or How I Learned to Stop Worrying and Love the Bouma." Microsoft Corporation, Redman, WA, 2004. Computer printout.

Lawson, Alexander S. *Printing Types.* Rev. ed. Boston: Beacon Press, 1990.

———. *Anatomy of a Typeface.* Boston: David R. Godine, 1990.

Loxley, Simon. *Type: The Secret History of Letters.* New York: I. B. Tauris & Co. Ltd., 2004.

McLean, Ruari. *The Thames and Hudson Manual of Typography.* New York: Thames & Hudson, 1980.

———. *Typographers on Type.* New York: W. W. Norton & Co., 1995.

Meynell, Sir Francis, and Herbert Simon. *Fleuron Anthology.* Boston: David R. Godine, Publisher, Inc., 1979.

Morison, Stanley. "First Principles of Typography." *The Fleuron* 7 (1930): 61–72.

———. "On Script Types." *The Fleuron* 4 (1925): 1–42.

———. "Towards an Ideal Type." *The Fleuron* 2 (1924): 57–75.

———. *Type Designs of the Past and Present.* London: The Fleuron, Limited, 1926.

Muller, Marion. "Prof File: Herb Lubalin," *Upper and Lower Case* 8, no. 1 (March 1981), 4–5.

Parker, Roger C. *Looking Good in Print: A Guide to Basic Design for Desktop Publishing.* 3d ed. Chapel Hill, NC: Ventana Press, 1993.

Perfect, Christopher, and Jeremy Austen. *The Complete Typographer.* Englewood Cliffs, NJ: Prentice Hall, 1992.

Phinney, Thomas W. "TrueType, PostScript Type 1, and OpenType: What's the Difference?" Adobe Systems, Inc., San Jose, CA, 2004. Computer printout.

Rand, Paul. *Design, Form, and Chaos.* New Haven, CT: Yale University Press, 1993.

Smith, Peggy. *Mark My Words: Instruction and Practice in Proofreading.* 2d ed. Alexandria, VA: EEI, 1993.

Snyder, Gertrude. *Herb Lubalin.* New York: American Showcase, 1985.

Soppeland, Mark. *Words.* Los Altos, CA: William Kaufmann, 1980.

Sumner, Stone. "Notes from Parma," *Upper and Lower Case* 21, no. 2 (Fall 1994), 8–14.

Swann, Cal. *Language & Typography.* New York: Van Nostrand Reinhold, 1991.

Tinkel, Kathleen. "Typographic 'Rules,'" *Aldus Magazine* 3, no. 3 (March/April 1992), 32–5.

Tschichold, Jan. *Treasury of Alphabets and Lettering.* 1966. Reprint, with an introduction by Ben Rosen, New York: Design Press, 1992.

Updike, Daniel Berkeley. *Printing Types: Their History, Forms, and Use.* 2 vols. 1937. Reprint, New York: Dover Publications, Inc., 1980.

Warde, Beatrice. *The Crystal Goblet: Sixteen Essays on Typography.* Cleveland, OH: World Publishing Company, 1956.

———. *Hands Off or Hands On?* New York: The Typophiles, Inc., 1969.

———. *Printing Should Be Invisible.* New York: The Marchbanks Press, 1937.

INDEX